What Is **monk** ?

Monk is the saga of two men, James Crotty and Michael Lane, who quit their jobs, sold everything they owned, hit the road with their cats Nurse, Nurse's Aide, and Dolly Lama, and for 12 years gallivanted across America, publishing *Monk,* the world's only mobile magazine. They traveled first in a '72 Ford Econoline van and then a 26-foot Fleetwood Bounder motor home ("the Monkmobile"), reporting on the incredible people, places, and phone booths they encountered along the way, until they drove each other crazy living in such cramped quarters, especially after New York, where one too many breakdowns wiped them clean, sending the Monks on a long backwards spin as Dolly furtailed it back to Arkansas, where yellowing back issues of *Monk* were held captive, awaiting a quantum shift in world consciousness.

Then, suddenly, from out of the deepest darkness, came the vision of a unique guidebook series spreading like a laser beam of light across the mallified American landscape, beckoning the Monks to pick themselves up by their hoods and trust that by spreading a message of peace, love, and excellence, while living their motto of simple, mobile, and true, all their needs would be taken care of right down to their very next carton of soy milk.

So, the journey continues . . .

the Mad

MONKS'

guide to

›New York City

by James Crotty and Michael Lane
(The Monks)

MACMILLAN • USA

MACMILLAN TRAVEL
A Simon & Schuster Macmillan Company
1633 Broadway
New York, NY 10019

ISBN 0-02-862755-5
ISSN 1520-5517

Editor: Matt Hannafin
Production Editor: Carol Sheehan
Photo Editor: Richard Fox
Design by Michele Laseau
Digital Cartography by Roberta Stockwell
Front cover photo by Barry Munger

Manufactured in the United States of America

Note

Travel information is subject to change at any
time—and this is especially true of prices. We
therefore suggest you write or call ahead for
confirmation before making your travel plans.
The authors, editors, and publishers cannot be
held responsible for the experiences of readers
while traveling.

Credits

Introductory essays, guide descriptions, insets, and
reviews by Jim Crotty, unless otherwise indicated. *On
the Road* by Michael Lane. People profiles by the Monks.

Reviews of Ellis Island and the Statue of Liberty
Museum and "Fishing" section by Reid Sherline.
"Radio" section and "Hatspotting" by Michael Kassner.
"Zines" section by Michael Kassner and Jim Crotty.
Reviews of The Fulton Fish Market Tour and the Phun
Phactory by John Kennedy. Review of Flosso
Hornmann Magic Co. by Fred Kahl. Reviews of the
Transit Museum, Red Hook, the Dream House,
Downtown Music Gallery, the Peacock Caffe, Moshe's
Falafel, Helianthus, Gryphon Bookshop, Astoria Park,
Hell Gate Bridge, and Riverside Park by Matt Hannafin.
"Transportation" and "Sex" sections by Monks and
Hannafin.

Special thanks to Reid Sherline, Michael Kassner,
Kerry "Nation" Mullett, Gayle Mayron, Seth King, John
Kennedy, Danial Glass, Terrence McGarty, Margot
Weiss, Anne Cassidy, and Pamela Warren for invaluable
editorial and research assistance.

Photo Credits

All photographs by Barry Munger except as follows:
Photos on pages 60, 62, and 189 by the Monks; 11 and
87 by Jim Crotty; 64 by Randl Bye; 24 and 146
by Michael Kassner; 223 by Reid Sherline; 193 by
Lisa Kristal; 15, 244, and 290 by Matt Hannafin;
68 courtesy of the Lowell Hotel; 104, 105, 107, 195,
201, and 218 courtesy of the New York Convention
and Visitors Bureau.

Acknowledgments

This book was born of the extraordinary faith and deter-
mination of several people, most notably our beloved
agent, Jane Dystel; our gracious and talented editors,
Matt Hannafin and Cheryl Farr; the incomparable Reid
Sherline and his brilliant sidekick, Barry Munger; and
the "Mom and Pop" of Monk Media, Doris and Jay
Bouma.

Dedication

This book is dedicated to every person who's ever
dreamed of quitting their job, selling everything they
owned, and hitting the road. Do it now!! But not in a
used 1986 Fleetwood Bounder motor home, bought
from Leach Camper Sales in Lincoln, Nebraska.

>contents

MONKS' NEW YORK, A TO Z 52

>contents

WE *Shot Andy Warhol:*

A Preface

This guide attempts to rescue New York from the ghost of Andy Warhol, the cold, distant, disingenuous face of Popism who has haunted alternative culture in this city for 4 decades. Before Warhol, the cool cats around here had genuine heart and big love. The fiery engine of New York brought forth a great wide embrace. Warhol killed all that. Not consciously, but the force of his distant personality was so great that it overwhelmed the big-hearted New York spirit and slashed its soul and dulled its wisdom and in its place gave us image for image sake, beauty for brains, celebrity worship, irony as its own reward, and love as an advertising gimmick.

You dispute my claim? Look around you at the state of New York's alternative press, all aping this sleek and empty Warholian ethic. Unwittingly, of course. Because the ethos is so pervasive amidst all the "cool people" in this town, they have no clue as to its roots. Look at the club kids, needing ecstasy to open their hearts. Look at the velvet rope establishments, meanness masquerading as hip.

The Mad Monks' Guide to New York City pulls the mask off these dead souls and shines a light on their emptiness. A true underground has life, and even a smile. A true underground is inclusive, not exclusive. A true underground fights the status quo elitism with all its might, challenging us to tackle our prejudices and resistance. A true underground is not the Spy Club or Bowery Bar or drug-dependent raves or well-dressed people that won't look you in the eye. A true underground does not come from advertising culture or fashion mags or Hollywood. A true underground is not overpriced and cruel.

A true underground is not mediocre either. A true underground has style—but with heart. A true underground has humor, often outrageous and absurd humor, and a genuine passion for authentic people, places, and events. A true underground is not shut down, shut off, or controlled. Above all, a true underground is not phony.

This is a guide to the vintage New York you won't read about in *Paper* or *Interview* or whatever cultural agent you employ. Some of their favorites will appear here, not because they are "cool" but because they represent the best of their kind.

Blame it on us—*we* shot Andy Warhol. And reclaimed the generous, big, and noble spirit of the greatest city on earth.

›on the road

speeding across four lanes of traffic with oil sputtering out the bottom, we cruise over worn roadways suspended by a bridge and catch our breath from the view. In the distance, rising out of an apocalyptic glow, a towering Babylon of lights thrusts skyward. Like forlorn sailors left ashore, the amassed buildings of Manhattan crowd to island's edge, over-seeing tugboats sailing out to sea.

It's dusk, and the urban skyline radiates below the fading sun.

The Monkmobile, its bottom ripped by highway refuse, bleeds a trail of debris. A storage bin near the left rear tire hangs gape-mouthed, tumbling out batteries and tools, oilcans and rags along the Verrazano Bridge. The Monks drive oblivious to the chaos underneath.

Mike intently eyes the road as he swerves around stalled traffic, descending into the honeycomb network of roadways that wind through Brooklyn. The Monkmobile rattles over Olympic-size potholes merging toward the bridges of Manhattan.

"Which bridge, Jim?!"

"Ah, ah, Williamsburg!"

Mike swerves onto the crusty, cool Williamsburg Bridge. Held back by just a short railing from the river below, the Monkmobile plunges into the bowels of the city.

We've finally arrived in New York.

Delancey Street looks like a war zone. Block-long fire trucks, racing cabs, and daredevil pedestrians clog the streets. Corner markets are lit up and crowded with night crawlers. Trash overflows to the gutter. Up Bowery, a stalled car hogs center lane, blaring horns passing on both sides. Over on Houston, triple-parked delivery trucks, flashers blinking, crowd toward the curb. Down Broadway, roller bladers hang on the tail of vans hitching free rides. Bug-eyed office drones stumble out of buildings into the dusk, cursing cars, screaming into the cacophony of sound.

Suddenly a van cuts in front.

"Mike, watch it! Shit!"

Thump, thump.

"Hey," Mike leans on the horn, "what the hell is he doing?"

"He's trying to get around."

"Did I hit him?"

"Yeah, but he doesn't seem to care."

The van driver leans on his horn, edging past the Monkmobile. More traffic makes its way around. People back away from the curb as the Monkmobile comes to a radiator-popping, oil-hissing, back-firing stop near Broadway and Prince. It sits beached on the curb like a giant pink whale, with foul smoke belching out the exhaust. The Monks turn off the ignition and step out to the street.

"New Yawk!" says Jim.

"New York!" echoes Mike.

"Meork," purrs our resident feline, the great Dolly Lama.

Talking Trash

After 7 years of criss-crossing the country, sampling love and lies in several different ports, we're back on the streets of the naked city. A blast of warm stale air rises from the subway grates, billowing our loose shirts open to the neck. Jim screams with delight, high off the air-conditioned buzz.

Mike takes off to retrieve a Western Union money wire. He steps out in the street with a hand outstretched towards careening cabbies, now more Pakistani than Haitian, and doubly deranged. One swerves dangerously close to Mike's thumb. A well-dressed, maximum wage earner exits towards traffic, and like a revolving door, Mike gets in. The cab speeds away beneath the tall shadows cast by the canyons of steel.

Meanwhile, Hell bellows from below.

The worst heat wave in memory is in full gear, and Mike's choking on his spit, swallowing gray air, longing for iced tea, gallon-tall at that. It's a scorcher. The gates of Hades swing wide, as a million swollen feet hoof across hard summer pavement. Mike's Kmart loafers feel like they're glued to the floor of the cab, sweat pooling up between his legs.

"Could you crack a window please?!"

The turbaned cabbie grips the wheel and says nothing. He smells like rotting beef, and is dressed in a wrinkled silk shirt with a pencil stuck behind his ear. His mustache has bits of mustard curdled on the end. Crazy mother. He's Pakistani, uses his horn for a brake, and burns a stick of musky rose incense that fogs the air of his mobile ashram.

Outside, swarms of deli-fed, suit-and-tie Wall Street refugees are moshing in the streets, weaving through cars like matadors eluding a bloody bull. They're loose on the avenues, filing into pubs, snorting like hogs.

Mike likes that.

The cab pulls over and deposits Mike at Sixth in the 40s. The cabbie's off work and turns east across 42nd, refusing to go west. Mike exits 3 blocks short of the 24-hour Times Square Western Union.

No tip for this guy.

Outside, he falls into formation approaching Times Square. Giant buildings with million-watt corporate signs blare hard upon the streets. Traffic slows to a crawl. The magic touch of Broadway lures in purse-clutching, bus-touring hordes in their button-down best. Clumps of tourists, fifty strong, herd beneath the brazen towers of show biz, eyes skyward, mouths agape and cameras flashing.

Two black girls with curlers lodged in their hair cruise down the sidewalks, tapping their nails, scuffling high heel proud, talking trash.

Mike's caught between the two of them, and is about to ask directions.

The one on the left wears a gold-plated vest and satin honey pants cut close to the crotch. She's on a mid-sentence rant ". . . and I's goin' downtown Four for the cross-town to the One at Sixth when I see that girl like she be doing that shit down First and I'd be like, wassup with that?"

"Uh huh, you mean that same one that be down Second and Tenth?" says the one on his right, wearing a skimpy blouse, belly button bared.

"No, what chu talking, I mean that one, you know, the other day down First and Third."

"You crazy, that was Tenth!"

"No, Third."

"Second and Tenth, you crazy?"

'No, no, no, you're thinking that shit we saw up Third and Tenth, you know what I'm talking?"

"I don't know what you're talking, that shit wasn't never down First."

"Oh, maybe Third?"

"No, girl, 'less you're talking Second and Third like that day you and I saw her and that shit."

"That wasn't even me, who you thinking?"

"Down Second?"

"No, down Third with that piece from Canal. Girl, you're rockin' my heels, where's your head?"

They're talking around Mike, walking Midtown, clickity-click, heads bobbing up and down. Suddenly the right side girl takes a look at gape-mouth, angular Mike, who's trying to make sense of them.

"What chu lookin' at?" She cast a pursed lip snarl at Mike's bald head, bloodshot eyes, and week-old beard. "You a junkie?"

Mike's washboard wrinkles bunch on his brow. He can't believe what he heard. "What'd you say?"

The three of them approach a light and are dodging through traffic toward the other side. "Listen, old man, you look at my titties any more you're gonna have to pay."

"I'm not looking at your . . ."

"How much you got? Forty dollars and you can look at mine too," the other cackles loud, snapping at the sky.

Now they're both chortling wet donkey laughs, spitting in the air and holding their sides. "How 'bout sixty, old man? You can look at all four. That's fifteen each!"

"I am not looking at your titties," Mike says forthrightly, leaving them at the corner, where they're slapping their thighs.

Half a block away, in a traffic island, stands a big-breasted Amazonian sculpture with silver ribs, guns, and bullets, for comic relief. A preacher stands at a nearby curb

shouting through a bullhorn, converting lost souls. Crowds of street merchants are hawking Asian-made wares. Mike continues walking across 42nd, past abandoned theaters and bare-boned marquees, when something seems wrong.

"Hey, where's all the sleaze?" he asks to no one, and no one cares.

Up and down the street it looks like everything's closed. The old show palaces, with their triple-X features and late night treats, are all shut down, boarded up and dark as night.

"My god, what is that over there? *Beauty and the Beast*?! Jesus, what's going on here?" Mike asks again.

A broken man, wearing cardboard shoes, with bad teeth and stinking of rum, shuffles by with a hand on his groin. His teeth clack in his head.

"Anything loose, anything? Quarter, dime?" His hands stretch out but his face moves on.

"Hey, what happened here, this place is, like, cleaned up!"

"Disneyfied," says the poor man, as he rambles off. "Disney owns the block."

Horny German with Wife

It's the start of the night. Gummy hot shoes stick to the pavement and the streets smell of decay. Turning the corner, looking up Eighth, suddenly the porn shops pop into view. Show World, Show Palace, XXX; the neon signs, pink and green, blaze against the asphalt, casting the word "sex" onto the pavement. Mike feels a sense of relief. At least Disney didn't buy this block, too.

Going up the 40s, the arcades boast buddy booths and theaters for private viewing pleasure. Inside the sleaze palaces, past the big-suited barkers, the strong smell of Pinesol disinfectant wafts up from the floors. There's a perversion for everyone among the collections of videos lining the walls. Gay, straight, lesbian, people into fat, teen porn, leather, water sports, S&M, transvestites, midgets. It's dinner time, and the suited commuters are catching a sexy snack before heading back out to the 'burbs.

Mike takes a stroll into Playland. An older German couple lean on a counter where the clerk sits on his stool. They are wrinkled and clutching their cameras tightly. The man cups his ears to hear. The woman holds onto the man's arm.

"It's like this," the clerk is saying to them. "The booths cost money. You go in, you put in some quarters, the window opens up, and a girl dances on the other side. Can't touch, just look. OK?"

The German couple don't understand. The wrinkled woman looks around the shop with Old World eyes, staring toward the back. Her husband asks in broken English what the girls do and what the customer does.

"Look," the clerk says again. "You go in, you shut the door, you put in some quarters, and a naked girl appears. She is behind a window. Then she dances while you watch. You just can't touch. OK?"

The couple look more confused then ever. They stand shoulder to shoulder, afraid to retreat back to the street. The clerk is impatient. He wears a skinny tie and rolled up sleeves, pleated pants with no pocket in back. His Chinese dinner sits on the counter, throwing off steam.

The couple are slowly nodding their heads, not saying a word. Customers side-step the two, heading en masse back to the booths as music pumps through the air.

"OK, let me explain it again." He leans down toward the wife, talking louder this time. "Tell your husband he goes in that room, he puts in some quarters, and a naked girl appears. A window is there. He looks through the window and she dances for him." The clerk shimmies his chest for added effect.

The wife looks bewildered.

"'Veely?' says the wife."

The clerk is rolling his eyes, nostrils flaring, buttons about to pop. A line of customers has now formed behind the German couple, and he's about to tell them to leave. Others are getting nervous because they have to stand waiting in plain view from the street.

"Lookit, one more time," his voice is direct. "Your husband goes in the room, puts the quarters in the machine, he sees the naked girl through the window. The girl dances. Your husband can play with his willy."

"Veely?" says the wife.

"Willy. Now make up your mind, I don't have all day."

The couple huddle. This time they talk quickly and quietly. The wife is carefully explaining it all to the husband in solemn words. His ears bend toward her mouth, catching the meaning.

Finally, a look of recognition sweeps across his face.

"Oh! . . ." he says finally.

The wife digs through her purse and comes out with a handful of quarters, which she carefully counts out one at a time. She drops them into his palm and then squeezes his cheek. The husband cautiously turns and goes into a booth, closing the door. The wife, alone and out of place, stands out among the video racks, dutifully waiting for her husband to watch a naked dancer beyond the window inside.

"Sehr gut," the clerk mumbles, as he finishes his Chinese dinner.

Hot Streets, Cold Meat

Williamsburg's Bedford Avenue rolls up its steamy carpet and tucks in for bed by 1am. The SoHo of Brooklyn is a miniature UN in a 20-block sprawl. Five-story brownstones, immigrant homes, and old industrial lofts house block after block of an interracial mix. Puerto Ricans, Haitians, Poles, Russians, Italians, and Hasidic Jews, along with migrant art types, are slumming together for the downscaled rents and the funky river views.

The Monkmobile sits slumbering peacefully in the yellow zone of a corned beef factory. Spicy meat fumes mix with exhaust in the early hour. We've been given generous free reign to a ground floor studio apartment on North Eighth, complete with loft bed, kitchenette, mice, loads of books, cockroaches, no cable, and no air conditioner. Mike guards the Monkmobile while Jim takes a shower. Rotting garbage from the East River's edge sends a death aroma throughout the 'hood. It's 95 degrees, and flies pick through the rot of waiting trash bins.

By 2am Mike's asleep in the loft bed. Jim crashes below on a folded out mattress thrown on the floor. It's thigh-sticking hot, and wetness is everywhere. Wet sheets, wet walls, sticky pillows, and sweaty socks. Blasts of hot air come off the street, through the windows and up the stairs.

At 3am Mike awakes with a start, bumps his head on the low ceiling, and knocks a wall of books onto the loft bed. Lying in a puddle of sweat, he's panting like a hot cat. The air tastes like plastic and the room feels like a death camp. He feels like he's dying, and the breaths come in gasps, searing the lungs.

He stumbles down the stairs like a blind man, groping for the kitchen, pausing at the sink. He dunks his head under the tap. He's turned on the cold water, but it's hot. No matter how long the water runs, the water stays warm. Mike stands in his shorts, toes curled on the floor. The fridge beckons like a whore from the cool side of town. The top freezer door, adorned with magnets and cut-out cartoons, is saying, "Open me, open me."

As the freezer door opens, Mike's long, skinny frame is engulfed by a cold blast of Arctic air. Mike furiously empties the freezer of ice trays, old meat, and a pint of ice cream. He sticks his head, shoulders, and arms deep inside, propping his chin on his hands. The cold engulfs him like a winter night full of sweet mountain air. He leans against the refrigerator door, breathing long and deep.

"Breathe," he whispers as his shoulders slump further in. He's so far in that his toes barely touch the floor. "Breathe." He stays in there, deep, smelling stale freezer air, falling asleep.

>>>•<<<

At 7am, North Eighth becomes a thoroughfare of delivery trucks dropping meat at the corned beef factory. Heavy metal gates bang open. Garbage trucks crash down the block, and the building shakes alive. Both Monks, zombies at best, hear the brusque voices of the morning carry through the grated window.

"Whose pink piece of shit is this? M-O-N-K. What the fuck is this, a circus?"

"Call the city. Get it towed outta here," yells a heavy voice.

Mike jerks awake to an open freezer door. His right ear is stuck to the inside, and he slowly pulls it away, tearing skin at the lobe.

"Christ, my head's freezing. What the hell am I doing?!"

Mike pulls frozen whiskers off his chin. A crust of ice outlines the brows. The right arm is blue from freezer burn. He stands in a pool of water at the base of the fridge.

"Oh my god. Jim! I fell asleep in the freezer!"

Jim's sprawled out on the floor in the front room, a bowl of millet at his feet. He lays snoring on his side, two stacks of *New Yorker* magazines surrounding his head.

"Whose pink piece of shit is this? M-O-N-K. What the fuck is this, a circus?"

Mike stumbles around him and pokes his eyes out the window at the commotion on the street.

The Monkmobile is surrounded by a crew of short, grumpy men, wearing white aprons splattered with corned beef.

"Get it towed," one short, bearded man is saying to the others. He wears a baseball cap and has a stomach as round as a beach ball.

Mike bolts through the apartment, shaking Jim awake. He pulls on some pants and steps outside. The right side of his face is still red and splotchy from the freezer.

He walks up to the crew, barefoot and red-eyed, pointing to the Monkmobile and forcing words from his throat. "It's mine," he says. "We're staying here."

"Listen, you get this outta here or we're having it towed. This is illegal. NO COMMERCIAL PARKING on the streets."

"Huh?" Mike looks up and down the street at the trucks parked everywhere. "But I'm not commercial. It's my home," he says, pointing to the pink Monkmobile.

"No living on the street. That's illegal." The short bearded man leans heavily toward Mike, his nose pointed to the curb, sneering at the pink.

"Well then, I mean, uh, I'm staying in that apartment."

"OK. No commercial parking. Do you hear me?"

"But it's not commercial, it's privately owned."

"No private vehicles. This is for COMMERCIAL!" he yells.

"Huh? But I thought you said no commercial . . ."

"Get it outta here or we're calling the cops. We own these buildings and we say who parks here. Fuckin' gypsies."

Mike stands confused, shakes his thawed head, and resigns to move the Monkmobile before the yellow tow trucks come roaring down the street to take the pink beast away.

Twenty minutes later the Monks park 2 blocks away on North Sixth. Jim and Mike crunch across a street paved in broken glass. Early morning neighbors sit on their stoops sipping tea, reading the Polish press. Down the way, Tops Supermarket is opening its doors. Built inside a warehouse, it could be a car shop from the looks of the outside.

Walking into Tops, the Monks notice an abrupt temperature change.

"This place is 30 degrees cooler," Jim exclaims.

The store has concrete floors and harsh lights that hang from above. More of an oversized corner market, it has only a few long rows. Ever curious, Jim decides to

look around a left corner and discovers a frozen paradise. Through plastic curtains draping heavy to the floor is another room that's ICE COLD. Here all of the refrigerated goods are stacked along shelves and across the floor. It's a butcher shop, cheese shop, and full of sodas, too. The temperature plunges to the 40s, cold enough to see your breath. Dozens of people are slowly pushing carts around, shopping for meat.

"Let's shop," says Jim.

"It's nice and cold," chatters Mike.

The Monks settle in at the Top's Supermarket meat department for the next half hour. Carefully reading labels, taking plenty of time, Mike studies everything from pirogi to beef tongue to those "family paks" of Perdue chicken wings. Jim finally notices that the other 20 people in there are basically doing the same thing, stalling for time, hoping to catch relief from the insufferable heat.

"Great place to chill," says Mike. "But looks like we're sharing it with half of Williamsburg."

Joe's Truck Repair

"Hello, I was wondering if you do repairs on motor homes? I've got a 26-foot Fleetwood Bounder that sounds like a lawnmower, loses power when driving in traffic, and is blowing huge clouds of black smoke out the rear. Can you help me?"

Click.

Mike's gone through the entire Manhattan phone book under "Automobile and Truck Repair" and has found, with little surprise, no results.

"Hello, do you do truck repairs?"

"Yeah, we work on trucks. Whaddaya got?"

"I have a 26-foot motor home."

"A what?"

"A motor home."

"Take it to Jersey."

Click.

"Hello, do you repair motor homes?"

"What's wrong, you need tires?"

"No, it's the engine, I want to take it to someplace close."

"Yeah, what's wrong?"

"It sounds like a lawn mower and it's blowing black smoke."

"Dump it in the East River!"

Click.

Mike's hands are getting chapped from clutching the phone as he stands outside at a 25-cents-a-minute phone booth that keeps eating his coins. He's next to a Laundromat where dour young Polish wives are doing loads of laundry and smoking cigarettes out on the curb. A midget man is practicing swings with a base-ball bat. The Monkmobile sits on the street, smirking.

"This is the last time I'm ever driving this thing to New York," Mike mumbles to himself.

He dials the 30th number, to a garage out in Jamaica Plains, and finally gets a friendly ear.

"Yeah, it's a Fleetwood, 26-foot."

"Oh, yeah, what is it, like one of those party jobs, seats eight people?" the voice chimes on the other end.

"Sort of; it's a 26-foot Fleetwood," says Mike.

"Yeah, whatever, just bring her in. We'll take a look at it."

"You sure?" Mike asks.

"Yeah, yeah, yeah, just bring it in. We got caddies all over the place."

"Cadillacs?"

"Yeah, yeah, yeah."

"I said this is a 26-foot Fleetwood *motor home*!" Mike is starting to yell, his face turning blue.

"What," yells the man at the garage. "Whaddaya talkin' about?"

"A *motor home*," fumes Mike.

"Take it to Jersey."

Click.

Finally Mike hits pay dirt on his 31st number and last quarter. Less than 15 blocks away, up Metropolitan Avenue, is Joe's Truck Repair.

"Yeah, I do trucks. Yeah, I've had a motor home or two, a few years back; you know, like for the movies."

Mike jumps in the motor home and cranks up the engine. Clouds of black smoke swirl up from behind as the Monkmobile turns the corner and heads toward Brooklyn's Metropolitan Avenue. The engine bellows down the street, sounding like a cross between a lawn mower and a chainsaw. But no one raises an eyebrow or turns a head. Nearly every car in traffic sounds exactly the same.

Joe's garage sits right on the avenue. Its building stops at the sidewalk, and a tall wide gate opens onto the street, revealing a narrow driveway crowded with four trucks and a bus. Mike edges the pink beast through the nose of the gate but then has to stop. There is nowhere to go. The tail of the Monkmobile sticks out in the street as traffic swerves around.

Mike walks in through the gates as the Monkmobile backfires and dies on the spot. Inside, the compound looks like an industrial Armageddon. Broken engine parts, discarded tires, and rivers of oil streak along the ground.

"There's more oil here than in all of Texas," Mike mutters as he enters the dark-ened garage, looking for Joe.

Inside is a labyrinth of grease monkey hell. Skeletal engine parts are everywhere. Half-opened carcasses of trucks lie abandoned like fetuses at a back alley abortion clinic. There is no order to the garage save for a wall of tires stacked toward the back.

An assortment of delivery trucks from Brooklyn, Manhattan, and Queens are parked inside at haphazard angles. Some are partly jacked up, others lay low, some are tireless with lights strung underneath. A pair of legs roll from underneath a large van.

"Is Joe here?" Mike yells.

"He's in the office!" a voice yells back.

Mike trips around more debris, the grease building up on his shoes. Now his feet squish as he walks, and the fine stitching at the bottom of his jeans is getting covered in black.

Walking deep into the building, Mike finds Joe separated from the garage by only a file cabinet and a bare light. He sits at a desk stacked high with catalogs and paper, grease covering everything.

"You Joe?"

"Uh," he grunts.

Joe's on the phone, swearing about a part. When he gets off he leaps up with a big smile, clenching his jaws and offering his grease-caked hand. "What can I do for you?"

"I brought the motor home," says Mike, "but there's no room to drive it in."

Joe walks out a side door that leads back to the compound into the searing bright sun. He splashes through a grease puddle and sees the pink Monkmobile nosed in through the gate.

"Jeez, you buy it like that?" he asks, looking at the electric pink walls and mural-ized sides of the motor home.

"No, I painted it."

"You mean you wanted it this way?" Joe shakes his head.

He's soon poking his head under the engine, sniffing the metal and banging on parts. "Start her up," he says.

Mike climbs in. The Monkmobile won't start, grinding the starter with each turn of the key. Finally, with a big pop, it starts, then goes completely dead, starter and all.

"Now what?" asks an exasperated Mike.

Joe whistles a shrill dog whistle and soon enough three big guys, six-foot four each, with a half ton between them, come ambling out, greasy rags in the pockets of their jumpsuits. Their arms are as big as Mike's waist. The biggest one walks with thighs rubbing hard, making a sandpaper sound. They butt their shoulders up against the front of the Monkmobile while Joe stands in the street stopping traffic. Within minutes they've pushed the beast out on the street while another guy backs out two trucks to park up the block. Then with a massive shove they all muscle the Monkmobile back into the compound until it is all the way in, like they'd done this a hundred times before.

"Whatcha got in there," one of them hollers as he returns to the garage. "Smells like shit."

"It's my holding tank," says Mike, "you know, my sewage."

"Should've dumped it in the river!"

›Here comes everybody

New York's Emerging Mono-Culture

Mallified in Manhattan

Unshaven, fat, and dressed in authentic pirate attire, Captain Hook harangues any-one who enters his maritime junk shop at the South Street Seaport: "Any money to help save the seaport?" When a middle-aged man balks, Jim Monk intervenes: "Anything will do. Give him a penny." The man gives two—big mistake.

"I don't want your pennies," Hook growls. "If that's all you think this shop is worth, get out!" The man, with his cookie-cutter family in tow, happily obliges, and Captain Hook turns to Jim. "I'm not a monkey. I don't take pennies. He can shove them up his ass."

Hook owns the last authentic shop at the South Street Seaport. The rest are chains, the same retail outlets you'll find in any mall in America. "They are trying to implant suburbia into urbia," Captain Hook tells Jim. "The cancer started in 1990 when they brought in Country Road, J. Crew, Liz Claiborne."

"They" is the Rouse Corporation, mall developers who have earned a name gen-trifying old seaports and landmarks, like Boston's Fannueil Hall and Baltimore's Inner Harbor. They've all but gutted New York's South Street Seaport, turning it into a white-bread tourist trap. Now the landlord is eyeing Captain Hook's. According to a sign hanging in the store's window, Rouse is threatening to increase the rent to $19,780 a month. Hook is fighting back. Donations from visitors help defray legal expenses, which so far have amounted to $75,000. "I'll move out of here when the courts tell me," Hook says. "Then they can put in their damn clothing store."

Captain Hook may be gruff, but he has certainly hit the nail on the head. The "cancer" he talks about has spread, to SoHo, Greenwich Village, Midtown, and beyond. In the 7 years since our last visit to New York, the city has been hit by a tidal wave of mallification, gentrification, and homogenization. Union Square has shorn its radical roots to make room for the Zeckendorf Towers, the Heartland Brewery, Toys 'R' Us, a Starbucks, and a Virgin Megastore. Lower Broadway, in SoHo, is now home not only to discount jeans outlets but also to the Pottery Barn, Williams Sonoma, Armani Exchange, and Eddie Bauer, among others. (The last time we were in town, the classiest place on the street was the Canal Jean Company.) The All-Star Cafe and Disney's *Beauty and the Beast* have colonized the down-and-dirty milieu of 42nd Street. Fifty-Seventh Street has become a row of theme restau-rants. Starbucks clones are fast replacing standard-fare coffee shops, imposing the words "grande" and "Americano" where "regular" once ruled the day. And the list goes on.

Old New York vs. New New York

The Deuce	The "New" 42nd Street
Stuffy old shoe *New Yorker*	Tina Brown's *New Yorker*
Village Voice	*Time Out*
Hotel Chelsea	The Gotham Group
The Ziegfeld	Sony Imax
Character	Convenience
Original Ray's	Domino's
Ebbet's Field Donut Shop	Krispy Kreme
Happy Land	Disneyland
Carmine Street Y	Reebok Fitness Center
Cafe Reggio	Starbucks
Dr. Zizmor's single-panel subway ads	Full-Train brand ads
Checker cabs	Pedicabs
"Regular"	"Frappuccino"
Tad's Steaks	All Star Cafe
The Subway Inn	Heartland Brewery
Art in the streets	Street artists in jail
Paris Is Burning	The Life
AIDS	Tibet
LES tenements	LES 1BR compl ren $1600
The Melting Pot	The Welfare Bill
Squatters	Dog runs
Immigrants	Tourists
"I Love New York"	"Polite New Yorker"
One of a kind	Something for everyone
Jackie O	John-John
Downtown Beirut	Standard
Hell's Kitchen	The Broadway Initiative
Times Square	"Square Times"
In the life	Quality of Life
Princess Pamela's	The Motown Cafe
Palladium	NYU
Writers	Content providers
Warhol	Warhol wannabes
Bernie Goetz, the Subway Vigilante	Rudy Giuliani, Mayor Cop
The Garage	Condos
Skateboarders at the Cube	Operation Civil Village
New York as a real place	New York as Seinfeld—a smug city, no longer about anything

See Ya' Later, Mom and Pop

New Yorkers are divided on the subject of their city's fast-changing landscape. They remain socially tolerant yet are tired of squeegee people mucking up their windshields; they relish the city's unique retail climate but are comforted by the presence of the nearby Barnes & Noble; they appreciate the city's funky, dark esthetic but are appalled by the desecration of its parks and buildings; they want to partake of a little herb but are tired of drug traffickers swirling around the 'hood. In other words, today's New Yorkers are no longer afraid to admit a few bourgeois conceits, which national chains and a pro-growth mayor have been all too happy to supply.

This mainstreaming of the city, what *The New York Times* calls the "remodeling [of] New York for the bourgeoisie," is not a throwback to the materialist self-aggrandizement of the 1980s. New Yorkers in that edgy, go-go decade liked the city the way it was; they just wanted to reward themselves for their hyperdrive. Nineties New Yorkers, chastened by the excesses of the past, are more bucolic, more middle American. They want the good life—the good suburban life, that is. But the new suburban-minded New Yorkers are still New Yorkers: Their one-stop shopping has to be gourmet; their clean streets have to be lively; they like graffiti but want it in art galleries instead of on subway cars; they want their homeless to be entertaining. Above all, they want a manicured, comfortable, sanitized urbanity, with pockets of orchestrated weirdness to keep everyone happy and spendy.

The city has become, as the economists say, risk-averse. The signs are everywhere. David Letterman, whose early days were so pioneering, has lost his edge. His show, now at CBS, mirrors the city's cultural makeover: It is more accessible, more predictable, and far less confrontational. Even Madonna, hardly a cultural critic, has noticed. "You really changed since the last time I was on the show," she told Letterman back in 1994. "Money's made you soft. . . . I see all these, like, you know, movie stars coming here and you're just all ga-ga." On Broadway, new plays are a rarity these days; instead we get reissues of such standard fare as *A Funny Thing Happened on the Way to the Forum; Victor, Victoria; Annie;* and *The King and I.*

V. S. Pritchett once wrote (in *New York Proclaimed*) that there is no city outside New York where newness is so vigorously pursued. But the newness of '90s New York is safe, manageable, antiseptic; the type of thing—albeit with a "hip," "fresh," "urbane" twist—that you'd expect to find in Epcot Center, Mall of America, or Nike Town. It's newness as marketing concept, not organic reality.

While New York has always been a battleground between the forces of sameness and diversity, there seems to be something palpably different this time around. Mainly it's because, after years of knocking on the door, mainstream America has finally broken into the city. Here comes everybody—and with their arrival, there goes a lot of what made New York *New York.*

Call us nostalgic, anti growth, or simply out of touch, but we think what is currently happening to the city is tragic. We liked the frumpy mom-and-pops, the quirky novelty stores, the grungy markets, the ethnic emporiums; we liked it that in the country's largest city you had a hard time getting a Wendy's hamburger or a Seattle-style latte or a Kmart blue-light special; we were relieved to find no microbreweries to speak of and so few megastores (Macy's and Bloomies are beloved, Filene's Basement and Old Navy are not).

After many years, we returned to our favorite American city. We visited the Barnes & Nobles, the Starbucks, the Bed, Bath & Beyond, and although we enjoyed their virtues, we knew we'd find them in any city in the country. So we turned our backs and sought out the funky, frumpy, eccentric New York of old. Our prognosis, at the end of our search, is a qualified mix of doom and delight. The bad news: A lot has been lost to the fast-emerging mono-culture; a lot has been squashed by giganticism run amok. The good news: Some genuinely great things still survive. The city may have lost Annie Sprinkle, the legendary porn star turned performance artist, but it still has Miss Vera's School for Boys Who Want to Be Girls, perhaps the world's only cross-dressing academy. It still has Jennifer Miller's funky, gender-bending Circus Amok; Raven Chanticleer's African-American Wax Museum; and a host of one-of-a-kind characters such as Quentin Crisp, Gene Pool, Lady Bunny, Joey Arias, and Gary Panter.

Coney Island's Sideshows by the Seashore may have lost its lease to a souvlaki stand (if the landlord hadn't been so obstreperous, the new tenant would be McDonald's instead), but it's managed to find a new space just off the dilapidated boardwalk. Adam Purple may be gone, but the Mosaic Man is still around, beautifying the East Village with makeshift art (despite the city's repeated attempts to force him out). On subway cars, the likes of Nike, Swatch, and Fruitopia may have knocked out many single-panel ads for hair replacement, AIDS prevention, and M.D. Tusch (hemorrhoid healer), but the inimitable Dr. Zizmor's unforgettably funky ads for laser dermatology live on. The Bowery Bar represents all that's gone wrong in the East Village, yet, in a gratifying sign that the radical spirit of the Village is still alive, the next-door neighbors have hung a sign in their window that reads: "Lifestyles of the $ick and Shameless—Cooper Union, How Could You Have Done This to Our Neighborhood?"

Cookie-cutter, L.A.-style cocktail lounges are ubiquitous throughout the city, but you can still find authentic dives like the Parkside Lounge and the Subway Inn. While on October 19th, 1997, 42nd Street's Grand Luncheonette served its last greasy hot dog and took down its famed "No Spitting," "No Water," "No Loitering" signs for eternity, the irrepressible Tad's Steaks and Holy Cross Church survive despite the Disneyfication of the area. The Bread Shop in Morningside Heights, where I first discovered molasses-flavored granola and natural bread while coaching

Velvet ropes. Give us a break. The 80s are over.

Mafia-like magazine distributors, who demand that you, the publisher, pay them to distribute your title.

The downtown press's overuse of the following: "gettin' busy," "flava," "Prada-clad" anybody!

The New York press's obsession with the following overexposed personalities: Marla Trump, Tina Brown, Mort Zuckerman!

Bodegas. The Korean green grocers beat them hands down in quality, selection, and service. They serve one useful purpose—drug distribution.

Condé Nasty.

Squeegee people, and the old-line New York liberals who defend their right to dirty your windshield.

Any kid that acts like an extra from *Kids.*

Frat boy cum stock broker cum bridge-and-tunnel weekend hangouts that line the Upper East Side.

The whole outmoded **club-kid thing.**

Beautiful young models. They don't know what to make of the Monkmobile. Should they ignore it, casually note it, or pose in front of it so they can appear more "downtown" in their portfolio?

West Broadway. Eurotrash trough. Will you people please take your Gucci purses, your Italian loafers, your cancerous tans, your unfiltered cigarettes, and your lines of cocaine

and go live someplace else. This is America, damn it, not Monte Carlo.

Bridge-and-tunnel creeps in Jeep Cherokees. Take your mindless house music, your booming loudspeakers, and gedouttahere. You give this city a bad rap.

Faux Tibetan Buddhists. Poor New Yorkers. They don't have a clue about true Buddhism. They think it's some new social club with a charming Tibetan pretext. The Tibetans are so desperate to get back their 'hood, they play along with the charade. For the real thing, try Korean Zen—no Japanese chauvinism, no celebrity chic, no feel-good causes. Just brass tacks Buddha way. And lots of kimchee.

Knee-jerk liberalism. Rudy Giuliani is the best thing for this city in 2 decades, and still liberals moan about "the cuts." Yeah, The Hunchback's a bit excessive at times, but he's a good man, doing a thankless job, making courageous choices, and *he should be given his due.*

Elitism. Though New York has mellowed as the digital ethos moved East, it still clings to a repugnant cheekiness that can totally spoil the fun. In more genuine parts of the planet, quality is quality, priced accordingly. New York seems intent on adding a veneer of shallow snobbery (models, velvet ropes, and overtanned celebs, oh my!) over what is simple excellence, destroying whatever natural appeal a place might have had. Perhaps the **Bowery Bar** serves very good food, but who in their right mind would go there with all the idiotic attitude attached to it. Of course, L.A. is just as noxious, but it is still embarrassing to find a city with such brains as New York reduced to such needless insolence.

Silicon Alley hype.

debate at nearby Columbia, is gone, but Peter and "Ma" Sylvestri's lovable Whole Earth Bakery is still cookin' at 130 Saint Marks Place. B. Altman's may be out of business, but the New York Doll Hospital, founded in 1900, is still around—as is CBGB's, which opened its doors in 1973, unleashing punk rock on the world; as is Schapiro's House of Kosher Wines, since 1899 serving wine "so thick you can cut it with a knife."

In this guide, we pay tribute to these people and institutions, and to others like them. We hope that, far from fragile relics of a fast-disappearing past, they are evidence of a still-diverse, still-offbeat, still-authentic present. Sadly, only time will tell.

Dear Monks,

Thanks for sending me Jim's essay. I like it, and applaud your intentions, though I suspect I'm so far from your target audience that my map of the city would look like a map of pre-sand Egypt to them.

What I miss in New York are two broad categories: (A) I miss that period when money and power seemed to be giving up or had given up on NYC, when living downtown was like living in some kind of hip North Dakota, when it was all scavenger culture and recycling and making do and using your imagination rather than your wallet; and (B) I miss all the traces of the really old New York. In the far downtown, say, I used to go to Mendoza's Bookstore on Ann Street, which was overpriced and run by misanthropic snobs, but on the other hand it had been there *since the 1840's*—you could imagine that Melville had browsed there. I went by there maybe four years ago on my way back from the motor vehicle bureau, and it had vanished (high rent the culprit, as usual). In South Street Seaport I had long wanted to have dinner at Sweets, upstairs in the last building on your right as you come down the Fulton Street Mall. It opened in 1842, and died about two years ago.

I miss all the designated trade zones of the city, which tend to be marked—if at all—by mere traces. Does anybody who frequents the Babyland bar on Avenue A realize that it owes its name to the former occupant, back when Avenue A was, officially, the baby furniture district? Broadway between Union and Madison Squares in the trendoid Flatiron District was the toy and novelty district. SoHo incorporated part or all of the cap and hat district, the second-rung cloak-and-suiters, the agricultural machinery (!) district. And those still hung on fifteen years ago. I miss the Bellmore Cafeteria (featured in *Taxi Driver*), Hubert's Museum on 42nd Street, movie houses that had balconies where you could smoke, all the pleasantly vile coffee shops and bars, the two Jewish coffee shops—one on Canal Street and Broadway, the other, Moishe's, on Bowery and Grand—that both falsely claimed to have invented the egg cream (but made excellent ones nevertheless). I miss local color, the small-time in all its many forms, eccentric local characters who were not media personalities, hand-painted signs, ancient garish neon, all the stuff that was New York City's equivalent of roadside attractions, and the whole idea that with only a small nest you could set up your own attraction. I guess that still exists to some extent on side streets in the East Village (a name I never use, by the way, because it was cooked up by visionary real estate gentrificationists in the 1960s and had no organic origin), but not for long, or not for poor people, anyway.

Yeah, I'm bitter about the city, about the world when you come down to it (I lived in Paris in 1974 when it still had a lot of rough edges and real life, and was lived in by people who hadn't inherited anything but debts). I hate every aspect of the culture of money, and that means I feel less and less a part of this city . . .

—Luc Sante

Luc Sante is the author of *Low Life* (Vintage), *Evidence* (Noonday), and *The Factory of Facts* (Pantheon).

Ontario

Lake Superior

Sault Ste. Marie

Quebec

Montreal

New Brunswick

Quebec

Ottawa

ME

Augusta

Paul

WI

Lake Huron

Lake Michigan

NH

VT

NY

Albany

Toronto

L. Ontario

MA

Boston

Cape Cod

Providence

Milwaukee

MI

Niagara Falls

Detroit

Chicago

L. Erie

Cleveland

PA

New York City

Pittsburgh

Philadelphia

NJ

Atlantic City

Indianapolis

OH

Baltimore

Cincinnati

IN

WV

MD DE

IL

Washington DC

St. Louis

Charleston

VA

Richmond

Louisville

KY

Atlantic

Ocean

Nashville

TN

Charlotte

NC

Raleigh

AR

Memphis

Little Rock

Birmingham

SC

Jackson

MS

AL

Atlanta

GA

Charleston

LA

Savannah

Mobile

Jacksonville

New Orleans

›mοnk mαρs

Arrival

The average arrival to New York flies into one of the three main airports—**Kennedy International** (JFK) (☎ **718/244-4444**) or **La Guardia** (☎ **718/533-3400**), both in Queens, or **Newark International** (☎ **201/961-6000**), in New Jersey—and hops either a taxi or a cushy bus to get right to the heart of things in Manhattan. There are drawbacks. One, the taxis aren't cheap: You'll drop at least twenty bucks to get to Midtown from La Guardia and around $30 from Kennedy, plus tolls and tip. Buses are about half that, but you'll be riding mostly with salesmen from Wisconsin, in town to try and make the payment on their kid's braces.

There are other ways to arrive, of course.

You could drive, for one, though if you're staying in Manhattan you'll have to deal with the hellish and/or expensive parking situation. (See "Transportation.")

Or you could take the bus, arriving at the **Port Authority Bus Terminal,** Eighth Avenue between 40th and 42nd streets (☎ **212/564-8484**). With luck, you'll be in time to see the twice-daily commuter races.

Ditto for arriving by train. By Amtrak (☎ **800/USA-RAIL**) you'll arrive at **Pennsylvania Station,** Seventh Avenue between 31st and 33rd streets, which is just about the ugliest imaginable entree to a major city.

Assuming you do arrive by air, and assuming that air deposits you at either La Guardia or JFK, you might want to take the adventurous (and, at $1.50, cheap) route and head for the city by means of **public transportation.**

From JFK, that means the **A train**—as in the Ellington/Strayhorn song. To get to the station at Howard Beach, you have to grab one of the free shuttle buses that runs between the terminal and the parking lots, but ask the driver if it's the right one for the subway (some only do the parking lot route). Once on the train, it's about an hour's ride into town, passing 22 stops (including Brooklyn's own Broadway, where many a tourist has been suckered into disembarking) before even getting to Manhattan. **Big plus:** The ride is above ground for much of the way, allowing you to see something of Brooklyn. **Big minus:** It takes friggin' forever.

From La Guardia, you can take the **M60 bus** right from the terminal to the city, but it'll only bring you as far as 105th Street and West End Avenue on the Upper West Side, right close to Columbia University. From there, you can catch the M104 bus into Midtown or the 1 or 9 subway all the way downtown and into Brooklyn. (Be sure to ask the driver for a free transfer when you get on at the airport—that way you won't have to blow the extra $1.50.) **Big plus:** The ride from La Guardia to the Triborough Bridge is usually pretty fast, and once in Manhattan it runs all the way across fabled 125th Street—Harlem's main drag—before cutting south at Amsterdam Avenue. **Big minus:** If you have much luggage, there's nowhere to put it where it won't be in other peoples' way.

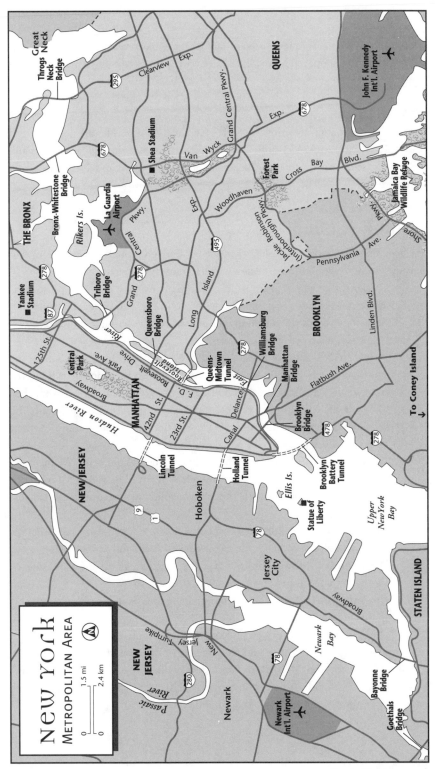

New York
METROPOLITAN AREA

⊕

0 ___ 1.5 mi
0 ___ 2.4 km

THE BRONX

Great Neck

Throgs Neck Bridge

295

Clearview Exp.

QUEENS

John F. Kennedy Int'l. Airport ✈

Bronx-Whitestone Bridge

678

Shea Stadium ■

Van Wyck

Grand Central Pkwy.

678

Exp.

Rikers Is.

La Guardia Airport ✈

Forest Park

Bay Blvd.

Cross

Jamaica Bay Wildlife Refuge

Yankee Stadium ■

278

Triboro Bridge

Grand Central Pkwy.

Exp.

Woodhaven

Jackie Robinson (Interborough) Pkwy.

Shore Pkwy.

87

278

278

495

Pennsylvania Ave.

Long Island

BROOKLYN

Linden Blvd.

125th St.

Queensboro Bridge

Central Park

Park Ave.

Roosevelt Island

F.D. Roosevelt Drive

East River

Williamsburg Bridge

278

Flatbush Ave.

Broadway

MANHATTAN

42nd St.

23rd St.

Queens-Midtown Tunnel

Manhattan Bridge

To Coney Island →

Hudson River

Delancey

Canal

Brooklyn Bridge

478

278

NEW JERSEY

Lincoln Tunnel

Holland Tunnel

Ellis Is.

Brooklyn Battery Tunnel

Hoboken

Statue of Liberty ■

Upper New York Bay

9

11

78

Jersey City

STATEN ISLAND

NEW JERSEY

New Jersey Turnpike

Newark Bay

Broadway

Passaic River

280

Newark

78

Newark Int'l. Airport ✈

Bayonne Bridge

Goethals Bridge

From Newark, you're pretty much stuck with the bus services or a taxi. The former will run you about ten bucks, the latter between $30 and $40, depending where you're going in the city.

Practicalities

For transportation information for JFK, La Guardia, and Newark airports, call **Air-Ride** (☎ **800/247-7433**) for a taped message that runs through all the bus and private car service companies registered with the New York and New Jersey Port Authority.

Getting Around

In the ("Transportation") section later in the book we go though the various ways of getting around town, but here's some practical info.

First, pick up a subway map at the ticket booth of any subway station. Buses generally have pockets of bus maps right inside the door. The **subway map** gives routes for all the boroughs, but the **bus map** will only be for the borough you're in.

Here are some main routes to remember:

- **The N and R subway lines:** Monk faves. In Manhattan, they follow the same route, only diverging in Long Island City on their northern (Queens) end and in Bay Ridge on their southern (Brooklyn) end. In between, they take you to a helluva lot of central New York spots: Coney Island, the Brooklyn Bridge, Tribeca, SoHo, NYU, Union Square, the Flatiron District, Times Square, the south end of Central Park.
- **The L subway line:** Williamsburg lifeline. Runs straight across Manhattan's 14th Street, across the East River, through Williamsburg, through a corner of the Queens/Brooklyn border, then heads south to Canarsie, near Jamaica Bay.
- **The B, D, F, and Q subway lines:** For access to Coney Island and Brighton Beach, and all the Brooklyn that lies between them and Manhattan.
- **The 1 and 9 subway lines:** For transportation along the west side of Manhattan and up to Van Cortlandt Park in the Bronx.
- **The 4 subway line:** For transportation along the east side of Manhattan and up through the South Bronx.
- **The M4 bus:** Maybe New York's most all-inclusively scenic bus ride— if you've got a lot of time and the patience of a Zen master.

Subways accept the **Metrocard** farecard or tokens. Buses accept Metrocard or exact change. A ride (to anywhere) costs $1.50. You can also get weekly or monthly Metrocards that will save you a bundle.

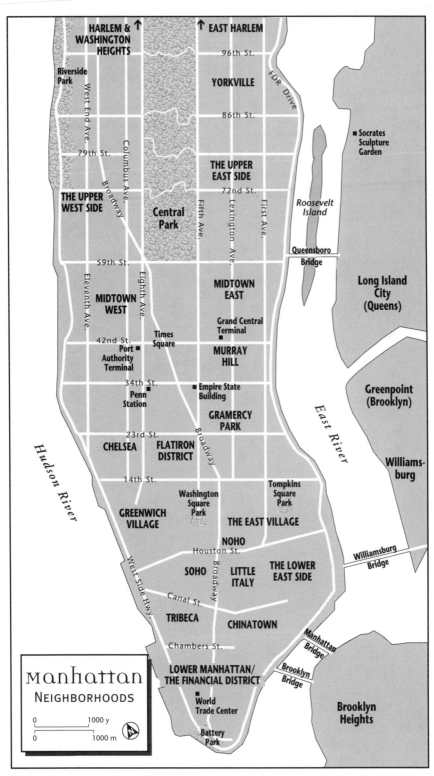

**HARLEM &
WASHINGTON
HEIGHTS** ↑

↑ **EAST HARLEM**

Riverside
Park

96th St.

YORKVILLE

West End Ave.

FDR Drive

86th St.

79th St.

Columbus Ave.

■ Socrates
Sculpture
Garden

**THE UPPER
EAST SIDE**

**THE UPPER
WEST SIDE**

Broadway

**Central
Park**

72nd St.

Fifth Ave.

Lexington Ave.

First Ave.

*Roosevelt
Island*

59th St.

Eighth Ave.

**Queensboro
Bridge**

Eleventh Ave.

**MIDTOWN
WEST**

**MIDTOWN
EAST**

**Long Island
City
(Queens)**

42nd St.

Times
Square

Grand Central
Terminal
■

Port
Authority
Terminal ■

**MURRAY
HILL**

34th St.
Penn
Station ■

■ Empire State
Building

**Greenpoint
(Brooklyn)**

East River

**GRAMERCY
PARK**

Broadway

23rd St.

CHELSEA

**FLATIRON
DISTRICT**

**Williams-
burg**

14th St.

Hudson River

Washington
Square
Park

Tompkins
Square
Park

**GREENWICH
VILLAGE**

THE EAST VILLAGE

NOHO

Houston St.

**Williamsburg
Bridge**

SOHO

Broadway

**LITTLE
ITALY**

**THE LOWER
EAST SIDE**

Canal St.

West Side Hwy.

TRIBECA

CHINATOWN

Chambers St.

**Manhattan
Bridge**

**Brooklyn
Bridge**

**LOWER MANHATTAN/
THE FINANCIAL DISTRICT**

**Brooklyn
Heights**

■ World
Trade Center

Battery
Park

ⲘⲁⲛⳂⲁttⲁⲛ
NEIGHBORHOODS

0   1000 y

0   1000 m

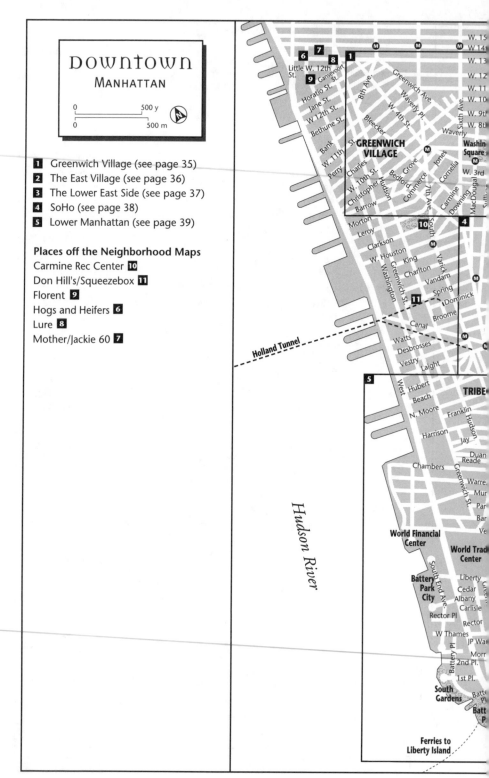

DOWNTOWN
MANHATTAN

0 — 500 y
0 — 500 m

1 Greenwich Village (see page 35)
2 The East Village (see page 36)
3 The Lower East Side (see page 37)
4 SoHo (see page 38)
5 Lower Manhattan (see page 39)

Places off the Neighborhood Maps
Carmine Rec Center **10**
Don Hill's/Squeezebox **11**
Florent **9**
Hogs and Heifers **6**
Lure **8**
Mother/Jackie 60 **7**

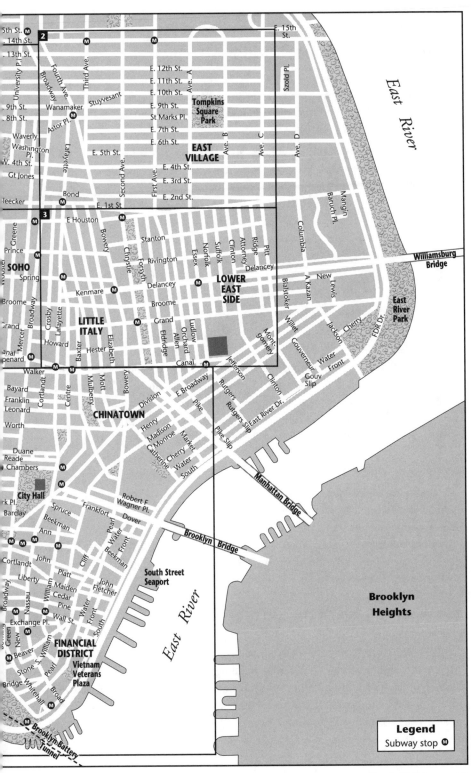

5th St. Ⓜ
. 14th St. Ⓜ
. 13th St.
University Pl.
. 9th St.
. 8th St.
Waverly
Washington Pl.
W. 4th St.
Gt Jones
leecker
Bond

2
Broadway
Fourth Ave.
Astor Pl.
Wanamaker
Lafayette
Third Ave.
Stuyvesant
E. 5th St.
Second Ave.
First Ave.
E. 1st St
E. 12th St.
E. 11th St.
E. 10th St.
E. 9th St.
St Marks Pl.
E. 7th St.
E. 6th St.
E. 4th St.
E. 3rd St.
E. 2nd St.
Ave. A
Ave. B
Ave. C
Ave. D
E. 15th St.
Szold Pl.

Tompkins Square Park

EAST VILLAGE

East River

Mangin
Baruch Pl.
Columbia

Williamsburg Bridge

SOHO
Greene
Prince
Spring
Broome
Grand
Mercer
Crosby
Lafayette
Howard
anal
openard
Walker

3
E Houston
Bowery
Chrystie
Forsyth
Kenmare
Baxter
Hester
Elizabeth
Mott
Mulberry
Bowery
Centre

Stanton
Rivington
Delancey
Broome
Grand
Canal
Stanton
Norfolk
Suffolk
Clinton
Attorney
Ridge
Pitt
Delancey
Essex
Ludlow
Orchard
Allen
Eldridge
Jefferson
Montgomery
Clinton

LOWER EAST SIDE

LITTLE ITALY

Blaistoker
Willet
A Kazan
New
Lewis
Jackson
Gouverneur
Cherry
Water
Front
Gouv Slip
Water

East River Park

FDR Dr.

CHINATOWN
Division
E. Broadway
Henry
Madison
Monroe
Catherine
Cherry
Water
South
Pike
Rutgers
Rutgers Slip
Pike Slip
Market
Monroe
East River Dr.

Duane
Reade
Chambers

City Hall
rk Pl.
Barclay
Spruce
Beekman
Ann
John
Cortlandt
Liberty
Frankfort
Dover
Robert F Wagner Pl.
Pearl
Water
Front
Cliff
Beekman
John
Fletcher
Platt
Maiden
Cedar
Pine
Wall St.

Manhattan Bridge

Brooklyn Bridge

South Street Seaport

East River

Brooklyn Heights

Broadway
Green
New
Nassau
William
Exchange Pl.
Beaver
Stone S.
Pearl
Broad
Whitehall
Bridge
Wall St.
Water
Front
South

FINANCIAL DISTRICT

Vietnam Veterans Plaza

Brooklyn Battery Tunnel

Legend
Subway stop Ⓜ

Downtown Neighborhoods

WEST VILLAGE. (aka Greenwich Village). For Monk purposes, the Village starts at Sixth Avenue in the east and runs to the Hudson River. In the other direction, it runs from 14th St. down to Houston.

The West Village is civil, livable, neighborly, and a perfect spot for people who want to retain their humanity while living within the city's vortex. The quaint little streets wind in and out, the place has a sense of history, there are surprising little pockets of beautiful architecture, and there's a total absence of towering apartment complexes.

EAST VILLAGE. Bowery/Third Ave. eastward, between Houston and 14th St.

Under attack for a decade from the forces of gentrification, the East Village still barely holds out as a bastion of eccentricity and diversity, providing a lot of the character and rawness that keeps New York City new. For now anyway, it's attained that rare and elusive quality of being both livable and exciting.

LOWER EAST SIDE. Houston toward Canal, east of Allen St.

This was New York's original immigrant neighborhood, where the poorest of the poor scraped by in cold-water tenements, with shared bathrooms and little heat. A few of the area's original Jewish establishments remain, but at this point the Lower East Side is evolving into a place where New Jersey comes to be entertained. Still, for the moment the place retains its gray, dark, and funky ethnic ambiance.

SOHO. Area around West Broadway, between Houston and Canal sts.

This famous artsy boho mecca has rapidly transformed into a conventional art and shopping district catering to one commercial fetish or another. The cobblestone streets and amazing cast iron architecture remain, but the stores are way overpriced, and on weekends the neighborhood is filled with people you just don't want to know. Stay away from West Broadway at all costs—it's schmoozing grounds for a sizable quotient of Eurotrash.

FINANCIAL DISTRICT. From the Battery up to around Chambers St. and from river to river.

The pot from which New York sprouted, and still the city's seat of power, all narrow streets, twisting canyons, towering buildings, and money, money, money. During the day it's all hustle-bustle, but at night most of the area is a ghost town, so quiet you can almost imagine what it was like a hundred, two hundred, three hundred years ago.

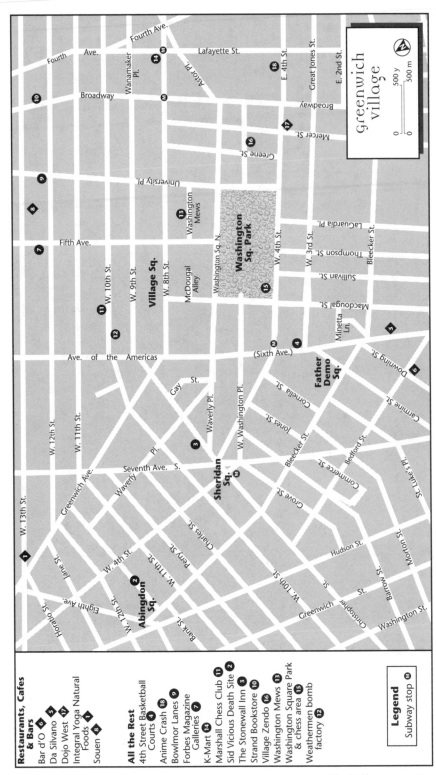

Greenwich village

0 ___ 500 y
0 ___ 500 m

Legend
Subway stop Ⓜ

Restaurants, Cafes & Bars
Bar d'O ❻
Da Silvano ❺
Dojo West ⓱
Integral Yoga Natural Foods ❶
Souen ❽

All the Rest
4th Street Basketball Courts ❹
Anime Crash ⓲
Bowlmor Lanes ❾
Forbes Magazine Galleries ❼
K-Mart ⓮
Marshall Chess Club ⓫
Sid Vicious Death Site ❷
The Stonewall Inn ❸
Strand Bookstore ❿
Village Zendo ⓰
Washington Mews ⓭
Washington Square Park & chess area ⓯
Weathermen bomb factory ⓬

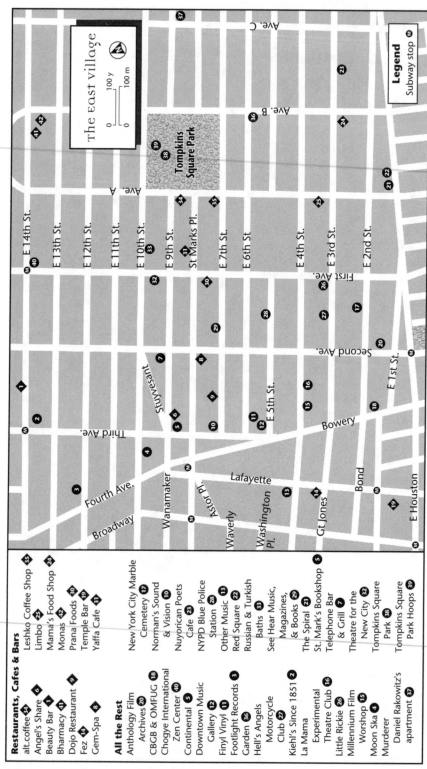

The East Village

0   100 y
0   100 m

Tompkins Square Park

Legend

Ⓜ Subway stop

Restaurants, Cafes & Bars
- alt.coffee 34
- Angel's Share 6
- Beauty Bar 35
- Bharmacy 42
- Dojo Restaurant 9
- Fez 24
- Gem-Spa 8
- Leshko Coffee Shop 43
- Limbo 25
- Mama's Food Shop 24
- Monas 42
- Prana Foods 30
- Temple Bar 19
- Yaffa Cafe 41

All the Rest
- Anthology Film Archives 20
- CBGB & OMFUG 18
- Chogye International Zen Center 40
- Continental 5
- Downtown Music Gallery 12
- Finyl Vinyl 11
- Footlight Records 3
- Garden 36
- Hell's Angels Motorcycle Club 27
- Kiehl's Since 1851 2
- La Mama Experimental Theatre Club 16
- Little Rickie 26
- Millennium Film Worshop 15
- Moon Ska 4
- Murderer Daniel Rakowitz's apartment 37
- New York City Marble Cemetery 17
- Norman's Sound & Vision 10
- Nuyorican Poets Cafe 23
- NYPD Blue Police Station 28
- Other Music 13
- Red Square 22
- Russian & Turkish Baths 33
- See Hear Music, Magazines, & Books 29
- The Spiral 21
- St. Mark's Bookshop 5
- Telephone Bar & Grill 7
- Theatre for the New City 32
- Tompkins Square Park 38
- Tompkins Square Park Hoops 39

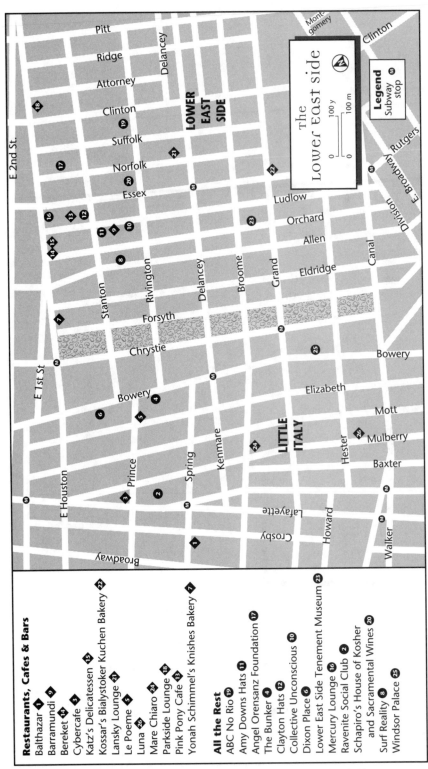

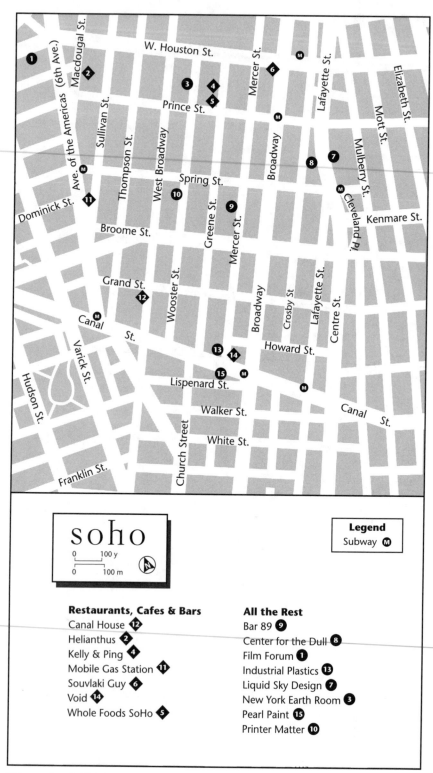

soho

0   100 y
0   100 m

Restaurants, Cafes & Bars
Canal House **12**
Helianthus **2**
Kelly & Ping **4**
Mobile Gas Station **11**
Souvlaki Guy **6**
Void **14**
Whole Foods SoHo **5**

All the Rest
Bar 89 **9**
Center for the Dull **8**
Film Forum **1**
Industrial Plastics **13**
Liquid Sky Design **7**
New York Earth Room **3**
Pearl Paint **15**
Printer Matter **10**

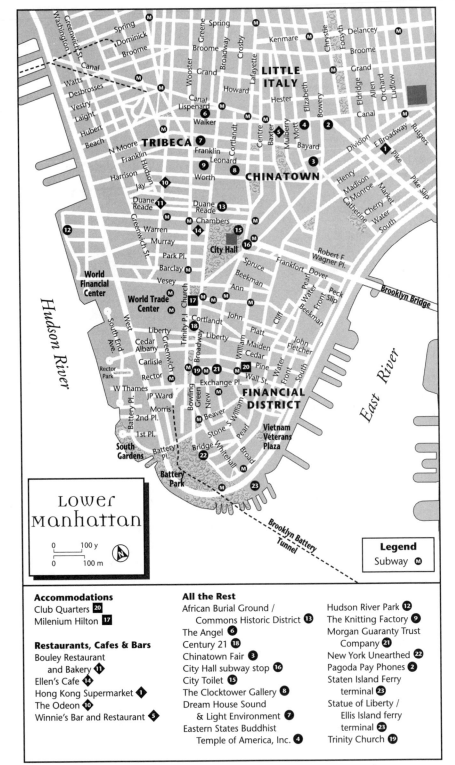

Lower Manhattan

0 — 100 y
0 — 100 m

Legend
Subway Ⓜ

Accommodations
Club Quarters 🎯20
Milenium Hilton 🎯17

Restaurants, Cafes & Bars
Bouley Restaurant
  and Bakery 🎯11
Ellen's Cafe 🎯14
Hong Kong Supermarket 🎯1
The Odeon 🎯10
Winnie's Bar and Restaurant 🎯5

All the Rest
African Burial Ground /
  Commons Historic District 🎯13
The Angel 🎯6
Century 21 🎯18
Chinatown Fair 🎯3
City Hall subway stop 🎯16
City Toilet 🎯15
The Clocktower Gallery 🎯8
Dream House Sound
  & Light Environment 🎯7
Eastern States Buddhist
  Temple of America, Inc. 🎯4

Hudson River Park 🎯12
The Knitting Factory 🎯9
Morgan Guaranty Trust
  Company 🎯21
New York Unearthed 🎯22
Pagoda Pay Phones 🎯2
Staten Island Ferry
  terminal 🎯23
Statue of Liberty /
  Ellis Island ferry
  terminal 🎯23
Trinity Church 🎯19

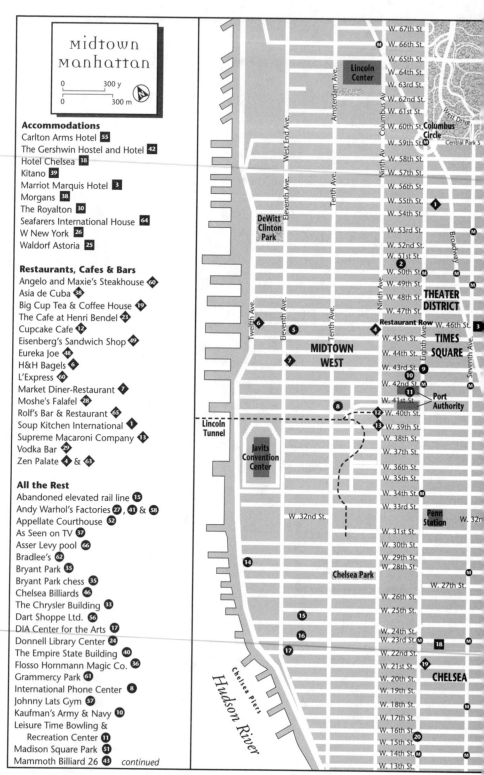

midtown manhattan

0 ___ 300 y
0 ___ 300 m

Accommodations
Carlton Arms Hotel **55**
The Gershwin Hostel and Hotel **42**
Hotel Chelsea **18**
Kitano **39**
Marriot Marquis Hotel **3**
Morgans **38**
The Royalton **30**
Seafarers International House **64**
W New York **26**
Waldorf Astoria **25**

Restaurants, Cafes & Bars
Angelo and Maxie's Steakhouse **60**
Asia de Cuba **38**
Big Cup Tea & Coffee House **19**
The Cafe at Henri Bendel **23**
Cupcake Cafe **12**
Eisenberg's Sandwich Shop **49**
Eureka Joe **48**
H&H Bagels **6**
L'Express **60**
Market Diner-Restaurant **7**
Moshe's Falafel **28**
Rolf's Bar & Restaurant **65**
Soup Kitchen International **1**
Supreme Macaroni Company **13**
Vodka Bar **29**
Zen Palate **4** & **63**

All the Rest
Abandoned elevated rail line **15**
Andy Warhol's Factories **27**, **41** & **58**
Appellate Courthouse **52**
As Seen on TV **37**
Asser Levy pool **66**
Bradlee's **62**
Bryant Park **35**
Bryant Park chess **35**
Chelsea Billiards **46**
The Chrysler Building **33**
Dart Shoppe Ltd. **56**
DIA Center for the Arts **17**
Donnell Library Center **24**
The Empire State Building **40**
Flosso Hornmann Magic Co. **36**
Grammercy Park **61**
International Phone Center **8**
Johnny Lats Gym **57**
Kaufman's Army & Navy **10**
Leisure Time Bowling &
  Recreation Center **11**
Madison Square Park **51**
Mammoth Billiard 26 **43** continued

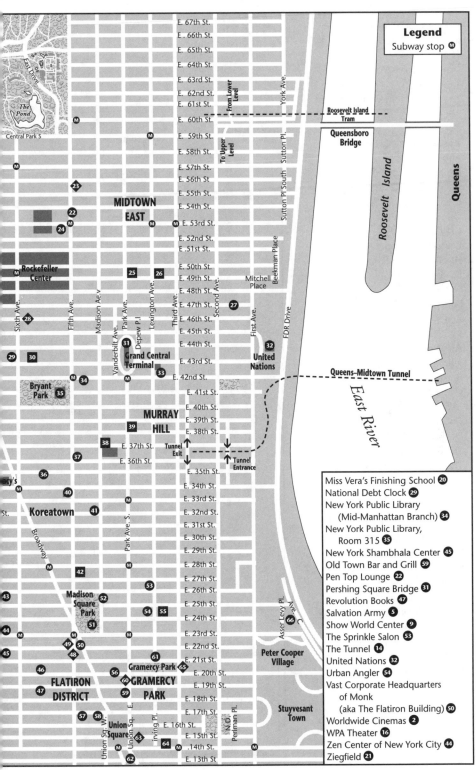

E. 67th St.
E. 66th St.
E. 65th St.
E. 64th St.
E. 63rd St.
E. 62nd St.
E. 61st St.
E. 60th St.
E. 59th St.
E. 58th St.
E. 57th St.
E. 56th St.
E. 55th St.
E. 54th St.
E. 53rd St.
E. 52nd St.
E. 51st St.
E. 50th St.
E. 49th St.
E. 48th St.
E. 47th St.
E. 46th St.
E. 45th St.
E. 44th St.
E. 43rd St.
E. 42nd St.
E. 41st St.
E. 40th St.
E. 39th St.
E. 38th St.
E. 37th St.
E. 36th St.
E. 35th St.
E. 34th St.
E. 33rd St.
E. 32nd St.
E. 31st St.
E. 30th St.
E. 29th St.
E. 28th St.
E. 27th St.
E. 26th St.
E. 25th St.
E. 24th St.
E. 23rd St.
E. 22nd St.
E. 21st St.
E. 20th St.
E. 19th St.
E. 18th St.
E. 17th St.
E. 16th St.
E. 15th St.
.14th St.
E. 13th St

Legend
Subway stop Ⓜ

East Drive
The Pond
Central Park S

York Ave.
From Lower Level
To Upper Level
Sutton Pl.
Sutton Pl South
Beekman Place
Mitchell Place
Second Ave.
First Ave.
FDR Drive

Roosevelt Island Tram
Queensboro Bridge
Roosevelt Island
Queens

MIDTOWN EAST

Rockefeller Center
Sixth Ave.
Fifth Ave.
Madison Ave.
Park Ave.
Vanderbilt Ave.
Depew Pl.
Lexington Ave.
Third Ave.

Grand Central Terminal

United Nations

Queens–Midtown Tunnel
East River

Bryant Park

MURRAY HILL

Tunnel Exit
Tunnel Entrance

Koreatown
Broadway
Park Ave. S.

Madison Square Park

Gramercy Park
FLATIRON DISTRICT
GRAMERCY PARK

Union Square
Union Sq. W.
Union Sq. E.
Irving Pl.

Asser Levy Pl.
Peter Cooper Village
Stuyvesant Town
N.D. Perlman Pl.

Miss Vera's Finishing School ⓴
National Debt Clock ㉙
New York Public Library
   (Mid-Manhattan Branch) ㉞
New York Public Library,
   Room 315 ㉟
New York Shambhala Center ㊺
Old Town Bar and Grill ㊾
Pen Top Lounge ㉒
Pershing Square Bridge ㉛
Revolution Books ㊼
Salvation Army ⑤
Show World Center ⑨
The Sprinkle Salon ㊾
The Tunnel ⑭
United Nations ㉜
Urban Angler ㊴
Vast Corporate Headquarters
   of Monk
   (aka The Flatiron Building) ㊿
Worldwide Cinemas ②
WPA Theater ⑯
Zen Center of New York City ㊹
Ziegfeld ㉑

Monk Maps   41

Accommodations

International Student Center **5**
The Lowell **36**
Malibu Studios Hotel **2**
The Mark **27**
The Sherry-Netherland **35**
The Westbury **30**

Restaurants, Cafes & Bars

Augie's Pub **1**
Big Nick's Burger **11**
Candle Cafe **28**
E.A.T. **23**
Elsie's **24**
Gray's Papaya **16**
Grossinger's Home Bakery **4**
H&H Bagels **7** & **26**
La Caridad **10**
Phil Hughes **20**
Subway Inn **38**
Zen Palate **12**

All the Rest

79th St. Boat Basin **9**
Amsterdam Billiard Club **12**
Carl Schurz Park **25**
Central Park **21**
Chabad of the West Side **3**
Dai Bosatsu Center **31**
The Dakota **14**
The Delacorte Clock **33**
Dr. Zizmor **34**
Gryphon Bookshop **6**
Hotel Ansonia **15**
Islamic Center of New York **18**
John Jay Pool **29**
Madonna and child **17**
New York Doll Hospital **37**
Queensboro Bridge **40**
Riverside Park **8**
Roosevelt Island Tram Station **39**
The San Remo **13**
Seventh Regiment Armory **32**
Smithers Treatment Center **19**
Stanhope Hotel **22**

Legend
Subway stop **M**

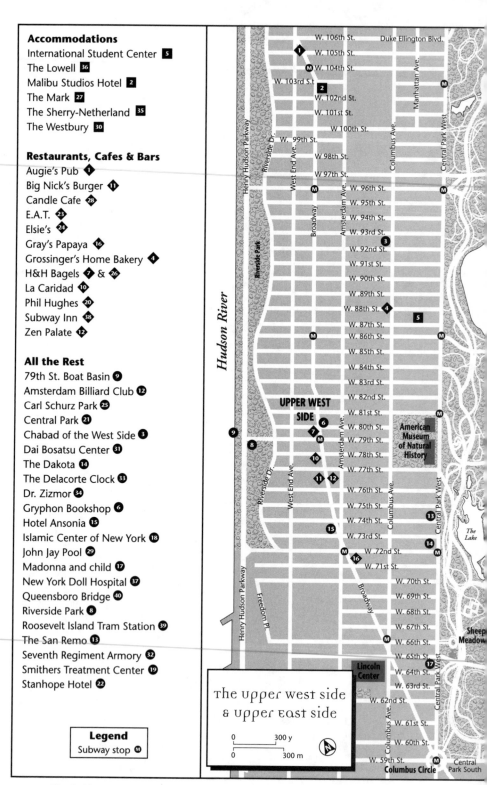

The upper west side
& upper east side

0   300 y
0   300 m

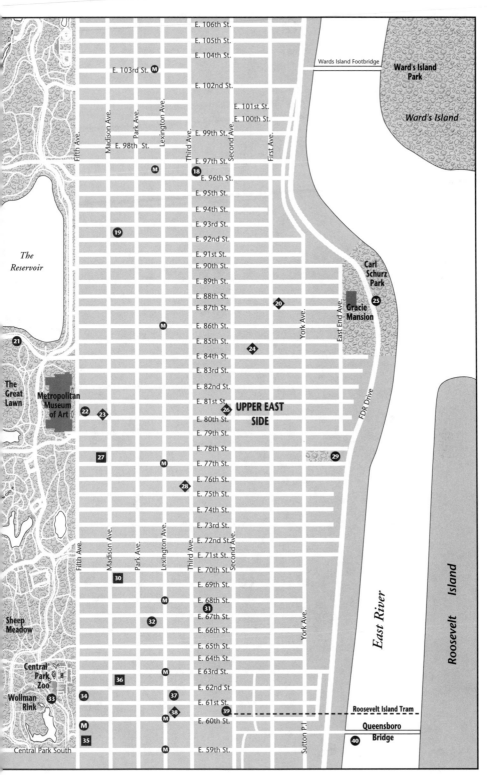

E. 106th St.
E. 105th St.
E. 104th St.
E. 103rd St. Ⓜ
E. 102nd St.
E. 101st St.
E. 100th St.
E. 99th St.
E. 98th St.
E. 97th St.
Ⓜ **18**
E. 96th St.
E. 95th St.
E. 94th St.
E. 93rd St.
19 E. 92nd St.
E. 91st St.
E. 90th St.
E. 89th St.
E. 88th St.
E. 87th St.
20 E. 86th St.
Ⓜ E. 85th St.
24 E. 84th St.
E. 83rd St.
E. 82nd St.
E. 81st St.
26 **UPPER EAST**
E. 80th St. **SIDE**
E. 79th St.
E. 78th St.
27 E. 77th St. Ⓜ
E. 76th St.
28 E. 75th St.
E. 74th St.
E. 73rd St.
E. 72nd St
E. 71st St.
E. 70th St.
30 E. 69th St.
E. 68th St. Ⓜ
31 E. 67th St.
32 E. 66th St.
E. 65th St.
E. 64th St.
E. 63rd St. Ⓜ
36 E. 62nd St.
34 E. 61st St. **37**
39 E. 60th St. **38** Ⓜ
Ⓜ E. 59th St.
35
Ⓜ
Central Park South

Fifth Ave.
Madison Ave.
Park Ave.
Lexington Ave.
Third Ave.
Second Ave.
First Ave.
York Ave.
East End Ave.
FDR Drive
Sutton Pl.

The Reservoir

21

The Great Lawn

Metropolitan Museum of Art

22 **23**

Sheep Meadow

Central Park Zoo

Wollman Rink **33**

Wards Island Footbridge

Ward's Island Park

Ward's Island

Carl Schurz Park

25 Gracie Mansion

29

East River

Roosevelt Island

Roosevelt Island Tram

Queensboro Bridge **40**

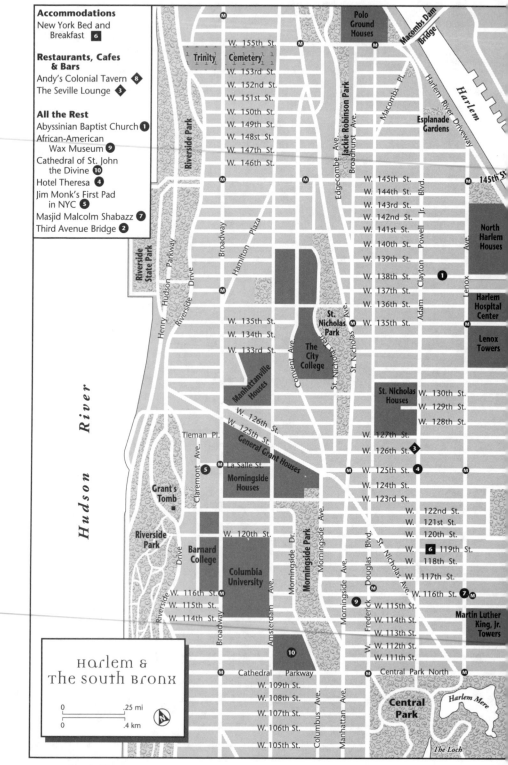

Accommodations

New York Bed and
  Breakfast **6**

**Restaurants, Cafes
  & Bars**

Andy's Colonial Tavern **8**
The Seville Lounge **3**

All the Rest

Abyssinian Baptist Church **1**
African-American
  Wax Museum **9**
Cathedral of St. John
  the Divine **10**
Hotel Theresa **4**
Jim Monk's First Pad
  in NYC **5**
Masjid Malcolm Shabazz **7**
Third Avenue Bridge **2**

Hαrlem &
The south Bronx

0   .25 mi
0   .4 km

Trinity Cemetery

Polo
Ground
Houses

Macombs Dam
Bridge

Harlem River

W. 155th St.
W. 153rd St.
W. 152nd St.
W. 151st St.
W. 150th St.
W. 149th St.
W. 148st St.
W. 147th St.
W. 146th St.

Riverside Park

Jackie Robinson Park

Macombs Pl.

Harlem River Driveway

Esplanade
Gardens

Edgecombe Ave.
Broadhurst Ave.

W. 145th St.
W. 144th St.
W. 143rd St.
W. 142nd St.
W. 141st St.
W. 140th St.
W. 139th St.
W. 138th St. **1**
W. 137th St.
W. 136th St.
W. 135th St.

145th St

North
Harlem
Houses

Lenox Ave.

Adam Clayton Powell Jr. Blvd.

Harlem
Hospital
Center

Lenox
Towers

Broadway

Hamilton Plaza

Riverside
State Park

Henry Hudson Parkway

Riverside Drive

St. Nicholas
Park

The
City
College

St. Nicholas Ave.
St. Nicholas Ave.

W. 135th St.
W. 134th St.
W. 133rd St.

Convent Ave.

Manhattanville
Houses

St. Nicholas
Houses

W. 130th St.
W. 129th St.
W. 128th St.

W. 126th St.
W. 125th St.
General Grant Houses

Tieman Pl.

W. 127th St.
W. 126th St. **3**
W. 125th St. **4**
W. 124th St.
W. 123rd St.

La Salle St. **5**

Morningside
Houses

Claremont Ave.

Grant's
Tomb

Riverside
Park

Riverside Drive

Barnard
College

W. 120th St.

Columbia
University

Morningside Ave.

Morningside Park

Morningside Ave.

W. 122nd St.
W. 121st St.
W. 120th St.
W. **6** 119th St.
W. 118th St.
W. 117th St.

Douglas Blvd.

St. Nicholas Ave.

Amsterdam Ave.

Broadway

W. 116th St.
W. 115th St.
W. 114th St.

W. 116th St. **7**
W. 115th St. **9**
W. 114th St.
W. 113th St.
W. 112th St.
W. 111th St.

Frederick Douglas Blvd.

Martin Luther
King, Jr.
Towers

Cathedral Parkway **10**

Central Park North

W. 109th St.
W. 108th St.
W. 107th St.
W. 106th St.
W. 105th St.

Columbus Ave.

Manhattan Ave.

Central
Park

Harlem Mere

The Loch

Hudson River

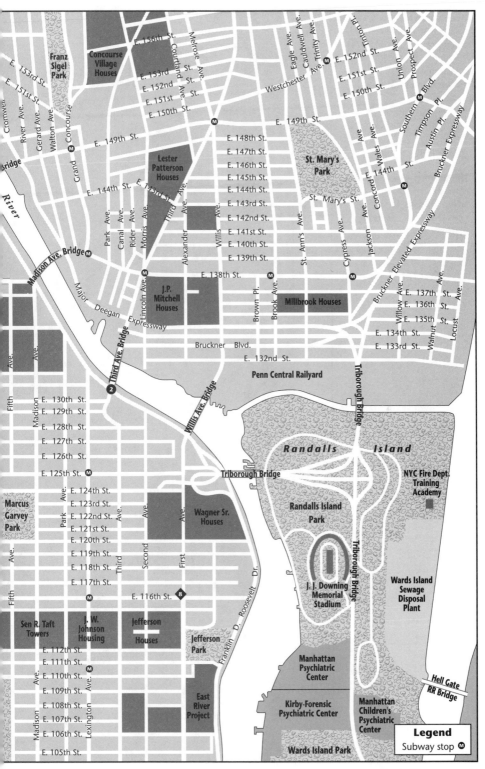

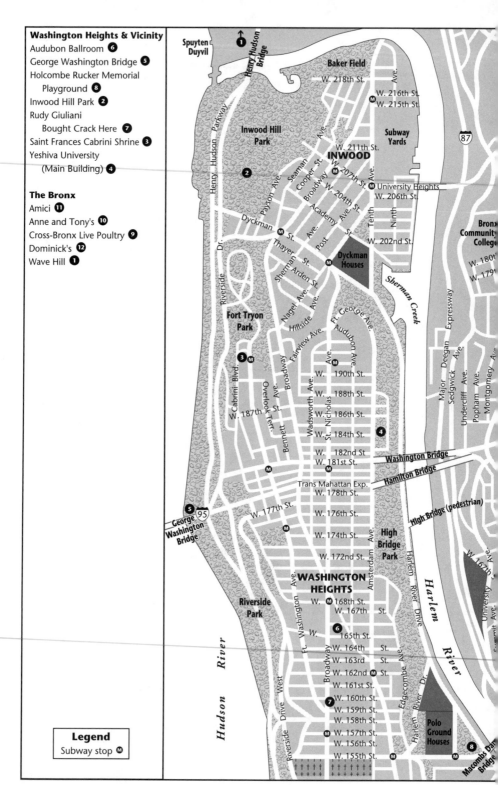

Washington Heights & Vicinity

Audubon Ballroom **6**
George Washington Bridge **5**
Holcombe Rucker Memorial
  Playground **8**
Inwood Hill Park **2**
Rudy Giuliani
  Bought Crack Here **7**
Saint Frances Cabrini Shrine **3**
Yeshiva University
  (Main Building) **4**

The Bronx

Amici **11**
Anne and Tony's **10**
Cross-Bronx Live Poultry **9**
Dominick's **12**
Wave Hill **1**

Legend
Subway stop **M**

Spuyten
Duyvil **1**

Henry Hudson Bridge

Baker Field
W. 218th St.
W. 216th St.
W. 215th St.

Inwood Hill
Park

Subway
Yards

I-87

INWOOD
W. 211th St.

2

Seaman Ave.
Cooper St.
Broadway
Academy St.
Post Ave.
Tenth Ave.
Ninth Ave.

W. 207th St.
University Heights
W. 206th St.

Dyckman St.

W. 204th St.

W. 202nd St.

Bronx
Community
College

Dyckman
Houses

Sherman Creek

Thayer St.
Arden St.
Sherman Ave.
Nagel Ave.
Hillside Ave.
Fairview Ave.

Ft. George Ave.

Audubon Ave.

Fort Tryon
Park

W. 190th St.
W. 188th St.
W. 186th St.
W. 184th St.
W. 182nd St
W. 181st St.

3 M

W. Cabrini Blvd.
W. 187th St.
Overlook Terr.
Bennett Ave.
Broadway
Wadsworth Ave.
St. Nicholas Ave.

Riverside Dr.

4

Washington Bridge
Hamilton Bridge

Trans Mahattan Exp.
W. 178th St.

High Bridge (pedestrian)

W. 177th St.

W. 176th St.

High
Bridge
Park

W. 174th St.

5 I-95
George
Washington
Bridge

W. 172nd St.

Major Deegan Expressway
Sedgwick Ave.
Undercliff Ave.
Popham Ave.
Montgomery Ave.

W. 180th
W. 179th

Harlem River Drive

Harlem River

WASHINGTON
HEIGHTS

W. **M** 168th St.
W. 167th St.

6
165th St.

W. 164th St.
W. 163rd St.
W. 162nd **M** St.
W. 161st St.
W. 160th St.
W. 159th St.
W. 158th St.
W. 157th St.
W. 156th St.
W. 155th St.

7

Riverside
Park

Hudson River

Ft. Washington Ave.
West End Ave.
Riverside Drive
Broadway
Amsterdam Ave.
Edgecombe Ave.

Polo
Ground
Houses

8

Macombs Dam Bridge

University Ave.

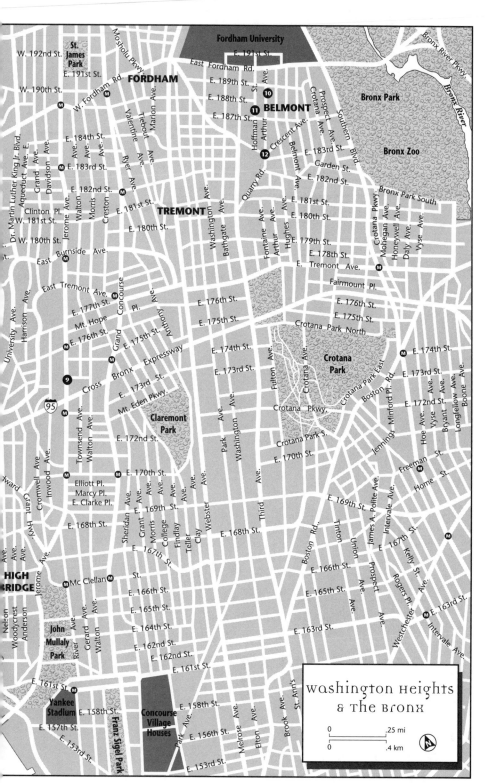

St. James Park
W. 192nd St.
W. 190th St.
E. 191st St.
Mosholu Pkwy.
FORDHAM
W. Fordham Rd.
Fordham University
East Fordham Rd.
E. 191st St.
E. 189th St.
E. 188th St.
E. 187th St.
⑩
⑪ BELMONT
Bronx Park
Bronx River Pkwy.
Bronx River
Bronx Zoo
Dr. Martin Luther King Jr. Blvd.
Aqueduct Ave. E.
Grand Ave.
Davidson Ave.
E. 184th St.
E. 183rd St.
Clinton Pl.
W. 181st St.
W. 180th St.
Valentine Ave.
Tiebout Ave.
Marion Ave.
Walton Ave.
Morris Ave.
Jerome Ave.
Creston Ave.
Ryer Ave.
E. 182nd St.
E. 181st St.
TREMONT
E. 180th St.
Bathgate Ave.
Washington Ave.
Hoffman St.
Arthur Ave.
Crescent Ave.
Crotana Ave.
Southern Blvd.
Prospect Ave.
Belmont Ave.
Quarry Rd.
⑫
E. 183rd St.
Garden St.
E. 182nd St.
Bronx Park South
Crotana Pkwy.
Mohegan Ave.
Honeywell Ave.
Daly Ave.
Vyse Ave.
E. 181st St.
E. 180th St.
E. 179th St.
E. 178th St.
E. Tremont Ave.
Fontaine Ave.
Arthur Ave.
Hughes Ave.
East Burnside Ave.
East Tremont Ave.
Harrison Ave.
University Ave.
E. 177th St.
Mt. Hope Pl.
E. 176th St.
Grand Concourse
Anthony Ave.
Bronx Expressway
Cross
E. 173rd St.
Mt. Eden Pkwy.
Claremont Park
E. 172nd St.
Townsend Ave.
Walton Ave.
Fairmount Pl.
E. 176th St.
E. 175th St.
Crotana Park North
E. 174th St.
E. 173rd St.
Fulton Ave.
Crotana Ave.
Crotana Park
Crotana Park East
Crotana Park Rd.
Boston Rd.
Crotana Pkwy.
Crotana Park S.
E. 174th St.
E. 173rd St.
E. 172nd St.
Hoe Ave.
Vyse Ave.
Bryant Ave.
Longfellow Ave.
Boone Ave.
9
95
E. 176th St.
E. 175th St.
E. 174th St.
E. 173rd St.
Park Ave.
Washington Ave.
Jennings St.
Minford Pl.
Freeman St.
Home St.
E. 169th St.
E. 170th St.
E. 169th St.
E. 168th St.
Elliott Pl.
Marcy Pl.
E. Clarke Pl.
Sheridan Ave.
Grant Ave.
Morris Ave.
College Ave.
Findlay Ave.
Teller Ave.
Clay Ave.
Webster Ave.
Third Ave.
E. 168th St.
E. 167th St.
Boston Rd.
Tinton Ave.
Union Ave.
Prospect Ave.
James A. Polite Ave.
Intervale Ave.
Kelly St.
Rogers Pl.
Westchester Ave.
Intervale Ave.
E. 167th St.
E. 163rd St.
HIGH BRIDGE
McClellan St.
Jerome Ave.
Nelson Ave.
Woodycrest Ave.
Anderson Ave.
River Ave.
Gerard Ave.
Walton Ave.
E. 166th St.
E. 165th St.
E. 164th St.
E. 162nd St.
E. 161st St.
John Mullaly Park
Grant Hwy.
Cromwell Ave.
Inwood Ave.
E. 166th St.
E. 165th St.
E. 163rd St.
Melrose Ave.
Elton Ave.
Brook Ave.
St. Ann's Ave.
E. 161st St.
Yankee Stadium
E. 158th St.
E. 157th St.
E. 153rd St.
Park Ave.
Franz Sigel Park
Concourse Village Houses
E. 158th St.
E. 156th St.
E. 153rd St.

washington Heights & the Bronx

0 — .25 mi
0 — .4 km

Monk Maps **47**

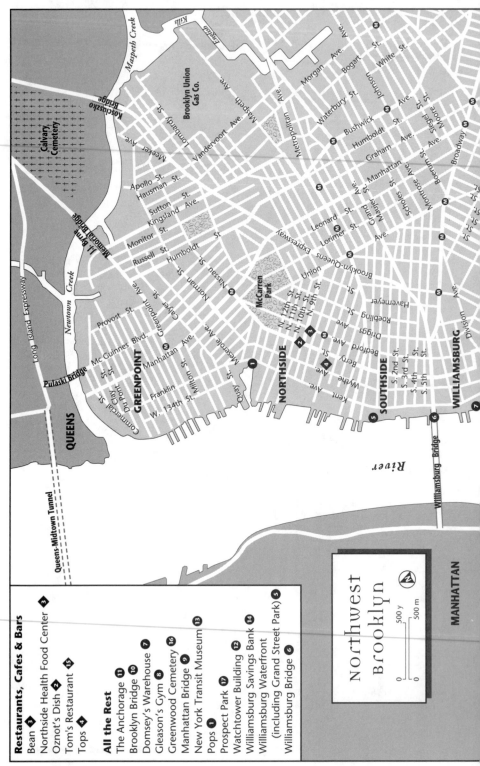

Northwest Brooklyn

Restaurants, Cafes & Bars

Bean ④
Northside Health Food Center ③
Oznot's Dish ②
Tom's Restaurant ⑮
Tops ④

All the Rest

The Anchorage ⑪
Brooklyn Bridge ⑩
Domsey's Warehouse ⑦
Gleason's Gym ⑧
Greenwood Cemetery ⑯
Manhattan Bridge ⑨
New York Transit Museum ⑬
Pops ①
Prospect Park ⑰
Watchtower Building ⑫
Williamsburg Savings Bank ⑭
Williamsburg Waterfront
(including Grand Street Park) ⑤
Williamsburg Bridge ⑥

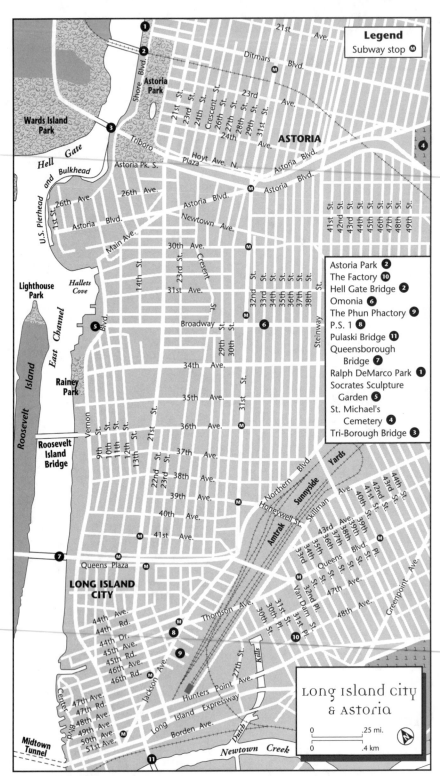

Legend
Subway stop Ⓜ

21st Ave.
Ditmars Blvd.

21st St.
23rd St.
24th St.
Crescent St.
26th St.
27th St.
28th St.
29th St.
31st St.
23rd Ave.
24th Ave.

ASTORIA

Astoria Blvd.

41st St.
42nd St.
43rd St.
44th St.
45th St.
46th St.
47th St.
48th St.
49th St.

Ⓜ ④

Shore Blvd.
Astoria Park
Triboro

Wards Island Park

Hell Gate and Bulkhead

Astoria Pk. S.
Hoyt Ave. N.
Plaza

Astoria Blvd.

U.S. Pierhead

1st St.
26th Ave.
26th Ave.
Astoria Blvd.
Newtown Ave.

Astoria Blvd.

Main Ave.

30th Ave.

14th St.
23rd St.
Crescent St.
31st Ave.

32nd St.
33rd St.
34th St.
35th St.
36th St.
37th St.
38th St.

Steinway St.

Lighthouse Park

Hallets Cove

Broadway

29th St.
30th St.
31st St.

6

Astoria Park ②
The Factory ⑩
Hell Gate Bridge ②
Omonia ⑥
The Phun Phactory ⑨
P.S. 1 ⑧
Pulaski Bridge ⑪
Queensborough
   Bridge ⑦
Ralph DeMarco Park ①
Socrates Sculpture
   Garden ⑤
St. Michael's
   Cemetery ④
Tri-Borough Bridge ③

East Channel

Roosevelt Island

Rainey Park

34th Ave.

35th Ave.

Vernon Blvd.

9th St.
10th St.
11th St.
12th St.
13th St.
21st St.

36th Ave.

37th Ave.

22nd St.
23rd St.
38th Ave.

39th Ave.

Northern Blvd.
Yards
Sunnyside
Honeywell St.
Skillman Ave.
Amtrak

44th St.
43rd St.
42nd St.
41st St.
40th St.
39th Pl.
39th St.
38th Ave.
37th St.
36th St.
35th St.
43rd Ave.
34th St.
33rd St.
32nd Pl.
31st St.
Queens Blvd.
47th St.
48th Ave.

Greenpoint Ave.

Roosevelt Island Bridge

40th Ave.

41st Ave.

⑦

Queens Plaza

LONG ISLAND CITY

44th Ave.
44th Rd.
44th Dr.
44th Ave.
45th Ave.
45th Rd.
46th Ave.
46th Rd.

Ⓜ ⑧

⑨

Thomson Ave.

27th St.
30th St.
30th Pl.
31st St.
31st Pl.
Van Dam St.

⑩

Jackson Ave.

Center Blvd.

47th Ave.
47th Rd.
48th Ave.
49th Ave.
50th Ave.
51st Ave.

Hunters Point Ave.

Long Island Expressway

Borden Ave.

Dutch Kills

Midtown Tunnel

⑪

Newtown Creek

Long Island City & Astoria

0 — .25 mi.
0 — .4 km

Everyplace Else

If we'd tried to map every area of New York, we wouldn't have had room in the book for anything but maps. Those we've provided show locations for most of the attractions listed in the book, but we had to rationalize not plotting a few of the most far-flung places.

For really obsessive location-finding, we suggest picking up one of the detailed atlases that are available, such as the *Hagstrom New York City 5 Borough Pocket Atlas*. With one of these, a subway map, and a bus map, you can't go wrong, and if you do, you can find your way back again.

›monks'
New York,
A to Z

Traditional travelers visit a place to fulfill expectations. Others, though, travel in search of the unknown, to experience "the shock of the new," in Robert Hughes's treasured words, to return home transformed by the experience.

In April 1986, following our credo of "simple, mobile, and true," we left San Francisco on an open-ended journey in search of the soul of this country, and when we began publishing *Monk* magazine from the dashboard of the Monkmobile, the credo became the magazine's mantra as well.

"Simple" and "mobile" are pretty self-explanatory, but, as our readers quickly learn, we mean "true" in more than the literal sense. We mean true from the heart, true from a sense of humor, true from a perspective on a place, showing its warts and its wackiness. It is this broader sense of truth that we have used as our compass as we traversed the country for the past 12 years.

When we look to see if a place is true, if it is Monk-worthy, we first and foremost determine if it has heart—and we don't mean that in any New Age or politically correct way. We mean humanity. Gusto. Love in the largest sense. This can come across as brusqueness or even rudeness, and just as often as exuberant passion. All Monkish places have it.

In addition, almost all Monk places demonstrate an unmistakable originality. Not trendiness, not novelty for novelty's sake, but a disarming "otherness" that provokes a visitor to ask "WHAT . . . IS . . . *THIS?*" The ability of a place to engender a kind of dumbstruck curiosity, a "don't know mind" in the words of Zen Master Seung Sahn, is the ultimate mark of its Monkness.

When it comes to people, the same criteria apply. At *Monk,* we end up interviewing folks who are extraordinary, though not necessarily famous. Men and women who are big enough to see beyond themselves and their schtick—who, more than "exposure," crave the adventure.

The spirit of a place must come from the street, growing naturally out of its fabric and the character of its people. But to find it, you often have to probe beneath the surface, which is precisely what real Monks are called to do.

Do you want to perceive a place like a Monk? Here are some questions to ask: (1) Does the place display an audacious originality? (2) Is the owner operating out of a marketing plan, or is there something more organic, more humane, going on? (3) Is the place accessible? Does it have a breadth of vision that allows even the most expensive hotels, stores, and restaurants to treat everyone with a degree of flexible civility? and (4) Does the place reflect the heart and soul of its locale?

In *The Mad Monks' Guide to New York City* we apply the above criteria to "the greatest city on earth." Sadly, we discovered that New York City has never been more ruled by the bottom line than it is today. It has become safer, more lucrative, and more livable, but it has also become more mechanistic, more predictable, less real. In other words, less Monk.

Originality, authenticity, and a flair for the true spirit of the city are qualities many of the chains now invading New York City simply lack. And that is why, even while creating convenient and pristine places to meet and shop, they leave an emptiness in their wake. The sense of local ownership starts to wane. The sense of "otherness," too.

The question is, can you have prosperity, safety, and standards and still preserve a passionate, innovative, and broad-minded culture? We believe so. Do people and places that reflect the quirky Monk spirit still survive in mallified New York? We believe they do.

And so, here you have it: Monks' New York, A to Z.

Accommodations

The most important decision you'll make in considering a trip to New York is where you will stay. And, in most cases, what you'd consider high-priced elsewhere—say a single room at over $200 a night—is considered the norm here. High rates have usually been the rule in the city, but never more so than now. Ask any hotelier. There has never been a better time for the New York hotel business. Most hotels in town run at over 70% occupancy all the time—which means higher tariffs for you.

In searching for a reason for this booming market, start with Mayor Giuliani's successful efforts to reduce crime, which have created an hospitable climate for visitors and dramatically increased the lure of New York as a tourist attraction. In addition, the robust U.S. economy has not only given more spending power to tourists, but has allowed major renovations of New York's existing hotel stock.

Think carefully about your choice of accommodations. It's your shelter from the 24-hour New York storm. For slightly more money you can get the comfort, quiet, location, and amenities that can turn a tolerable foray into the vacation of your life.

Atmosphere and Design

The Monkish traveler is not only after quality and bargains, but character and design. The following supply both in spades.

> **Kitano.** 66 Park Ave., between E. 38th and E. 39th (Midtown). ☎ 212/885-7000.

The operative description here is tasteful understatement. The Kitano is a peaceful Japanese hotel only a few blocks from the commotion of Grand Central. The highlight, and the reason the Kitano makes this list, is their traditionally appointed

Japanese suite (a mere $1,350 per night). It's all here: shoes left at the door (removed with an elegant shoehorn), tatami mats on the floor, zabutons for sitting, his-and-hers futons for sleeping, a tearoom, a traditional Japanese bathtub. Each element is a perfectly realized example of ingenious Japanese simplicity. The beds are a bit small for the average American cowboy, and the suite seems a bit tiny for the hefty price tag, but maybe the Kitano is banking on all the headroom that comes with sitting on the floor. Downstairs is a very traditional restaurant, Nadaman Hakubai, which serves several different variaties of the deadly blowfish.

> **The Royalton.** 44 W. 44th St., between Fifth and Sixth aves. (Midtown). ☎ 212/869-4400.

If choosing a hotel were purely a question of looks, this Starck-designed and Schrager-owned masterpiece would be a five-star winner. But factor in size of room, reasonableness of price, and general feeling of warmth and comfort, and this cool cat sinks to a three. This doesn't daunt the Brit pack and the Condé Nast pack and the terminal trendoid pack from calling it home, however. They just miss a fundamental point: Trendiness and hipness do not equal greatness. Still, on its own terms (image over substance), The Royalton succeeds, especially in the completely novel rest room, the world-renowned Vodka Bar, and the mind-bending lobby, with surreal sofas, lights shaped like Rhino horns, and white-clothed chairs that looked like they were personally wrapped by Christo himself.

> **W New York.** 541 Lexington Ave., at E. 49th St. (Midtown). ☎ 212/755-1200.

We get nervous when the name David Rockwell comes up in regards to any business. (The designs for Snobu and the Suit Monkey Bar are unique in their way, but the clientele they attract is absolutely scary.) And so here he is again—as Barry "Starwood" Sternlicht's pal in a creative venture with restaurateur Drew Nieporent (Tribeca Grill) and nightclub impresario Rande Gerber (L.A.'s Sky Bar), who've all teamed up to renovate and relaunch the former Doral Inn. The result is a full blown "New Age hotel," a very dangerous proposition in general, but especially when dealing with Midtown real estate. We hope the W team pulls it off, since there are some decidedly Monkish elements here: a soft soothing color scheme, avant yet not oppressively hip design, lovely wood cabinetry, elegant drapery, sharp and smart lighting, a complete juice bar in the lobby, and little flourishes like flower boxes of very green grass in each room (a nightmare to maintain, said our guide, but then, to paraphrase the late Viktor Fidele, "no pain, no concept!"). There are some gauche elements too: The inverted lamp shades above the bed look like those giant cone-shaped breasts Madonna made famous a couple of trainers ago, and Rockwell's well-intentioned theme of "earth, air, fire, and water" is a bit too woo-woo and, at times, dumbly executed. (We could have done without the wallpaper leaf motif in our suite.) However, we fell for the lovely enlightened inscriptions on the edge of the bed's comforter, mainly because the bed itself was so fluffy, comfy, and inviting. Which really cuts to the core of what this place is about: a comforting "oasis" amidst the hustle and bustle of midtown Manhattan. Take our word for it: To block out the noise, block out the funk of the busy traffic below, you will *need* W New York.

Budget

As the adage goes, "New money goes to the Four Seasons, old money goes to the St. Regis, and The Monks go wherever they can plug in a pressure cooker." The following are the best cheap accommodations in the city. And all of them will allow you to plug in a pressure cooker.

> **Carlton Arms Hotel.** 160 E. 25th St., between Third and Lexington aves. (Gramercy). ☎ **212/679-0680.** www.hotwired.com/gallery/96/04/carlton.html.

This is Hotel Chelsea's poor cousin, yet it's got the community spirit the Chelsea has long since lost. A pretty hard-core place until manager Eddie Ryan encouraged visitors to paint their rooms in exchange for rent. The results, while perhaps not high art, are definitely a hoot. And at these prices—$76 for a double room, with bath and a good, firm mattress—you can hardly complain.

> **Club Quarters.** 52 Williams St., at Pine St. (Financial District), and 40 W. 45th St., off Fifth Ave. (Midtown, Fri–Sun night only). ☎ **212/443-4700** (reservations).

The NYU Guest Suites used to be the best bargain in town—all you needed was a familiar face or some tangential NYU association. It was quiet, cheap, and clean, with kitchenettes and new furniture, and located right in the heart of Union Square. Unfortunately for you, the Suites have been converted back to dorms. In their place, NYU is steering folks to the slightly higher priced (though by today's standards, still ridiculously cheap) accommodations at Club Quarters. Single queen bed rooms run $119 a night during the week, and only $95 a night on weekends. Ditto for rooms with two single beds. Suites, which come with one queen and another roll-out queen,

Hotel Trivia

One of the artists who decorated the rooms at the **Carlton Arms** *was Senator Daniel Patrick Moynihan's son, Mendel Moynihan.*

are only $179 during the week and $149 on weekends. If you can prove some form of NYU affiliation (attending a Beat conference, looking like a prospective film student in a black leather jacket), then you can stay. It's possible without any NYU affiliation, but it requires Monk-style maneuvering.

› **Ganas Community.** 135 Corson Ave., near the intersection of Jersey St. and Victory Blvd. (Staten Island). ☎ 718/720-5378. www.well.com/user.ganas.

This is the only "intentional community" in the city. (For the layman, that's what communes were called before Jim Jones and the Baghwan ruined the term.) Officially, Ganas, "a residential facility of the Foundation for Feedback Learning," is "dedicated to developing responsible autonomy and caring relationships based on problem-solving dialogue that joins reason with emotion in daily interaction"— whatever that means. The central idea is that members are expected to share their problems with the group. Ganas explicitly warns all newcomers, however, that "we are not a therapeutic community," so don't go hoping for some kind of free shrink service, buddy.

The community welcomes visitors (hell, sometimes they stay for years), and is a seductive possibility, especially if you don't have friends or haven't eaten for a while, or both. To get there, take the ferry to Staten Island, turn left on Bay Street, then, at the Every Thing Goes store, mention that you want to visit the "community" (just like in a spy novel), and they'll take it from there.

Beyond curiosity, there's a good reason to check out Ganas: It may well be the rock-bottom cheapest accommodation in the city. If you stay from 1 to 7 days, it'll cost you $25 per night (you'll also be asked to help out); if you stay longer, it'll cost you about $150 a week.

› **The Gershwin Hostel and Hotel.**
7 E. 27th St., between Fifth and Madison aves. (Gramercy/Murray Hill). ☎ 212/545-8000.

Publicist Jules Filer calls it an "upscale budget hotel"—something of a contradiction, but you get the idea: It is for people with lots of style but less cash. Although a bit enamored of the

Observation

"LA...[is] one big hassle—it's the most frenetic, seething, hostile city on the face of the Earth under the guise of being this laid-back, cool place, which it is not by any stretch of the imagination. New York is calm and sweet compared to this place."

—David Bowie, *Seconds Magazine*

Warhol/Factory thing (the walls pay slavish tribute to the man and his mystique, including massive Pop Art murals in the lobby and photographs by Warhol protégé Billy Name), it more than makes up for the schtick in price, service, and quality. There is an art gallery, a performance area (on Thursdays, regulars from Saturday Night Live try out new sketches, and other standups appear too, including "eccentric billionaire" Abe Hirschfeld), a rooftop garden, a bar, a cafe and—gulp—a floor reserved for models. Mind you, this is not as lame as it sounds: It seems agencies, wanting to keep tabs on their young talent but not wanting to spend big bucks on expensive apartments, put them up here, in bunk beds. For $25 a night, you, too, can get a bunk (although your neighbor isn't likely to be a model). The Gershwin's guests are about 60 percent foreign, and—a la Hotel Chelsea and the Carlton Arms—a fair number are "artists" who, in exchange for free rent, help around the place. Thankfully, despite the paean to Warhol, the place is not overrun with club kids. Actually, it's pretty diverse. And with the recent upgrade in room quality (now $89 a night for a private room and bath) it's still a decent bargain.

> **International Student Center.** 38 W. 88th St., between Central Park West and Columbus Ave. (Upper West Side). ☎ 212/787-7706.

A preposterously low-priced option, smack in the center of some of the world's most expensive real estate. And it's just a hop to Central Park. The rooms—a mere $15 a night—aren't half bad, even if they are jammed with bunk beds. Alas, it's open only to under-30 foreigners (especially foreigners with an extraordinarily high liquor tolerance); no Yanks, or even Canucks, allowed.

> **Malibu Studios Hotel.** 2688 Broadway, at 103rd St. (Upper West Side). ☎ 212/222-2954.

Cheap hotels in New York specialize, it seems, in surly Brits at the front desk. The clean, colorful Malibu is no exception, although it's no match for the cantankerous snootiness of Hotel 17. In a town where $150 a night is considered cheap and $250 is about average, this place is a bona fide steal, offering small, basic rooms (with or without a bath) for really decent rates ($58 a night, single, communal bath; $92 a night, single, private bath). As an added bonus, the rooms are decorated with airbrushed artwork that would make your grandmother go weak in the knees. Unfortunately, the secret is out. Call in advance, since it's booked solid for months.

> **New York Bed and Breakfast.** 134 W. 119th St., at Malcolm X Blvd. (Harlem). ☎ 212/666-0559.

"I've got enough business," the proprietress told us over the telephone. "I don't want people coming up here and not knowing what Harlem is like. I've had people

New Yorker Trailer City, aka New Yorker RV Park and Campground

coming up here and getting scared and crying. It just goes to confirm all the stuff the guys hanging out on the street believe about white people." We assume the rates are reasonable.

> **New Yorker RV Park and Campground.** 4901 Tonnelle Ave., North Bergen, New Jersey. ☎ 201/866-0999. From Manhattan, take the Lincoln Tunnel to New Jersey, stay on Hwy. 3 West, exit at 1-9 North, go to 49th St. and look for park on the left side of Tonnelle.

This huge parking lot of an RV park is strategically situated next to Tonnelle Avenue, the New Jersey Turnpike, and a busy railroad yard (sleep to the music of trains butting heads all night). Very New Jersey and only a short bus ride from Port Authority, which seems like the Promised Land by comparison. We used to stay here years ago, until Don Francis and his Greenpeace posse informed us that environmental engineers had discovered mercury buried beneath the soil. Gives new meaning to the concept of mutant trailer trash.

> **Seafarers International House.** 123 E. 15th St., between Irving Place and Third Ave. (Union Square/Gramercy). ☎ 212/677-4800.

This place is cuckoo, but cheap ($46 a night for a single). The high-strung desk clerk was battling some cranky maritime lobby rats the night we arrived. It's run by the Evangelical Lutheran Church of America, and you must have some student, church, or maritime affiliation to stay here. The rooms are small and clean, and they reminded us of a college dormitory, but the cheap price tag and the incredible location (near Gramercy Park) more than make up for any deficiencies.

> **White Pickets.** 67 Brewster St., between Bay St. and Victory Blvd. (Staten Island). ☎ 718/727-9398. Call for directions.

Funky, friendly, very low-key, clothing-optional bed-and-breakfast in the heart of dowdy middle class Staten Island. It's an odd juxtaposition of competing sensibilities, but if you're looking for a freak show, you'll probably be disappointed. More like backyard sunbathing than eccentric nudism. Jesse Tree (listed as Ian J. Tree in the phone book) is your host. His fastidious neighbor runs a cleaner, straighter B&B next door, catering mostly to Belgians and other Europeans.

Historic

New York is the defining city of the 20th century, taking over from Paris and now passing the torch to Los Angeles. The first portal through which visitors perceive the historic magnitude of New York is in their accommodations. For me, it was the 34th Street YMCA. I never forgot it. But for many others, the choices were far more colorful and illustrious. Of the many historic New York digs, these are the most significant.

> **Hotel Chelsea.** 222 W. 23rd St., between Seventh and Eighth aves. (Chelsea). ☎ 212/243-3700.

A few artist-decorated apartments and a rich history are the drawing cards, although, at $150 a night, you're essentially paying for folklore, not amenities. Still, for some, it's worth the price to inhabit the same derelict quarters as the likes of Candy Darling, Bill Burroughs, Edie Sedgwick, or Sid and Nancy. In point of fact, though, the Chelsea isn't really about any of the luminaries who have crossed its door; it's about managers Stanley Bard and his son David, who've seen them come and go and

The legendary Hotel
Chelsea

who, despite it all, remain gentle and tolerant. Check out the wrought iron spiral staircase, akin to L.A.'s Bradbury Building in sheer jaw-dropping beauty.

› **Waldorf Astoria.** 301 Park Ave., between E. 49th and E. 50th sts. (Midtown). ☎ 212/355-3000.

If Liberace were looking for a place to sleep, he might choose this ornate wonder. (In fact, at one time he *did* choose this ornate wonder.) There is something heart-warmingly nostalgic about the Old World touches at this grande dame of New York hotels: the cordial, delightfully obsequious, and completely useless elevator operators; the dramatic entrance on Park Avenue; the tall ceilings and antique wood furnishings; the fabulous complimentary breakfast in the 26th floor Astoria Lounge;

the history! However, its days as a world-class destination for world-class celebrities is long gone (though the current $60 million upgrade might change all that). Today it is the preferred destination for well-heeled Midwesterners looking for that tony New York experience they've seen in all those '40s movies, and for the Japanese and Euro tourists who've read about the Waldorf in all the conventional guidebooks. It's also the permanent residence of dozens of well-heeled couples, widows, and corporate execs. In fact, Herbert Hoover once lived here. The Royalton this is not. And, frankly, we like it that way.

Mid-Range

I'm a middle child, from the Middle West, with mainstream middle-of-the-road looks. I know all about Mid-Range. I feel comfortable there—though, of course, I've spent my life railing against it. Here's what is considered "Mid-Range" by New York's rather skewed standards.

> **Marriott Marquis Hotel.** 1535 Broadway, between W. 45th and W. 46th sts. (Times Square). ☎ 212/398-1900.

Michael Monk on this architectural and interior design wonder: "Very typical Barbie doll architecture, circa 1979. Notice the permanent Christmas lights. Even in the South that is considered poor taste; here we are in New York City, and they're leaving the Christmas lights up year round. We're sitting on leatherette cushions. All we need is a disco ball." As Middle America as you're going to find in New York.

> **Millenium [sic] Hilton.** 55 Church St., across from the World Trade Center (Financial District). ☎ 212/693-2001.

There are only three reasons to stay at the Millenium Hilton: (1) you have an important meeting with a Wall Street brokerage first thing in the morning; (2) you are a tourist and want to take advantage of the low weekend rates; (3) the view. Let me tell you, this is the mother of New York hotel views, with over 180-degree vistas from our suites on the 50th and 49th floors. As for the decor, Millenium has that chrome-and-wood feel of a "snazzy" Chicago hotel circa 1975. No need to upgrade here: The place will soon be unwittingly camp. Besides, this 54-story black glass structure would take *forever* to renovate. We like it this way. Unlike the Mark, you don't feel you're competing with unparalleled excellence. You can relax, and do like most hotel visitors: Use your room as a place of business, even a little sordid business. Or do like Michael Monk (who is deathly afraid of heights): Shut the curtains and blockade the windows with chairs.

The mother of New York hotel views: out the window of the Millenium Hilton

› **Morgans.** 237 Madison Ave., between E. 37th and E. 38th sts. ☎ **212/686-0300.**

Though a reputation for snooty service hangs over (Ian) Shrager-Land like a pesky virus, Morgans—the first property in Ian's "boutique hotel" empire, and perhaps the most intimate—has always shocked visitors with its first-class treatment of guests. Goes to show, you can't always judge a book by its author.

Overrated, Overpriced, Overdone, or Just Flat-Out Annoying

New York is rough enough as it is. Make it easy on yourself: Don't stay in places that make your stay even rougher.

› **Hotel 17.** 225 E. 17th St., between Second and Third aves. (Gramercy). ☎ **212/475-2845.**

Hip and trendy, or so the Hotel 17 brochures say, but the fact that they say so is a pretty good indication that it's neither. The Eurotrash and Yank tourists who fall for

I have a major bone to pick with most Ian Schrager properties, whether it be Delano in Miami, Mondrian in Hollywood, or Royalton in New York: The problem, dear compassionate sir, is "attitude." Your hotels REEK of it. And in all the wrong ways, and in every nook and cranny of their being, from the wait staff to the desk help to the doormen to the bartenders to the publicists to the managers. It's unfortunate, for if one were to remove the completely gratuitous snobbery, one would find several compelling innovations at all Schrager-owned properties. At **Morgan's,** the originality is in the communal seating at the Asia de Cuba restaurant, and the barless Morgan's Bar; at the **Royalton** and **Paramount,** it's "the hotel as theater," taken to its full creative extension. Unfortunately, despite their painfully articulated panache, these hotels remind me of an elegant funding proposal, held together by precious bamboo, printed on carefully aged parchment, in a hip new calligraphy, with a simple message inside: "We Don't Like You." Quite beautiful, quite clear—yes, even quite "chic"— but, one must ask, "Where's the beef?" Or, rather, "Where's the love?" Despite French designer Phillipe Starck's sweet rhetoric about creating an "oasis of sympathy, of love, of tenderness," there is, in practice, absolutely no soul in any Schrager property, only concept—"Modern hotels for modern people" (roughly translated: arrogance, empti- ness, and casual service for people who deliver the same). Concept, dear sir, no matter how beautifully designed, will only get you so far.

this gimmick deserve what they get: average, undistinguished rooms and shabby ser- vice. The hotel does have one legitimate claim to fame: it appeared in Woody Allen's *Manhattan Murder Mystery* as the Hotel Waldron, where Allen and Diane Keaton discover a dead body.

> **Hotel Gramercy Park.** 2 Lexington Ave., at E. 21st St. (Gramercy Park).
☎ 212/475-4320.

Gramercy Park is so genteel. The surrounding town houses are so upper crust. And the view, especially on a snowy winter night, is so magical. So why is this hotel so shabby? A smart investor would buy it up, give it some class and pizzazz, and you'd have one of the finest places to sleep in Manhattan. Right now, it's barely suitable for a Moose Lodge Convention. The one redeeming feature is that guests get key privileges to the park, which is otherwise only open to neighborhood residents.

> **The Inn at Irving Place.** 56 Irving Place, between E. 17th and E. 18th sts. (Gramercy). ☎ 212/533-4600.

This B&B has the Victorian decor to go with the Gramercy Park location. Only one problem: The rooms feel so stiff and the beds so short, I can't imagine trying to sleep here. Better as a museum piece than a place to truly unwind. Besides, you've got to wonder about a place that lists its rates as "tariffs" (and at $325 per night, these tariffs make Smoot-Hawley look benign by comparison).

› **Paramount.** 235 W. 46th St., at Eighth Ave. (Theater District). ☎ 212/764-5500.

This fashion industry favorite is the antithesis of the Old World charm and splendor of hotels like the Carlysle and Essex House. Every chair, table, bed, and corner screams "I'M DESIGNED!" The hotel's interior is darkly lit, lending an impression there is more here than meets the eye. Same goes for the closet-sized rooms, which are like well-appointed coffins. The thinking seems to be: "We know the rooms are a joke, but don't they look fabulous!" As one would expect from such a place, the doormen and elevator boys are rumored to be the best looking in the city, aspiring models and actors all. Check out the kiddies' playroom, designed by Gary Panter, and the elevators (there's a weather report on each floor).

› **The Pierre.** 795 Fifth Ave., at E. 61st St. (Upper East Side). ☎ 212/940-8101.

Though it is rumored to have been Salvador Dali's favorite New York hotel, the kind of people who now frequent the Pierre are the same as those who stay at San Francisco's Fairmont: clueless rich Yanks and misguided foreign tourists. It's all about bands playing Sinatra in the back, couples in their golden years all boozy and slow dancing, and a gaudy Baroque decor that's just too much to be even decent camp. So completely lost in its out-of-touch time warp, the Pierre clientele doesn't even know there's a downtown to worry about. This is *the* place for spendy stiffs from suburbia: all the pretense of old-style elegance with not an ounce of true finesse.

› **The Plaza Hotel.** W. 59th St., at Fifth Ave. (Midtown). ☎ 212/759-3000. www.fairmont.com/newyork.

In each room of this temple of swankness there is a minibar, a few selections from which will cost you more than we make in a day. One suite is available at the reasonable rate of $15,000 *for a single night.* We suggest you see it our way: from the outside.

› **Soho Grand.** 310 W. Broadway, at Canal St. (SoHo). ☎ 212/965-3000. www.sohogrand.com.

It's a sad day when one longs for the Paramount. But not only is this pathetic attempt at a "nightclub hotel" way behind the curve, it is so lacking in design sense, it will be lucky if it survives as a budget hotel in a few years. The combination of Industrial, Art Nouveau, and oversized Minimalism is disturbing at best. The hip fashionistas the owners of this brick elephant hoped to attract have obviously deserted en masse, leaving vacationing Brits from Birmingham, turtlenecked jitteratti, and Joisey trash desperately seeking a "scene." This place reeks of marketing concept right down to the model-worthy bell boys, who looked like they were lifted in one fell swoop from Schrager Inc. When hotel staffers are bitching about the clientele in the elevators, you know the attention to detail is slack. And when the tiny gray rooms look like they were trashed by an Aerosmith party, with frayed robes, chairs with wood chipped out, dented air vents, and—the piece de la resistance—a hook that fell completely out of the wall when Michael Monk tried to hang a robe on it, you know you have amateurs running the place. This would all be tolerable if the Soho Grand were charging Gershwin rates, but at $299 to $379 for the lowest priced rooms and $1,049 for a suite, and with bonsai beds too small for Anna Paquin, this place ranks as one of the true unabashed rip-offs in the entire city. In other words, Eurotrash always welcome.

World Class

A great hotel makes you want to be a great guest. All of these hotels operate on such high and exacting standards, it makes even the most punctilious and proper among us want to spruce up our act a bit. As my mother always said, surround yourself with people that challenge you to be your best. All of these hotels do just that.

› **The Lowell.** 28 E. 63rd St., between Park and Madison aves. (Upper East Side). ☎ 212/838-1400.

Like any major tourist destination, New York has its fair share of the rich rube contingent. These waste-management executives and their wives need a "fancy" place to stay, and places like the Plaza, the Waldorf Astoria, and lesser lights like the Ritz-Carlton meet their needs perfectly. Then there are those entertainment and fashion executives and "stars" who do not want to meet up with Mr. and Mrs. Rube, no matter how wealthy, and certainly do not want to meet up with Mr. and Mrs. Hoi Poloi. For these rare few there is the Lowell, a 62-room former "apartment hotel" that prides itself on its intimacy, familiarity, and marked absence of the rube contingent. The Lowell is not snobby—in fact, it is generally hard to find such effrontery in even the priciest of Manhattan's hotels—however, it is discreet. Actually, it's hard to think of the Lowell as a hotel. It's more like a country inn. An expensive country inn, mind you: For 4 of the last 5 years the Lowell has had the highest average room rate of any hotel in America (somewhere around $550 a night). And with well above 80%

The Lowell

occupancy, 80% repeat customers, and the enormous difficulty one finds in making reservations, the Lowell is clearly one of the prime luxury destinations in the city. Do not, however, go looking for the crisp, tight, well-oiled machine and state-of-the amenities one expects from such places as The Mark or Four Seasons, which cater to far more business travelers. At the Lowell, the doormen, concierge, and waiters are a bit more, shall we say, schlumpy. The decor of the rooms is decidedly English manor. In fact, half the rooms have woodburning fireplaces. The managers like to think of a room at the Lowell as a warm, quiet, comfy apartment, "an oasis in the city," a "Pied-a-terre," rather than a hotel room. In other words, more Northeast Harbor than Newport. More cardigan than Armani. More old-school English than cutting-edge American. In fact, a fine English tea is served in the hotel's opulent

Pembroke Room, including delicious scones, clotted cream, champagne, and hot toddy (a strange and uneventful drink that mixes butter, rum, and sugar). The Lowell does have its share of quirky features: the *tres* gauche Hollywood Room (with Lana Turner's datebook and poker chips, plus a giant-screen TV, stereo system, and blinds all controlled by a push-button remote console); a conservatively furnished—but highly recommended—luxury suite with a beautifully landscaped terrace or two; and "the gym suite," which, like the name implies, includes full workout equipment. No surprise that obsessive-compulsive fitness freak Madonna Ciccone stayed in the gym room. (She also hiked the 12 flights of stairs to her room every time she returned.) Stars like Cretin Tarrantino also allegedly prefer the Lowell—which is the only good reason to avoid the place.

> **The Mark.** 25 E. 77th St., between Fifth and Madison aves. (Upper East Side). ☎ 212/744-4300.

If you are a Monk, namely a Jim Monk or a Michael Monk, the first thing you feel upon entering this refined "deluxe boutique" hotel on the Upper East Side is that you are decidedly *underdressed.* Your cheap loafers, recently bought for $10 at the Huntsville Walmart—not to mention your black-and-white checked Republican golf slacks bought for 25¢ at a thrift store in Berryville, Arkansas—aren't quite up to the formal attire of the well-trained hotel management, nor the fine Italian marble floor upon which they stand. There is a sense of insecurity that enters your soul: "I'm Not Worthy . . . I'm Not Worthy." This self-loathing is subtly inculcated by the bright, well-scrubbed, and attentive staff, to such an extent that one starts to feel the urge to tip for every minor act of obeisance, as a preventive measure against the horrible judgment you feel coming your way: "These Monks guys are paupers, without a penny to their name, and undeserving of the high standards of the The Mark Hotel, and the Junior Suite to which they have been assigned." This poverty-born fear is only deepened by said Monks' lack of a credit card to cover "the cost of incidentals." As a result, a new mindset starts to appear in the Monk subconscious: *"I dare not leave my room."*

It feels safe inside that $550 Junior Suite, with the complimentary blue bottle of Ty Nant spring water from Bethania, Wales (except when a Monk thinks of Wales, the first thought isn't of clean water), and the endless supply of snacks (only one problem—just a few of those snacks, say a bag of Oreos and a bar of Toblerone Swiss chocolate, would eat up the $20 deposit the front desk clerk allowed each Monk to leave as a deposit). And then there's the phone. It would seem perfectly natural for a Monk, safely ensconced in his luxury Junior Suite, to want to call a few Monkettes. Unfortunately, a local call runs $1.75 a pop, and a long-distance call substantially more. So, the Monk decides it is best to lay low.

Until he gets bored, and decides to sneak downstairs for some fresh air. On his way out through the lobby he discovers that far from world-class lookers, his fellow Mark patrons are as frumpy as he. Plump Midwest matrons, schlocky doctors, nouveau riche Brits, French families on vacation—with their kids outfitted in the requisite Nike Wear—businessmen in town for a convention of window frosters. *Wait a minute.* The Monk starts to feel more at ease. The Monk rushes up the spiral staircase, past the suits, past the intoxicating smell of chocolate emanating from the second floor pastry kitchen, past the stately banquet room. He changes into his gray Nike shorts and Grey tank top, his bright red Air Jihad Nike sneakers, and rushes back downstairs and heads out for a run in the park.

And not one member of the staff, not even world renowned Clefs d'Or concierge Giorgio Finocchiaro, looks askance. The staff at the Mark know they're good, they know their hotel is top of the line, so they don't need to lord their greatness over the clientele. It is such good-hearted tolerance of the sometimes tasteless qualities in its guests—matched with up-to-date amenities like complimentary cell phones, cell phone forwarding, gorgeous suites with large bathtubs, tall showers, several phones, and incredible views—that makes the Mark hotel our favorite luxury hotel in all of New York.

Devotees of the Shrager-led trend towards deliberately "informal and untrained" service may scoff at what appears to be the rote "institutionalized" formality of the Mark and its meticulous owner, the Rafael Group of Hoteliers, but we'll take professional deference over stylish lassitude any day. In fact, we'd like to see Georg Rafael and his eclectic international team of co-preneurs show Mr. Shrager how a hip modern hotel is really done. Go for it, Georg!

› **The Sherry-Netherland.** 781 Fifth Ave., between 59th and 60th sts. (Upper East Side). ☎ 212/355-2800. www.sherrynetherland.com.

The Sherry-Netherland always gets described as a more restrained and "elegant" alternative to the brash excess of the Plaza across the street. Our take is slightly different. We like the Sherry because it doesn't try to be anything but a quiet, beautiful hotel right on Central Park. With spacious rooms and attentive but not overbearing help, Sherry-Netherland is the kind of place one can slip in and slip out without a whole lot of fuss. But the main selling point is that, despite its obvious class, the Sherry-Netherland never tries to be anything but an American hotel. The lobby aesthetic may be Louis XIV, but the help is decidedly Noo Yawk. I like it when hotels are not embarrassed that the bellmen have a thick accent. I like it when hotels don't feel obligated to hire Europeans as desk attendants. The Sherry-Netherland does not put on airs. This is so unique in a city completely in thrall of all things European, it's positively revolutionary.

> **The Westbury.** 15 E. 69th St., at Madison Ave. (Upper East Side).
☎ **212/535-2000.**

A small, cozy, and luxurious Upper East Side find, whose noble mission is to make all guests feel cared for and right at home. That may sound like some hotel group rhetoric, but in this case, it's no marketing gimmick. You really do feel at home in this traditionally appointed, though newly renovated, oasis. And in a nice touch, if the Westbury doesn't have the regular room you reserved, they will put you up in one of their gorgeous suites at no extra charge.

Addresses

One of the problems with a city like New York is that so much happens behind closed doors, in buildings with impenetrable security—and there are often no clear demarcations telling you what happened or who lived inside. That's why we've created a section of important addresses, so, at least in your own imagination, you can re-create the scene for yourself.

Sites of Death, Violence, or Other Mayhem

> **18 W. 10th Street,** between Fifth and Sixth aves. (West Village).

The Weathermen used it as a bomb factory in the '60s. The facade had to be rebuilt after three died in a blast.

> **63 Bank Street,** at Bleecker St. (West Village).

Sid Vicious died here, of a heroin overdose, on February 2, 1979. Months earlier, as anyone who has seen *Sid and Nancy* knows, he'd murdered his girlfriend, Nancy Spungen, in the Hotel Chelsea.

> **700 E. 9th Street,** at Avenue C (East Village).

The scene of perhaps the most gruesome murder in East Village history: On August 19, 1989, self-proclaimed messiah Daniel Rakowitz murdered his dancer roommate, boiled her remains in a large pot, and, allegedly, served them up as soup to the homeless of Tompkins Square Park.

> **Audubon Ballroom.** 166th St. and Broadway (Harlem).

Malcolm X was shot and killed here on February 21, 1965.

> **The Dakota.** 1 W. 72nd St., at Central Park West (Upper West Side).

John Lennon, who was a resident, was murdered outside the building by one Mark David Chapman, a deranged fan and Holden Caulfield wannabe who is now incarcerated in Attica state prison. Yoko still lives in the Gothic landmark, as do other celebs, including Connie Chung, Rex Reed, John Madden, and Lauren Bacall.

> **Morgan Guaranty Trust Company.** 23 Wall St., at Nassau St. (Financial District).

Site of an anarchist bombing on September 16, 1920. Scorch marks are still visible on the building.

> **Stanhope Hotel.** 995 Fifth Ave., between 80th and 81st sts. (Upper East Side).

Jazz legend Charlie "Bird" Parker died here of a heart attack.

> **The Stonewall Inn.** 53 Christopher St., just east of Seventh Ave. (West Village).

Few places evoke more profound memories in the struggle for gay rights than the site of this former West Village bar, the scene of 2 days of rioting following a police raid in the summer of 1969. Many claim it marks the beginning of the Gay Rights Movement.

> **Windsor Palace.** 103 Bowery, above Hester St.

Former haunt of Ludwig the Bloodsucker, who got his kicks from drinking the blood of wounded patrons.

Addresses that Are Interesting for One Reason or Another

> **Andy Warhol's Factory (or Factories)**

The Factory had a lot of homes over the years. The first was at 231 E. 47th St., between First and Second avenues (1963–68), followed by 33 Union Square W. (1968–74). The third was on the tenth floor of 860 Broadway, at 17th Street (1974–82), and the fourth was inside the Con Edison building (*all* of the Con Edison building) at 19 E. 32nd and 22 E. 33rd streets, at Madison Avenue.

> **The Bunker.** 222 Bowery, at Stanton St., 2nd floor. No phone.

Most of the famous junkie artists came to this former YMCA locker room to see the ultimate junkie artist, William S. Burroughs. There's no question Burroughs was a beguiling genius, but what's usually forgotten is that he was an emotional-spiritual kindergartner who never got beyond 1940s existential nihilism. Despite his exultation by the alterna-nation in recent years, there is nothing hip or even remotely admirable about the late author of *Naked Lunch*. He was a bitter man, hopelessly addicted to smack, who had the coldness of heart to write about "the total need of heroin addiction," thereby inspiring lesser intelligences to copy his method of personal destruction.

It was a testament to Kerouac's greatness that he at least attempted to forge a new direction before succumbing to his own personal demon, alcohol. Ginsberg, the least compelling of the Beat triumvirate, was, not surprisingly, the most functional. He made Buddhism the center of his life, at least on the surface, and probably went the furthest in tackling the addictions that felled his Beat brothers.

Star Maps Here

For listings of celebrities' homes (if you're into that sort of thing) try New York City Star Walks (St. Martin's Press) or The Official Map of Movie Star Homes.

But Burroughs will always carry the mystique—mainly because he stuck so firmly to his routine, his schtick, and his dark, sorry point of view. Much like the accouterments of artist Joseph Beuys, the elements of the Burroughs aesthetic are now burned into our psyche: the felt hat, the cane, the suit, the black Olympia manual typewriter, the revolver. And they are all preserved lovingly at the Bunker, which served as Burroughs' refuge for 22 years, every time he visited New York.

› **Hotel Ansonia.** W. 73rd St. and Broadway (Upper West Side).

Its primary achievement: The walls are so thick it's almost totally soundproof. Perhaps that's why the Ansonia has been home to leading talents like Enrico Caruso and Igor Stravinsky.

› **Hotel Theresa.** 2090 Adam Clayton Powell Jr. Blvd., at 125th St. (Harlem).

Now just an office building, but in its heyday it housed such notables as Dizzy Gillespie, Cab Calloway, and, in 1960, Fidel Castro (who, we're told, cooked live chickens in his room).

› **Jim Monk's First Pad in NYC.** 125th St., just west of Broadway, above a car repair shop (Harlem).

Lama Pema was a twenty-something Tibetan monk studying English, whose family had all been killed during the Chinese occupation. Jim Monk was a young disciple filled with chela fever for the Buddha Dharma, whose family all voted Republican. Jim acted as Lama Pema's assistant while coaching debate at nearby Columbia. Pema's devotees tired of Jim about the same time Jim discovered Zen.

> *NYPD Blue* **Police Station.** 321 E. 5th St., between First and Second aves. (East Village).

Every foreign tourist recognizes this 5th Street station as the exterior for what is called "the 15th Precinct Station" in the TV police drama *NYPD Blue*. As with almost every recent sitcom "set" in New York, interiors are shot in an L.A. studio.

> **Rudy Giuliani Bought Crack Here.** 160th St. and Broadway (Washington Heights).

Back in 1986, as a publicity stunt to prove how easy it was to procure drugs on the streets of New York, federal prosecutor Rudy Giuliani and Senator Alfonse "Al" D'Amato journeyed up to Washington Heights to buy some crack cocaine. In what some might consider a strangely prophetic move, Rudy went undercover in a Hell's Angels leather vest adorned with swastikas, while Al went with simple sunglasses and military fatigues. The two scored not only major headlines, but several vials of rock.

> **San Remo.** 145 Central Park West, at 75th St. (Upper West Side).

This building houses, among others, Diane Keaton, Dustin Hoffman, Mary Tyler Moore, Elaine May, Barry Manilow, and either Demi Moore or Bruce Willis (depending on the divorce settlement). Madonna wanted to live here, but the board turned her down—they thought she'd bring too much commotion. Diane Keaton was the only member to vote on behalf of the Material Girl. (Just in case you need to know, Madonna and child now reside at 1 W. 64th.)

> **The Seinfeld Restaurant (Tom's Restaurant).** 2880 Broadway, at 112th St.

Fans of the sitcom *Seinfeld* will recognize this Columbia University area restaurant, from the exterior at least. It's where Jerry and his buddies gathered once a week to neurotically kibitz about endless ephemera. To avoid paying exorbitant usage fees, the producers of the show deliberately only shot the word "restaurant" in Tom's sign.

> **The Sprinkle Salon.** 90 E. Lexington, at 26th St.

Famed apartment of porn star turned post-porn modernist turned tantric nature girl Annie Sprinkle (nee Ellen Steinberg), who introduced The Monks to the fascinating world of the New York sex industry. We saw it all here—from Danny the Wonder Pony to Les/Linda, a lesbian separatist who trannied into a full-fledged full-chested man, so he/she could "get more respect in a male-dominated world." The Factory of '80s New York, but with a lot more love and kindness.

In 1997 there were 767 murders in New York, the lowest total since 1966, and a radical decrease from a high of 2,245 murders in 1990. It's a staggering statistic that can actually be felt on the streets. Believe it or not, New York City is now one of the safest cities on the planet.

And that is thanks to one simple fact: the election and reelection of Mayor Rudy Giuliani. Achieving what the colorful Koch and the dapper Dinkins could not, Giuliani successfully lobbied for more cops, better training, aggressive policing, and a new attitude that prosecutes quality of life misdemeanors as a way of discouraging an overall criminal climate. The strategy has worked.

It is most noticeable on the New York subways, where cops can be found at most major stations all hours of the day. How gratifying to get off the cross-town L at Bedford Street in North Brooklyn and find two cops getting off with you. How amazing to find several cops patrolling the area around Union Square after dark. How utterly refreshing to not be accosted by drug dealers as one strolls through Washington Square Park or heretofore sketchy parts of the East Village.

These aren't Gestapo tactics, as the liberal press would have us believe. (Though reports of excessive force have dramatically increased during Giuliani's tenure, the gruesome beating of Haitian Abner Luima is still a rare exception, not the norm.) While New York cops are not unobtrusive, and the *Gattaca*-like patrols outside city nightclubs can be a bit ominous, if you aren't flagrantly breaking the law, they generally stay out of your way. In fact, I've noticed a palpable change of tone from the city's police in just 2 years. Most are helpful, kind, with a witty remark, too. They are happy—and will be much happier if they are now given the raise they have rightfully earned.

Yes, it is possibly true that because of the new Giuliani-Disney regime, New York is "over" as a dangerous creative cauldron. Anarchy had its day. The city is becoming something different. Safer, cleaner, more hospitable. While the jury is still out on what cultural price New York will pay for this historic transformation, it's definitely time to drop the habitual moaning and groaning and admit that in a city where it is heresy to admit that the government gives out too much welfare and is too soft on thugs, Rudy Giuliani had the guts and intelligence to tackle the conventional wisdom. He is rightfully winning kudos for his courage—not forgetting significant reductions in crime.

Art in Public Places

There's art inside buildings, where you pay a fee to see work that you generally can't photograph or touch, and which can only be viewed on certain days at certain hours. This sort of art is on display at the many places listed in our Museums, Galleries and Landmarks section. Then there's "art in public places," a fancy way of classifying art that can be viewed, touched, played on, and even occasionally added to. Accessible art. Below we've listed the best of these.

Art on the East River: The Socrates Sculpture Garden

> **The Factory.** 47–44 31st St., at 47th Ave. (Long Island City, Queens).

It's been called a lot of things: "Coney Island on acid," "an exuberant construction crafted from some 50 tons of recycled junk" (*ARTnews*), "a pastiche of recognized clichés" (Hilton Kramer), and "staggering in terms of sheer lunatic invention" (Robert Rosenblum). Whatever it may be, one thing is sure: You won't find anything else like it, in New York or anywhere else.

In 1991, a group of artists who called themselves "The Three Js" was commissioned to mount an installation in the 18,000-square-foot lobby of a former Macy's warehouse. They took their mission seriously, gathering junk—soda machines, safes, bathroom fixtures, even a school bus—and bolting it to the floors, walls, and ceiling. The result is hard to describe (Disneyland meets *Waterworld*, with a little Lower East Side junkie thrown into the mix?); let's just say it's got to be seen to be believed.

Not so long ago, the warehouse stood at the center of a nasty legal battle. It seems the nefarious Helmsley-Spear had taken over management of the building and wanted the work dismantled. The Three Js went to court—and won. Now, the strange lobby of 47–44 31st St., in Queens, is protected until the artists' deaths. Apparently, the ruling was the first test of an amendment to the federal copyright act called the Visual Artists' Rights Act. So now and then the little guy *does* win. (Be sure to ride the elevators.)

> **National Debt Clock.** 43rd St. at Sixth Ave. (Midtown).

Sponsored by real estate developer Seymour Durst to remind us how much further we plunge into debt each nanosecond (owing in large part to interest on the debt itself). Factoid: 60% of the federal budget goes to the Pentagon. (The War Resisters League has the solution—see the sign in their window at Bleecker and Lafayette.)

> **The Phun Phactory.** 45–14 Davis St., at Jackson Ave. (Long Island City, Queens). ☎ 718/482-Phun.

The innocent days of bombing lay-ups and subways are making a comeback, and if you got a burner that you want to stay sitting, it's the phattest free wall space in the world. In 1990, Pat Dilillo, the founder and president of the Phun Phactory, scored the outside of a commercial warehouse in the bottom tip of Queens and fast turned it into the largest open-air graffiti gallery in the world. Pat figures that the space the Phun Phactory provides for murals, characters, and "burners" (slang for great graffiti, with all the customary elements) gives these artists a legal channel to vent their talents, and also a way for them to advertise their art in the hopes of infiltrating other free spaces and keepin' it legal.

> **Socrates Sculpture Garden.** 31–34 Vernon Blvd., at Broadway (Long Island City, Queens). ☎ 718/956-1819.

What makes this sculptural oasis so special is its quiet position adjacent to the East River, in a neglected corner of Queens, abutting a notorious housing project. This is an art place that restores the spirit, clears the mind, and tickles the funny bone. The inspiration of sculptor Mark DiSuvero, who lives nearby, The Socrates Sculpture Garden rates as one of the finest places in the city to not only quickly get away from it all, but perhaps, as we did, to meet fellow New Yorkers losing themselves amidst the beguiling sights, sounds, and views found there.

Mad Monks and Mosaic Man:
The *Jim Powers* Interview

There was a time in the 1960s in the East Village when the barriers between commerce, property, and the people were less rigid. It was a special place where like-minded residents resided, sharing a common language, goal, and sacrament. But as that like-minded feeling broke down, the force field that held this community together began to crack as well. Today, time and gentrification have taken their toll. Starbucks, Tower Records, and the Virgin Megastore are the new gathering places. What was original and quirky and small-scale is quickly being bulldozed or replaced by the growing mono-culture sweeping the area.

But one man is determined to keep the old flame alive, and he's doing it one tile at a time. His name is Jim Powers, though everyone knows him as The Mosaic Man.

The Mosaic Man crouches on a litter-strewn sidewalk amidst discarded butts, glass, wrappers, dirt, and grime, scraping a trowel against the wall of an Avenue A storefront. Nearby is a bucket full of broken glass, colored tiles, plates, saucers, and other ceramic artifacts. Some pieces are donated, the rest are scavenged.

The Mosaic Man wears his long hair in a ponytail and kneels before his work. It's a skyline of New York that emerges along a wall, complete with skyscrapers and landmarks set against a glittering sky.

For decades he has applied his discarded ceramics to the lampposts of the East Village. Growing from their base like a city-born fungus, they spread up the poles, giving a signature funkiness and artful humanity to the often barren and bleak streets of the neighborhood. Yet it's been an unending battle with city bureaucrats, who at their best turn their heads, but at their worst engage in a tug-of-war battle of citations, removals, and threats.

In following the letter of the law, the city is missing the bigger picture. For despite their grassroots spirit—no, because of their grassroots spirit—the mosaics serve an important purpose. The intricate, carefully laid tiles, with their swirling patterns, asymmetrical designs, and clever street scenes that incorporate real people from the neighborhood, are not just one man's art-in-your-face obsession but a personal idiosyncratic counterpoint, if not a symbolic roadblock, against the increasing mallification of Manhattan.

We follow Mosaic Man around his East Village Mosaic Trail, where he touches up on a few pieces (including a mosaic dedicated to the late Jerry Garcia), points out the ghosts and skeletons of others, and proudly takes us to a commercial project where his latest commission graces an eyewear shop's outer walls. He is a committed street artist and has given decades of his life to fusing art with community. He talks as we walk.

"Public art is, to me, an answer to the kind of problems you have in New York City."

Monk: How did you get started?

Mosaic Man: I started in 1985. I went down to St. Marks Place and did around the tree stumps. I mean, completely around. We built little houses and castles. Some of them got huge. Castles you could look inside. It was great. People brought down tons of stuff. I literally had about a ton of stuff. So it had the flavor of the neighborhood, you know—all kinds of stuff that they brought down. The city came and removed it. We had a police problem at the time. It was over—well, the thing got too high. They actually told me to knock it down like 6 inches from the top. It wasn't until I left town that they removed the whole thing. The neighborhood just seemed to get sick after that. They also started spraying the light posts silver. But that's easy to clean. It's just a matter of going out there with a high-power spray or with cleaning stuff.

Monk: You should get this artwork protected.

Mosaic Man: Well, we're trying to do just that. It could take a long time; it could take a short time. I'm trying to get it to take as short a time as possible.

Monk: Is it bureaucracy you're fighting against?

Mosaic Man: Mostly the bureaucracy. I don't think anybody sees it the way I do. This is an opportunity to move forward. Otherwise, what happens is you end up with heroin, somebody standing here watching that way, watching that way. Another guy over there. Before you know it, the tourists are gone. It's purse snatchings, fights—stupid stuff. What you've got here are 20 or 30 or 100 blocks, 40 or 50 different neighborhoods, and the mosaics tie them all in. I've had people say to me that when they come up out of the subway at the end of the day and they see a mosaic, they know they're home, they're in their neighborhood. Just working out here last week for 4 or 5 days, I stayed out until midnight, and I was amazed how many people I hadn't seen in years who came up: "Oh, you're back." It was nice to see that connection.

Monk: You went to Woodstock—for how long?

Mosaic Man: I was up there for 4 years. I have a mile of stuff right through the town. Big huge cement planters, which I want to introduce into New York. They have really nice scenes on them.

Monk: Why are you doing this?

Mosaic Man: I believe artists have to make a statement of some sort. I'm talking about people who come out here on the street and actually do something. My idea is that instead of having a building or a mural or something, which you walk by—and it's wonderful, a particular building is beautiful or whatever—but when you walk through something that's spread out for a mile, it takes on a different flavor. I actually think it keeps the streets a little bit nicer, a little saner, a little happier. It may even keep them a little safer. I believe in *public* art. Public art is, to me, an answer to the kind of problems you have in New York City. It reduces the anxiety, it makes people feel better. I'm having a great time all day. I really do like what I'm doing. I just wish I was getting paid for it.

Interview

Bars

Everybody has their favorite New York watering hole: **Ace**, 531 E. 5th St. (kiddie lunch pails, werewolf hologram, oh my); **Art Bar**, 52 Eighth Ave. (Last Supper on the wall); **Birdland**, 2745 Broadway (Edmund Wu is a regular); **The Casablanca**, 1553 St. Nicholas Ave. (a black man's hunter's "lounge"); **Ciel Rouge**, 176 Seventh Ave. (Jacque Brel on mournful accordion); **Dublin House**, 225 W. 79th St. (hypnotic flashing neon); **The Ear Inn**, 326 Spring St. (built in 1817, and still roaring); **55 Bar & Grill**, 55 Christopher St. (grungy blues bar with killer jazz jukebox); **Fraunces Tavern**, 54 Pearl St. (George Washington drank here); **Gold Bar**, 345 E. 9th St. (watch out for the hole in the floor); **The Great Jones**, 54 Great Jones St. (Jenkins, McClain & company); **Heartland Brewery**, 35 Union Square West (symbolizes the end of downtown as we knew it); Jack Dempsey, 61 Second Ave. (that's Miller on tap, not Harp); **Joe's**, 560 E. 6th St. (Ernie Steele's of the East Village, where New York newcomers come to pick each other up); **Korova Milk Bar**, 200 Avenue A (okay, we get the Lucy reference from *A Clockwork Orange*); **Landmark Tavern**, 626 Eleventh Ave. (pressed tin and mahogany, third oldest bar in the city); **Live Bait**, 14 E. 23rd St. (hip waitresses, lots of TVs); **Lucky Cheng's**, 24 First Ave. (Asian drag queens—a tired schtick); **Lucy's**, Avenue A between St. Marks and 9th St. (a slice of Broken Bow); **Mars Bar**, 25 E. 1st St. (Euro art punk refugees); **Max Fish**, 178 Ludlow St. (big deal); **Merc Bar**, 151 Mercer St. ("50s Adirondack," with a rather un-rustic clientele); **Milano's**, 51 E. Houston St. (nifty hole in the wall now colonized by Wall Street); **Monkey Bar**, 60 E. 54th St. (once host to Tallulah Bankhead and Tennessee Williams, now ruined by developers); **Morgans**, 237 Madison Ave. (Schrager-owned Temple Bar wannabe); **Mugsy's Ale House**, 9th St. and Bedford, Williamsburg (lots of choices); **n**, 33 Crosby St. (Spanish sherries and an exquisitely tiled wash basin); **The Oak Room**, at the Plaza Hotel, Fifth Avenue and 59th Street (what The Donald might call "classy"—for tourists who say the same); **Peter McManus**, 152 Seventh Ave. (drunkass locals bar lifted from the Smith's school of tavern decor); **The Raccoon Lodge**, 480 Amsterdam (erstwhile rough and tumble dive, now popular with bankers); **Raul's**, 180 Prince (if posing with well-tanned Eurotrash and overaccessorized knuckleheads is your thing, make this a stop along the Delia's–Bowery Bar–Lucky Strike trail); **Riverrun**, 176 Franklin St. (*NY Press's* Mugger is too soused to see there's absolutely *nothing* extraordinary about the place, which, of course, might be its appeal); **The Sapphire**, 249 Eldridge St. (boxy space made to look like an L.A. lounge bar, with cookie cutter couches, patrons and decor); **Sophie's**, 106 Greenwich St. (snide Brit Packers mourning the demise of punk); **Spy**, 101 Green St. (more Studio 54 snobbery

from people who still don't get that "in" and "out" lists are at least 10 years out of date); **Teddy's Bar and Grill**, 96 Berry St. (Cheers-like Williamsburg stronghold, with a mix of starving artists, Polish longshoremen, and the local Spanish league baseball team; bartender Spike is a huge Bucs fan); **10th Street Lounge**, 212 E. 10th St. (sleek sofa bar with altar candles all around—in the old East Village it stuck out like a Mormon missionary; not anymore); **WCO (aka Tile Bar)**, northwest corner of 7th Street and First Avenue (Gabby Glaser was a former bartender); **The Townhouse**, 206 E. 58th St. (The Log Cabin Republican Club of gay male bars: suits and ties, a piano bar in back, executives making out downstairs, a secret exit for extreme closet cases); **West End Gate**, 2909–11 Broadway (Columbia hangout that's a far cry from the Beat Era—highlight is a report card dated June 29, 1896); **White Horse**, 567 Hudson St. (bathroom graf: "Joel Schwaab rules much. More than you would think [fact]"); **Zinc**, 90 W. Houston (quality jazz in an itsy-bitsy space) . . .

I've seen them all. I've even been in a major car wreck looking for more. So don't go wagging your New York finger at me, trying to ferret out what I missed. I'm Jim the Mad Monk, damn it, and I know what's best . . . and . . . worst.

The Best

> **Bar d'O.** 34 Downing St., at Sixth Ave. (West Village). ☎ 212/627-1580.

Without the husky cabaret voltage of the beloved Joey Arias, Bar d'O would be a small, dimly lit neighborhood couch bar. But with Joey and his torch pals, the place takes on a kind of Weimar mystery and melancholy. With everyone bunched in close, smoke clouding the air, and the spotlight on the diva, Bar d'O is the perfect setting for a drag queen's naughty brilliance.

> **Elsie's Okie Dokie.** 307 E. 84th St., between First and Second aves. (Upper East Side). ☎ 212/650-9424.

In theory, this is a public bar—except the public, by and large, is not invited. The night we peeked in, a chunky, grumpy, and decidedly tough-looking woman was tending bar to a posse of young straights, who were no doubt clucking over their good fortune in being admitted to this relatively nondescript hole-in-the-wall. Owner-operator Elsie keeps her customer base to a bare minimum, unlocking her door only for patrons she likes the looks of. She didn't like the looks of us, apparently. Waiting outside, we could hear the conversation inside. It seemed to center around what we were doing—which, in short, was standing around waiting to be let in. This may well be the focus of entertainment at Elsie's. It's hard to know where to put this place: Is it the very best, by virtue of its uncompromising meanness, or is it the very worst, by virtue of the same quality? We leave that to you. Just write us, if she lets you in.

He Plays a She: *Joey Arias*

"Today's the incarceration look," Joey Arias tells us. "It's a little striped number. Put you in chains and then chop your head off." (This is a reference to Marie Antoinette and Florent restaurant's Bastille Day celebration, where Arias is performing this evening.)

"Kind of a Flying Nun look," Jim Monk says—which it is, in a manner of speaking: the Flying Nun in prison stripes and chains. For a long time, in 1994, Arias performed his act, "Strange Fruit," at Astor's on Lafayette Street, but he has since moved further west, to the smoky, intimate Bar d'O, where he has been entertaining crowds Saturday, Sunday, and Tuesday nights for months. Arias doesn't just lip-synch Billie Holiday; he doesn't even just sing her. Although he is a white man in drag, dressed (at least tonight) like the Flying Nun in chains, he seems, oddly enough, to embody Holiday, or at least to be possessed by her spirit. Fans say he "channels" her. The voice, if not Holiday's exactly, captures the soulfulness and melancholy.

Michael Monk with Joey Arias and friend

> Interview

84

"How do you know Florent?" Jim asks.

"Ah, we used to hang out in a back room years ago."

"In a back room? Which back room was that?"

"Oh, no. Oh, you're—no, no seriously, I stole his car years ago."

"No way."

"On Bastille Day about 8 years ago. He would—he drove up to the restaurant looking incredible in a pink Cadillac, and I walked out with Elvira."

"Oh, God."

"And he got out there, and we got in the car and drove, like, for about half an hour, and came back and he was screaming and yelling at me. He never—to this day he has never known it's me. And I'm telling you, this is an exclusive. So you guys tell him I'm going to kick your butt."

"How was he screaming at you and he didn't even know you did it?"

"He'd never associated my face with Joey Arias. I looked a bit different in those days, also."

"Oh, you did?"

"More a Spanish woman, with her spit curls and this little eyeliner and all in black and very bony, like thin—thinner—a lot thinner. I'm more chunky now."

"Yes, you are."

"It's a little striped number. Put you in chains and then chop your head off."

> **Hogs and Heifers.** 859 Washington St., at W. 14th St. (Meatpacking District). ☎ 212/929-0655.

In the heart of the meatpacking district, this redneck-cum-hipster hangout has a kick-ass Country Western jukebox and a down-and-dirty atmosphere. It's also got a beautiful bartender with a foul mouth and a bad attitude. Of course, the whole thing is a charade: The rednecks are probably paid for their services. Dancing on the bar was a rite of passage for most female patrons, until Rudy cracked down—you see, H&H didn't have a cabaret license. Now they do. Yee Haw!

> **Phil Hughes.** 1682 First Ave., at 87th St. (Upper East Side). ☎ 212/722-9415.

The most authentic watering hole on the Upper East Side. Not only that, it's one of the few bars in the city named after its bartender. Outside, the place resembles a VFW social club; inside, it feels like a gathering spot for the modern militia movement. On one wall hangs a large, framed American flag. At the bar, tending the few serious inebriates who frequent the place, is Phil Hughes himself, a reserved, serious, and oddly proper man, given his clientele.

> **The Seville Lounge.** 126th St. and Adam Clayton Powell Jr. Blvd. (Harlem). No phone listed.

We guarantee a minimal hipster quotient at this Harlem original. First off, the doors are locked, especially late at night—a device used by many area "lounges" (there aren't "bars" in Harlem) to keep out the riffraff. But if you pass several criteria—(1) you are about to be mugged by a crack addict; (2) they aren't too busy; (3) you're damn lucky—then you're reluctantly let in. Inside it's a comforting hideaway from the hard-core street life outside. They serve you Budweiser in an elegant champagne glass; Barry White's on the jukebox; and everything is cool, calm, and aqua blue. On a cold winter's night, it's a bit of Heaven in the heart of the 'hood.

> **Subway Inn.** 143 E. 60th St. and Lexington Ave. (Upper East Side). ☎ 212/223-8929.

There are plenty of dive bars in New York. In fact, dive-bar diving has, for a long time, been a pastime of slumming celebrities (consider Madonna, R.E.M., and Drew Barrymore). Julia Roberts is reported to have been spotted at the Subway. Yet this place manages, despite Roberts's appearance, to retain its ambiance. More than any other, this is *the* dive bar of New York City. The regulars come in all shapes, sizes, and ages, but for the most part they're commuters who are here to get sloshed before the long trek home. The aged tile floors and wood bar, the Hopper-esque vibe, the film-noir feel of the neon out front, the Willy Loman pathos of the soused and sappy patrons, the dollar glasses of Bud—all would make the Subway a winner in anybody's book. But what tips this place into the top 10 is the inimitable hardass charm of owner-operator Charlie Ackerman. I tried to ask Charlie a few questions. "I've got enough trouble answering questions," he told me. "Got environmental people, police. Leave me alone."

"How long has this place been here?" I asked.

"Talk to me about something that's interesting."

"Did Julia Roberts tip?"

"No! The only guy you ever tip is the rabbi who cuts your dick off." And then, finally, he asked me a question: "Where do you live?"

"Williamsburg, Brooklyn," I told him.

"That's not New York!"

Charlie wouldn't let up. He disagreed with everything I said, no matter how accurate or complimentary; finally, as I was leaving, he said, "You have a nice approach."

Don't miss this place.

Julia Roberts didn't tip here: The Subway Inn

> **Temple Bar.** 332 Lafayette St., at Bleecker St. (NoHo). ☎ **212/925-4242.**

A handsome, dark, wood-paneled uptown bar serving top-of-the-line drinks in a downtown locale. It has the feeling of a private men's club, but is filled with enough of the hip slacker quotient to make Jim Monk, the strange bridge between these two worlds, feel right at home. This place was Cocktail Nation before Black Velvet Flag was even born.

> **Vodka Bar.** At the Royalton Hotel, 44 W. 44th St., between Fifth and Sixth aves. (Midtown). ☎ **212/869-4400.**

A stylish little hideaway tucked off to the side of the Royalton Lobby serving only—of all things—vodka and champagne. *A Clockwork Orange* meets *The Jetsons.*

> **Void.** 16 Mercer St., between Canal and Grand (SoHo). ☎ **212/941-6492.** www.escape.com/~void.

Although it's become popular with the young, ironic, *South Park*–loving, *Simpsons*-quoting, Web-designer crowd, Void is, at least for now, the perfect SoHo gathering place. And it's Bridge-and-Tunnel proof, for the simple reason that it's next to impossible to find. Wonderfully dark and spacious, Void is artsy without being pretentious. Plus, it's on the Web. Hit the copper flower for a devilish surprise.

The Best of the Rest

> **Angel's Share.** Inside the Village Yokocho Restaurant, 8 Stuyvesant St., between 9th St. and Third Ave., 2nd floor (East Village). ☎ **212/777-5415.**

This place is a true find—that is, it's hard to find. Who would think that behind a wooden door in an upstairs Korean barbecue joint would sit one of the most romantic hideaways in the East Village? It features a spectacular view of the street scene below, and top-line bartenders who know how to mix a fine cocktail.

> **Augie's Pub.** 2751 Broadway, at 106th St. (Upper West Side). ☎ **212/864-9834.**

Of all the Columbia area hangouts, this small, funky, brick-walled jazz joint is the one Kerouac would most likely have frequented were he alive today. Then again, any place that served liquor would probably have been fine by Jack. No outrageous cover, excellent performers, an eclectic clientele, plus more beautiful and bright Barnard "womyn" than other spots in the area.

> **Barramundi.** 147 Ludlow St., at Stanton St. (Lower East Side). ☎ 212/529-6900.

Named after an Australian fish sacred to aboriginal peoples, the place is filled with handcrafted furniture, sculpture, and treasures from owners Shane and Ana's travels. The overall effect is dark, cool, and glowing like an underwater cave. The highlight is a cozy, coven-like back room where scorpion-like slackers trade stories into the night. Rumor: free pot brownies at the club's summer Sunday barbecues.

> **Beauty Bar.** 231 E. 14th St., between Second and Third aves. (East Village). ☎ 212/539-1389.

It's a retired beauty salon, as the name suggests, complete with hair dryers and manicure tables. On Thursdays and Fridays, Flo, the owner of the place when it was a beauty salon, gives manicures for $7 (includes a drink). Not bad, and as high as a high concept is likely to get you.

Patrons at the Beauty Bar

The Worst

› **Chumley's.** 86 Bedford St., at Christopher St. (West Village). ☎ 212/675-4449.

We're sure the middle-brow, middle-class collegiate types who populate this former speakeasy are, for the most part, decent people who will raise fine, upstanding babies in Eau Claire, St. Paul, or wherever the hell they settle down, but their loud Bud Lite demeanor ruins what must have been a compelling little find decades ago. Skip it with all your might.

› **Heartland Brewery.** 35 Union Square West (Union Square). ☎ 212/645-3400.

If one place symbolizes the end of downtown Manhattan as we knew it, it's the Heartland Brewery. Everybody we can't stand find his or her way here: fratheads, stockbrokers, bridge-and-tunnel creeps. They all cram into this clean streamlined space. You half expect the local college football team to charge through the door any minute. Who cares if the place has 537 different microbrews on tap; it belongs in the heartland, not in New York.

› **The Hi-Life Bar and Grill.** 477 Amsterdam Ave., at 83rd St. (Upper West Side). ☎ 212/787-7199.

The epicenter of New York's mindless Neanderthal breederdom. Upon seeing me enter, with my recently shaven head and a bag of groceries, the bouncer shouted, "Hey, look, it's Timothy McVeigh, here to blow the place up! Hey, you got a bomb in there, Timothy?" I joked about how much I loathed the federal government and how I was perturbed by the raid at Waco, as the bouncer said, "Yeah, oppressed by the black man." *WHA?* Like most bars and restaurants in this No-Monk's land, it's a Bud Lite ad gone bad.

› **Julius.** 159 W. 10th St. (West Village). ☎ 212/929-9672.

Our theory is that if a gay man drinks enough, he'll turn straight, and from what we've seen of this dingy losers' den, Julius is the place for men ready to make the transition. Few people know that this pugnacious pithole predates Stonewall. The opening shot of *Boys in the Band* was filmed here, back in 1969; it seems the bar never recovered.

› **McSorley's Old Ale House.** 15 E. 7th St., between Second and Third aves. (East Village). ☎ 212/473-9148.

It doesn't get more frightening than this, especially on a Saturday night when the frat boys are in town. One look into their drunk-ass faces should send you screaming out of the place. Lounging like cows around the wooden tables, hoisting enormous mugs of beer, and shouting in that inimitable white frat boy way, they seem poised either for a good fight or a gang rape. Like Chumley's, McSorley's is a great old bar (one of the oldest in the city) whose present clientele is undeserving of its history and character. Check it out, but only when it's empty.

> **Monkey Bar.** 60 E. 54th St., between Madison and Park (Midtown). ☎ 212/838-2600.

A sad story. When we visited not so many years back, it was a real find. Faded and nearly forgotten, in the lobby of the Hotel Elysée, the Monkey Bar, with its famous jungle motif, had once been host to the likes of Tallulah Bankhead and Tennessee Williams. We were the place's only patrons that day, and the bartender engaged us for nearly an hour with stories of the hotel's famous denizens. A couple of years ago, the developers got hold of it, and, in short order, ruined the place.

> **Pete's Tavern.** 129 E. 18th St., at Irving Place (Union Square/Gramercy). ☎ 212/473-7676.

Who knows, maybe this historic 1864 Gramercy Park tavern was special once upon a time. Today, it's crowded with young Republicans and their homely dates, getting soused like it was some Duke frat party. Hey, how about them Blue Devils! Give it a miss.

Bars for the Brainless

Where do they get the people that frequent places like **Bowery Bar, Monkey Bar, Au Bar,** and these other vacuous model showcases with the braindead dullards who grovel after the shut-down babes in black, and the Mafia-like bouncers who think the place is very special. And how is it they all seem like a weird fusion of *Central Park West, Melrose Place, Beverly Hills 90210,* and some horribly snotty sorority prom? Like, who the fuck are these people, and why are people like David Rockwell (Le Bar Brat, Snobu) designing places for them? And who, in God's good name, would wait outside for an hour to get into a place to mingle with people you absolutely despised in high school, and the older Anthony Haden-Gest types who prey on them now? This elitist trendiness for the truly non-elite is one of New York's most egregious failings.

> **Shark Bar** (officially known as Spring Lounge). 48 Spring St., at Mulberry (Little Italy). No phone listed.

Formerly a divey neighborhood bar popular with rich rockers and twenty-something poseurs looking to slum it up with Mulberry Street drunks. In those days, back in the '80s, the cranky bartenders didn't quite get what all the fuss was all about. Then it was featured in the R.E.M. video "Near Wild Heaven," and now, true to bogus NoLita form, it's been bought out, refurbished, and populated by the very people those original drunks probably most despised: yuppie art scum.

> **Spy.** 101 Greene St., at Prince St. (SoHo) ☎ 212/343-9000.

More Studio 54 snobbery from people who still don't get that "in" and "out" lists are at least 10 years out of date. What self-hating simpleton would wait outside a place that declared "Guest List Only Tonight"? Elitism is a virus, and Spy is a carrier.

Concept Bars of the Village and Lower East Side

Now that the East Village and Lower East Side have been thoroughly tamed and claimed, there has arisen a slew of concept bars to woo twenty-nothings eager for that antiseptic downtown thing. We don't think much of them, and we've seen them all. However, there are a few that are above average. For example:

> **Bharmacy.** 538 E. 14th St., at Avenue B (East Village). ☎ 212/BA8-2240.

Everyone in the Village probably has their story about this place when it was Wright's pharmacy. I used to buy my dermatological gloves here. What's great is that the aesthetic, if not the spirit, of the old drugstore remains. As far as concept bars, this one works better than previous attempts like the Sci Bar, mainly because the owners have adroitly worked the pre-existing elements into the current design: glass cases of combs, pills, mortars, pestles, Maalox, and other pharmacological items line the place; drinks are served in beakers. Unknown to most regulars, though, the items actually came from a pharmacy in Philly, not the original Wright's. The music—Henry Mancini and other trippy retro pop faves the night we were there—ain't bad, but underneath the concept, Bharmacy is a striking symbol of what the East Village has become: less of a place where real people live and build a community, a place where drugstores *are* drugstores, and more of a conceptual place for the world to come and "party."

> **Fez.** 380 Lafayette St., at E. 4th St. (NoHo). ☎ 212/533-2680.

We were a bit disappointed with the Time Cafe, so we were surprised to find how much we enjoyed the Cocktail Nation, faux-Beat ambiance of its back-room adjunct, Fez. There are plenty of goatees—not to mention some Sturm und Drang—in this well-appointed Moroccan casbah, but it's somehow tolerable. The downstairs performance area is cozy and fun.

> **Lansky Lounge.** Norfolk St., between Rivington and Delancey (Lower East Side). ☎ 212/677-9489.

Named for the legendary Jewish gangster Meyer Lansky, the scene at this former bar mitzvah room in the rear of Ratner's Deli begins every night except Friday (when it's closed for Shabbos) at 11pm, after the old deli closes its doors. Then, a far younger crowd descends. They enter through a speakeasy-like entrance, down a back alley, up some stairs through a nondescript entrance, near where pot smoke wafts through the air. Inside is a busy bar scene filled with fresh-faced twenty-somethings in '40s and '50s style threads, lounging at the bar or dancing to big band tunes, and knowing the steps, too. No wonder the local news media claims this generation has no beef with their parents. They are aping their parents' entire schtick, emulating an era when hard drugs weren't de rigeur and dancing cheek to cheek was the norm. Of course, the retro swing thing and faux illicit nature of the place perfectly encapsulates how safe the Lower East Side has become.

> **Lure.** 409 W. 13th St., at Greenwich St./Ninth Ave. (Meatpacking District). ☎ 212/741-3919.

The ultimate leather boy meat market. You'll find all ages among this tough-as-nails-until-they-open-their-mouth crowd. Don't miss foot-fetish night.

> **Mare Chiaro.** 176½ Mulberry St., at Broome St. (Little Italy). ☎ **212/226-9345.**

Legends abound about this place (a deaf bartender, a three-legged cat). Although it's supposedly known to regulars as Phil's, Mare Chiaro is really Tony's place. He's the owner, and believe us, he is not a man to mess with. Perhaps the only bar in Little Italy that hasn't been overrun by tourists.

> **Monas.** 224 Avenue B, between E. 13th and E. 14th sts. (East Village). ☎ 212/353-3780.

The bar at the end of the universe, if the universe was the East Village—come 14th street, a whole new world begins. The regulars who inhabit this grungy cave of a joint seem to relish this fact. It's a safe warm world inside Mona's. A place where alcoholic young Brits and Paddies mingle with East Village punk and slacker slime, shooting pool, shooting shit, and shaking to the tunes on the excellent jukebox. Cheap Guinness on Thursday nights.

> **Parkside Lounge.** 317 E. Houston St., at Attorney St. (Lower East Side).
☎ 212/674-9308.

A bona fide New York dive bar, with dusty buck and trout mounted on the wall, bright neon out front, and a crowd of seriously inebriated Latinos and white trash.

> **Winnie's Bar and Restaurant.** 104 Bayard St., at Mulberry (Chinatown).
☎ 212/732-2384.

We are often asked: What qualifies something as a Monk bar? We reply that it's an intuitive thing, and best explained by example. Take, for instance, this Chinatown hole in the wall. Winnie's has that special gnarly something that stops you in your tracks and forces the question: WHAT . . . THE HELL . . . IS . . . THIS? The ability of a place to engender a kind of dumbstruck curiosity—a beginner's mind, to borrow Suzuki Roshi's treasure phrase—is a key ingredient in determining if it is Monk-worthy. It may be because we are Caucasian, but the sight of drunk Asians greatly enjoying an evening of karaoke as if they were teenagers at their first prom, while a posse of other oddballs lounged at the darkly lit bar, struck us as strangely compelling. They didn't want us there snooping on their scene ("We don't want any amateurs!!" one patron shouted), which only fueled our desire to see more. But be careful: The place attracts the fringes of the Chinatown galaxy and has been the scene of two gangland murders.

Jim at Mare Chiaro

Boroughs

In most other cities of America, the five boroughs of New York would be considered separate cities. In fact, the city's second largest borough, Brooklyn, would be among the country's largest cities if it hadn't merged with the rest of New York over 100 years ago. Though ostensibly all part of this one great entity we call "New York," each borough has its own distinct identity. In fact, Staten Island considers itself so distinctive it wants to secede. Only in New York . . .

The Bronx

Though at various junctures in its history the Bronx has been both a safe suburban haven and a bucolic residence of the city's best and brightest, in the last 3 decades it has devolved to such an extent that it is now considered the very symbol and reality of the city's worst urban nightmares. Forget the bourgeois pleasures of the Zoo, City Island, and Riverdale on the northern tip of this borough (they belong to some other world)—the Bronx is essentially a Third World country. On some winter days, it looks like the aftermath of an apocalypse. While Brooklyn at least carries some emotional resonance with native New Yorkers, in recent years the Bronx has only carried pure dread. No sympathy, just revulsion. Interestingly, the despair has its own captivating aesthetic. Probably our favorite borough of the moment because it is so routinely dissed,

Observation

"There is something about this ceaseless buzz, and hurry, and bustle, that keeps a stranger in a state of unwholesome excitement all the time, and makes him restless and uneasy, and saps from him all capacity to enjoy anything or take a strong interest in any matter whatever— a something which impels him to try to do everything, and yet permits him to do nothing. He is a boy in a candy-shop—could choose quickly if there were but one kind of candy, but is hopelessly undetermined in the midst of a hundred kinds. A stranger feels unsatisfied, here, a good part of the time."

—Mark Twain in _Travels with Mr. Brown_

James Boyvin,

Staten Island Resident and Nudist Bed-and-Breakfast Owner

Jim Monk: Secession, Staten Island secession. Everybody talks about it. How real is it? What are you doing to stop it?

James Boyvin: Well, I'm not doing anything to stop it. I'm in favor of it.

Jim Monk: Oh, you are?

James Boyvin: For the following reason: Staten Island, being the smallest of the five boroughs, has been traditionally grossly underserved by the city of New York. We are only 400,000. By other cities' standards that's a relatively large place; however, by New York City standards that's nothing. Consequently, we always end up with the short end of the stick here. We give more tax dollars to the city than we get back in services. And after all the studies that have been done, there is a secession commission on Staten Island, and the process is now going through the legislature and the courts to establish whether that's even going to be a possibility. Staten Islanders voted overwhelmingly for secession, but it's in the courts right now as to whether we will be able to get through the legislature to be able to secede.

Jim Monk: Well, what will happen to the great resources of Staten Island, like the Fresh Kills Dump, if you become your own city?

James Boyvin: We will close it.

Jim Monk: You will?

James Boyvin: Most emphatically.

Jim Monk: No kidding.

James Boyvin: In fact, one of the issues at the conference, the island-wide conference in 1995, was very specifically the Fresh Kills Dump. I personally feel that I am amazed that the folks that live out there haven't en masse gone across the street and closed the damn thing.

Jim Monk: It's definitely not good for their health, is it?

James Boyvin: It's not only not—it's primarily not good for their health.

Jim Monk: Because of the methane, or what is it?

James Boyvin: Well, because it hasn't been properly studied, the effects of it in such a highly and densely populated urban area. No one considered that, as usual. So consequently, now, finally, some studies are being done, which haven't been completed. But all

Interview

you have to do is drive through that area with your windows closed, air vents closed. It's [nauseating]. It's staggering. Again, since I've been back on the island, it amazes me that the folks that live out there haven't just gone over and closed it. That is one of our prime problems here on the island.

Jim Monk: Why don't you just turn it into a tourist attraction and make money off of it?

James Boyvin: Well, I've thought it would be a great ski area.

Jim Monk: Yeah.

James Boyvin: For instance.

Jim Monk: Yeah.

James Boyvin: I'm serious. And it is something that actually is being looked at. Because the hill is now a hundred and fifty, two hundred feet high.

Jim Monk: Right.

James Boyvin: So you may think it's funny but—

Jim Monk: At least snow boarding.

James Boyvin: Exactly.

though an influx of federal dollars and a renewed sense of community pride are finally transforming the borough for the better.

Brooklyn

The Sad Sack Borough. Everyone seems to remember it with forlorn nostalgia. Historically, the great ethnic home for scores of writers, artists, and musicians, from Spike Lee to Marianne Moore, today Brooklyn is a wounded animal—poor, decrepit, lacking in the spark and sparkle of Manhattan across the way, never fully recovered from the loss of its one cultural common ground, the late Ebbet's Field. It has its pockets of wealth (Brooklyn Heights), popularity (Park Slope), ethnicity (Carroll Gardens, Bedford Stuyvesant), and decayed industrial beauty (Williamsburg, Greenpoint, and Coney Island), but essentially Brooklyn hobbles along on one leg, without much pride, without much hope, without even a major daily newspaper. Which, in a perverse way, is why we like it. Manhattan can hide its disease and decay beneath a wall of gentrification. Brooklyn never lies.

Manhattan

The epicenter of the planet. No matter what they say in Paris, L.A., or London, if you want to be among the chosen, you have to come here. But, unless you are terrifically adept, you will be hard-pressed to create family, community, *and* career in the Naked City.

Queens

This is the new Ellis Island, where every type of ethnic immigrant learns the ropes before being let loose on the cold-hearted crap shoot of Manhattan. There are some lily-white couples and their kids scattered hither and yon, as well as a few artist types around Long Island City, but essentially Queens is where the newly arrived "wretched of the earth" huddle together in dense tribal units to scratch out a little home and happiness in "The Land of Endless Possibilities."

Staten Island

God created Staten Island so Manhattanites would realize what a great deal they had. The place has enormous camp-lite appeal, but woe to anyone who thinks they can live here. It's really more of a Jersey suburb than a New York borough (with the sort of right-wing values one would expect from such a place). Ask any teen who grew up there, for whom the place is worse than Riker's. Ironically, on the surface anyway, it would seem that Staten Island would be the ideal residential retreat from the city, but it doesn't work out that way. It's a poorly maintained bastion of closed-mindedness, with a few highlights (Snug Harbor, the Jacques Marchais Museum of Tibetan Art, even the the Fresh Kills Dump) sprouting up through the mediocrity. The ride there (aboard the Staten Island Ferry) is much more exciting than the eventual destination. *Caveat:* Staten Island's woeful condition may have to do with getting short shrift from the city, which is why residents recently voted to secede.

Bridges

Though New York is often seen as a city of skyscrapers, it is actually a city of bridges—because it is New York's bridges that carry the greatest emotional and aesthetic significance with lifelong residents. Starting with the "BMW" bridges (Brooklyn, Manhattan, and Williamsburg), for decades it has been bridges that have carried upwardly mobile immigrants from the high rents and squalor of lower Manhattan to a "new life" in the outer boroughs. Each of New York's bridges has a unique story to tell. We encourage you to view them, stand on them, and walk across them, as did your forebears many years ago. (See Monk Maps for exact locations.)

› Brooklyn Bridge

The bridge of dreams, literally and figuratively. It lacks the monumental scale of the Golden Gate, but it carries great symbolic significance for generations of New Yorkers who made Brooklyn their home. Take it by cab with the one you love late some night—by far the most romantic back-window view of Manhattan. The next night, stroll from Brooklyn Heights back over to Manhattan, and enjoy the most romantic *walk* in the city.

In 1883, when it was completed, the Brooklyn Bridge was the first bridge in the world to use steel cable. In addition, it is the only bridge to employ a spider-like cable design, one of its major visual hallmarks. Most importantly, when her husband was too sick to finish overseeing the final construction, Mrs. Washington Roebling messengered instructions over to the construction crew in her husband's forged handwriting, knowing that at the time the instructions would not have been followed were they seen coming from a woman.

› Casciano Memorial Bridge

You will take this bridge any time you are heading from Newark into New York, and vice versa. Incredible views of the New York City skyline and the astounding Verrazano Bridge.

› George Washington Bridge

Massive grand connecting point between Jersey and Upper Manhattan. Try it riding on top of an RV. We did. See "On The Road," 1990 New York issue of *Monk* (at www.monk.com).

› Hell Gate Bridge

You can't drive across or walk it (it's a railroad bridge crossing the East River between Astoria, Queens, and Wards Island), but it's one hell of a sight anyway—especially paired with the relatively sleek and modern Triborough Bridge, which stands between it and the Manhattan skyline. The bridge's huge stone towers rise on one side right out of Astoria park, looking like enormous elephant feet. Years ago, somebody spray-painted the word "Bustle" up on the north face of one tower, and it's stayed there ever since, way up above everything else in the neighborhood, like a rarely followed command.

› Manhattan Bridge

The most overlooked bridge in the city, and the underappreciated sister of the Brooklyn Bridge. Most people don't even know how to get to it, and hipsters only think of it because of the Dumbo (Down Under the Manhattan Bridge) Area. *Caveat:* Michael Monk once got pneumonia from riding atop the Monkmobile as it crossed the Manhattan Bridge in the dead of winter, for a *People* magazine story about the Monks, which never ran. We find that anecdote rather emblematic of the bridge as a whole.

› Pershing Square Bridge

Brings the traffic of Park Avenue around the sides of Grand Central Terminal. One of our favorite drives in town.

› Pulaski Bridge

The bridge connecting north Brooklyn to Queens. An ugly concrete bridge admittedly, but it has a footpath along the side and it isn't a bad walk from hip North Brooklyn to the Phun Phactory. From this scenic vantage point you can view both a chemical plant bellowing thick plumes of toxic steam and the old train depot, which has rusting spaghetti strands of rail tying themselves into three lines to go under the East River to Manhattan. A good place to view the haves and the have-nots, with the picturesque, rich Manhattan skyline over the river on your west and unused factories, railroads, truck lots, and the rest of lower Queens all around you. The water underneath is about as disgusting as New York water can get.

> Queensborough Bridge

Definitely has the best view of Midtown, totally immersing you into the buildings and letting you feel like you're arriving in the Metropolis with a capital M. This is the big brother of New York bridges—wider and stronger than the rest.

> Third Avenue Bridge

Hard to believe this little Harlem drawbridge is the main thoroughfare to get you from the FDR Drive to the Deegan Expressway. Fascinating in a funky, rusty, rickety sort of way.

> Triborough Bridge

Another modern, large-span bridge similar to the Throg's Neck Bridge. Officially named because it splits three ways to three of the boroughs of New York: Manhattan, the Bronx, and Queens. It also separates to the three boroughs of rich suburbia around New York: Long Island, Westchester, and Connecticut (87 to upper New York State, 278 to 95 to Connecticut, or 278 to 295 to Long Island, see?). Use this as a good marker: When you get to the Triborough Bridge, turn back at the next exit!

> Verrazano Narrows Bridge

Huge, otherworldly, and towering connection from Brooklyn to Staten Island. Our favorite bridge in the city.

> Williamsburg Bridge

New York's answer to the Huey P. Long in New Orleans, this rusty ugly mother feels like it's going to collapse at any moment. In fact, on several occasions, parts of it have. In the last 12 years, 6 feet of roadway and two 30-pound steel support bars have fallen into the East River. It's so bumpy you actually bob up and down as you drive. Like walking a high wire, the side lanes feel like an afterthought of bridge engineering, rattling and shaking as you cross. One of those bridges that makes you ponder what it would be like if you were really planning your final exit. The oft-repaired walkway is now open, which offers its own special kind of thrill. However, be careful when you get to the other side: Gangs of Hispanic teenagers await your arrival (ask Mike Connor). The great anti-Situationist and archenemy of Guy Debord, Glen Adams, was hallucinating one of the times he drove across the Williamsburg Bridge, and swore he saw silhouettes of men jumping out before the car—no doubt the spirits of the souls still confined to architect Leffert L. Buck's spooky and dangerous contraption.

Buildings

and Other Compelling Structures

There are scads of excellent architecture books about this architecturally rich city, but they are often so vast and detailed, one is left daunted by the prospect of using them at all. This section cuts New York architecture down to bite-size chunks. We've applied a simple Monkish criteria: The structure, for better or worse, must have completely blown us away.

> **Abandoned elevated rail line.** Between Tenth and Eleventh aves., from 14th St. to the 30th St. Rail Yard.

Unofficially open to the public, this is the abandoned remains of a rail line that ran to the meatpacking district up to the old east side lines that were shut down in the '50s. It's trippy to see this steel structure elevated over the traffic, with trees sprouting from the extended tressel.

> **The Anchorage.** Brooklyn Bridge Reception Hall. Cadman Plaza West, between Hicks and Old Front sts. ☎ **718/206-6674.**

This huge and beautifully built hall is actually *within* the Brooklyn Bridge (on the Brooklyn side). Supposedly a place for art exhibits and the occasional rave, we recommend it for the Founders Day Dinner of the Brooklyn Cacophony Society.

> **Angel Orensanz Foundation.** 172 Norfolk St., just below E. Houston (Lower East Side). ☎ **212/780-0175.** www.orensanz.org

The Sephardic Spanish sculptor Angel Orensanz's studio and foundation are housed in an old synagogue (the oldest Reformed temple in New York, according to Angel). Designed by Alexander Seltzer, the German architect who also designed the Astor Library on Lafayette Street and the Academy of Music on Irving Place, the space is impressive. It is being renovated (slowly), and continues to be used for exhibitions and performances (the artists' collective P. S. 1 has held openings here, and the place hosted the 1998 Vision Festival of jazz and experimental music). Angel is colorful and might even be certifiable; his brother, Al, is a little easier to talk to (either because he's got a firmer grip or because his English is better). You've got to wonder how the two brothers will ever come close to restoring the rickety, decayed former synagogue in this or any lifetime. Not a problem, really, since the eerie, unfinished quality of the space makes it the ideal setting for music videos, fashion shoots (with the likes of Linda Evangelista and Naomi Campbell), live concerts (Kronos Quartet), and even an occasional wedding.

1849: The Anshei Slonim Synagogue. 1998: The Angel Orensanz Foundation

Angel Orensanz: I bought this.

Jim Monk: You bought this?

Angel Orensanz: Yes, that's right.

Jim Monk: Because you want to restore it?

Angel Orensanz: Yes, restore it. Expensive. Everything. Administration, materials. Making sculptures, movies, sitar concerts, exhibitions—here, here. Is coming Whitney Houston, Lou Reed, Martin Scorsese.

Jim Monk: You did a Lou Reed video here?

Angel Orensanz: Already. They have already.

Jim Monk: So you own this and rent it out—that's how you make a living?

Angel Orensanz: Many people, artists. You no imagine. Everybody like this place, and is coming and coming and coming to make exhibition from Vienna, Germany, Paris, Roma.

> **Appellate Courthouse.** 25th St. and Madison Ave. (Midtown).

Imposing Greco-Roman structure that gives off an impenetrably forlorn air. On a Saturday, when no one is around, it feels eerily post-apocalyptic (think *12 Monkeys*), with pigeon droppings covering the stairs. One of the exterior highlights is a stone sculpture of a man reading from a giant tablet, with the inscription "Every Law Not Based On Wisdom is a Menace to the State." Equally powerful is a sculpture on the east side of the building called "Auschwitz, August 25, 1994," which includes a model of the concentration camp, with demarcations for the Commandant's House, Torture Chamber, Gas Chamber, and Crematorium. The inscription reads: "Indifference to injustice is the gate to Hell."

> **The Chrysler Building.** Lexington Ave. and 42nd St. (Midtown).

They just don't build them like this anymore. As great as the Empire State is, there is something incomparably majestic about this art deco masterpiece. At 77 stories, it is still higher than most of its neighbors, and for sheer architectural elegance, not to mention invention (those are gargoyles shaped like hood ornaments), it's perhaps the greatest building in all of New York.

The Chrysler Building

> **City Hall subway stop.** End of the 6 Line. City Hall (Financial District).

The oldest subway station in the United States. While it's been officially closed to the public for the last 50 or so years, you can catch a glimpse of the station if you paste your face to the window of a number 6 train as it makes its loop of lower Manhattan heading back uptown. Notice the terra-cotta brickwork and tiling.

> **The Empire State Building.** 34th St. and Fifth Ave. (Midtown).

An obvious selection? A paean to tourists? No way. The Empire State Building transcends all that. Second only to the Chrysler in pure epic beauty, the Empire State is the keeper of New York City dreams. Loaded with lore, it anchors us to the past, and is a symbol of New York in its glorious forward-moving prime. Like a Masonic temple, it carries almost metaphysical significance, standing proudly and distinctly with no architectural competitors in sight. You catch glimpses of it down avenues, from office windows, from airplanes, from boats. It is the grand reminder of who we are as New Yorkers and what this city is in the eyes of the world: the capital city of the 20th century.

The Empire State Building

> **New York Public Library, Room 315.** 42nd St. and Fifth Ave. (Midtown).

Let's don't even debate it: This is the greatest public room in all of New York, where many a manifesto and great literary work has been born. We are of the less than humble opinion that all other city services should be cut first, but library hours should never *ever* be shortened. They are the ticket out of idleness, stupor, and poverty for so many. Of course, nobody listens. I would have preferred the city spend less money gentrifying Bryant Park and more money ensuring long library hours. The two lions guarding the entrance to the library represent Patience and Fortitude.

> **Red Square.** 250 E. Houston St., at Norfolk Ave. (Lower East Side/East Village).

The hallmark here is the enormous rooftop statue of a saluting Vladimir Lenin. Lenin presiding over a condo complex on the Lower East Side? How's that for adding insult to injury?

> **Seventh Regiment Armory.** E. 66th to E. 67th St., between Lexington and Park aves. (Upper East Side).

You've got to see it to believe it. Like a Scottish Castle on the outside, and a giant airplane hangar on the inside. The National Guard is headquartered here. Amidst huge hallways and imposing portraits of American war heroes, there's a whole lot of slacking going on. The Armory Bar seemed to be a popular destination. There's also a restaurant open to the public, with brusque Scottish waitresses at your service. One came up to me and snorted, "What ya take'n notes for?" "Isn't this open to the public?" I replied. "Yes, but I don't want ya take'n notes." So I proceeded to take lots of notes. In particular, I noted what must be New York's largest concentration of mounted moose. There's also a massive hall where our boys do their marching, though today the space is mostly used for antique fairs and drunken Tailhook-type gatherings. Right in the heart of ritzy Park Avenue.

> **United Nations.** First Ave., between 42nd and 46th sts. (Midtown).

Americans have grown a bit impatient with the vast paper bureaucracy of the U.N. The can-do spirit of this country butts up against the inherent loquaciousness of an institution that believes talking things out works far better than fighting them out. Because of America's short-sighted resistance, the very existence of this well-intentioned body often gets grossly overlooked. In the minds of most New Yorkers, it's just another subculture within city life, where good-hearted, French-speaking world federalists go to posture and pontificate. However, seen from 43rd or 44th and First Avenue on a full moon, blue sky night, the beautifully designed Secretariat and green-tinted General Assembly take on a lovely spiritual glow. On such a mystical eve, the whole United Nations complex, so artfully designed by a team of architects including Le Corbusier and Niemeyer, possesses a soft, ethereal quality that beckons the viewer to contemplate loftier ideals and perhaps, if the mood is right, to truly perceive *the U.N.'s primary role in this warring world:* a great place for horny diplomats to pick up altruistic interpreter chicks. Officially, the grounds of the United Nations is international territory, so the laws of the United States don't apply!

› **Vast Corporate Headquarters of** *Monk,* **the Mobile Magazine.** 175 Fifth Ave., Suite 2322, New York, NY 10010. ☎ **212/465-3231.** www.monk.com. E-mail: monk@monk.com.

Okay, so it's just a mailbox at Mail Boxes Etc., but it's in the Flatiron Building, and, more to the point, it's a great place to drop off your subscription check (only $10 for four episodes, $18 for eight, and $100 for a lifetime-after-lifetime subscription).

The United Nations

> **Washington Mews.** Between Fifth Ave. and University Place, just north of Washington Square Park (West Village).

A bit of the Cotswolds in the heart of the Village. The cobblestone streets and the quaint cottages make this a highly coveted residential street. Alas, one must have some major NYU affiliation to reside in these turn-of-the-century row houses. Formerly known as Washington Alley, the Mews was where residents of Washington Square kept their stables of horses.

> **Watchtower Building.** 25 Columbia Heights, right by the Brooklyn Bridge (Brooklyn Heights). ☎ 718/625-3600.

This is a strange location for an evangelical Christian organization, just a hop, skip, and a spiel from Norman Mailer's pad on the promenade. The Seventh Day Adventists also own a lot of the other buildings in the area—one reason Brooklyn Heights is no longer considered such a coveted address.

> **Williamsburg Savings Bank.** 1 Hanson Place, at Ashland Place (Brooklyn).

This is the tallest structure in Brooklyn, built in 1929 just before the Crash, at a time when it was conjectured that one day Brooklyn would be filled with skyscrapers. The bank has a church-like interior, with huge hanging lamps, but its primary attribute is that it's near the intersection of Flatbush and Atlantic, where 10 subway lines (the B, D, M, N, R, Q, 2, 3, 4, 5) and the Long Island Railroad cross. The clock on the tower tells reasonably accurate time.

> **Yeshiva University (Main Building).** 500 W. 185th St., at Amsterdam Ave. (Washington Heights).

This orange-brick structure, adorned with minarets and turrets, is one of the strangest in the city, but don't bother trying to gain entry unless you're wearing a yarmulke. The campus police will harass you if you even look at them funny, and the orthodox kids at the Deli Kasbah across the street aren't much nicer.

Cafes

Long before Seattle-style latte bars swept the city, New York was the center of authentic cafe culture. What's an "authentic" cafe? A place where a genuine community still prevails. Here are some that pull it off, and some that fail miserably.

> **Big Cup Tea & Coffee House.** 228 Eighth Ave., at 22nd St. (Chelsea).
☎ **212/206-0059.**

You'll probably find a stronger gay community vibe at cafes in San Francisco, but this is about as close as you're likely to get in New York. It's vibrant, colorful, and genuinely eclectic, except for the relative absence of female customers. When we visited, a few tables had been pushed together and a grave, whispered discussion was underway about the future of the gay movement.

> **Eureka Joe.** 168 Fifth Ave., at 22nd St. (Flatiron District). ☎ **212/741-7500.**

The place is unimposing, and the serving staff is pleasant, not snotty. Even better, it's pretty empty, and the couches are comfortable. Eureka's even got a liquor bar, the sort of makeshift thing your father might have erected in your suburban basement. In fact, the whole place has a thrown-together, impromptu feel, as if it's just for one night—no doubt the source of its appeal.

Patrons at the Big Cup Cafe

> **Limbo.** 47 Avenue A, at 3rd St. (East Village). ☎ 212/477-5271.

A whole crew of so-called hipsters was photographed out front this place for *The New York Times Magazine.* The photo's caption called them "the new Beats" and catalogued what they were wearing (mostly Banana Republic). We don't feel much about Limbo either way, but that photo is damning enough.

> **Omonia.** 32–20 Broadway, at 33rd St. (Astoria, Queens). ☎ 718/274-6650.

Although the once vibrant Greek community of Astoria, Queens, has, for the most part, dispersed, there's at least one place where Greeks, old and young, male and female, still gather. It's nothing special in the decor department, but that doesn't stop it from being packed all weekend. Nowhere in the city will you find a cafe with a similar electricity and sense of community.

> **Peacock Caffe.** 24 Greenwich Ave., just west of Sixth Ave. ☎ 212/242-9395.

One winter night, bitter cold, the snow falling outside. Soft lights glow off heavy wooden tables. The waitress comes over slowly, foot-weary; speaks with some vague European accent. Marlene Dietrich as the old woman broken by regret. Behind the counter in back, a man stares off into the middle distance. We order coffee, then sit and contemplate the storm outside. How long will it be, we wonder, before the partisans arrive to liberate the town?

> **Pink Pony Cafe.** 174 Ludlow St., at Stanton (Lower East Side). No phone.

Thumbs up, even if the place was vacant when we visited. Everyone seemed to know each other. A big green painting in the back read "Fuck." The counter guy had both a Fu Man Chu and a shaved head (apart from a single curl). Bathroom graffiti: "Wake up! Reject the way things are" and "Hey you! Watch out for the video cameras"—sentiments that might soon be quaintly anachronistic in this rapidly gentrifying neighborhood.

Cybercafes

At last count, there were about half a dozen Internet cafes in New York. We have seen things come and go and don't think much of any of them. "Cyber cafes are just another oxymoron," Michael Monk said philosophically, one afternoon. His hands were clasped behind him; his lips were pursed and his head was contemplatively inclined. We were not far from one of the cafes, on the corner of Lafayette and Spring Street. Jim nodded and, a moment later, frowned; Jim turned to Michael, perplexed: "An oxymoron?"

"Yes, oxymoron—for moron. Why would you go to a cafe where there are living flesh-and-blood human beings sitting right next to you, to carry on with and talk to and touch and smell their sweat, and then plug into a computer so you can talk, by computer, to the same people?"

"No, it's different people," Jim corrected. "People who aren't there."

"It doesn't matter."

"Say you're a bunch of really snobby, uptight Condé Nast British people who came here and worked, and you wanted to talk to your other uptight, snobby, I-hate-America British people, and they're in London. So you get all your friends—Miranda and Amanda and Nigel—and you sit around the computer, and you talk to your friends in London."

"There's no reason to do it."

"What are you talking about? It's a perfect thing to do at the cyber cafe."

"You should go to a cafe to interact with people."

"You're interacting with your fellow uptight, snobby—"

"If you want to be snobby, go to a cocktail party and be snobby there. You don't have to use a computer to do that."

We were outside the cafe now, facing each other. Jim bounced, light on his toes, like a boxer feinting and jabbing. Michael was still, his fists clenched at his sides. Inside the cafe, at a computer, a man and woman were head to head, quietly at work.

"These are people from England, and you can't reach them. . . . You come here, and you look at the computer screen together, and you talk to your idiotic, anal-retentive, uptight, I-hate-New-York and I-hate-America British friends who are in London."

"The British people love America." With that, Michael turned and walked away.

> **alt.coffee.** 139 Avenue A, at 9th St. (East Village). ☎ **212/529-2233.** www.altdotcoffee.com.

The funkiest, comfiest, and thus the best of the cybercafes. The interior is like the back room of an antique store, and the computers (which emit fish-tank sounds) are hidden in corners so as not to be eyesores. The bathtub in the restroom is filled with old Commodore 64 parts. Jazz on Monday nights. One major drawback: no Macs, and no helpful geeks, which means the place isn't recommended for serious Webheads. Try the Cybercafe at 273 Lafayette, Cyberfeld at 20 East 13th St., or Kinkos if the net is your main focus.

> **Cybercafe.** 273 Lafayette St., at Prince (SoHo). ☎ **212/334-5140.** www.cyber-cafe.com.

SoHo, how we despise you. $1.62 for a small coffee? No, thanks. The upside: They have nice computers, and are about as slick of an operation as you are going to find in the world of New York cybercafes—though, unfortunately, only one Mac.

› **Kinkos.** Locations all over town.

Probably the most convenient and reliable option in the city, though at $12/hour, not as cheap as other options. At most other cafes, the Internet is a second thought; cafe culture comes first. Not here. Disadvantage: The help is often so frenzied they give you very little assistance.

Calendar

Forget standard fare like Greenwich Village Halloween (horribly suburban since it stopped being gay), Columbus Day, and especially New Year's Eve in Times Square (unless a more idiotic version of *Strange Days* is your idea of fun). Check out Monk's calendar of truly magnificent New York happenings—some quirky, some corny, all compelling.

Winter

› **The Westminster Kennel Club's Annual Dog Show.** Second Mon and Tues of Feb. Madison Square Garden, Seventh Ave. between 31st and 33rd sts. (Midtown). ☎ 800/455-3647.

Nutty canine owners from around the country get together once a year to determine who's groomed, breeded, and fluffed up Fluffy the best. An absolutely obsessive

The Westminster Kennel
Club Dog Show

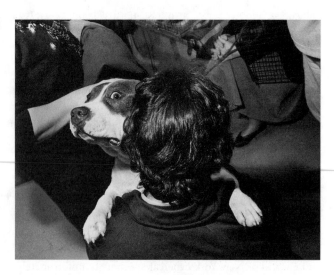

pastime is turned into twisted fun for all. Held for 121 consecutive years, the show is the second longest consecutive sporting event in the country, surpassed only by the Kentucky Derby, which was first run 1 year prior to "The Dog Show's" inception. Formed originally by a group of men who met at the Westminster Hotel (hence the name) and wanted to decide whose dog was the best, the event is now an exhibition of the nation's best breeding stocks.

> **International Cat Show.** First weekend of Mar. Madison Square Garden, Seventh Ave. between 31st and 33rd sts. (Midtown). ☎ 800/455-3647.

Let's talk obsessive-compulsive. Let's talk anthropomorphic. Let's talk the International Cat Show (known to insiders as simply "IN Cats"), the largest freak-show of fastidiously cared for felines and their eccentric caretakers in America. The winner of the 1995 International Cat Show was Yoyo, a Japanese bobtail. Jim Monk was on hand—on-stage, actually—for the award ceremony. He did not speak to the cat's owner, Allen Scruggs of Winston-Salem, North Carolina, but to a passing Brazilian journalist.

Brazilian Journalist: You are a relative of the owner of the cat, or no?

Jim Monk: Yes, I'm the one who gave him the money to buy it.

Journalist: Oh, really?

Jim: I'm the financier behind it.

Journalist: Oh?

Jim: I'm his lover, actually. We live in the West Village. We are very proud of that cat (pointing to cat).

Journalist: How old is she?

Jim: The cat? I think about 3 years old. We had another cat, Yo Yo Ma. We're going to have a new cat soon. We're going to call it Yo.

Advice on Bathing a Cat: Create a nice atmosphere, turn on music, and feed it turkey (it's a tranquilizer).

Factoid: Tabby is not a breed, it's a color.

Most Interesting Cat Name: Battle Hymn of Java, 5 years old; Battle Hymn's daughter is Battle Hur.

› **New York Underground Film Festival (NYUFF).** Third week of Mar. New York Film Academy, 100 W. 17th St. at Park Ave. ☎ 212/925-3440. www.nyuff.com.

"Not a one," they proudly declared when we asked if any famous directors or actors had been discovered there. The festival shows over 100 shorts, cartoons, documentaries, and features, both local and foreign, in nearly continuous rotation. It gained notoriety in 1994 for opening *Chicken Hawk,* a film about consensual man-boy love. *Frisk* and *Tattoo Boy* carried on the controversial tradition in 1996. "These are raw, vital works—not watered-down, multiplex-friendly products. Our films are not for Mr. and Ms. Mainstream, and we like it that way," said Ed Halter, Festival Director.

"The NYUFF is the epicenter of North America's anti-Oscar, do-it-yourself cultural tornado. Camera in hand, I'm diving into its vortex," said Canadian Ken Hegan, whose mocumentary *Aardvark!* appeared at the 1998 festival, and who is shooting a video journal of his cast and crew's journey to the event. The 1998 NYUFF lineup also included *The Erotic Adventures of Alex the Clown, Cotton Candy* (set in Japan's schoolgirl sex industry), and *Cannibal, The Musical,* the debut feature from Trey Parker and Matt Stone, the makers of the TV hit *South Park.*

Spring

› **Crest Hardware Show.** Third week of May through June. 558 Metropolitan Ave., at Union St. (Williamsburg, Brooklyn). ☎ 718/486-8386.

Curated by the Can Man himself, Gene Pool (see interview under "Parks"), this annual Williamsburg art happening is held in an actual hardware store. All the pieces fit comfortably in the store, and are often tucked beneath or beside hammers, nails, household appliances, and the like. Keeping with the spirit of the place, you can buy the art by the foot or the gallon.

> Rites of Spring (Procession to Save Our Gardens). Sun before Memorial Day. Gardens of the Lower East Side. Sponsored by Earth Celebrations, 638 E. 6th St., 3rd floor, New York, NY 10009. ☎ 212/777-7969.

Like a pagan Mardi Gras meets The Rainbow Nation, Earth Celebrations' Rites of Spring procession winds through the 50 or so community gardens of the Lower East Side to celebrate the beauty of green in this largely greenless area. Colorful and free-form, the freaky cast includes giant papier maché puppets, mudpeople, percussionists, nature spirits, and dioramas of community gardens long since destroyed (for example, Adam Purple's Garden of Eden on Forsyth between Stanton and Rivington). This colorful crew stops at each garden to enact rituals. At one garden Gaia is kidnapped by developers. At another, a huge psychedelic butterfly angel flies from the top of a building into the spectacular garden at East 6th Street and Avenue B (the thing even makes Mothra-like sounds). The procession eventually intermingles with the Loisaida Street Festival, making the whole day a unique community event, and in its earnest reverence for the natural world, a rare one for the city.

> Bang on a Can Marathon. Early June. Alice Tully Hall, Lincoln Center, Broadway and 64th St. (Upper West Side). ☎ 212/875-5050.

Artistic directors David Lang, Michael Gordon, and Julia Wolfe sample hundreds of tapes to narrow the eclectic, innovative program. With everything from new classical to post-grunge, it's a concerted and largely successful attempt to bridge uptown and downtown musical sensibilities. The three Yale graduates are composers in their own right and often include samples of their work on the bill.

> Change Your Mind Day. First or second Sat in June. Central Park. Sponsored by *Tricycle* magazine, 92 Vandam St., New York, NY 10013. ☎ 212/645-1143. Fax 212/645-1493. E-mail: tricycle@echonyc.com.

Held outdoors in a Central Park meadow, accurately mirroring the setting in which the Buddha first transmitted the dharma, Change Your Mind Day is the city's big-time Buddhist gathering, with over 2,000 new and old meditators in attendance. Sponsored by the award-winning *Tricycle* magazine, the event features speakers from a variety of traditions, including bodhisattva superstars Joseph Goldstein and Philip Glass. You certainly get a taste of what's out there, including an illuminating example of Tibetan dharma combat with monks from the Dalai Lama's own Gelugpa lineage, and you'll undoubtedly walk away with several meditation tools that will help you navigate the samsaric waters of New York's karmic landscape.

Quentin Crisp:

The Monk Interview

Out of the door into the bright East Village sun steps a short gentleman, and quite a dandy too. But they are one and the same. The gentleman is dapper, with a cleverly folded hat, the brim swooping down across an eye. He wears a well-appointed jacket, with a slight frilly collar, and scuffed shoes. He looks like a casual aristocrat out for a walk through the Commons on a warm sunny day.

The dandy? He's got just a touch of eyeliner. Mascara, too. His fingers are laden with rings, some with stones, and his withering hands are arched by his side, ready in a moment's notice to leap through the air in dramatic gesture. And the perfume. Oh my, he reeks of it.

These days it's hard to say precisely what Quentin Crisp is famous for. He used to be famous for writing books (*The Naked Civil Servant*), and then he was famous for appearing in movies (*Orlando*). Today he is just famous, and no one, it seems, much cares why. It's fun to have Quentin Crisp be famous. He's a generous celebrity, the kind who's listed in the telephone book, the kind you can call up and arrange to meet for coffee (as long as you pay for the coffee). We joined Mr. Crisp outside his apartment, as he was busily shredding his mail.

Monk: Why do you live in New York as opposed to other parts of America?

Quentin Crisp: Well, I live in Manhattan for the same reason that everybody lives here: so as to be ready to rule the world, should the opportunity arise. And you can't rule the world from anywhere else.

Monk: That's true.

Quentin Crisp: So you have to stay here.

Monk: What kind of ruler would you be?

Quentin Crisp: Very benign. I would let almost anything go, except the music. I would put a stop to the music.

Monk: All music, or just certain kinds?

Quentin Crisp: All music.

Monk: No music.

Quentin Crisp: No more music.

>Interview

Monk: Why's that?

Quentin Crisp: It's the cause of everything that's gone wrong in the world. The dirty music. The young are violent because they have no inner life. And they have no inner life because they have no thoughts. And they have no thoughts because they know no words. And they know no words because they never speak. And they never speak because the music's too loud.

Monk: But that's not true for classical music.

Quentin Crisp: Yes, good.

Monk: Now, if you were to give us a tour of your neighborhood and the places you would go on a typical jaunt around this area, where would we go?

Quentin Crisp: We would go to Second Avenue. That way is First Avenue, and there live the Angels.

> *"I live in Manhattan for the same reason that everybody lives here: so as to be ready to rule the world, should the opportunity arise."*

Monk: The Hell's Angels or the Guardian Angels?

Quentin Crisp: Yes, the Hell's Angels. They have a bad reputation. They've never murdered me. When I take my laundry to the laundry on First Avenue, I pass between their house and their row of Harleys. I pass with bowed head to show I accept their supremacy, and they've never murdered me.

Monk: That's because you've showed respect. So we go past the Hell's Angels, and if we go up this way?

Quentin Crisp: If we go this way, this is Second Avenue, which is nice, and the people have said to me, "Do you get stared at as much in New York as you did in London?" And I say, "There is nothing you could wear on Second Avenue that would make you remarkable." And there isn't.

Monk: Well, let's take a walk. Is this your birth name, Quentin Crisp?

Quentin Crisp: Quentin, no, it's so artificial. I dyed it. My original name was Dennis. And people said, "You can't be called Dennis." And I said, "What shall I be called?" And they suggested various names, and I tried to go along, and I thought Quentin was the best name.

Monk: What's your typical day like?

Quentin Crisp: I have no curtains to exclude the light. So in summer, I wake up around six and in winter probably eight. And when I wake, I get up. And I drink a glass of Guinness.

Interview

That's a great day shortener. If you drink a glass of Guinness, you don't know it's daytime until about five-thirty. And then, if I'm not invited out to lunch, I do a crossword puzzle. They're the aerobics of the soul. I have to do one a day to keep my soul slim and active. And crossword puzzles in America are different from ones in England. In England crossword puzzles depend on ingenuity, but in America crossword puzzles depend on general knowledge. If the capital of Uganda crosses with the name of a famous baseball player, you can't do it because you don't know the capital of Uganda and you don't know the name of the baseball player. So it's very disheartening.

Monk: So you would prefer the English type of crossword puzzle.

Quentin Crisp: I like the English ones.

Monk: So there are some things you do like about English culture as opposed to American culture.

Quentin Crisp: Yes. Crossword puzzles are better.

We arrive at the very pink Cooper Square Restaurant, one of Mr. Crisp's favorite haunts, and go inside for something to eat. All the waiters know and cherish him. Passersby see him in the window and wave or knock on the glass.

Monk: You've always been such a dapper dresser.

Quentin Crisp: You have to dress up, to preserve your image, because in America once you leave the front door, you're on. So you can't just creep out with dark glasses and your coat on. You see, I try to spend at least 2 days a week without ever leaving my room, because if I don't, when would I recharge my batteries? So I stay indoors two times a week, at least.

Monk: What sort of things do you do indoors those two days to recharge your batteries?

Quentin Crisp: Well, I sleep a lot, and I used to say I do a hell of a lot of nothing, but someone said to me, "Oh, I don't think you should say that. Couldn't you say you meditate?" So I meditate. Because you have to recover. I mean, in America, there's so much to do and you want to do it all, because I never say no to anything. And that's why you're here, because I never say no to anything. And that means you have to do a lot, because people want you to . . . they want a piece of you, they want you to belong to them.

Monk: When did you move here, by the way?

Quentin Crisp: I came to be here in 1981. I lived for 6 weeks in unaccustomed splendor on 39th Street with the man who constituted himself my manager. Then this room was found for me, and it must be one of the last boarding houses in Manhattan, because they'll turn anything into an apartment. There's a relationship between the people of a country and the system. Now, in England the people are hostile, but the system is benign. And in America the people are kind, but the system is ruthless. And once you are unproductive, you will end up living in a cardboard box at the corner of the street. So when people see my room, and they say, "You actually live here?" The answer is, "Yes, unless I knew I would die in the next two days."

Monk: You really consider New York your home, don't you?

Quentin Crisp: Yes, my whole world.

Monk: Would you ever move anywhere else?

Quentin Crisp: No. I've been to various places in America. I've been as far west as Seattle. When you look at a huge map, Seattle appears to be on the Pacific coast, but it isn't. It's on a lump of water which I cannot explain. And beyond that are the Cascade Mountains. And the people in Seattle are like an Englishwoman showing you her garden. When an Englishwoman takes you to a bare patch of earth and says, "This is where the begonias were. You should have been here last week. They were a blaze of color. And here, do you see that tiny—no, that's a weed. That little thing under there, that's a petunia, and there— you should be here next week, there'll be a blaze." People in Seattle say, "Over there are the Cascade Mountains, but you can't see them today. They're very beautiful when you can. And over here are the Olympic Mountains. You can't see them either, but they're beautiful when you can." Because it's wet; it rains all the time.

Monk: How far south have you gone?

Quentin Crisp: I've been as far south as you can go. I've been to Key West. And Key West is a holiday island—wide, flat, sunny. And no one ever works. There are eternal guest houses and piano bars. And it's a shrine to Mr. Hemingway. Every bar has a life-size photograph and the words "Hemingway lived here. Hemingway drank here. Hemingway fought here."

Monk: What about Los Angeles?

Quentin Crisp: I've been to Los Angeles. I loved Los Angeles. It's an earthly paradise. Everyone is beautiful, and everyone is rich. And when I said that on English television, I was co-star with a man called Mugarich, and Mr. Mugarich is born to disapprove. And he said, "They're not all rich, you live a show-biz life." And I said, "I looked out of my window in the Beverly Wilshire Hotel, and no poverty did I see."

Monk: So what are some of your favorite things about New York City?

Quentin Crisp: The people. Wherever I go, people are there. And an Englishman met me here and said, "You're the one who lives in New York, aren't you?" And I said, "Yes." "Well, why?" And I said, "Because everywhere I go everybody talks to me." And he said, "I can't think of anything worse."

A waitress approaches and takes our order.

Monk: If you had to name your three favorite places in Manhattan, what would they be?

Quentin Crisp: This place. That place. What else? I don't know where else. I do my shopping in the neighborhood.

Monk: So it's your room, the diner, and all the places in between.

Quentin Crisp: Yes.

> interview

Monk: Do you ever go to the Bar [a well-known East Village gay bar]?

Quentin Crisp: The Bar on the corner? I haven't been there, because the owner rushed out and invited me in, and I had my shopping with me and the milk, and I said, "I can't come in, I've got the milk with me, and the milk would go bad in your bar in half an hour." And the man said, "Why do you say that?" And I said, "Think of the people who have gone bad in half an hour in that place."

Monk: Who are your favorite New Yorkers?

Quentin Crisp: Miss Taylor.

Monk: Miss Elizabeth Taylor?

Quentin Crisp: She's wonderful. When she arrives at a fund-raiser, she doesn't wave and she doesn't ignore me.

Monk: Number two?

Quentin Crisp: Number two. Joey Arias.

Monk: What do you do for physical exercise?

Quentin Crisp: I don't take any physical exercise. That would be unthinkable. That would be like working. I haven't worked in fourteen years. Since I came to New York I have never, never worked.

Monk: So what do you think of the way people dress these days in the United States?

Quentin Crisp: Well, I like the way people dress. They wear any old thing, and I think it is a good idea. Everything I have on has been given to me by someone. You simply have to parade your hopelessness. If you fail to do that, people will not give you things. Money is for saving, not for spending. And therefore if you buy clothes, you spend money, and then you have less. I try to save money.

Monk: Do you have—how may I ask this, it may be too personal—but do you have a lover?

Quentin Crisp: No, I don't have a lover because it would cost me.

Monk: Have you at any point had a lover in America?

Quentin Crisp: Never. The other day someone said to me, "You decided to come to America when most people decided to go into a nursing home." That is true. I came to America instead of going into a nursing home.

"Wherever I go, people are there."

Jennifer Miller of Circus Amok

Summer

> **Circus Amok.** June. Various parks around the city. ☎ **718/486-7432.**

It may not seem obvious that circus and politics go together. It's hard to imagine clowns, animal acts, and stilt-walkers in, say, a show about the impact of New York City budget cuts; or a sword-swallowing, fire-breathing bearded lady in one about the darker, meaner side of New York's history. And it's almost mind-boggling to imagine a show containing these elements playing to anything but a downtown crowd—playing, for instance, in a park in Queens or the Bronx. Yet that's precisely what happens, every summer since 1989, in Jennifer Miller's Circus Amok. Circus Amok is a circus, with all the weirdness and splendor of the real thing, but it's a hard-hitting—not to mention queer—one. Does that create problems for Miller, in neighborhoods that may be hostile to her message? Not at all, she insists: "They're all queer for a day."

Miller has a beard. She has called the act of wearing one a radical feminist statement, and when she is performing—as she did for us, a band of neighborhood men, and several children—she both embodies and defies the role of the freak, the bearded lady of sideshow fame. "I call myself a woman with a beard," she tells the audience, "not the bearded lady. Why is that?" The rest of the time, however, she wears her beard rather blandly, if not indifferently. One gets the sense, talking to her, that she is a little tired of talking about the beard and would like to discuss other things. When asked to explain the difference between a bearded lady and a woman with a beard, she told us, "People actually call me Jennifer. They don't call me either one of those things."

› **Mermaid Parade.** Sat after the Summer Solstice. Between Surf Ave. and Riegelman Boardwalk (Coney Island, Brooklyn). ☎ **718/372-5159.** www.whirl-i-gig.com.

The Mermaid Parade dates back to 1980, when Dick Zigun and a few other Yale graduates started Coney Island USA, a nonprofit arts group dedicated to the revival of the amusement mecca by the sea. "We were looking for something big and splashy to be our calling card," Zigun explains. "We decided to take over the neighborhood for a day." The group's first choice, July 4th, was rejected because it is Coney Island's busiest day of the year. So Zigun and his crew decided to celebrate the summer solstice and hold their event on the weekend nearest June 21st.

Beneath its outlandish campiness, the parade does serve a purpose. After the eccentric parade has wound its way through the historic Coney Island amusement district, the Queen Mermaid, accompanied by her sometimes-handsome King Neptune and throngs of onlookers, waddles to the ocean. En route, she snips four ribbons, each signifying a season. The last represents summer, and after it has been cut, the queen, in a ritual reminiscent of old cheesecake publicity photos, plunges a giant key to Coney Island into the ocean and turns it . . . thus warming the waters and opening the Atlantic for summer.

Mermaids at the annual Mermaid Parade, Coney Island

› **Shakespeare in a Parking Lot.** Call for schedule. Sponsored by Expanded Arts, 85 Ludlow St., at Broome St. (Lower East Side). ☎ **212/249-6543.**

Every summer for who knows how many summers, the Joseph Papp Public Theater has sponsored free Shakespeare in Central Park. We've heard it's good, although we can't really say for sure, since the time we went the performance was in Portuguese. Free we like, but Central Park just isn't our stomping ground. More our speed is Expanded Arts' free Shakespeare in a frumpy, beat-to-heck municipal parking lot on the Lower East Side.

We saw *A Midsummer Night's Dream* there, to the accompaniment of screaming sirens, wailing car alarms, and barking dogs. The players made excellent use of parking meters, light poles, and, occasionally, cars. About three quarters of the way through the play a dump truck rolled into the lot, and the actors halted their performance and, in a brilliant absurdist touch, bowed before it.

In 1995, Expanded Arts, which is a not-for-profit arts group, moved into cramped quarters in a storefront on Ludlow Street. Almost immediately, the organization's founders, Jennifer Pias and Robert Spahr, began eyeing the abandoned parking lot across the street. It took a few months to clear things with the Department of Transportation, but now the group has use of the lot.

Performers in Expanded Arts' Shakespeare in a Parking Lot

› O'Giglio e Paradiso Feast and Bazaar. First Thurs in July, for 2 weeks (Giglio Sunday is the first Sun of the feast). Weekdays 7pm–midnight; Sat–Sun 9am–midnight. Our Lady of Mt. Carmel. Havemeyer St., between N. 8th and 9th sts. (Williamsburg, Brooklyn). ☎ 718/384-0223.

We're confused. We want to know what it all means, what's it all about. It's over a hundred degrees out, and we're on Havemeyer Street, in the Williamsburg section of Brooklyn. There is a large platform, and on the platform is a large band, and behind the band is a large monument (it's five stories tall, this monument—as tall as the tallest of the neighborhood's buildings), and at its apex is a statue of a saint. A man begins to pray: "Lord, we ask you to bless this Giglio. We ask you to bless and strengthen these lifters. As they lifted the Giglio over 1500 years ago in the town of Nola, help us to lift it today."

Lord, we ask you to bless this Giglio . . . whatever it means

With that, 165 men surround the platform, wedging their shoulders beneath the support beams. The band strikes up an ear-splitting march, and the men, grunting in unison, lift the stage—musicians, monument, and all—and carry it at intervals down the street. The saint teeters ominously. With a rhythmic bounce, the stage comes to rest at the end of the block. The crowd cheers. The lifters exchange hugs and high fives. But it's not over yet. Back and forth, up and down the block they carry their nearly 2-ton load.

But just what is the point of all this? One parishioner, who has been coming for 15 years, tells us it's about getting close to God. Another says it's in honor of the patron saint of Nola, a town in Italy. "Mediterranean pirates came and took all the manpower into bondage and slavery," the man says. "Saint Paulino went and freed all of the manpower from—probably from Libya or whatever. And everybody waited for him with lilies. 'Giglia' in Italian means 'lily.'"

Jim asks Michael what he thinks of this celebration: "I think it's a stupid thing to be doing on a 110° day. I can think of better ways to put all those muscles to work."

› **Nude Cruise in New York Harbor.** First and Second Sat in Aug. Sponsored by the Skinny-dippers, 51–04 39th Ave., Woodside, Queens, NY 11377-3145. ☎ 718/651-4689.

One thing from the start: Nudist gatherings are not orgies. It's a point any nudist (or naturist) would insist on, and one we can back up from personal experience. But nudism does have a fascinating appeal, and, believe it or not, can be enjoyed right here, once a year, in New York harbor.

In 1992, Jay Soloway and the Skinny-dippers' founder, Peter Kacalanos, came up with the idea of a nude cruise. They hired the *Richard Robbins,* a two-masted schooner built in 1902, and quickly filled the 50 spaces. For 1995 they had to hire four tall-masted vessels, and are hoping to have an entire fleet soon. It is the biggest 1-day nudist event in the Northeast.

› **Coney Island Tattoo Festival.** Early Aug. W. 10th St., in front of the Cyclone, Astroland (Coney Island, Brooklyn). Sponsored by Coney Island USA and Astroland. ☎ 718/372-5159.

While tattooing was until recently officially illegal in New York City, there would have been a transgender, polysexual, modern-primitive, heavy-metal riot if anyone had tried to put the kibosh on this scene. Once a year, in front of the Cyclone roller coaster, the folks at Sideshows by the Seashore showcase the very best in "body art." Some of the most amazing cutting-edge "tats" and scarification this side of the Zulu Nation.

> **Wigstock.** Sun nearest Labor Day. Venue changes, but generally Christopher St. piers these days. www.at-beam.com/Wigstock.

The world's largest outdoor dragfest has come a long way, perhaps too long a way, since it began in 1985. It used to be a small neighborhood gathering of a few friends and a few hundred onlookers in the East Village. Today it's a huge event of some 50,000 on the Christopher Street Piers. It has a Web site. It has spawned a line of products, including key chains by Todd Oldham, and a documentary film. Like the Village's Halloween parade—like the Village itself, not to mention SoHo—Wigstock started out modest and idiosyncratic, but once it was discovered by the media, it got chewed up, swallowed, digested, and spit out again as something with roughly the consistency of pabulum. It used to be weird; now it's just big—really big, like a giant fraternity party. Even still, it's a load of fun, mainly because of the magnanimous presence and riotous humor of its cofounder, Lady Bunny. (For more, see "Back on the Road" and the Lady Bunny interview in this section.)

> **West Indian–American Day Carnival (a.k.a. the West Indian Parade).** Labor Day. Westbound on Eastern Parkway, from Buffalo Ave. to Grand Army Plaza (Brooklyn). ☎ 718/773-4052.

A day-long, million-strong street party (part of a 5-day festival of West Indian music, arts, and crafts), featuring completely over the top performers and bands on large flatbed trucks. Still not co-opted by white people and mainstream media, the

The West Indian–American Day Parade

very size and magnitude of this parade is indicative of the enormous demographic shift occurring in New York City, where a new generation of immigrants from Russia, Asia, India, Pakistan, and, increasingly, the Caribbean, are once again reshaping the New York melting pot.

Fall

> **Professor Jackson's All-Night Bicycle Tour.** Late Sept, early Oct. Tour starts from Columbia University sundial, 116th St., between Broadway and Amsterdam Ave. (Upper West Side). To ascertain times and to possibly gain permission to attend, call Professor Jackson directly at ☎ 212/854-2555 (or the History Department at 212/854-7001).

Every other fall, as part of his History of New York class, Columbia University history professor Kenneth Jackson escorts 300 of his students on a midnight bicycle tour of the city. The tour starts from the university and heads to the tip of Manhattan, then it heads downtown and crosses the Brooklyn Bridge, exploring the city's historical sites along the way. Ostensibly open only to members of Professor Jackson's history class, you can easily sneak in if you bring a bike and keep a low profile.

> **Feast of Saint Francis (a.k.a. Blessing of the Animals).** First Sun in Oct. Cathedral of St. John the Divine, 1047 Amsterdam Ave., at W. 112th St. (Upper West Side). ☎ 212/316-7540, box office 212/662-2133.

In characteristic St. John the Divine fashion, the Blessing of the Animals during the Feast of St. Francis is completely over the top. It features every manner of God's creation: an elephant, a swarming beehive, a beaker swimming with several trillion blue-green algae—all marching down the nave and encircling the altar. Thousands of parishioners bring their pets—dogs, cats, ferrets, snakes, you name it—to have them blessed at this mass honoring the saint who was famous for talking to the animals.

St. John's—which, if it's ever completed, will be the largest Gothic cathedral in the world—is the city's capital of ecumenical, we-are-the-world, save-the-United-Nations-and-invite-Paul-Winter-to-play, feel-good celebrations. Many fail; this one works big time.

The cathedral has been hosting the Blessing of the Animals since 1984. To our knowledge, it's the only place in New York where you can take your goldfish to receive communion. But don't expect just to show up with your pet in tow: The mass, which starts at 11am, is free, but tickets are distributed on a first-come, first-serve basis, starting around 9am.

Feast of St. Francis,
St. John the Divine

An Interview with the One and Only

Lady Bunny

"I never ask a boy to do a man's job. You know."

If Wigstock is not what it used to be, if drag itself—ever since RuPaul became the celebrity spokesperson for MAC cosmetics—is not what it used to be, Lady Bunny, Wigstock's cofounder and chief promoter, seems only to get better with age. She alternately admits to being a mere 25 years old and to having been born in 1792. We tracked her down the week before Wigstock.

"My pussy she was sitting there under the tree, the rain came down and so wet got she, my wet pussy, meow meow, my wet pussy, meow meow. La la la la la la la la, la la la la la la la la, my wet pussy, meow meow, my wet pussy, meow meow, eiiiiiii . . ."

Wet pussy song finished, she glides off the stage and up the stairs under the glare of flashing bulbs. Her bouffant is so high she could sail the Hudson in a high wind. Ms. Bunny, or Lady Bunny as she's known, is a languid Southern girl with a nice bubble butt, an open airy dress, and a hem so high her titties are showing. She walks in a prance, side to side, with sleek mile-long legs, and wears thick-as-horse-hair eyelashes that would lift her off the ground, helicopter-style, if she blinked fast enough. Back stage, she swoons at a fawning fan, a nice guy in jeans and a Village clone tattoo. She looks straight through him, like she can taste his balls with a glance, and charms him with a big coquettish smile. Lady Bunny's a nice girl, comes from good Dixie stock, and can hog a camera like no other queen, giving glamour a new name, a new height. Yet with all her ranting and antics, and her dumb blond bitch-from-the-South routine, she can't mask the fact that she, the mother of all queens, with panties so tight they could crush a rib, is, in fact, a Diva, plain and simple, through and through.

We want to take a picture but the lights aren't right. She gasps and points to fluorescents like they're the devil's scourge. In all seriousness she squeals, "these lights are death to a queen. Where are your lights? I told you to bring them!"

She almost chases us away. But then we run down the stairs and around the block looking for the proper light. She's not about to let the cameras roll until we've

Interview

found the perfect glow with the right angle, no shadows, not too harsh. After 20 minutes we finally settle for a dim yellow street light. It casts just the right soft light, enough to erase a few lines and hide some bloodshot eyes.

Monk: Now, let's get to the facts here: How many years has Wigstock been on? I know you've been asked this question a million times, but we've got to know.

Bunny: How many dog years?

Monk: These are complicated questions.

Lady Bunny: And then she sang that pretty song, and the year I sang that other pretty song—so many pretty songs.

Monk: For awhile. It's been going on awhile?

Lady Bunny: This is going to be the 11th year.

Monk: So, you must have started this when you were 14.

Lady Bunny: That is correct.

Monk: Has Wigstock peaked for you?

Lady Bunny: Years ago, honey [she laughs]. No, it hasn't. When I'm being wheeled out in my wheelchair—next year—it will peak.

Monk: Now, Miss Bunny, we're all awaiting your next film. When are we going to see your next film, and what will it be?

Lady Bunny: Well, I played a lesbian aging porn star who runs for Congress and wins, and I got to break a sugar vase over my husband's head in a bridal gown.

Monk: And what's the name of the film?

Lady Bunny: Well, it seems they can't get a distributor for it. Imagine. My finest performance. No, it's called *Peoria Babylon,* and it was made in Chicago starring David Drake and Ann Cusack.

Monk: We can't wait to see that.

Lady Bunny: You might have to.

Monk: What are some things that Bunny looks for in a mate?

Bunny: Well, I like 'em breathin'. And, well, you know I'm a big girl. It takes a lot to satisfy me. And I never ask a boy to do a man's job. You know.

Monk: Do you have a current special someone in your life?

Bunny: Why do you ask? Several.

Monk: You're not a monogamous gal.

Bunny: No, I'm not. Honey, I can't find anybody—I can get 'em, but I can't keep 'em. I can't find anybody crazy enough to put up with me.

Monk: Who were some of your role models? Who influenced your growing career?

Bunny: Satan and Hitler. No. No. Um, Charo. And Carole Channing I love to death, and uh, uh—and, who else do I—Patty LaBelle. Love her to death. Barbara Eden.

Monk: Of course.

Bunny: Elizabeth Montgomery. Martha Ray. Tody Fields. My look-alikes.

Monk: Do you have any fashion tips for all these new wanna-be drag queens?

Bunny: No. I don't welcome the competition.

Monk: Do you have secrets of your own?

Bunny: Yes, I do.

Monk: You want to reveal just one?

Bunny: I will not.

Monk: Not one? Even one little secret?

Bunny: Certainly not. Wouldn't dream of it.

Monk: Okay, let's talk about food. What do you like to eat?

Bunny: Oh, God, I just got back from Dallas, where they served me only barbecue—don't tell PETA—beef. Mmm. I'm a PETA spokesmodel. Occasionally.

Monk: Are you really?

Bunny: I had barbecue beef with potato salad and coleslaw with those little poppy seeds in the coleslaw. Oh, my God. It was divine. Then we had Mexican one night and farted the house down. My idea of a bubble bath is to have Mexican food for lunch and take a bath at night.

Monk: Are you hungry, Bunny? What would Bunny like to have to eat right now?

Bunny: Honey, I'm going to head over to Cottonwood Cafe . . . over there [she waves], fried chicken, collard greens, some mashed sweet potatoes, sweet iced tea, and some fried okra. I love okra. Can there *ever* be enough grease. Well, I eat a lot of salads. Course, the dressing's my favorite part. I eat like a bird. A big bird.

Cemeteries

The Big Sleep always looms, even in the city that never sleeps (and where big tracts of soil are in short supply). Here's where the bodies are buried.

> **African Burial Ground and the Commons Historic District.** Broadway, between Reade and Duane sts. (Financial District).

Discovered during the construction of a federal office building, the site will be transformed into a museum devoted to colonial-era blacks, whose unjust and inhumane treatment few New Yorkers know much about.

> **Greenwood Cemetery.** Fifth Ave. and 25th St. (Borough Park, Brooklyn). ☎ 718/768-7300.

The final resting place of Montgomery Clift and Boss Tweed, among other notables, it is best known for crate full of parrots that actually fell off a truck a few years back and took up residence in the turrets of the Gothic gatehouse. Schedule a tour with the ranger; otherwise it's closed to the public.

> **Montefiore Cemetery.** 121–83 Springfield Blvd., at Merrick Blvd. (Cambria Heights, Queens).

Final resting place of Rabbi Menachem Mendel Schneerson, head honcho of the New York Lubavitchers (and about the closest Judaism is going to get to a messiah, for awhile anyway), who draws throngs of Hassidic faithful to his gravesite every day, just as he drew a crowd any time he was spotted in public while alive. A small, sealed room in one of the buildings overlooking the gravesite contains a fax machine, so believers around the world can fax their prayers to the "Rebbe's" grave. Contact the Lubavitchers through their web site, www.chabad.org, if you want more information.

> **New York City Marble Cemetery.** East 2nd St., near Second Ave. (East Village). Not officially open to the public.

This is our favorite cemetery in the city. An eerie, sparse vibe. Irish poets would love it. Go late at night in winter for the proper funereal atmosphere. Final resting place of Preserved Fish, a prominent merchant in Old New York.

> **St. Michael's Cemetery.** 72–02 Astoria Blvd., at the Brooklyn Queens Expressway (Astoria/Jackson Heights, Queens). ☎ 718/278-3240.

Among the many buried here is African-American Granville T. Woods, inventor of "the third rail."

> **St. Raymond's Cemetery.** 2600 Lafayette St., at the Cross Bronx Expressway (Bronx). ☎ 718/792-1133.
Billie Holiday is buried here, beside her mother, Sadie. She's in the St. Paul's section, row 56, plot 29.

> **Woodlawn Cemetery.** Webster Ave. and 233rd St. (Throgs Neck, Bronx).
☎ 718/920-0500.
Look for the burial sites of music legends Miles Davis, Duke Ellington, and W. C. Handy, the "father of blues," among others. It's not as well manicured as Greenwood, but the plots tend to be larger and the mausoleums are better. Plus, there's some unbelievably hideous sculpture.

Clubs (Both Night and Otherwise)

Most of the clubs we list here are too out of the loop to have a door policy, or too funky to care, unless you count the few gangster playpens, which should be visited in order to experience a *bona fide* door policy.

> **The Angel.** 44 Walker St., near West Broadway (Tribeca). ☎ 212/226-4977.

A strip club, yes, but not your average one. Wednesday nights feature "chicks with dicks," a.k.a. drag queens and trannies. Thursday is ladies-night only. The crowd seems game—sort of, some of them. Despite the place's efforts, there's still a fair number of leering, drunk men in cheap suits in the audience. The Angel (formerly known as the Blue Angel) is perhaps most famous as the place (one among many?) where actress Drew Barrymore is said to have flashed her tits in public.

Observation

"You see Berlin wake up in a way that New York does not wake up. New York never really goes to sleep."

—Clifton Hood, author of *722 Miles: The Building of the Subways and How They Transformed New York*, quoted in *The New York Times*, January 21, 1997.

> **Hell's Angels Motorcycle Club.** 77 E. 3rd St., between First and Second aves. (East Village). No phone.

You'll have to do a lot more than look fabulous to get past the doorman at this one. The 3rd Street club was founded by Sandy Frazier Alexander on December 5, 1969, and between then and now these well-armed tough guys have come to seem almost friendly. As Quentin Crisp, who lives around the corner, put it, "They've never murdered me." (See the interview with Quentin Crisp, under "Calendar.")

> **Jackie 60.** Held on Tues at Mother, 432 W. 14th St., at Washington (Meatpacking District). ☎ 212/366-5680. www.echonyc.com/~interjackie.

After several years, still the most original theme club in the city. We were there for Dead Elvis night, which featured not only the resurrected King himself but a knife-wielding Priscilla too, covered in blood, looking pale and cadaverous. Whether it's the Night of the 1000 Stevies (Nicks, that is) or JonBenetRamseyfest, you can *always* count on co-creators Chi Chi Valenti and DJ Johnny Dynell dreaming up some bizarre schtick guaranteed to melt your brain. They're also into the cyber thing, as their Jackie Hacker evenings attest.

> **Marshall Chess Club.** 23 W. 10th St., between Fifth and Sixth aves. (West Village). ☎ 212/477-3716.

On New York's Block Beautiful, under a canopy of trees, is where the true nerds hang. There's a kid in a corner in thick black aviator glasses and a wild tuft of curly black hair; there's pudgy middle aged men in thick Russian accents; and occasionally there's the faux skater boy, a bridge to the other downtown no one here knows or cares much about. This is a private world, devoted to pawns, kings, and Deep Blue. Leave your sensuality outside.

> **Ravenite Social Club.** 247 Mulberry St., between Spring and Prince sts. (Little Italy). No phone.

You're not likely to catch the sounds of DJ Dan or Frankie Knuckles here. This private men's club was made famous by John Gotti and his crew back in the

Mylar at Limelight

"How do you like my new nose job? I didn't have this the last time I saw you. I am no longer Blossom Goes Punk Rock. I am now Tank Girl. I'm part of this new modeling agency in New York, and it's all about freaks. It's all about club kids and transsexuals and pierced kids and tattooed kids. And we're actually getting a lot of work and a lot of calls from like major designers."

A Monk among the clubs kids

star-studded, freewheeling '80s. After beating raps, "The Dapper Don" and his cohorts would celebrate at the Ravenite. Long before Gotti, though, the Ravenite was a hangout for other area mobsters, including Lucky Luciano. Originally the Alto Knights Social Club, it was renamed the Ravenite by Mafia kingpin Carlo Gambino, after his favorite Edgar Allan Poe poem, "The Raven."

› **Squeezebox.** Held on Fri at Don Hill's, 511 Greenwich St., at Vandam St. (SoHo). ☎ 212/219-2850.

The hottest glam-rock, AC/DC, punk drag scene in town—not that there's a lot of competition for the honor. The night we were there we ran into both John Waters and Drew Barrymore.

Cyber New York

It's a little strange watching this city catch up with the high-tech digital wave. Hierarchical New York seems, at first, like a bad fit for such a refined and democratic ethos, but the city is adapting well, if a tad bit crassly. Unfortunately, it is quite possible that New York, with its addiction to celebrity worship, will transform the newly arrived digital revolution—which at its core seems so egalitarian and merito-cratic—into something stupidly elitist. We can only pray for sanity.

New York Resources on the World Wide Web

Most of the Web sites devoted to the city are wretched, retread bores, and even when they're okay, they tend to come and go, either dropping off the face of the earth or relocating to a new server (which often amounts to the same thing). So it's a bit tough to come up with anything that'll have a shelf life of more than a couple months. The most comprehensive index of New York stuff on the Web is by Clay Irving (www.panix.com/clay/nyc). There's also Yahoo! New York (www.ny.yahoo.com), Total New York/Digital City (www.totalny.com/www.dci-studio.com), CitySearch (www.newyork.citysearch.com), and the loathsome and banal Sidewalks.com (another middle of the road Microsoft marketing monster). Beyond that, there are several guides to the city on the Web. We like *Paper* magazine's (www.papermag.com) and *ALLNY* (www.allny.com)—the latter, in large measure, because it provides comprehensive listings of everything from bathrooms to museums. Beyond these, we offer a few suggestions of our own.

> **Abandoned Subway Stations.**
www.cc.columbia.edu/~brennan/rails/disused.underground.html.

Let's imagine for a moment that you're in dire need of an underground subway stop that is no longer in use. Perhaps you've run out of wall space and have a suitcase full of aerosol paint in bright neon colors. Or, suppose you just got evicted and need a place to move your meth lab, all four girlfriends, and 20 years of vinyl that you plan to auction off when the time is right. You detest the light, prefer life below ground, and hell, you even like rats. Where do you go? Abandoned subway stations on the net. They provide you with a complete inventory of existing underground stations in the New York area that are not in use. Sounds like a much-needed service. And don't laugh—you may be using it sooner than you think.

> **Club Culture.** www.clubNYC.com.

There is something so deliciously inane about the New York "club scene," based as it is on such outmoded definitions of "celebrities" and "elites." Which is why you have to check out this site, mainly for its hilariously literal-minded imbecility. Take, for example, this choice excerpt from the site's explanation of door policies:

Q: How do I know what the best clubs are?

A: It all depends on what you want. Do you want intense dancing? Do you want to be seen? Are you looking to meet someone?

Q: How do I get into "some exclusive" club? or How do I get picked from a line?

A: If you're a man, go with a couple of your female model friends. If they happen to be out of town, make sure that you go with a mixed group of women and men. Find some women entering the club, and start a conversation with them if you have to.

> **Echo (East Coast Hang Out).** www.echonyc.com.

The East Coast's version of the Well, founded and still run by a woman named Stacey Horn. Fairly stimulating discussions can lead you into fascinating urban esoterica. This is where we learned about the bar Elsie's Okie-Dokie.

> **Jewish Alternative Movement.** www.jewmu.com.

For years I've been saying those Hasidic boychiks are phat-ass cool. There was something righteously militant in their unmistakable garb and their clear disinterest in merging with mainstream American culture. Now, on two discs, Knitting Factory Records has seconded that emotion. *A Guide for the Perplexed* is a compilation of new vistas in "Jewish" music, including Jewish ambient, Jewish spoken word, Jewish dub, Jewish guitar rock, and Jewish psychedelia, and includes tracks by the likes of David Krakauer, Uri Caine, and the Klezmatics. The other disc is by a group called Hasidic New Wave. It's entitled "Psycho-Semitic." Learn all of this and much more on their Web site, which features many Up with Jews pieces, as well as details of the world's largest "cyber-seder" held at Lincoln Center. Mazel Tov, Yo!

> **Otaku.** www.iijnet.or.jp/tko.rockin/.

Web site for hipster Japanese exiles living in the East Village, officially known as "otaku."

> **Scarlett's Web.** http://marge.infohouse.com/nsal/scarlett.

You may remember the story of the cat Scarlett, who rescued its brood, one by one, from a burning garage in Brooklyn. This is the site of the North Shore Animal League, which offers updates on Scarlett and her kittens (look under News). Who got her? Who got the kitties? Also includes adoption info for strays and extensive coverage of other abused and abandoned pets.

> **The Telephone Exchange Name Project.**
http://ourwebhome.com/TENP/TENproject.html.

Robert Crowe, a 39-year-old computer consultant who grew up in SYcamore 4 (that's Pasadena) would like to bring back the good ol' days of descriptive telephone numbers (remember *Butterfield 8,* the movie starring Elisabeth Taylor?). Given that the telephone company wouldn't dream of going back to a mix of letters and numbers, he's pursued his alpha-numeric obsession by launching the Telephone Exchange Name Project on the Internet. Here, he gathers historical exchange names and provides a grid of numbers and exchanges that were used during the bygone days of character phone listings.

Apparently the response has been overwhelming, and for good reason: It's an interesting excursion into the past, where a telephone exchange said everything about your status in society. The names themselves are often dreamily '50s. So next time you dial 0 for the operator just ask for Klondike 2-3000 and see where it takes you.

Film

Los Angeles can stake its claim as the capital of the film "industry," but any thoughtful filmgoer knows that the most independent and innovative film fare, film schools, and film venues have always come out of Gotham.

Movies

Of the many thousand movies set in or made about New York City, the following, when seen in total, best capture the multi-faceted, multi-ethnic, multi-generational zeitgeist of the metropolis. While some succeed better than others, they are all required viewing for any true fan of the city.

After Hours (Martin Scorsese, 1985)

Alice (Woody Allen, 1990)

All About Eve (Joseph L. Mankiewicz, 1950)

Annie Hall (Woody Allen, 1977)

The Apartment (Billy Wilder, 1960)

Bad Lieutenant (Abel Ferrara, 1992)

Barefoot in the Park (Gene Saks, 1967)

Basketball Diaries (Scott Kalvert, 1995)

Basquiat (Julian Schnabel, 1996)

Batman (Tim Burton, 1989)

Bed Stuy Barbershop (Spike Lee, 1983)

Bell, Book, and Candle (Richard Quine, 1958)

Blue in the Face (Paul Auster and Wayne Wang, 1995)

Breakfast at Tiffany's (Blake Edwards, 1961)

Broadway Danny Rose (Woody Allen, 1984)

The Brothers McMullen (Edward J. Burns, 1995)

Chelsea Girls (Andy Warhol, 1967)

Crossing Delancey (Joan Micklin Silver, 1988)

Crowd (King Vidor, 1928)

Dead End (William Wyler, 1937)

Desperately Seeking Susan (Susan Seidelman, 1985)

Do the Right Thing (Spike Lee, 1989)

Empire (Andy Warhol, 1964)

Escape From New York (John Carpenter, 1981)

Eyes of Laura Mars (Irvin Kershner, 1978)

Fame (Alan Parker, 1980)

The Fisher King (Terry Gilliam, 1991)

Fort Apache, The Bronx (Daniel Petrie, 1981)

42nd Street (Lloyd Bacon, 1933)

The French Connection (William Friedkin, 1971)

Funny Girl (William Wyler, 1968)

The Godfather (Francis Ford Coppola, 1972)

Goodfellas (Martin Scorsese, 1990)

Green Card (Peter Weir, 1990)

Heavy Traffic (Ralph Bakshi, 1973)

The Heiress (William Wyler, 1949)

Hester Street (Joan Micklin Silver, 1975)

I Shot Andy Warhol (Mary Harron, 1996)

Jungle Fever (Spike Lee, 1991)

Kids (Larry Clark, 1995)

King Kong (Merian C. Cooper and Ernest B. Schoedsack, 1933)

The King of Comedy (Martin Scorsese, 1983)

Klute (Alan J. Pakula, 1971)

Last Exit to Brooklyn (Ulrich Edel, 1989)

Liquid Sky (Slava Tsukerman, 1982)

The Little Fugitive (Morris Engel, Ray Ashley, Ruth Orkin, 1953)

Looking for Mr. Goodbar (Richard Brooks, 1977)

Lords of Flatbush (Stephen Verona, 1974)

The Lost Weekend (Billy Wilder, 1945)

Malcolm X (Spike Lee, 1992)

Manhattan (Woody Allen, 1979)

Manhattan Melodrama (W. S. Van Dyke, 1934)

Marty (Delbert Mann, 1955)

Mean Streets (Martin Scorsese, 1973)

Metropolitan (Whit Stillman, 1990)

Midnight Cowboy (John Schlesinger, 1969)

Miracle on 34th Street (George Seaton, 1947)

Mixed Blood (Paul Morissey, 1984)

Moonstruck (Norman Jewison, 1987)

Moscow on the Hudson (Paul Marzursky, 1984)

My Dinner With Andre (Louis Malle, 1981)

Naked City (Jules Dassin, 1948)

Network (Sidney Lumet, 1976)

New York New York (Martin Scorsese, 1977)

Next Stop, Greenwich Village (Paul Mazursky, 1974)

On the Town (Stanley Donen, 1949)

On the Waterfront (Elia Kazan, 1954)

The Out-of-Towners (Arthur Hiller, 1970)

Panic In Needle Park (Jerry Schatzberg, 1971)

Party Girl (Daisy von Scherler Mayer, 1995)

Plaza Suite (Arthur Hiller, 1971)

Police State (Nick Zedd, 1986)

The Pope of Greenwich Village (Stuart Rosenberg, 1984)

Prisoner of Second Avenue (Melvin Frank, 1974)

The Producers (Mel Brooks, 1968)

Pull My Daisy (Robert Frank and Alfred Leslie, 1958)

Radio Days (Woody Allen, 1987)

Rear Window (Alfred Hitchcock, 1954)

The Roaring Twenties (Raoul Walsh, 1939)

Roseland (James Ivory, 1977)

Rosemary's Baby (Roman Polanski, 1968)

The Saint of Fort Washington (Tim Hunter, 1993)

The Salt Mines (Carlos Aparicio and Susana Aikin, 1990)

Saturday Night Fever (John Badham, 1977)

The Secret of My Success (Herbert Ross, 1987)

Serpico (Sidney Lumet, 1973)

The Seven Year Itch (Billy Wilder, 1955)

She's Gotta Have It (Spike Lee, 1986)

Sid and Nancy (Alex Cox, 1986)

Six Degrees of Separation (Fred Schepisi, 1993)

Smoke (Wayne Wang, 1995)

Something Wild (Jonathan Demme, 1986)

Sophie's Choice (Alan Pakula, 1982)

Straight Outta Brooklyn (Matty Rich, 1991)

Stranger than Paradise (Jim Jarmusch, 1989)

The Sweet Smell of Success (Alexander Mackendrick, 1957)

Superman (Richard Donner, 1978)

The Taking of Pelham One, Two, Three (Joseph Sargent, 1974)

Taxi Driver (Martin Scorsese, 1976)

Thelonious Monk: Straight, No Chaser (Charlotte Zwerin, 1989)

A Thousand Clowns (Fred Coe II, 1965)

Three Days of the Condor (Sydney Pollack, 1975)

Tootsie (Sydney Pollack, 1982)

Trash (Andy Warhol, 1970)

Wall Street (Oliver Stone, 1987)

Wanda Whips Wall Street (Chuck Vincent, 1981)

The Warriors (Walter Hill, 1979)

The Wedding Banquet (Ang Lee, 1993)

West Side Story (Robert Wise and Jerome Robbins, 1961)

When Harry Met Sally (Rob Reiner, 1989)

Where's Poppa? (Carl Reiner, 1970)

Wild Style (Charlie Ahearn, 1982)

Yankee Doodle Dandy (Michael Curtiz, 1942)

You Killed Me First (Richard Kern, 1985)

Theaters

Though Seattleites see more films in a given year, when it comes to genuine knowledge of cinema as an art form, no one is better than a New York film buff. Here are the places that consistently show compelling cinema and video. Some are more notable for their atmosphere than their content. All are worth visiting.

› **Anthology Film Archives.** 32 E. Second Ave., at 2nd St. (East Village). ☎ 212/505-5181.

This one is easy. There is only one truly unique and consistent place to view avant-garde/experimental films in Manhattan, if not America, and that's the Anthology Film Archives. The Angelika Film Center is very pleasant, with a latte bar, clean theatres, and a selection of mildly alternative films from Miramax and other leading independents, and the Film Forum and Cinema Village, while not quite as nice-looking, also dependably schedule indie favorites. But the Anthology, located in a grungy, dark, and easily missed part of the East Village, is the one true venue for underground film activity in the city. And, as such, not as likely to be part of the film-buying and film-going loop. Everyone from Saul Levine to Georges Melies to Anthology founder and artistic director Jonas Mekas (editor of *Film Culture* magazine) are regularly shown here. Rare, outstanding places like Anthology Film

October 7, 1997

Sir Crotty:

Whilst pursuing my own creative adventures, I partake in some temp work to pay the bills. During a recent assignment at *Entertainment Weekly*, I came across your book *How to Talk American* on the freebie table. Unfortunately for you, I don't know what that means review-wise, but for me it was an unexpected gold mine. I sincerely want to congratulate you. I'll be keeping it on my shelf to add some spice to my future writing. In fact, I've already made abundant use of the San Francisco chapter.

I would also like to take you up on your pleas for additional colloquialisms. The majority of these expressions stem from my three-plus years in the world of New York film production, which by its very nature is a different animal from its Hollywood sibling.

10CC: 10 Columbus Circle. The building where the majority of film productions have temporary offices because it is one of the few places in the city that allows short-term, month-to-month leases.

Columbus Circle Society: The highly unofficial fraternity of production offices in the building. Actually just another fancy excuse to have a party every other Friday. Resistance is Futile.

The Sisterhood: Local 161. The union of Production Coordinators, Auditors, and Script Supervisors. At last count, there were less than a dozen male members.

The Brotherhood: Local 644. The camera union. Just the reverse of the above.

Swim with the Sharks: To deliver something to Scott Rudin's office; also refers to the people who work at Rudin's, i.e. "Those Who Swim with Sharks" (from the movie of the same name).

House of Weinstein: Miramax, the "independent" film distributor headed by Bob and Harvey Weinstein. Aka "The Golden M."

The House That Bobby Built: The Tribeca Film Center, spearheaded by Robert DeNiro. The upscale prestigious downtown address for producers, directors, and rich kids who want to be in the film biz.

The Pier: Chelsea Pier Studios, home of NYC television shows *Law & Order* and *Spin City*, among others.

The Gallery: The Shooting Gallery, production company which is the self-proclaimed jewel of East Coast independent, low-budget film-making.

Saint Billy Bob: Billy Bob Thorton, the East Coast's answer to Quentin Tarantino.

Before Cell Phones: A term of endearment used to describe an old-timer in the industry.

Corky: A production assistant who doesn't get it. Cruelly lifted from the Downs Syndrome–afflicted main character of *Life Goes On.*

Color Commentary: Any memo from the West Coast studio. Stems from the belief that any L.A. studio executive wouldn't know how to make a film on the streets of New York. The best they can offer is x's and o's, like the diagrams sportscasters and coaches draw.

This is just the stuff I thought of in one afternoon. I could probably write a whole book myself just on film slang. Anyway, continued success, and I look forward to the second edition.

Sincerely, **Cheryl E. Compton**

Archives are clear examples of why intelligent, creative people feel the need to *live* in Manhattan, not just visit.

> **Donnell Library Center.** 20 W. 53rd St., near Fifth Ave. (Midtown).
☎ **212/621-0618.**

Strictly speaking, this is not a film theater—but it's probably better. With a simple New York public library card, you can choose from thousands of films and videos and watch your selection in your own private viewing station for *free*.

> **Film Forum.** 209 W. Houston St., between Sixth and Seventh aves. (West Village). ☎ **212/727-8110.**

We performed a simple litmus test on employees at several film theaters in town. Question: "Who was the sad sack hometown boy who was still in love with Mary McDonnell in the movie *Passion Fish?*" Among other roles, he also had a quick cameo as a fix-it man in *Home for the Holidays*. Only the Film Forum answered correctly (David Strathairn), just one of many small testaments to why it is the most intelligent and creative source of commercial movie programming in the city (and, along, with Facets in Chicago, among the best of its kind in the country). FYI: The folks at Angelika hadn't even seen *Passion Fish*.

> **Millennium Film Workshop.** 66 E. 4th St., at Third Ave. (West Village).
☎ **212/673-0090.**

There are several types of junkies in New York. Least recognized is the serious (and I mean *serious*) film fanatic. What I call "flickies." These are the kind of people who look at you rather dismissively if you don't know your Stan Brakhage from your Jerry Tartaglia, your Chick Strand from your Bruce Baillie. Second only to the Anthology in its commitment to truly independent video and cinema, the Millennium Film Workshop is a meeting ground for New York's serious flickies—folks who like to hand-paint their films, pixilate whenever the mood strikes, and generally experiment with the film form. Millennium also rents out its large screening room, the screening and film editing rooms, as well as film equipment, all at cheap rates. It also offers a wide variety of workshops and classes, from film editing to animation, all with an independent filmmaking slant. Thank God places like this still exist. Call for brochure.

> **Worldwide Cinemas.** 340 W. 50th St., between Eighth and Ninth aves. (Midtown).
☎ **212/246-1560.**

Three-dollar movies, six theaters, showing many of the year's great films just after their mainstream run. Because of the cheap price, Worldwide usually pack them in. The audience can be rather festive.

> **Ziegfield.** 141 W. 54th St., between Sixth and Seventh aves. (Midtown).
☎ **212/765-7600** or 212/765-7601.

One of the few remaining big screens in America, though it is now reserved-seating only. No big deal really—just show up, and pick the seat you want from the seating chart in the lobby.

Food

They say New York is a food town. They are incorrect. San Francisco is a food town. New York is a money town with lots of places to eat.

This is not a comprehensive, all-inclusive guide to the 15,000 restaurants in New York. We leave that up to the *Village Voice,* the *New Yorker,* and whoever has the time to sit through 99 mediocre meals for every good one (from what we've seen, only the folks at *New York Press* have that kind of time). Instead, this is the list of the most unique restaurants that New York has to offer—in not only food, but price and, most importantly, ambiance. After all, a Monk can't always afford to eat out, but at least he can stand and stare.

Atmosphere

> **Cross Bronx Live Poultry.** 1663 Jerome Ave., near the Cross Bronx Expressway, across from Ari Unger Used Police Cars (Bronx). ☎ **718/731-0976.**

Live chickens, hens, rabbits, turkeys, roosters, doves, and ducks, all waiting to be slaughtered for your dining pleasure. Have them killed kosher (knife), halal (sword), or do it yourself at home. The signs are in Spanish, but the owner is a Muslim from Uzbekistan.

Michael Monk at the Hong Kong Supermarket

"I've been to the Hong Kong market before. I used to come here and buy all my pig's feet. I grew up eating pig's feet. You're talking white trash here. I grew up eating pig's feet, pig head, pig tail, chicken feet. This was because my grandmother, who was a wanna-be Asian lady—she's from Germany, but she would spare no parts in the animal. That's why I like the Hong Kong market. You can buy any part of any animal inside." (109 E. Broadway, at Pike Street ☎ **212/227-3388.**)

You pick 'em, we pluck 'em: Cross Bronx Live Poultry

> Cupcake Cafe. 522 Ninth Ave., just south of the Port Authority bus terminal (Midtown). ☎ 212/465-1530.

It is easy to understand the appeal of the Cupcake: '30s jazz playing on what sounds like an antique radio, quaint paintings on the walls, and cake decorations that seem Old World without being yuppie gourmet. The steady stream of regulars regard it as their own slice of sugar heaven. But beware: The overly hip staff can act a little bored, tired, and above it all.

> Eisenberg's Sandwich Shop. 174 Fifth Ave., at E. 23rd St. (Flatiron District). ☎ 212/675-5096.

The food isn't much (in fact, the much-heralded tuna sandwich is nothing special at all), but the help is extra-friendly, and the grungy throwback interior, with its wooden walls and old-style diner tables, is the real article. After all, the place has been around since 1929.

> Ellen's Cafe. 270 Broadway, at Chambers St. (Financial District). ☎ 212/962-1257.

A single distinction, which more than makes up for the run-of-the-mill food: framed photos and bios of former Miss Subways. A perfect slice of the '50s mind-set—the decade's view of women in particular.

Inside Katz's
Delicatessen

> **Grossinger's Home Bakery.** 570 Columbus Ave., at 88th St. (Upper West Side).
☎ 212/874-6996.

A welcome antidote to Zabar's and other Upper West Side yuppie establishments.
It's old-time Jewish, straight down the line, from the hamentaschen to the babka to
the famous praline cake. Closed for Saturday Shabbos.

> **Katz's Delicatessen.** 205 E. Houston St., at Ludlow St. (Lower East Side).
☎ 212/254-2246.

The highlight is the World War II–era sign hanging from the ceiling: "Send a Salami
to Your Boy in the Army." It's also the site of Meg Ryan's famous faked orgasm in
When Harry Met Sally. Unfortunately, the prices are way out of line.

› **Luna.** 112 Mulberry St., at Hester St. (Little Italy). ☎ **212/226-8657.**

Nobody comes to Luna for the exceptional food, though it's passable. You come to Luna because it's the last authentic place on Mulberry Street. There's plenty of tourists for sure, but the waitstaff could care less who the hell they, you, or whoever are. They treat everyone with the same loving derision. (Don't know what I mean by "loving derision"? Stay in New York awhile. You'll get it.) Luna is the place to cut loose and party. The food tastes so much better when you do.

› **Mobil Gas Station.** 140–52 Sixth Ave., between Spring and Broome sts. (SoHo). ☎ **212/925-6126.**

What Mobil gas station have you frequented where chapatis are shelved next to Frappuccinos, and trays of chicken rolls, samosas, and pakora are placed above boxes of Spunkmeyer orange muffins? Listen to Pakistani and Indian cabbies kibitz around the refrigerator case, sprinkling "this motherfucker" and "that motherfucker" in amidst their native tongue. On your way to the counter, pick up some salted green peas, hot and spicy channa, and mango juice, rather than the customary Pringles and Snapple. This, my friends, is New York!

› **Rolf's Bar & Restaurant.** 281 Third Ave., at 20th St. (Gramercy/Murray Hill). ☎ **212/477-4750.**

Most of the year it's a worn-down German restaurant, with faded memorabilia in a glass case and a waitstaff that is no-nonsense and not much fun. But come Christmas, the place is decked out in elaborate and beautiful decorations. Suddenly, there are crowds waiting an hour or more for tables, with Yuletide music playing in the background. Nobody, we mean *nobody*, does Christmas like the Germans, and no restaurant in New York does it quite like Rolf's.

› **Supreme Macaroni Company.** 511 Ninth Ave., at 39th St. (Hell's Kitchen). ☎ **212/564-8074.**

The women could be extras in *Goodfellas;* the men wear rings on their pinkies. Although the fella who runs the bulk noodle department may not know fettuccine from linguine, it doesn't really matter: Any one of the selections is bound to be good. This place would certainly be touristy in another part of town, but here in Hell's Kitchen, it's relatively unknown—an authentic Guido treasure.

› **Yonah Schimmel's Knishes Bakery.** 137 E. Houston St., at Forsyth St. (Lower East Side). ☎ **212/477-2858.**

Beyond quaint. Yonah cooks up some pretty okay knishes (though not the best, mind you): huge mounds, made with everything from buckwheat (a Monk favorite) to spinach and sweet potato. Sit at a spacious table and watch the dumbwaiter haul the food up from the cellar bakery. A cozy, friendly artifact of Jewish culture circa 1910. And just down the street from Russ and Daughters—which is, according to the late tour guide Lou Singer, "the most authentic Jewish take-out deli in the city."

Bargains

> **Bereket Turkish Kebab House.** 187 E. Houston St., at Orchard St. (Lower East Side). ☎ 212/475-7700.

Not as cheap as it once was, but still a decent all-night bargain, and friendly service to boot. The fare is standard Middle Eastern stuff like falafel and kebabs, with some tasty Turkish delights like guvec and lahana dolmasi thrown into the mix.

> **Dojo Restaurant.** 24 St. Mark's Place, between Second and Third aves. (East Village). ☎ 212/674-9821. Dojo West: 14 W. 4th St., just west of Broadway (West Village). ☎ 212/505-8934.

Try as you might, you will not find a healthier food bargain in the city, which is why the place is packed with students, hipsters, and starving Monks at all hours. $2.95 gets you a veggie burger with salad and brown rice. "The Denny's of the East Village," according to local white-trash foodie Reid Sherline. Actually, Veselka is the Denny's of the East Village (Dojo serves far tastier fare), but we had to find a way to squeeze Sherline into this guidebook.

> **Gray's Papaya.** 2090 Broadway, at 72nd St. (Upper West Side). ☎ 212/799-0243; 402 Sixth Ave. at 8th St. (West Village). ☎ 212/260-3532.

This New York institution is a hundred times faster than any chain, and they do it with a smile and respect. Chili dog with kraut, only $1.25. Regular dog, only 50 cents. Not to be confused with Original Papaya, Papaya King, or Papaya Prince.

> **La Caridad.** 2199 Broadway, at 78th St. (Upper West Side). ☎ 212/874-2780.

Food Trivia

You can always get a free meal out of the **Hare Krishnas** *on Avenue B between E. 3rd and E. 4th streets, next to Blackout Books. They look at it as "prasad," or holy food. They also like it if you stick around and listen to their spiel.*

In an area lousy with yuppies, La Caridad comes as a welcome relief. A Chino-Latino thing, serving up a variety of dishes at cheap prices—almost everything is under $7.

> **Leshko Coffee Shop.** 111 Avenue A, at St. Mark's Place (East Village). ☎ 212/473-9208.

Super cheap 24-hour Eastern European restaurant on Tompkins Square Park. Four pirogi, stuffed cabbage, kielbasa, sauerkraut, and a baked potato—all for under six bucks. The breakfasts are even cheaper.

> **Mama's Food Shop.** 200 E. 3rd St., at Avenue B (East Village). ☎ 212/777-4425.

The guys who run this place never seem particularly happy, but they serve up unbelievably good comfort food at dirt-cheap prices. Everything in the small but mighty buffet is delicious, from Mama's fried chicken to the meat loaf to the mashed potatoes to the macaroni and cheese. Next door to the beautiful Miracle Garden.

> **Moshe's Falafel.** On the southeast corner of 46th St. at Sixth Ave. Mon–Fri only. No phone.

Since the Giuliani administration's misguided assault on street vendors seems to have fallen through, you can still nab the best falafel in town through the walk-up window of this little yellow trailer, which sets up every day on a busy corner 1 block off 47th Street, the main drag of the city's Diamond District. Inside, five frantic Israelis fling together softball-sized falafels topped with spicy pickles and hot sauce, all for three and a half bucks. Note: Don't go looking for them on any Jewish holidays, as they ain't gonna be there.

> **Soup Kitchen International.** 259A W. 55th St., just east of Eighth Ave. (Midtown). ☎ 212/757-7730.

He's had a bad rap ever since *Seinfeld* christened him the Soup Nazi, but it's not fair. Al Yeganeh is not a Nazi; Al is thinking of the next customer. His seven-second rule: "Order, pay, and step to the left in seven seconds." And he'll punish you if you are not mindful of it; this is New York, after all, not Santa Cruz. While this place is not a bargain, given the phenomenal soups, you'll think it is.

> **Souvlaki Guy.** Somewhere on Broadway between 4th and Prince. No phone.

The best fast-food deal in the city still remains street vendor souvlaki. The guy roaming lower Broadway between 4th and Prince is the cheapest—$2 with all the fixins', $1.50 on a stick, with a grateful smile to boot.

> **Tom's Restaurant.** 782 Washington Ave., at Sterling Place (Prospect Heights, Brooklyn). ☎ **718/636-9738.**

This classic diner and neighborhood fave is always packed, and features some of the cheapest deals ($2.95 hamburgers) and friendliest faces in New York. Gus, the owner, has a smile and a greeting that'll keep you from bitching too much while you wait for a seat, and his equally charming staff passes around orange slices and cookies. The crab cakes with eggs, hash browns, and toast make a killer breakfast. Wash it down with that almost-disappeared New York classic, the chocolate egg cream.

> **Tops.** 89 N. 6th St., between Wythe and Berry (Williamsburg, Brooklyn). ☎ **718/782-6660.**

When you want to cook, this is your best bet. Located on Williamsburg's booze and meatpacking row, Tops delivers a great variety of meat and vegetables at the cheapest rates in the city. But the big plusses are the mixed crowd (Polish regulars, Hispanic help, and local artsy boho types) and the cold meat room, which offers welcome respite from the summer's heat waves.

Jim at Tops

"What ya gonna do with that?" says a black man, laughing.

"With what?" Jim asks cautiously, carefully assessing the man's tone.

"Those collard greens," the man continues, laughing.

Jim picks up on it.

"Why, you think a white man don't know about collard greens?"

The black man laughs real hard. Jim continues.

"I may be white on the surface, but I'm a black man inside."

"Now you're talking some shit," the man says, laughing.

Natural Foods Restaurants

> **The Candle Cafe (formerly the Healthy Candle on Lex).** 1307 Third Ave., at E. 75th St. (Upper East Side). ☎ 212/472-0970.

There's a reason this vegan restaurant is immensely popular: Owner Bart Potenza is a total love spirit. His place is clean, elegant, happy, and friendly. A blessed vortex on the materialist Upper East Side, with more beautiful female customers than you can shake a chopstick at. Woody "Hemp" Harrelson and Julianna Margulies (Nurse Carol Hathaway on *ER*) are regulars.

› **Helianthus.** 48 Macdougall St., between W. Houston and Prince (SoHo). ☎ 212/598-0387.

Helianthus is a fancy way of saying "sunflower," and that's the theme here. Sunflowers everywhere. Walls, tables, menus. Everywhere. Sunny. Sweet. The whole place is sweet. The atmosphere and decor are sweet. The staff is sweet. You get the feeling if you told them you didn't like the food they might very well start to cry. Not much chance of that, though: This is some serious veggie cooking, in somewhat the same style as Zen Palate (see box), featuring dishes that resemble meat but are made from ingredients that never moved under their own power. Try the diced veggie chicken—yum.

› **Souen.** 28 E. 13th St., between Fifth Ave. and University (West Village). ☎ 212/627-7150.

One can't beat the city's original Japanese natural foods restaurant, made famous by John and Yoko when they were on heroin detox and backed by health-conscious New Yorkers ever since. We actually preferred the now-closed Soho location (we'll never forget the day Liza Minnelli dined nearby), but the Village version still hangs on, serving simple but strong rice and fish dishes, and, of course, miso soup.

Best Vegetarian Restaurant: Zen Palate

16 Park Ave. South (on Union Square), ☎ 212/614-9345; 663 Ninth Ave., at 46th St. (Midtown), ☎ 212/582-1669; 2170 Broadway, between 76th and 77th sts. (Upper West Side), ☎ 212/501-7768.

From design to speed to actual food, this place delivers big-time. The steamed brown rice is the best in town, and everything else here is imaginative and good. In all respects true to the concept of completely vegetarian Asian food—no meat, fish, dairy, or eggs in the whole joint. Hard to imagine there's that many vegans to keep a place like this rocking, but Zen Palate is always crowded. And what's more amazing, the prices are downright monkish.

Natural Foods Stores

For whatever reason, there has yet to appear a natural food store in New York that rivals the unparalleled selection and funky good vibe found at the legendary Rainbow Grocery in San Francisco. If someone could study what Rainbow does (at those amazingly low prices) and combine it with a well-stocked selection of organic meat and fish, one would have a true natural foods oasis on this island. It may never happen, though there have been recent attempts. Unfortunately, most are way overpriced with absolutely no heart, soul, or decent bulk selection.

> **Integral Yoga Natural Foods.** 229 W. 13th St., at Greenwich Ave. (West Village). ☎ 212/243-2642.

The folks that work here are very friendly, and the small store is relatively clean, uncluttered, and peaceful, but this is *not* the best health food option in the city: (1) The prices can't compare to Prana or Whole Foods or even Healthy Chelsea;(2) the selection isn't up to snuff (at Whole Foods you get organic and commercial varieties of grains, plus lots of other esoteric items); (3) it is strictly vegetarian (which fits nicely into the East Indian philosophy of founder Swami Satchitananda, but forces enlightened carnivores to shop elsewhere). One does have to cut Integral a little slack—because of their limited space, they've needed to ship the herbs and vitamins division across the street and the books department next door.

> **Northside Health Food Center.** 169 Bedford Ave., at N. 6th St. (Williamsburg, Brooklyn). ☎ 718/387-1078.

Netham, the Palestinian gentleman who manages this Williamsburg health food store, may be the most genuinely good-natured retailer in the city. He understands how to run a solid neighborhood business, treating regulars to price breaks and continual quality service.

> **Prana Foods.** 125 First Ave., St. Marks Place (East Village). ☎ 212/982-7306.

By far the cheapest health food store in the city. It's actually a co-op (which explains the dreadlocked checkout girls), but it's up to snuff, selling quality organic food at prices you can't find even in the deepest part of the Deep South. No clear sign out front, which excludes all but true Village insiders.

> **Whole Foods Soho.** 17 Prince St., just west of Broadway (SoHo). ☎ 212/982-1000.

There are health food stores sprouting up all over Manhattan, many trying to merge a Dean and Delucca aesthetic (and inflated prices) with organic quality, but all disappoint in the area of selection. And you just can't count on that neon pill joint having your favorite brand of soymilk. Whole Foods, however, will have it, and at a cheap price. As the rest of SoHo loses its heart and moderation, Whole Foods maintains its quality and integrity, though they wouldn't win any competition for neatness or maneuverability (the place is packed).

Overrated, Overpriced, Overdone, or Just Flat-Out Annoying

› **44.** Lobby of the Royalton Hotel, 44 W. 44th St., between Fifth and Sixth aves. (Midtown). ☎ **212/869-4400.**

If your idea of fun is listening to a babble of British editors curled up in lime-green banquettes, while you languish over overpriced vittles in restaurant Siberia, then go ahead, make a reservation now. Frankly, we've never been impressed by most of the products and people that come out of the Condé Nast empire. The Brits are alright when they venture out west to Los Angeles (the sun draws out their hidden tackiness and warmth), but, like most Europeans, they become positively unbearable when ensconced in Manhattan, which they increasingly regard as their own editorial fiefdom. 44, affectionately known as "the Canteen," or "the Commissary" by Condé Nast regulars, is where the Brit pack and their fashion industry backers gather—and where people like us come to use the extraordinarily crafted bathroom. See "Accommodations."

› **The Algonquin.** 59 W. 44th St., between Fifth and Sixth aves. (Midtown). ☎ **212/840-6800.**

The old literary landmark is way past its prime, which doesn't stop an endless parade of Dorothy Parker wannabes trying desperately to recapture the elegance and refinement of the legendary Roundtable.

› **Barney Greengrass, The Sturgeon King.** 541 Amsterdam Ave., between 86th and 87th sts. ☎ **212/724-4707.**

This is a "Yupper" West Side version of authenticity, symbolizing all that is wrong and greedy about the area. The locals pile in every Sunday thinking they are getting something special. What they're getting is a beautiful old storefront and a charming old New York interior that is completely self-conscious of its shtick. Telltale sign: astronomical prices for homeopathic portions of basic Yiddish folk food. This place is a phoney, right down to the deliberately brusque waiters.

› **Bean.** 167 Bedford Ave., at 8th St. (Williamsburg, Brooklyn). ☎ **718/387-8222.**

I don't think the staff at this quasi-vegetarian burrito place in the heart of hip and hardened Polish Williamsburg ever forgave us for trying to coax Dishwasher Pete into an interview. Weeks after I apologized for our strong-arm tactics (which really weren't that pushy), I kept running into a staff member with a perpetual hangover and a bad attitude. His revulsion (or maybe his hangover) was so strong it made me never want to even walk past the place. So, who knows, maybe the small and funky Bean has the best food in all of Brooklyn. We'll never know.

> **Bowery Bar.** 40 E. 4th St., at Bowery (East Village). ☎ **212/475-2220.**

This one takes the cake. In protest, the next-door neighbors have hung a sign in their window: "Lifestyles of the $ick and Shameless—Cooper Union, How Could You Have Done This to Our Neighborhood?" If you go in after seeing this bit of social commentary, you *are* a moron.

> **Cafe des Artistes.** One W. 67th St. between Columbus Ave. and Central Park West (Upper West Side). ☎ **212/877-3500.**

Pity those who lazily trust the mainstream restaurant reviewers, who all consistently list this outrageously overpriced dinosaur as one of the best dining experiences in the city. The much-lauded brunch is a joke, best appreciated by tacky tourists from Nebraska and Upper West Side doctor's wives on their third facelift. The smoked salmon benedict, at a hefty $19+, can be enjoyed at a far higher quality and far lower price at about 20 other locations around the city, including your local deli. The string beans and carrots taste like they came from a grade school cafeteria lunch line, and the much-talked-about "frolicking nude nymphs" that adorn the walls give a kind of old shoe cultured person's atmosphere that once upon a time was backed up by a waitstaff and patronage of real class and peerage. It is quite clear from one visit to Cafe des Artistes that those days are long gone.

> **Coffee Shop.** 29 Union Square W. (Union Square). ☎ **212/243-7969.**

The mediocre food may be Brazilian, but I've spent several months in Brazil, and the attitude of these vacuous patrons is definitely *not*. Coffee Shop is owned by the Gotham City Restaurant Group, and like all such "properties," the place reeks of marketing concept, right down to the "Jus" bar.

> **Fashion Cafe.** 51 W. 51st St., at Rockefeller Plaza (Midtown). ☎ **212/765-3131.**

This place—replete with runway—makes you wonder how America managed to come so far with so little class.

> **Korean Green Grocer Buffets.** 24 hrs., all over town.

These are, without a shred of doubt, the worst buffets in Manhattan: old, over-salted, yet too-sweet meats and vegetables that smell and look funny. With egg salad and crab salad that look like they came straight from a bucket. What's amazing is that this food *can* look tantalizing in its bountiful glory, especially to a starving writer at 1am, but when you bring it home you realize it's been sitting around in a state of rigor mortis for hours, if not days. How to treat a no-nonsense Korean Green Grocer: (1) have your change ready; (2) refrain from too much small talk (they won't play along anyway); (3) no eye contact. Then, as Korean Zen Master Dae Seung Sunim says, "no problem."

> **New York Kom Tang Soot Bul House.** 32 W. 32nd St., between Fifth Ave. and Broadway (Chelsea). ☎ 212/947-8482.

Don't go to *any* of the many 24-hour restaurants on this street, but particularly avoid Kom Tang Soot Bul. This food is ugly. The tofu soup is like brackish water from the Platte River. The beef is chewy and as old as Buddha. And everything else, from the kimchee to the daikon, appears to have come out of a can. In fact, cans are advertised prominently on the menu. As it turns out, the proprietor also owns a cannery. Yes, the same foul oxtail soup you wretched over last night can be had at home out of a *can!*

> **Official All-Star Cafe.** 1540 Broadway, at 45th St. (Times Square). ☎ 212/840-8326.

Anyone under the impression that plans for Times Square are at worst benign and may even be in the greater cultural interest need look no further. This place, a half-baked Nike Town with mediocre food, is hollow at the core—or merely greedy. Just to get to the dining room you have to pass two floors of merchandising. The food? Average hamburgers at ridiculously high prices. The patrons can't possibly be having fun. But, then, they probably didn't have fun in Las Vegas or Disneyworld, either.

> **Pastrami King.** 124-24 Queens Blvd., near 82nd Ave. (Kew Gardens, Queens). ☎ 718/263-1717.

Like Veselka, Odessa, and a host of other ethnic New York eateries, maybe Pastrami King was better before the renovation, but now it's not worth the hassle of getting there. And, let me tell you, it's a hassle getting anywhere in Queens. If this is the finest in Jewish deli food, it's a sad commentary on Jewish deli food. Call it the Veselka effect: ethnic emporiums spiffing up their image and losing their soul. (If you do go, order a Dr. Browns's Cel-Ray. It's made from celery extract.)

> **Royal Canadian Pancake House.** 1004 Second Ave., at 53rd St. (Midtown).
☎ **212/980-4131.**

This place has promise. The crowds out front testify as much. I came carrying fantasies of Dudley Do-Right and the Royal Canadian Mounties and what they might order on a bright, clear Sunday morning. Unfortunately, the Mounties seem to have a severe sweet tooth, as every pancake and waffle on the menu comes loaded with heaps of white sugar inside. The taste was closer to candy than authentic breakfast food. The vaunted Canadian bacon and sausage didn't compensate much either.

> **Tony's Seafood.** City Island in the Bronx. ☎ **718/328-5200.**

We pity any fool who drives all the way out to this tourist trap, which masquerades as an authentic fishing village. If you go to the end of the island hoping to find bona fide Manhattan Clam Chowder, you ain't gonna get it. Ours tasted like it was made in some poorly run Campbell's Soup factory, and for $3, a pathetic disappointment, though the regulars that come here probably didn't even notice.

Pricey, Scenesterish, Yet—Despite It All—Recommended

> **Asia de Cuba.** 237 Madison Ave., between 37th and 38th sts. (Midtown).
☎ **212/726-7755.**

Long communal table. High chairs. Inside Morgans. Owned by Schrager. Well-dressed stock brokers. Some scary. Asian/Latin cuisine. Blended, mixed, shaken up. Starck-designed. Friendly coat check. Trippy painting. Pricey. What would you expect?

> **Balthazar.** 80 Spring St., at Crosby St. (SoHo). ☎ **212/965-1414.**

We'd like to say this large, busy, high-energy French bistro is as snooty as Bowery Bar, but it is not. In fact, the hostesses and waiters are downright friendly to all, whether celeb or chump. And they seem to know what they are doing. You are going to pay a lot of money for the food here, but you are not going to find a more authentic reproduction of a Parisian bistro anywhere else downtown. The boulangerie next door is also recommended.

> **Bouley.** 120 W. Broadway, at Thomas St. (Tribeca). ☎ **212/964-2525.**

There has yet to be a restaurant in this city that merges humanity with greatness—in other words, a place that isn't full of itself. Bouley certainly doesn't blaze a new path in that department—the anal maitre'd didn't like the rain-soaked look of us (we assume he expected us not to sustain even one raindrop during the torrential down-pour that nailed us as we exited the car)—but let's forget all that, and cut to the point: The dude in back can *cook*.

> **The Odeon.** 145 W. Broadway, at Thomas St. (Tribeca). ☎ **212/233-0507.**

This is one of those rare Eurotrash restaurants that transcends trendiness. Like Florent (see "Open 24 Hours," below), it keeps plugging along for three simple reasons: warm inviting atmosphere, excellent service, and consistently great food (the free-range chicken and mashed 'taters are the best we've ever had). Not that the models in attendance would notice; they're having microscopic portions of salad, thank you.

Open 24 Hours

We visited the pricey pleasant Empire, the groovy pricey Moondance, the time-tested and beloved East Village kielbasa vortex, the after-hours chef scene at Blue Ribbon, even Uncle George's out there in Astoria, and have decided the places below are the most compelling late-night eating options in New York. Now shut up and don't argue the point.

> **Big Nick's Burger.** 2175 Broadway, at 77th St. (Upper West Side).
☎ **212/362-9238.**

Fast service, tasty grub, and great late-night dinner ambiance—all in a tight, cozy space. In an area long on fakery and fluff, Big Nick's is the real thing.

> **Florent.** 69 Gansevoort St., at Washington St. (Meatpacking District).
☎ **212/989-5779.**

The epicenter of late-night dining for years, Florent is genuinely friendly (a big surprise for a restaurant so perennially hip). It's all about community, and the patrons show their appreciation by returning, year in and year out. The lesson, unfortunately, has yet to rub off on other, snootier late-night eateries. Don't miss the restaurant's annual Bastille Day party, substantially scaled back to Bastille Lite now that co-sponsor Housing Works has lost its non-profit status, but still an outrageous hoot.

> **Gem-Spa.** 131 Second Ave., at St. Marks Place (East Village). ☎ **212/529-1146.**

Any New Yorker, especially any Jewish New Yorker, knows immediately why we list this crowded corner newsstand under "food." It's because Gem-Spa not only carries a range of domestic and international periodicals, it's also one of the few remaining

Florent in Marie Antoinette drag, Bastille Day

places in the city to get a beloved "egg cream." Don't know what an egg cream is? Mix seltzer water, milk, and Fox's U-bet chocolate syrup, and you got it, kid.

> **H&H Bagels.** 639 W. 46th St., at Twelfth Ave. (Theater District), ☎ **212/595-8000;** 1551 Second Ave., at 80th St. (Upper East Side), ☎ **212/734-7441;** 2239 Broadway at 80th St. (Upper West Side), ☎ **212/595-8003.**

The place's secret is well known to seasoned locals: sugar, and lots of it. It's open 24 hours and feels almost industrial inside—perhaps no surprise since over 60,000 bagels are baked at the 46th Street store alone every day. Call 1-800-NY-BAGEL to have these soft and addictive creations sent anywhere in the world.

> **Kossar's Bialystoker Kuchen Bakery.** 367 Grand St., at Essex St. (Lower East Side). ☎ 212/473-4810.

This place does for the bialy what H&H does for the bagel. What Kossar's has that H&H lacks is atmosphere: big brown sacks of bialys on the floor, flour dust over workers and machinery.

> **Leshko Coffee Shop.**

See "Bargains."

> **L'Express.** 249 Park Ave. South, at E. 20th St. (Flatiron District). ☎ 212/254-5858.

If this restaurant had regular hours, it probably wouldn't make the cut, but for a 24-hour place in the heart of the Flatiron District, it definitely does the trick. Excellent soups, a superb ravioli, plus very good pates and salads make this a reliable and reasonably priced standby for late-night dining.

> **Market Diner-Restaurant.** 572 Eleventh Ave., at W. 44th St. (Theater District). ☎ 212/695-0415.

Googie meets Joisey in this, The Mother of All New York Diners. The pretenders, lining the east side of Tenth and Eleventh avenues, include the **Empire Diner** (210 Tenth Ave., ☎ 212/243-2736) and the **River Diner** (454 Eleventh Ave., ☎ 212/868-1364), but this sucker beats them all. It has drive-up parking (a miracle for New York), tacky light fixtures, and gray booths, and it's packed with greasy, smoky, hard-nosed, and crumple-suited limo drivers. Not to mention the fact that it's right next door to Edelweiss, the best trannie bar in the city. Need we say the food is standard diner fare—nothing fancy, but it does the trick.

> **Yaffa Cafe.** 97 St. Marks Place, between First Ave. and Avenue A (East Village). ☎ 212/674-9302.

Yaffa is Dojo's glamorous cousin, which isn't saying much, if you've ever been to Dojo. The decor is American kitsch: Elvis paintings, fake fruit, plastic zebra-stripe couches. Dining options are middle brow and are almost all under $9. Very sweet open court in summer. Always packed. Unfortunately, the taste and quality of food is disappointing at best. Dojo wins in that department, hands down.

Best of the Rest

> **Amici.** 566 E. 187th St., near Fordham University and the New York Botanical Garden (Bronx). ☎ 718/584-6167.

Famous because actor Joe Pesci worked here as a maitre'd and lived upstairs back in the late '70s. You walk in the door, and three waiters approach you immediately like you were the Godfather himself. No surprise, given the reputation of the place.

> **Angelo and Maxie's Steakhouse.** 233 Park Ave. South, at 20th St. (Gramercy Park). ☎ **212/220-9200.**

The downtown version of Smith and Wollensky's, with the requisite cigar bar, giant slabs of steak, and throwback clientele, both young and old, gnawing on fat stogies, and indulging in their very best Joisey-speak and Long Guyland–ese. There's something likable about these stockbroker types—Goodfellas gone legit, the Brothers McMullen gone Wall Street. And there's something remarkable about this corner— every place that has *ever* located on the east side of the street has packed 'em in. On Thursday's they really pack 'em in, when Angelo and Maxie's becomes the epicenter of the angry male universe. No doubt Mickey Rourke and Rush Limbaugh would receive standing ovations were they to dine here. Go before the cigar craze takes a nosedive.

> **Anne and Tony's.** 2407 Arthur Ave., just south of Fordham University and the New York Botanical Garden (Bronx). ☎ **718/933-1469.**

Like a lot of things in the Little Italy of the Bronx, the place and the people who run it were a trifle scary. Great granddad Napolitano founded the place and son Ralph made it famous when he played the character Gino in Bob De Niro's *A Bronx Tale*. Nearby Amici's has the rep, but you get the idea that "the boys" may have dined here as well.

> **Canal House.** In the Soho Grand Hotel, 310 W. Broadway at Canal St. (SoHo). ☎ **212/965-3588.**

Given the way I chastised the Soho Grand Hotel (see "Accommodations"), it may surprise you that I was pleasantly surprised by the hotel's restaurant. The entrees were light and fresh, if at times (as with so many gourmet restaurants in Manhattan) on the oversalted side. The desserts were richly decadent. The PIB (People in Black) quotient was tolerable, and, what's more, the service was genuinely cordial, border- ing on overtly friendly. In fact, genuine graciousness and cordiality is a characteris- tic of most of the very accommodating staffers associated with the Soho Grand. Folks, build on this strength, and drop the Shrager schtick.

> **Da Silvano.** 260 Sixth Ave., at Bleecker St. (West Village). ☎ **212/982-2343.**

Probably the best Italian food I've had in my life I had at this relatively pricey Village favorite. There's nothing special about the standard issue decor, but the service is beyond impeccable. A treat in all ways.

> **Dominick's.** 2335 Arthur Ave., at E. 187th St., just south of Fordham University (Bronx). ☎ **718/733-2807.**

Most people who make the trek out to this menu-less restaurant on Arthur Avenue swear it's the best Southern Italian food in the country. They will cook anything you want, but be sure to eat it all or the price doubles (no joke). Check out Mario's, too, while in the Belmont area. It's where Al Pacino shot the cop and capo in *The Godfather*.

> **E.A.T.** 1062 Madison Ave., at 80th St. (Upper East Side). ☎ **212/861-2544.**

$14 for a 3-pound loaf of bread is a bit much. But this is the Upper East Side, where everything is double . . . just on principle. This Dean and Delucca's of Madison Avenue does deliver on one thing—taste. Martha Stewart is a regular.

> **Kelly and Ping.** 127 Greene St., between Houston and Prince (SoHo). ☎ **212/228-1212.**

Brainchild of Brad Kelley and Lee Ping (Khin Kao and Bop), Kelly and Ping opened in 1993, offering pan-Asian cuisine at surprisingly decent prices (for SoHo anyway). It's not so much the food that makes this restaurant so compelling, it's the exquisitely realized Asian realism that inhabits every fiber of the place, from the selection of moon cakes in aged wicker to the very walls, chairs, and light.

> **Le Poeme.** 14 Prince St., at Elizabeth St. (Little Italy). ☎ **212/941-1106.**

To me, this is the Beatrix Potter of Little Italy cafes. It's that precious. Of course, I've always wandered how the sweet and delightful Corsican owner, Martine "Mais Oui" Abitbol, makes any money. Everything is done on such a low-key, scattered level here, as if you were dropping in to say hi and you caught her getting her children off to school. I'm not even sure she has a cash register. And I'm sure credit cards are out of the question, though I've never tried. The hunk in charge of selecting your items speaks with a very thick, almost impenetrable accent, but the food is out of this world. And no sugar. So sweet, so friendly, such high quality, it would break our hearts to see it swept away by the tidal wave of gentrification sweeping the area.

> **Oznot's Dish.** 79 Berry St., at N. 10th St. (Williamsburg, Brooklyn). ☎ **718/599-6596.**

We don't know who the heck Oznot is (and neither do the owners), but her funky namesake serves semi-natural food, and occasionally gets it right on the pierced nose (especially the Afghani bread, which is made off-premises). Along with Teddy's and Plan-Eat Thailand, the major hipster hangout in the hood.

> **Sweet and Tart Cafe.** 76 Mott St., at Canal St. (Chinatown). ☎ **212/334-8088.**

Depending on your point of view, this Chinatown favorite has either the most intriguing or the most disgusting menu in New York. Take a look at some of the options: Noodle with braised pork leg, jumbo shrimp with intestine, broiled frogs, pond fish, pig's blood, broiled pork intestine, shredded jelly fish, duck's blood with ginger and scallion, pig knuckle with ginger. Not getting enough variety in your diet? Try the pork belly and liver combo.

Worst of the Rest

> **Dine By Design.** 252 Elizabeth St., below E. Houston St. (Little Italy).
☎ **212/965-9182.**

This place is everything Le Poeme (see above) is not. The woman handling our requests appeared to be somewhere left of a lesbian separatist, all set to join the Society for Cutting Up Men. Not a positive experience. A place we will not frequent, despite the tasty food and the highly recommended personal chef service.

> **Navia's Diner.** 133 Ludlow St., at Rivington St. (Lower East Side). No phone listed.

After a late-night run through the Lower East Side we stumbled into this brightly lit vegetarian restaurant. There were lots of people hanging out, waiting for something to happen (perhaps a police bust of the place for serving liquor without a license). That it was actually a restaurant seemed an afterthought. The star of this makeshift enterprise is Asian model, cook, and owner Navia Nguyen. In between dishing up some pretty decent grub, the charismatic Leo (born on August 4th, Michael Monk's birthday) and local girl (she grew up a few blocks away) vogues up and down her kitchen runway. Her audience is a bored and boring club kid/supermodel clientele that seemed they were here primarily to pay homage. These folks were not the friendly types you'd expect from a vegetarian restaurant, and, like Navia, were awfully full of themselves—the main reason we will not return, though the beautiful Nguyen did make a decent interview.

"How old are you?"

"26," she replied.

"I thought the press said you were 24."

"Model years are like dog years."

"What is this place all about?" I asked over the pounding rap music.

"Healthy vegetarian without being righteous," she shouted while dancing and smoking. "A crossover restaurant."

Museums, Galleries, and *Landmarks*

› **African-American Wax Museum and History Museum of Harlem.** 316 W. 115th St., between Manhattan Ave. and Frederick Douglass Blvd. (Harlem). ☎ **212/678-7818.** Open Tues–Sun 1–6pm (by appointment only).

Forget MoMA, forget the Met—we've all been there, done that. Instead, try Raven Chanticleer's African-American Wax Museum and History Museum of Harlem. The place is inimitable, all right. It's not cheap (10 bucks a head), and it doesn't keep regular hours (call ahead for an appointment). But you'll be investing in perhaps the strangest museum-going experience New York City has to offer.

Pointer in hand, tall, thin Raven will give visitors a guided tour of African-American history, illustrated with a wall-to-wall collection of artifacts, sculptures, and paintings (most of them by Raven himself). There are illustrations of the black family "on their way to town to sell their wares of cotton and whatnot," not to mention photographs of Raven's family ("This is me, the radical artist, and this is my sister, who is an RN"). There is a bust of Josephine Baker carved—by Raven, of course—from stone, and one of Whoopi Goldberg ("the greatest diva since Moms

African-American Wax Museum and History Museum of Harlem

Mabley") in wax. But the real attraction is the "main hall"—actually it appears to be Raven's living room—arrayed with life-size, if not exactly to-scale, wax figures: Malcolm X, Martin Luther King Jr., Adam Clayton Powell Jr., Mary McLeod Bethune, Harriet Tubman ("the diva who was on the underground railroad"), Duke Ellington, Fannie Lou Hamer, David Dinkins, and Nelson Mandela, among others—all poured and sculpted by Raven.

We visited Raven Chanticleer in his neat museum, his very neat museum, so neat he insisted we wear paper shoe covers to keep from scuffing the hard-wood floors. "You're about to see the wax museum," he said to us, "referred to as one of its kind in the world. It is the museum of *he*roes and *she*roes of African ancestry."

"You're about to see the wax museum referred to as one of its kind in the world . . ."

Raven Chanticleer with Monks

Jim Monk: How long has the museum been here?

Raven Chanticleer: Since 1989.

Jim Monk: And you started it yourself.

Raven Chanticleer: Yes, sir.

Jim Monk: What inspired this innovation?

Raven Chanticleer: Well, it was my dream to have the first black wax museum.

Jim Monk: How do you make the wax figures?

Raven Chanticleer: I first make the model, and they are made out of chicken wire and papier maché and plaster. Then I do my research. I get the photos. I do the studying of figures like Harriet Tubman and Whoopi Goldberg and whatnot. Then I have my studio downstairs. I put them together. You cook the wax and you take the instruments and you create the whole figure. When you know what you're doing, it's very simple.

Jim Monk: Have any of the figures you've done been here?

Raven Chanticleer: Let's see who has been here. Oprah Winfrey has been here and Sheri Belafonte, Malcolm X's daughter, and Dr. King's daughter. One of Calvin Butts's parishioners used to live here, Sister Souljah. Do you remember her? She wouldn't pay her rent. But let's not talk about that.

Jim Monk: How has Harlem changed?

Raven Chanticleer: Oh, my God, it's changed. It's changed completely. You know the Kennedy boy was arrested out here on the corner. Do you remember? Did you hear about it? That was back in the '70s. The park has been redone. We have a lot of Columbia University students who used to be afraid to live here. A lot of the kids from the Village are living all around here in these different houses. We are highly integrated here now.

Jim Monk: You must be an inspiration to the people around here. Or do they think you're crazy?

Raven Chanticleer: I don't care. I have my friends. I don't care. You know Virgos.

> **The Delacorte Clock.** Central Park Zoo and Wildlife Center. Fifth Ave. at 64th St. ☎ 212/861-6030.

Every half hour near the Tisch Petting Zoo, a circle of 4-foot bronze animals—a goat playing pipes, a hippo doing the fiddle, and a bear banging on a tambourine—do a quick ditty around the clock.

> **Dream House Sound & Light Environment.** 275 Church St. (bell no. 3), between White and Franklin sts. (Tribeca). ☎ **212/925-8270.**

What we have here is an attempt—largely successful—to turn an empty loft in Tribeca into an alternate universe. Created by composer LaMonte Young ("the father of minimalism") and visual artist Marian Zazeela, and running for a solid 7 years, what it is is Young's sound environment paired with Zazeela's magenta-hued lighting in a plushly carpeted but otherwise bare white room. The effect of the music is immediate and stunning—what sounds like a drone at first actually changes depending on your movement within it: Swirl your hand, and the music shimmers and swirls; stop, and it stops. Stay a while, though, especially around sunset, for the total effect: The city outside the magenta windows starts to seem distant and unreal, the circular sculptures suspended from the ceiling start to look less solid than their shadows on the wall, and you begin to drift into another world. (The Environment is open Thursday and Saturday 2 to 9pm and by appointment. Closed in the summer.)

> **Ellis Island National Monument and Museum of Immigration.** ☎ **212/363-3200.**

It's late afternoon. We are driving to Ellis Island. We have gone to elaborate pains to drive there. It has cost us nearly 2 hours, $20 in tolls, and $150 in bribes to the National Park Service. It seemed like a good idea at the time. Millions of immigrants have arrived at Ellis Island, all of them by boat. We wanted to be different; we wanted to arrive by car. It's important to us. We don't go anywhere without our motor home.

Michael is driving (he almost always drives, 99 percent of the time); Jim is in the passenger seat. Her holiness the Great Dolly Lama is nowhere to be found. The route is circuitous: over the Brooklyn Bridge, over the Verrazano Narrows Bridge, through Staten Island and into New Jersey. (On the Brooklyn Bridge we nearly lose the roof of the motor home; clearance is, at first, 11 feet, then—once we have committed and there is no turning back—only 10.)

For us it's another day, another road trip. "We've driven over 225,000 miles," Michael says. "That's what?" He makes a calculation in his head. "Eleven times around the earth. We could have been to the moon and back." (It's actually closer to nine times around the earth, and we might have gotten to the moon—just barely—but not back.)

A little-known bridge connects Liberty State Park, in New Jersey, to Ellis Island. It's a service bridge, and it is not open to the public. But Jim is persistent and will not leave well enough alone. The Park Service said no 10 times and on the 11th suggested a small donation. The donation, as it turns out, has not bought much. We arrive at 6:45pm, well after the park has closed; we have access to the loading dock

Marvin Schneider,

New York's Father Time

They call him Father Time, although his actual title is City Clock Master and his actual name is Marvin Schneider. It's a big job, but somebody's got to do it—and often. Approximately once a week the clocks need to be tended to. Otherwise they won't keep accurate time, if they'll keep it at all. What they'll do is just stop, which is what they had done when Schneider began to unofficially perform his duties in 1979. He thought it was a shame that the city's old clocks were not ticking, and so, in his spare time, he took to fixing and winding them. In 1992 he was officially appointed to the post. (Before him, New York's last City Clock Winder was Victor Wahlberg, appointed exactly a century earlier, in 1892.)

We caught up with Marvin Schneider in the clock tower of the former New York Life Insurance Company building (346 Broadway, at Franklin Street) in lower Manhattan, where he was winding one of the six city-owned clocks that he tends.

Jim Monk: Is there a simple way to explain the operation of this clock?

Marvin Schneider: It's powered by gravity. It's much like a grandfather clock. The pull of gravity on weights gives the gears power, and all these various gears and different ratios distribute that power. The clock would strike for 8 days, plus a few hours, without rewinding. What happens after that point is the weights bottom out, they land on the floor, and there's no more power. So the clock won't strike. When it comes to the time part, there's a little more leeway; we can get about 11 days out of it.

Jim Monk: So you have to keep coming back every week.

Marvin Schneider: Every week. Basically it's every week. Yes.

Jim Monk: What's the name of this clock?

Marvin Schneider: Well, it doesn't have a name.

Jim Monk: The building it's in—

Marvin Schneider: The building is the former New York Life Insurance Company building. And the New York Life Insurance Company had its offices here until 1928. They owned the building until 1945. The clock was manufactured by the E. Howard Company, which any clock or watch collector will tell you was, and still is, one of the top-notch clock firms and watch firms in American history. And this particular model is called the Number 4, which is pretty much the largest of the mechanical clocks that they made. And if I'm not mistaken, this particular clock is the largest mechanical clock in New York City.

Jim Monk: Do you have a particular fascination with time itself?

Marvin Schneider: Not more than anybody else, I don't think. Of course, we become a little more cognizant of the passage of time as we grow older.

Jim Monk: How does working with clocks affect your relationship to time?

Marvin Schneider: I try to conserve it.

Michael Monk: Are you on time? Can you make an appointment?

Marvin Schneider: You saw that I was today. But in New York City it's very difficult. You've got to allow a 15-minute window at least. Because you are not your own boss. You're either getting on a highway where they may be doing some construction, and that throws you off, or you get on the subway where something goes wrong, so you can't be 100% sure.

Jim Monk: You're a rabbi, I hear.

Marvin Schneider: Yes, by training. [Schneider hears a click.] There we go. Excuse me. Let me just get over there, because we've got 30 seconds before she's going to go off.

Jim Monk: Thirty seconds.

Marvin Schneider: Okay, we made it.

Photographer: What is going to happen now?

Jim Monk: It's going to be really loud?

The bell tolls.

Marvin Schneider: It's loud enough.

Jim Monk: For whom does the bell toll?

Marvin Schneider: For one and for all. If the bell tolls, listen. . . . That's it.

Jim Monk: Do you know any good poems about clocks or time?

Marvin Schneider: There's a famous Hebrew saying that we tend to fret about our loss of wealth, not noting time's march of stealth. To return our days will fail, but our wealth is of no avail. Something like that.

Field notes from Conversation with Marvin Schneider

Spoke w/MS. MS listed numerous interesting clocks:

• Silk clock, Park Avenue. Remnant of the silk trade, which was housed in the building the clock adorns. The clock has an Arthurian theme. When it strikes, various things happen—Merlin comes out, Guinevere dances around, someone bangs on an anvil. MS thinks the clock is 1 story up. He's fairly sure one has to look up from street level to see it.

• Williamsburg Savings Bank, downtown Brooklyn. Was in the Guinness Book of World Records as world's tallest 4-sided clock tower.

• St. Theresa's Roman Catholic Church, Rutgers Street, Lower East Side. Oldest working mechanical clock in city. Someone from church winds it.

• Pier A clock at Castle Clinton monument. Four-sided, not working. What makes it interesting is that it's a ship's clock, and it's very unusual to find nautical chimes on land.

• E. Howard, model 70 wall clock outside City Council Chamber on 2nd floor of City Hall. Semipublic; diameter is about equivalent to the height of a small adult.

• Street clocks. About 10 of them left, one at Fifth Avenue and 23rd Street, another (now privately owned and maintained by York College) was moved from a city street near York College in Jamaica, Queens, to a private arcade on campus.

• Trinity Parish, St. Paul's, Fulton Street. Oldest clock in NYC (1798), not working, badly rusted out, neither rehabilitatable nor removable, hidden behind louvers in the clock tower—so it's this great monument that no one knows about; need special appointment to view.

• Trinity Parish, Trinity Church, Wall Street and Broadway. Old (mid-19th-century?) clock with distinctive chimes, and working—overhauled/rehabbed several times.

• Con Edison clock, East 14th Street

• Met Life clock, East 23rd Street and Madison Avenue

Proof that you can drive to Ellis Island

and the parking lot only; we can stay for 15 minutes; and we cannot record for posterity our passage over the bridge.

There is some lesson to be learned in all of this. For $150, two men who live in a pink motor home can, indeed, drive—from New Jersey—to Ellis Island. We arrive surreptitiously, after the island has closed. We sit in the parking lot, near a garbage bin, guarded by two park rangers, for a quarter of an hour, then turn around and go back where we came from.

Nevertheless, we proved that—at least in theory—it is possible to drive (or even to walk) to Ellis Island. It'll cost you, though, and we can't promise you'll get your money's worth. We recommend the more standard approach, via the Statue of Liberty Ferry from Castle Clinton in Battery Park, during regular business hours (9am to 6pm in summer). It's a lot cheaper, and you'll get to go inside and walk the walk the immigrants walked.

Liberty State Park, from which there is a service bridge (with guard) to the island, is worth a visit in its own right, if only for the view of Manhattan from the esplanade. The park, located off exit 14B on the New Jersey Turnpike in Jersey City, New Jersey, is open 6am to 10pm daily. ☎ **201/915-3400** for a machine, **201/915-3401** for a human. Admission is free.

> **Forbes Magazine Galleries.** 62 Fifth Ave., at W. 13th St. (West Village). ☎ **212/206-5548.**

On the surface, a conventional stop, but when you consider Malcolm Forbes's almost insatiable appetite for weird stuff, you start to appreciate the place for what it is: an eclectic melange of strange esoterica. How about 12,000 toy soldiers, 500 toy boats, or 12 priceless Fabergé Easter eggs!

> **Historic Richmond Town.** 441 Clarke Ave., between Richmond and Arthur Kill roads, near the United Hebrew Cemetery (Staten Island). ☎ **718/351-1611.**

Set in 100+ acres of otherwise undeveloped land, this slice of colonial New York consists of 28 buildings, all fully restored to their 17th-, 18th-, and 19th-century splendor. Like Williamsburg, Virginia, the place is staffed by interpreters in period costume. However, the ones we met, although friendly, sounded an awful lot like people you'd meet on-line at the Duane Reade. Supposedly, George Conlon, the tinsmith, does a better job "when he's around."

Monks at the Jacques Marchais Center of Tibetan Art, Staten Island

> **Jacques Marchais Center of Tibetan Art.** 338 Lighthouse Ave., at Windsor Ave. (Staten Island). ☎ **718/987-3500.**

It may seem strange to find a Tibetan center anywhere on Staten Island, much less on a residential street, but there it is: one of the Western Hemisphere's largest collections of Tibetan art. This remote hilltop museum is a perfect stop for Buddhists, faux or otherwise. Commune with devilish entities; meditate in the sweet, peaceful garden; maybe catch a few real live Tibetans dressed in orange robes. Curator/director Barbara Lipton seemed a trifle touchy, but if you'd been hanging around Yama, the god of death, and Maha Kala, the wrathful Chenrezig, as long as she has, you might be a little touchy, too. She's quite knowledgeable, however, if you can bring her out. The museum's founder, Jacques Marchais, was a woman; her real name was Edna Coblentz. Don't miss the Tibetan Harvest Festival every October.

> **Barbara Lipton:** The collection basically was made by Jacques Marchais herself, the founder of the museum. But we add pieces from time to time, by donations or gifts, or occasionally I'll purchase something. But we are a very, very poor institution, and funds are so severely limited. That's why I have to pray every day to White Mahakala—for the museum, not for me. It's not a private collection anymore, it's a public institution, what's called a private, nonprofit institution. We're certainly not the biggest public collection, nor are we the biggest private collection.

> **Jim Monk:** Are there rituals held here?

> **Barbara Lipton:** We have monks who come to chant here several times a year. They answer questions for the public as well. Once in a while, a great while, we'll have a Lama do a special kind of ritual, but that happens very, very rarely. It's not a religious organization, you have to understand. This is a cultural museum. But Tibetan culture is totally intertwined with Buddhism, so you can't ignore one for the other.

> **Jim Monk:** How does it feel to be around all of this powerful art that has such a spiritual quality to it? I mean, it must do something to you.

> **Barbara Lipton:** Well, I hope so.

> *". . . I have to pray every day to White Mahakala—for the museum, not for me."*

> **Lower East Side Tenement Museum.** 90 Orchard St., at Broome St. (Lower East Side). ☎ **212/431-0233.**

A reality check after the likes of the Met and the Frick. This restored and preserved tenement house gives a taste of what life was really like for the thousands of immigrants who came to New York in the late 19th and early 20th centuries. The rent was cheap, but the conditions were abysmal. Most visitors to the museum are descendants of immigrants; some, our guide told us, weep during the tour.

> **New York Transit Museum.** At the corner of Boerum Place and Schermerhorn St. (Brooklyn Heights/Downtown Brooklyn). ☎ **718/243-8601.**

Museums are, by definition, funhouse mirrors of real life, taking the commonplace and making it archetypal, taking the exceptional and making it EXCEPTIONAL— literally putting it on a pedestal. Think of all those Georgian-pillared edifices of culture uptown, all those wide, Romanesque steps leading to the Official Human Story. It's what you expect.

Then you get to the corner of Boerum and Schermerhorn. A couple big, impressive buildings around, but no museum—just a subway stop. Then you look again, realize: That subway stop *is* the museum. You smile. This will be different.

Housed in the decommissioned Court Street station, the Transit Museum contains a collection of subway cars dating back to 1903 and all the turnstiles and "ticket choppers" ever used in the system, plus architectural drawings, historical maps, mosaics, historical films, and more. It's all full of texture, tough as nails, and you can almost feel the ghosts of a billion sweaty straphangers as you sit on the old rattan seats or contemplate the turnstile that drew its power—all 600 volts of it— right from the third rail.

Tip: The museum runs regular free guided tours. Take one, especially if Ken Kasowitz is the tour guide. A genuine transit zealot and real-life historian, Ken's at his best when railing against Robert Moses, Fiorello La Guardia, and other politicians who, under the influence of General Motors, did everything they could to kill public transit in favor of highways.

> **New York Earth Room (a.k.a. Walter De Maria's Earth Room).** 141 Wooster, between Prince and W. Houston (SoHo). ☎ **212/473-8072.** www.diacenter.org/ltproj/er/er.html.

It's dirt—280,000 pounds of it—filling up a well-lit, 3,600 square-foot SoHo loft 22 inches deep and wall to wall. Despite its sterility (not one sprout did we see, though there's plenty of natural light), you've gotta love the idea of a huge, expensive SoHo interior filled up with dirt. And they don't even charge admission. The whole thing must gall the hell out of the real estate lobby.

> **New York Unearthed.** 17 State St., at Bridge St. (Financial District).
☎ **212/748-8628.**

Anticipating a dig, we eagerly descended the stairs of this building, expecting to see archaeologists swarming around in lamp-hats with pick and shovel. Instead we found a clean, well-lit place, very much a museum, with displays of fascinating artifacts dug up during excavations of the city. Inside a sizeable glass cubicle sat the "archaeologist" toiling away at a find. A Fordham grad, he doubled as a cute tour guide, too, revealing that the owners of the building originally tried to cover up the historic artifacts they found when erecting the building. They were called to the mat on it, and had to build this excellent museum as penance. Holy schist!

> **P.S. 1 and the Clocktower Gallery.** P.S. 1: 22–25 Jackson Ave., near the Pulaski Bridge (Long Island City, Queens). ☎ **718/784-2084.** Clocktower: 108 Leonard St., at Broadway (Tribeca). ☎ **212/233-1096.**

These two go together. P.S. 1 is out in the boonies of Long Island City, but it's worth the trip. It's a 19th-century public school (the first in Queens) converted into artists' studios and exhibition space. The Clocktower Gallery is in the tower room of an old office building. Both are run by the Institute for Contemporary Art.

> **Queens Museum of Art.** New York City Building, Flushing Meadows–Corona Park (Queens). ☎ **718/592-5555.**

The highlight here is the world's largest scale model, the 9,335-square-foot Panorama of New York City. This monster (it's got over 800,000 buildings represented) was built for the 1964 World's Fair. In 1994 it was completely renovated and updated. Every single detail is here—including airplanes landing at La Guardia. New York is so vast it is difficult to get a firm handle on its geography. But after visiting the Panorama, one leaves with a deep sense of what it means to live in the greatest city on earth. Added highlight: The museum is located in Flushing Meadows, which features trippy abandoned relics from the 1964 World's Fair.

> **Sideshows by the Seashore and the Coney Island Museum.** 1208 Surf Ave., at W. 12th St. (Coney Island, Brooklyn). ☎ **718/372-5159.**
www.coneyislandusa.com. Call for hours and schedule.

It might be a fact that more cherries have been popped per capita on the Coney Island Boardwalk than any other boardwalk in the world. At least that's a theory from a little research and a lot of hearsay. Today the mobs are weathering the heat, clutching Nathan's hot dogs, cotton candy, and giant pretzel sticks. They stroll back and forth amid the hawkers, the greasy sleazy drifters, old Russians, sun worshippers, and old New Yorkers dragging their next of kin for a nostalgic walk at the beach.

Kiva the Fire-Eater, Sideshows by the Seashore, Coney Island

Scores of male breeders-in-training out on a date walk the same walk as four generations before, groping their sweeties under the defunct roller coaster tracks that climb to the sky. Off in the distance the fatal parachute drop, long since closed, stands like a forlorn insect walking towards the sea.

The boardwalk seems all new and improved. Gone are the old winos and tattooed gangs, and in their place are the kinder, gentler, Disneyfied versions of a carnival crowd. Circus colors offset the haze, but there's still enough funk to set the stage for occasional freaks.

Dick Zigun's Sideshows by the Seashore is full of them. Here the freaks are urban renegades, coming from the pierced, tattooed, hard-rock crowd. In front of the sideshow, the Human Blockhead barks in a twangy nasal voice at the meandering crowd, advertising the freaks inside—people like Todd Robbins, the Glass-Eater. Zigun: "Todd is an ordinary-looking Joe, but he's got a weird diet. We call him the Glassy Gourmet. . . . He chows down on broken bottles and light bulbs, and it will send chills up and down your spine when you hear him chew up that glass in his mouth."

Then there's Kiva, the Fire-Eater. Zigun: "This one here, our fire-eater, [is] the combustible Miss Kiva. She bathes that beautiful body of hers in flames and eats flaming torches like you'd eat an ice cream cone. . . . They call her the Human Volcano."

Zigun is also responsible for the annual Mermaid Parade. See the "Calendar" section for the parade and an interview with Zigun later in this section for more info.

› The Statue of Liberty Museum. Liberty Island. ☎ 212/363-3200.

We went to the Statue of Liberty, but, for a number of reasons, all having to do with Michael, we did not go up in it.

1. Michael did not want to go if Jim went.
2. Michael felt the Statue of Liberty was sacred ground, and it was sacrilegious to tread on it.
3. Michael is afraid of heights.
4. "The Statue of Liberty is not my color. I do not do well in green."

Take the **Statue of Liberty Ferry** (it combines trips to both Liberty and Ellis islands) from Castle Clinton in Battery Park. Hours and departure times vary seasonally; call for current schedule (☎ **212/269-5755**). Round-trip fare: adults $7, seniors $5, children $3. Once you are out there, the Lady herself costs nothing and is open 9am to 6pm daily in the summer (9am to 5pm during off-season). Call to confirm schedule.

Give me your tired, your poor, your Monked

An Interview with

Dick Zigun

of Sideshows by the Seashore

The bearded, low-key Dick Zigun came to New York from the Yale School of Drama, where he had studied to be a playwright, and set about almost single-handedly reviving and preserving the culture of the sideshow. He launched the annual Mermaid Parade (see the "Calendar" section), and 2 years later, with funding from arts organizations, opened Sideshows by the Seashore, where, for more than a decade, performers like the Illustrated Man and Demonica, the snake charmer and part-time Satanist, have been entertaining audiences with 12 shows a day.

In addition to operating the museum and sponsoring the Mermaid Parade (and Coney Island's Tattoo Festival), Sideshows by the Seashore gets credit for a singular—though perhaps dubious—achievement: It has encouraged a young generation of performers to do twisted tricks like swallow fire, eat light bulbs, electrocute people, or, as the case may be, get electrocuted themselves. As Zigun explained to us, "We've got a new generation of circus idiots for the 21st century."

We saw the show. We even volunteered to be guinea pigs for the electrocution episode, during which Jim was chosen to sit in the electric chair and get fried—by Michael. ("He's been wanting to do this for years," Jim said.) Our visit came at a precarious moment in the sideshow's history: The organization's funding had been cut, it had run into trouble paying rent, and ever-voracious McDonald's was eyeing the property. The sideshow, the last of its kind in the country, was in court, fighting to hold on to its lease. In the end, Zigun and his crew lost, but they managed to secure a new space, from which they continue, in Zigun's words, "to defend the honor of American popular culture."

Michael Monk: Okay, we've just seen the fire woman, the elastic woman, the blockhead, the contortionist—what do you do?

Dick Zigun: I write the checks, feed the dog, clean the toilets and try and keep this place going. Primarily, my big job is to provide intellectual justification.

Jim Monk: And how long have you been doing this?

Dick Zigun: Fifteen years now.

Jim Monk: Right here? Was there a sideshow here before you?

Dick Zigun: No. I showed up in the neighborhood 15 years ago. We got some grant money, and we've been full-time here in the building for 11 years.

Jim Monk: But you created the whole thing. There was nothing here before you.

Dick Zigun: Right.

Jim Monk: There had to be some sideshow at Coney Island, right?

Dick Zigun: Last sideshow before us in Coney Island ended late '60s, early '70s.

"Primarily, my big job is to provide intellectual justification."

Jim Monk: What invigorated your interest in carnival culture, freak-show culture?

Dick Zigun: I grew up in P. T. Barnum's hometown, Bridgeport, Connecticut, so I was obsessed by it when I was a little boy from the time I was midget size.

Jim Monk: Seriously?

Dick Zigun: Seriously.

Jim Monk: In what kind of way? Did you collect things related to the circus, or what?

Dick Zigun: When I was 8 years old I was going to sideshows. And P. T. Barnum ended up mayor of Bridgeport. He was the patron saint of Bridgeport, so it's the one place in America where it's patriotic to believe in elephants and freaks. So I was obsessed with all of that. I actually have an academic background in theater. As a playwright, I have an MFA from the Yale school of drama, and I was writing plays about vaudeville, about amusement parks, about Barnum, about ventriloquists, and when I moved to New York, like most thespians do, to do theater, instead of aspiring to Broadway, I thought Coney Island was some kind of incredible staging ground.

Michael Monk: When you took over here, what was going on?

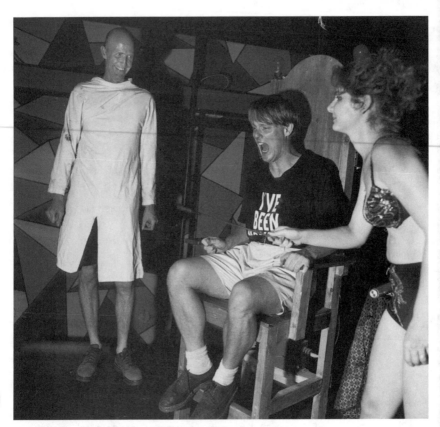

Michael Monk gets his revenge at Sideshows by the Seashore

Dick Zigun: This was a big empty barn of a building. It was a penny arcade that had been full of pinball and video machines, so we just had some very clever designers and architects renovate the place to look like it's been here since the 1930s, but all the work was actually done recently.

Michael Monk: Did you ever bring back some of the older freaks that used to do carnival sideshows?

Dick Zigun: Well, when we started in '85, the first time we did the sideshow 11 years ago was with veteran performers in their 60s, in their 80s. We opened just as the largest sideshow traveling on the road, the James E. Straight carnival, shut down for economic reasons, so all the performers from the James E. Straight show came to work for us and finished their careers here, and then younger people started showing up and learned the old-fashioned way—by oral tradition, how the acts passed down almost as folk art. And now we've got a new generation of circus idiots for the 21st century working.

Jim Monk: Now, you're saying this is the only sideshow in the United States left?

Dick Zigun: It's the only—well, the traditional format of a sideshow is a 10-in-1. Ten live acts in one show. We're the only people who still do that. You go to a carnival, you see a tent, you see the sideshow banners. You think it's a sideshow. You pay your money, you go inside, it's all photographs, wax dummies. Maybe there's one bored person doing something inside. You still have the grind shows or what they call the single lows. Jamaica Joe or somebody like that. You pay a dollar, you go in, and you see one person. But a traditional sideshow is 10 live acts, and nobody else in the country still does it but us.

As freaky as it all seems, this is a nonprofit community arts center. We're an arts group. Like every other arts group in the country, we lost our NEA funding, we lost our state funding. All the grant money disappeared. We still have our city grant. It's cut in half. Instead of shutting down, we tightened the belt, trimmed payroll, cut programs. We're making it again, but we have old debts that we're paying off. We're paying off a lot of the money we owe. We will survive. We're not going bankrupt.

Jim Monk: You still love it? You're not burned out on doing this freak show thing?

Dick Zigun: Not with a front yard like this [he indicates the beach and boardwalk. Not with the fun we have, no.

Jim Monk: Can you describe some of the performers that have performed here that are really dear to your heart and what their act is all about.

Dick Zigun: Melvin Burkhardt, who's still alive. He lives in Florida, he's in his 80s. The original anatomical wonder, or anatomical blunder. He is the man who did the blockhead here, worked as a magician. We've shamelessly ripped off all of his dialogue. Melvin is wonderful. Otis Jordan worked for us as the human cigarette factory. Otis passed away 4 years ago. He worked in carnivals all his life. Until he worked for us he was exploited a bit in the sideshow business. They used to call him the frog boy. He wasn't froglike, he wasn't a boy. He was a wonderful man. He was handicapped. Using nothing but his tongue and his mouth, he would roll and light a cigarette and perform cigarette tricks.

Jim Monk: Wow.

Dick Zigun: And Otis was wonderful, and it was an honor to have him finish his career here and extend a certain amount of dignity to him that was an opportunity he did not have most of his life.

Jim Monk: That is really great.

Michael Monk: So, do you think there's any tricks that we should learn for the road?

Dick Zigun: Regurgitation. Learn how to swallow cockroaches, coins, rats, bring them up in whatever order the crowd wants. You know, you can travel all over America, go to bars, and drink for free. Regurgitate.

Michael Monk: Thank you for the tip.

Music

When we visit New York, we rarely listen to music. The sounds coming off the streets are so captivating, we rarely feel the need. But there inevitably comes a time when one wants the New York aural landscape articulated a bit more precisely, a bit more profoundly, a bit more, shall we say, brazenly. The following clubs, radio stations, and stores will completely meet your need for the New York sound.

Radio

Radio around these parts just doesn't live up to the city's cultural richness. The reasons are largely economic. Like property in Midtown, bandwidth is lucrative real estate; with financial stakes being what they are, few stations are willing to take risks. The city's top-heavy topography makes matters even worse: reception of lower-wattage stations is difficult and, even in the best circumstances, can vary wildly (sometimes within the same building). Nevertheless, there are a few good broadcasters out there.

› **88.3 FM WBGO.** www.wbgo.org.

One of the nation's few remaining all-jazz stations (the station's collection is among the largest in the world). The highlight is "Birdologist" Phil Schapp—he can tell you just about everything you'd ever want to know about Charlie Parker—like what, for instance, the Bird had for breakfast before a recording session: "Bird was late for this particular session, trying to score, but the cut sure swings once he showed up."

The Love Doctor

Overheard while checking out Greek Restaurants in Astoria on a rental car radio: "Alright, we want the men out there to call now. Only men. No women. Unless you're walking on Dykman Street."

    The Love Doctor is asking listeners what they physically like in a woman. After debating the merits of busts and butts, Dr. Love chimes in in a thick Caribbean accent, "If she does not have a nice bus [bus = butt], she not get even one penny from the Love Doctor." Do NOT miss the Love Doctor, and his sidekick "intern," Prince Kalunda. (Sundays 6–8pm, WPAT Radio, 930 on your AM dial. ☎ 718/778-7846.)

> **88.7 FM Steal This Radio (Friday nights).**

Broadcasting from "an undisclosed location on the Lower East Side," Steal This Radio carries on a proud Yippie tradition, featuring whoever stops by from the neighborhood. The emphasis is on community news, poetry, and live music. Too bad the FCC doesn't like this sort of thing.

> **89.1 FM WNYU.** Radio station of New York University. www.rockonline.com/wnyu.

Slicker than your average college station, but it still manages to play a broader range of new music than the city's commercial options. Some highlights: *The New Afternoon Show* (4pm), an essential promo stop for bands on the college circuit; and *Club 89* (10:30pm), dance music broadcast live from nightclubs. Down time (which is anything *not* between 4pm and 1am Monday through Friday) is leased to WFDU, a much lower-wattage college station.

> **91.1 FM WFMU.** P.O. Box 1568, Montclair, NJ 07042. ☎ **201/678-8264.** www.wfmu.org. E-mail: wfmu@wfmu.org.

Once the best college station in the region, its playlist continues to be fearlessly diverse and noncommercial (a typical lineup might include the Ramones, the Residents, Steve Reich, and Sonny Rollins). It's also known for being just about impossible to find on the dial. We wonder how many loyal fans have plunged to their deaths trying to jury-rig an antenna.

Some highlights from the program guide: *The Floating Pad,* "A spicy paella of vinyl finds from moldy basements, dusty attics, and greasy garages"; *Give the Drummer Some,* "The finest in Micronesian doo-wop, Appalachian mambo, Turkish mariachi, tuba choirs of Mozambique, Portuguese juju, pigmy yodeling from Baltimore, Inuit marching bands, Filipino free jazz, and throat singing of the Lower East Side"; and *Radio Thrift Shop,* "Discarded musical treasures." (Most of the shows change their broadcast times every few months, so check the Web site or program guide to track them down.) The station's 'zine, *Lowest Common Denominator,* and its Web site aren't half bad, either.

> **99.5 FM WBAI.** www.wbai.org.

The city's last remaining community radio station. An institution—and a beloved one, at that—it's been around for more than 30 years and is entirely listener supported (no commercials). Programming highlights include *Shocking Blue* (Wednesdays–Fridays

Music Trivia

Barry Manilow grew up in Williamsburg, Brooklyn.

10am–noon, great music DJed by a sexy-voiced lesbian) and *Mass Backwards* (Mondays 4am, a weekly "word of Satan" drama). But our favorite is Emmanuel Goldstein's *Off the Hook* (Tuesdays 8pm–9pm). The legendary hacker, phone freak, and technopunk (he's the editor of *2600: The Hacker Quarterly*) takes to the air to answer tough questions about the information superhighway. He's often assisted by the infamous Phiber Optik. The show has a cult following of geeks, freaks, and disgruntled employees.

› 93.0 AM WPAT.

Listen for "legendary" Gil Bailey afternoons and evenings on "Caribbean Blend." As his voice dances over soca and calypso, calls pour in from Brooklyn, the Bronx, Queens, and Jersey to "represent your island"—usually Barbados, Dominica, Jamaica, and Belize (which, OK, isn't an island, but who cares)—with greetings to friends and family. This is real community radio, with singing ads for immigration lawyer David Scheinfeld, tickets to Beenie Man, and information on how to ship that piano to Guyana. It's happy music, too. Listen for Indian music from Trinidad, a unique style combining the syrupy, high-pitched excesses of the mother country with the "jump jump, everybody jump jump jump" soca beat. The late, late night reggae shows are marvelously incomprehensible to the outsider, a reminder that Planet Brooklyn is the real capital of the West Indies. Seen.

› 97.1 FM "Hot-97."

Love it or hate it, this is the New York shit, the soundtrack to urban life. "Representing ALL the flavors of Hip-Hop," Hot-97 is popular music in the best sense. "I'd like to make a shout out to my crew Mr. Freeze, Pee Wee, Snuggles, and D up in the Boogie Down and, uh, to my Moms." For the great unwired, this is interactive media. Hot-97 plays a freely calculated mix of hard beats, funk, disco, R&B, go-go, whatever. They have good dance mix, reggae, dance hall, and oldies shows too, playing what the listeners request. It's hard to believe that hip-hop's been around for almost 20 years. With the first generation now hitting middle age, Hot-97 brings a multi-layered mix of old-school and the latest rhymes.

Morning show hosts Dr. Dre and Ed Lover's ugly mugs are familiar to all subway riders. On good days, they can be very funny in between the traffic reports; on the other days, they're just loud.

Hot 97's incredible success may be its own weakness. When these well-paid DJs use street slang as lead-ins for corporate commercials, what exactly is "keeping it real"? Still, Hot-97 is like classic radio from an earlier time: kids calling in to rap or sing along to their favorite songs, notices of upcoming dance contests and concerts, etc. Of course, the lyrics do present a problem with the FCC. Fortunately, Hot-97

Road Mix — A Bunch of Songs by, for, and/or about New Yorkers

"Asshole," by Local Oddness

"Bell Bottoms," by John Spencer's Blues Explosion

"The Blank Generation," by Richard Hell and the Voidoids

"The Bottle," by Gil Scott Heron

"Bronx Cheer," by Mercury Rev

"Brooklyn Blues," by Barry Manilow

"Brooklyn Zoo," by Ol' Dirty Bastard

"Chelsea Girls," by Nico

"Chelsea Morning," by Joni Mitchell (Chelsea Clinton was named after the song)

"Chinatown," by Bloody Minded (the best there is for unlistenable electronic squealing)

"Crack City," by Space Hog

"Fairy Tale in New York," by the Pogues

"First We Take Manhattan," by Leonard Cohen

"Fuck Compton," by Tim Dog

"Harlem River Drive Theme," by Harlem River Drive

"I'm Waiting for My Man," by Lou Reed and the Velvet Underground

"Italian in New York," by Chicago

"Kool Thing," by Sonic Youth (with Chuck D.)

"Little Johnny Jewel," by Television (the first punk single, from 1976)

"A Love Supreme," by John Coltrane

"Machine Gun," by Jimi Hendrix and the Band of Gypsies

"Manhattan," by Richard Rodgers and Larry Hart

"Max's Kansas City," by Wayne County

"New Jack Swing," Wreckx-n-Affect

"New York Fever," by the Toasters

"New York Is Now," by Eddie Ornette

"New York, New York," by Nina Hagen

"New York," by the Sex Pistols

"On the Corner," by Miles Davis

"On the Subway," by The Last Poets

"Pacifics," by Digable Planets

"Pennsylvania 6500," by Glenn Miller

"People Who Died," by the Jim Carroll Band

"Rapper's Delight," by the Sugarhill Gang (widely considered the first true rap recording)

"Rapture," by Blondie (includes the best-ever white-girl rap about Fab Five Freddy)

"Rockaway Beach," by the Ramones

"Shattered," by the Rolling Stones

"Staten Island Hornpipe," by Tony Elmer

"Straight from tha' Bronx," by D-Nice

"Subterranean Homesick Blues," by Bob Dylan

"Subway Train," by the New York Dolls

"Supermodel," by RuPaul

"Uptown Girl," by Billy Joel

"Wu Tang Clan Bring Da Ruckus," by Wu Tang Clan

has some of the city's best DJs on staff to unobtrusively put a beat, scratch, or "yeah" over the offending expletives.

> **92.3 K-Rock.** The Howard Stern Show.

To better understand the dynamics of contemporary American apartheid, alternate between Hot-97 and K-Rock in the mornings, where the Howard Stern Show holds court as about the most symbolic representation we've got of suburban Long Island white people's uneasy relationship with the great non-white metropolis to the west. Though the show is national, Howard, unfortunately, comes from here.

Mr. Stern has a symbiotic relationship with his vast and troubled following. The more self-deprecating and virulent he gets, the more they love him. His fans are such fucking retards I'm embarrassed to say I kinda like him. He's a dickhead and a racist to be sure (though he's got his own human shield, cohost and official black person Robin Quivers—the same way Hot-97's Dr. Dre and Ed Lover have a blond white woman as cohost), but he has his moments of twisted brilliance. He understands radio and what the market will bear. If he really is today's Lenny Bruce—and I hope he's not—it's only a sign of the times.

Stores

> **Downtown Music Gallery.** 211 E. 5th St., just east of Third Ave. ☎ **212/473-0043.** Fax 212/533-5059. E-mail: dmg@panix.com.

This tiny little basement place is to record stores what the Knitting Factory is to performance venues, stocking disks and vinyl from the whole downtown improv/experimental/jazz/whatzit scene. Don't go if you're looking for pop; do go if you want the complete works of John Zorn, Christian Marclay, Thomas Chapin, William Hooker, Elliott Sharp, and the like. Bruce Gallanter, store owner and all-around passionate über-booster of the so-called "downtown" scene, programs in-store concerts on Sunday nights and sends out an electronic weekly newsletter (drop an e-mail to get on the list).

> **Footlight Records.** 113 E. 12th St., between Third and Fourth aves. (East Village). ☎ **212/533-1572.** www.footlight.com.

Footlight's claim to fame is soundtracks and original cast recordings—4,000 of them, the largest stock in the country.

> **Moon Ska.** 84 E. 10th St., between Third and Fourth aves. (East Village). ☎ **212/673-5538.**

Further proof that when it comes to subspecialties of subspecialties, New York has it covered. This store is devoted exclusively to ska. That would be specialty enough for just about any other city in the country, but Moon Ska goes even further, specializing in small-label ska. So no 2Tone, the major marketers of the ska sound, whose acts have included Madness, the Selector, and the Specials. Amazing.

> **Other Music.** 15 E. 4th St., between Broadway and Lafayette (West Village). ☎ **212/477-8150.**

Carries everything that nearby Tower does not, including CD reissues of '60s and '70s Kraut rock, plus French pop and Japanese avant-garde. The boys who run this place make their selections by "a gut thing." Don't come looking for Graham Parker or Southside Johnny.

> **St. Marks and Vicinity.**

There's nothing at all flashy, or even inviting, about the array of record shops on this street, but they're all better than they look. It's difficult for us to say this, but start with **Mondo Kim's Video & Music** (6 St. Marks, ☎ **212/598-9985**), the new alternative superstore. Not only does the place consistently pay more for your used CDs, the staff just knows its stuff. We also recommend **Joe's Compact Disc Corp.** (11 St. Marks, ☎ **212/ 673-4606**), **Venus Records** (13 St. Marks, ☎ **212/598-4459**), and, more

Music Trivia

The "sound" part of LaMonte Young and Marian Zazeela's Dream House Sound of Light Environment (see "Museums, Galleries and Landmarks") is titled "The Base 9:7.4 Symmetry in Prime Time When Centered above and below The Lowest Term Primes in The Range 288 to 224 with The Addition of 279 and 261 in Which The Half of The Symmetric Division Mapped above and Including 288 Consists of The Powers of 2 Multiplied by The Primes within The Ranges of 144 to 128, 72 to 64 and 36 to 32 Which Are Symmetrical to Those Primes in Lowest Terms in The Half of The Symmetric Division Mapped below and Including 224 within The Ranges 126 to 112, 63 to 56 and 31.5 to 28 with The Addition of 119." No foolin'.

tentatively, **Sounds** (20 St. Marks, ☎ **212/677-2727**) and **Norman's Sound & Vision** (around the corner at 67 Cooper Sq., ☎ **212/473-6599**). Norman's also buys used CD-ROMs and laser discs at its new store on St. Marks. For vinyl we refer you to **Finyl Vinyl** (204 "Positively" E. 6th St., ☎ **212/533-8007**), whose motto is "eat, sleep, just records," and the legendary **Bleecker Bob's** (in the West Village at 118 W. 3rd St., between Sixth Avenue and MacDougal Street, ☎ **212/475-9677**), where the perfectionist "Bob" will literally find any record you want, which is why people like Martin Scorsese turn to him for hard-to-find music.

Performance Venues

› **ABC No Rio.** 156 Rivington St., at Suffolk St. (Lower East Side). ☎ **212/254-3697.**
CB's (see below) is mainstream compared to this legendary anarchist/punk/squatter oasis. Poetry, too.

› **CBGB & OMFUG.** 315 Bowery, at Bleecker St. (East Village). ☎ **212/533-0456.**
www.cbgb.com.

CBGB's has been a fixture for so long scarcely anyone knows what its name stands for. "Country, Bluegrass, and Blues" is what it stands for. Actually, the full name is CBGB & OMFUG. OMFUG stands for "Other Music for Uplifting Gourmandisers," which might be an allusion to the space's eclectic programming. The cradle of punk, this dump has launched everyone from the Ramones to Blondie to the Talking Heads. But there's always been one important condition: Acts must perform original material. It's been a creative challenge for owner Hilly Kristal, but he's stuck to his guns. (See interview with Kristal later in this section.)

› **Continental.** 25 Third Ave., at St. Mark's Place (East Village). ☎ **212/529-6924.**
www.nytrash.com/continental.

This raucous hole-in-the-wall has seen some very rocking entertainment over the years, including the legendary New York Dolls guitarist Johnny Thunders, who played here before he OD-ed. If you're in the neighborhood, it's always worth a peek before you head home for the night. And right next to a new McDonald's!

› **Knitting Factory.** 74 Leonard St., between Broadway and Church St. (Tribeca).
☎ **212/219-3055.** www.knittingfactory.com.

At the intersection of jazz, rock, folk, and performance art, the Knitting Factory acts as a kind of conduit, feeding out-of-the-mainstream artists to the public. And the strategy seems to have paid off. A couple of years back, the club moved from its beloved space on East Houston to newer, larger, many-storied digs in Tribeca.

> **Mercury Lounge.** 217 E. Houston St., at Essex St. (Lower East Side).
☎ **212/260-4700.**

There's nothing spectacular about the room, although devotees claim the sound system and sight lines are great. Fairly interesting booking policy, plus special events like the celebration of the Bureau of Alcohol, Tobacco, and Firearms (all performances had to celebrate one of the three). For us, though, the place lacks character.

> **The Spiral.** 244 E. Houston St., at Avenue B (Lower East Side). ☎ **212/353-1740.**

The bottom of the venue barrel. Many New Jersey bands start here. The Spiral's policy is first come, first serve; it'll sign anyone and everyone, without even a listen. Which means those in attendance are usually friends of the band.

> **Squeezebox.** Held on Fri at Don Hill's, 511 Greenwich St., at Vandam St. (SoHo).
☎ **212/219-2850.**

The hottest glam-rock, AC/DC, punk drag scene in town—not that there's a lot of competition for the honor. The night we were there we ran into both John Waters and Drew Barrymore.

Music on the streets: E-Man in Midtown

Hilly Kristal

Papa of Punk Rock

Hilly Kristal, founder and owner of the legendary CBGBs, is the calm antidote to the music and scene he shepherds, the still center of the raging punk and alternative storm. And though a man trained in classical music and jazz, and looking ever so much the professor of both, he has come to appreciate the subtle and rather not-so-subtle nuances of rock and roll.

Hilly Kristal: I opened it to do country, bluegrass, and blues. That's what I thought would be the pop music of the country.

Jim Monk: Who was the first band that ever played here? Rock band?

Hilly Kristal: Rock band I don't know. We had a band called Squeeze, Tight Squeeze. A couple of the members are still around. The first, I guess you would say new wave of music, I guess—they weren't really punk but, you know, that kind of band—was Television.

Jim Monk: So when did they first perform here?

Hilly Kristal: I think it was about April of '74.

Jim Monk: So Television was April of '74. Interesting.

Hilly Kristal: And they were terrible.

Jim Monk: Tom Verlaine would love to hear that.

Hilly Kristal: Well, they were then.

Jim Monk: He got better.

Hilly Kristal: He sure did. And then I wouldn't let them play anymore—and their manager persuaded me to let them play—because nobody came and they were awful. So he said, "I have this band from Queens, and they have a following." So the next week we had Television and this other band from Queens, which was the Ramones.

Jim Monk: Oh, my God! This is great.

Hilly Kristal: But they were worse.

Jim Monk: They hadn't perfected that inimitable Ramone style yet, huh?

Hilly Kristal: No. You know, Dee Dee couldn't play at all. He made sounds.

Jim Monk: Joey couldn't sing? Well, Joey never could sing, but I mean in a certain way he could.

"You know what's enjoyable? If you can help a band get signed. . . . The joy is discovery, finding something new and trying to help."

Hilly Kristal: But they were pretty sloppy. And they got better. You know, and then we had the Stilettos, who were very good. They were kind of campy. That's where Debbie Harry and Chris Stein and all those people—they were kind of fun. Well, the scene became profitable in '77. The scene started back in '75, '74. Actually, it started after Patti Smith. She played here 7 weeks in a row, and she got signed out of here. Clive Davis came down. But then I had a festival. The top 40 unrecorded New York rock bands. And people took out big ads in the *Voice* and the *SoHo News*. I mean, huge ads. Nobody realized there were all these bands. They'd never heard of them. There were certain times, certain bands, certain performances, I think, that were just special. I think the last time the Police came in they were just great. Patti Smith almost always was great. The Talking Heads in the beginning I loved a lot. The Stilettos were fun, and then when they became Blondie after a while, it was nice, nice to hear. You know, through the years there was—John Cale did some great performances here. One time they wouldn't let him off, and I think we ended up closing the doors, and he played until about 5, 5:30 in the morning. He just played and played and played. Nico was a little interesting once in a while. AC/DC was undoubtedly the loudest band we ever had here.

Jim Monk: How's the neighborhood changed in the last 20 years?

"There are so many awful stories, and I hear a lot of them—most of them."

Hilly Kristal: They're real people. They're not derelicts.

Jim Monk: It was derelicts in '73?

Hilly Kristal: Oh, yeah. '74, '75, '80, '85. Then you had a big epidemic of crackheads here a few years ago. It was awful. Absolutely awful.

Jim Monk: They were all over the place.

Hilly Kristal: All over the place. They used to hang out. We had a flop house upstairs. Four or five hundred people just out of jail or out of—I used to spend more time taking knives away from derelicts and throwing people out.

Jim Monk: Has that calmed down now, the crack scene?

Hilly Kristal: Oh, yeah. Well, now it's worse. Now it's heroin and crack. Sid Vicious was a problem here for a while. He used to hang out, tried to hang out, and I had to literally throw him out.

Jim Monk: You had to throw him out a lot.

Hilly Kristal: A couple of times, yeah. He threw a beer mug at Cheetah Chrome. Hit him. He was wild. He hated people. He disliked everybody.

Jim Monk: Did the Pistols play here ever?

Hilly Kristal: No.

Jim Monk: They never did? He did, though.

Hilly Kristal: No. He said he did. Actually, there's a record out that he supposedly did here, but he never did. It's a lie. Johnny Lydon, when they broke up, he sat right at the bar for 2 weeks, he and Joe Stevens of NMA—just sat there night after night, sulking. You know, there are so many awful stories, and I hear a lot of them—most of them. You know, I'm right here, street level. They can come right in the door and talk. I mean, people die of drug overdoses, people—all kinds of things happen. So I feel the frustration, I feel their frustration, and that's pretty unpleasant.

Some bands have disappointed Hilly over the years. The Ramones didn't show up for the 20 year reunion but in 1995 asked Hilly if they could book the club for the final two dates of their upcoming farewell tour.

Hilly Kristal: They said I could keep the bar and they would keep the door. I said, "forget it." Are you kidding. These guys are millionaires and they're worried about $400 or $500 from the door? I told them no. Now Patti Smith has always been good. She always came back after she got big. She came around recently and gave me a big hug. That's the first hug she ever gave me in her life. She didn't come around for years. I just learned recently that was because he [her deceased husband, Fred "Sonic" Smith] kept her on a tight leash. He wouldn't let her see anybody. I always thought he was clean, but I guess he was a serious drinker. Used to drink a case a day. And wouldn't let her out. Only recently she reconnected with Lenny Kaye.

I've always liked Sonic Youth. They've never been really big. But they've stuck together. They're wonderful people.

Patti Smith performing at CB's, late '70s

Neighborhoods and Streets

New York no longer has neighborhoods; it has real estate designations. That's because, as any New York artist knows, it's property value—not community—that determines "character" in the city.

The primacy of real estate over people is a phenomenon that has slowly crept up on New York. For years, most New Yorkers didn't care what realtors did with Midtown or Battery Park City. Nobody lived there. But in the last decade, aided and abetted by Mayors Dinkins and Giuliani, traditional development restrictions have been lifted, and with that change has come not only chain stores and mini-malls, but restaurants, boutiques, and other high-ticket specialty stores catering to the moneyed class. What we see as a result is the death of diversity, if not the obliteration of entire neighborhoods. Jeremy Rifkin would have a heyday with this development—an entire city built around consumption, a community of consumers.

The sad part of this trend is that there really is no one part of the city that feels like "the place to be." The whole concept of "places to be" seems to have died forever with the '80s. In its place, one finds in New York several decent compromises, but no place that pulls you in and says "this is home; this is my beloved 'hood."

We have listed various sections of the city, some authentic neighborhoods, some real estate fictions. All of them speak to the radically changing "character" of the New York melting pot.

See the Manhattan Neighborhoods map in the "Monk Maps" section for many of these locations.

> **Arthur Avenue.** Arthur Ave. between Crescent Ave. and E. Fordham Rd. (Bronx).

Mott Street of the Bronx. Former home to your host, the late movie mogul cum crane operator, Joseph Denti. Check out Santobello's Social Club, a friendly place with all manner of listening devices, and Amici's Restaurant, where struggling actor Joe Pesci served as maitre d' during the 1970s (Pesci also lived in an apartment upstairs). (See Amici's under "Food." See also Belmont neighborhood.)

> **Astoria.** Area around Jackson and Astoria Blvd. (Queens).

This is New York's Greek community in name only. Some restaurants and a few cafes remain, but most of the locals have headed out to the burbs or to better parts of the city. Akin to Little Italy, except, instead of Asians, the Greek community is

Lower Manhattan Island, with Battery Park in left foreground

surrounded by a sea of Hispania. The epicenter of what remains can be found at the Omonia Cafe on weekends. (See listing under "Cafes.")

> Atlantic Avenue. Lower Atlantic Ave. (Cobble Hill, Brooklyn).

There are some truly outstanding businesses in Brooklyn's Middle Eastern mecca: nondescript restaurants, with a menu scribbled on some butcher paper that only Arabic-speakers understand; markets with dozens of varieties of olive oil and chick peas. All at ridiculously low prices.

> Battery Park City. Area around West End Hwy., near the World Trade Center (Financial District/Downtown Manhattan).

An artificially created neighborhood for Wall Street types who want to live in the city but not experience what the city is really about. For that very reason, this Financial District residential 'hood is perhaps the most un–New York part of the city—safe, suburban, and very borrrring. It is where the ultra-rich yuppies hang out before they buy their cottage in Westchester County. One upside is the Promenade—infested with power joggers though it is, it is well-maintained and offers excellent views of the Colgate sign in New Jersey across the way.

> Bedford-Stuyvesant. Area around Lafayette and Marcy aves. (Brooklyn).

The second largest community of African-Americans in the country (next to Chicago's South Side) is known as a crime-ridden hell, though it is actually far more economically and culturally rich than it is given credit for. Check out the

Caribbean District along Flatbush. If you tune into the right local radio station as you cruise along, you can actually mind-meld with the happy jump'n vibe of the locals. And I don't mean that in some stereotypical way, either! (See 93.0 AM WPAT under "Radio.")

› Beekman Place. E. 49th to E. 51st sts. at First Ave. (Midtown Manhattan).

Nestled into a larger neighborhood known as Turtle Bay, filled with consulates for countries like Luxembourg and Tunisia, this UN-adjacent little block is a tender slice of old refined upper-crust New York overlooking the grimy, less-than-refined East River. The park down below is a bit noisy due to its proximity to the FDR, but the walkway overhead is a real find—you can watch the speeding traffic as it zooms by below.

› Belmont. Area around Southern Blvd. at E. Fordham Rd. (Bronx).

The poor man's Little Italy. Basically an Italian shopping mecca, though most of the Italian families have long since moved out. But refreshing for the lack of tourists that normally descend on such spots (that's why we like the Bronx—it weeds out all but the diehards). There's some peculiar charms that set it apart—a place where you can buy live chickens and geese; a meat store with lambs hanging in the window, fur and all (Q: "Why do you leave the fur on?" A: "So people know we sell lamb"); and Italian restaurants where Mafia guidos have hung out for years. The soccer clubs that line the area have throngs of Italian and now Albanian men who like to hang out and shoot the shineola. Some of them truly are interested in soccer, but you suspect something more sinister also goes down. No wonder the Belmont area is preferred by Scorsese for genuine Mob scenes.

Other traditional Italian neighborhoods to check out: Bayside (near the Verrazanno's Bridge) and Bensonhurst (though, sadly, not if you're black). See also Arthur Avenue.

› Bensonhurst. Area around upper Bay Ridge Parkway (Brooklyn).

African-American Yusef Hawkins came into the neighborhood in 1989 to buy a bike. He didn't leave alive. This should tell you a lot about the character of this Italian-American stronghold.

› Boat Basin. 79th St., beside Riverside Park (Upper West Side, Manhattan).

People live here in their boats. Neat, huh? The northernmost pier was open to the public on weekends when we typed this, though it was "on a trial basis." If the public passes the trial, take a walk out—it's a 100-meter vacation from the city.

> **Borough Park.** Area around mid–New Utrecht Ave. (Brooklyn).

Fundamentalist Jewish community. You can buy the *New York Post* and several different publications of the Jewish press, but no *New York Times*.

> **Brighton Beach.** Area around Brighton Beach Ave. (Brooklyn).

Non-Russian New Yorkers rave about Brighton Beach. They love its "authenticity"—the Russian restaurants with the awful pickled food; the cheesy nightclubs (try Tonsost; it's run by the Russian Mob) with performers singing Bee Gees covers; the elderly Russian immigrants kibitzing on benches, going on about the "Old Country"; the omnipresent air of vodka. But talk to an intelligent Russian émigré who's been here a few years, and he or she doesn't want to come within a hundred kilometers of this neighborhood. To them the residents of Brighton Beach are lost in some Odessa time warp, completely out of touch with the rest of New York and completely uninterested in the cultural riches found here. Because of the determined insularity of the natives, Brighton Beach, like many other ethnic areas of the city, is more Russian than Russia actually is today.

> **Brooklyn Heights.** Area around lower Henry St., just southwest of the base of the Brooklyn Bridge (Brooklyn).

This is the moneyed section of Brooklyn, though it has a rather schizophrenic character. On the one hand, some truly rich and renowned do live here—Norman Mailer for one. But the area near the Promenade is heavily populated by the 7th Day Adventists (the Watchtower people, who you see peddling their Christian propaganda at train stops all over the borough; see the Watchtower Building under "Buildings and Other Compelling Structures"). On weekends, the aristocracy that should naturally claim this area is nowhere to be found, and the Promenade becomes home to poor couples necking and strolling with their dates. Fact: Ho Chi Minh once lived in Brooklyn Heights

Neighborhood Trivia

In 1929 in the **Old Brewery,** *an overcrowded housing tenement in the notorious Five Points areas of lower Manhattan (at Point, Baxter, and Worth streets), there was an estimated one murder every night for over 15 years.*

An Interview with Owner of the

Nam Wah Tea Parlor

(13 Doyers St., between Pell Street and Bowery, in Chinatown)

Jim Monk: Did they film a movie in here once?

Man: Who?

Jim Monk: Didn't they film _Reversal of Fortune?_
This is—what is the name of your restaurant?

Man: It's the Nam Wah Tea Parlor.

Jim Monk: How long has it been here?

Man: This tea parlor? Seventy-five years.

Jim Monk: That's all? How long you been here?

Man: Who?

Jim Monk: You.

Man: Forty-five years.

Jim Monk: Where are you from?

Man: China.

Jim Monk: Do you serve special teas?

Man: Chinese tea.

Jim Monk: Did they film _Reversal of Fortune_ here?

Man: Lots of movies.

while a seaman. Beautiful residential streets to check out include Grace Court Alley and Hunts Lane, off Montague Street.

> **Chelsea.** Area around Eighth Ave. at 23rd St. (Manhattan).

The newly gentrified gay party and residential part of town, with a slew of bright new contemporary restaurants and shops that are quickly turning this former drug-and-hooker hood into the Castro Street of Manhattan. Quite appropriately, beneath the clean and tidy makeover, there's a vast trove of emptiness—unless Bed, Bath and Beyond is your idea of nurturing spirituality, which it is for many Chelsea locals. Chelsea is the first area Michael Monk stayed in in New York, at Sandra Holtzman's apartment, back in 1980.

> **Chinatown.** Area around Canal St. at Bowery (Manhattan).

There's more here than meets the eye. You've got your requisite dim sum palaces, your hanging chicken feet, your Buddha shrines and exotic herb stores. But let's get real: This place is corrupt. Beneath the tinsel-thin gloss and schmaltz, the merchants are dealing in hot illegal merchandise, often right out in the open. Sure they've closed all the illegal opium dens and many of the gambling clubs, but the Chinese of Chinatown make only a vague attempt to cover up the fact that they are selling illegally cloned goods, from computers to handbags to clothes. Police busts are a matter of course. As far as the herb stores, more than a third of the over-the-counter potions are derived from endangered species.

> **City Island.** At the end of City Island Rd. (Bronx).

This place makes me depressed. The restaurants are so tacky, and the fast-food seafood places so ridiculously overpriced one just feels sorry for the poor suckers who come here expecting a good time. There is nothing to this island, except the feeling of ennui and shattered illusions. Yes, how nice it would be to have a place in the Bronx with the charm of a New England fishing village. Unfortunately, City Island has about as much charm as former senator Alphonse D'Amato, many of whose die-hard supporters are among those who make the trek.

› **Nathan's Famous.** Surf Ave. at Stillwell Ave. ☎ 718/946-2202.

Michael Monk: We are at Nathan's world-famous hot dogs. This is the most pathetically small hot dog I've ever seen in my life. Nathan's used to serve really big hot dogs. Look at this. [He points to his hot dog.] I said with onions. This is not a healthy portion of onions. And this is just basic, low-grade Velveeta. It's not even the high-grade stuff. It's the low-grade Velveeta. High-grade Velveeta wraps around the bottom, and it doesn't drip like that.

› **The Cyclone.** Surf Ave.

Michael Monk: We are about to ride the world's scariest roller coaster. It's a wooden roller coaster. A lot of people have died on it, actually. In one instance, two highly intelligent people decided to stand up in the back and raise their hands up, and they lost their heads.

This roller coaster is the heart and soul of Coney Island, and it is not so much fun. It just yanks you around. Until the late '60s, it was the world's tallest first-drop wooden roller coaster. The first drop is around 95 feet, and it has a right-angle turn, which gives a wicked pitch to the spine. It also has two surprise little twists to the left and one to the right. All of this adds up to a very bad back.

The worst place to sit on a roller coaster is not in the front—that's the scariest place—but the very last seat, because then you take the full shock of every twist and turn and bump in the ride. That's where we're not going to sit today.

Let me tell you one little anecdote. The last time we were here, we rode the Cyclone five times in a row, and there was a little baby bird down on the tracks, and the riders were all looking at the baby bird, and they said, "Oh, the baby bird, the baby bird." And the operator said, "Kill it," and just pulled the switch, and the car rolled over and killed the little bird.

If anything happens to me, let the—what's that thing called?

Jim Monk: It's like a vegematic.

Michael Monk: It's like a vegematic, but it's called something else. If anything happens to me, let the thing that's like a vegematic go to my Mom, and all of my personal diaries—they're under the bed on the right-hand side, way back in a shoe box—those go to my literary agent. The RV takes unleaded regular.

The Cyclone, Coney Island

> **Coney Island.** Along Surf Ave. (Brooklyn).

Paul Lukas of *Beer Frame* (one of the top three 'zines in New York) puts it best: "Once upon a time, Coney was the entertainment center of the city, with Steeplechase, Dreamland, and Luna Park all competing to spin the best fantasy. These days, Coney is a burned out husk of its former self, with just a few rides (including the Cyclone, around 70 years old and still the world's most terrifying roller coaster) and LOTS of cool industrial decay. It's still a blast during summer (especially on the first Saturday after June 21st—date of the annual Mermaid Parade), but Coney is at its most surreal during the late fall and winter, when it's largely deserted and makes an ideal setting for black-and-white photography."

The Dutch named it Konijn Island, or island of rabbits. There's about a thousand theories why.

> **East First Street.** Between Bowery and Avenue A (East Village, Manhattan).

This stretch near Houston and Alphabet City contains a growing variety of "cool" restaurants and shops—from Lucky Cheng's (24 First Ave., ☎ 212/473-0516) to Maria Del Greco's Hats (70 E. 1st St., ☎ 212/505-3304). Where the newly shaved and pierced zomboids go to feel hip and "downtown."

> **East Village.** Bowery/Third Ave. spreading eastward, between Houston and 14th St. (Manhattan).

For those with a taste for adventure, eccentricity, and diversity, the East Village is the last great holdout in the city. It will take a few more years of gentrification before its core personality completely disappears, though it is coming, and with a vengeance. The rest of New York is white bread by comparison. SoHo is dead, ruined by high prices and Eurotrash. The West Village hasn't been truly alive for over 2 decades, home now to the gay and liberal bourgeoisie. Much of the Upper West Side is yuppie hell, boring and white. Ditto the Upper East Side, which has no guiding light. There is some hope in Williamsburg and Red Hook, Brooklyn, and perhaps in some forgotten part of Queens, but it is the East Village that provides the character and rawness that keeps New York City new. Unfortunately, until recently it was often Hell on earth to live there. From the endless parade of beggars and slackers and crazed crackheads and sirens and shouting and partying, it was trying to both mind and soul.

Alas, my dear old East Village, land of the pharmaceutical professional and various levels of New York low-life, has seemed to spontaneously gentrify during the Giuliani years. Some of this is for the better. Fortunately, some of the funkier, more enduring highlights of the village remain, from the irreplaceable and timeless CBGB's to the tried and true benefactor of the poor, the Catholic Worker House on East 3rd Street. For now anyway, the East Village has attained that elusive and short-lived quality of being both livable and exciting.

> **Financial District.** Below Chambers St. to the Battery (Manhattan).

The pot from which New York sprouted, this roughly triangular piece of expensive real estate all the way at the south end of the island is still the city's seat of power, both in terms of government (City Hall) and finance (Wall Street). This is the New York of 1930s American movies, all twisting canyons between towering buildings that scream "Powerful men toil here!" During the day, it's populated by well-dressed people with cell phones and by not-so-well-dressed people (also with cell phones) who keep those others in coffee and donuts. At night, though, most of the area is a ghost town, so quiet you can almost imagine what it was like a hundred years ago.

> **Flatiron District.** Area around 23rd St. and Fifth Ave. (Manhattan).

Like so many neighborhoods in the city, the Flatiron is a real estate distinction. At one point it had pretensions of being SoHo North, but now most of the blocks are taken up by expensive gourmet restaurants, though a few funky shops remain. The architecture in this area is stunning and at times forbidding, anchored around the fascinating Flatiron Building ("home" of *Monk* Magazine). But as for real teeming human life, you must look elsewhere. The narrow streets and tall structures make for lots of darkness, which has a certain appeal, though I think living here would bring on Seasonal Affective Disorder quicker than any spot in the city.

> **Fort Green.** Area around Lafayette Ave. and Fulton St. (Brooklyn).

If you're looking for the hippest black neighborhood in the city, this is it. The late Spike's Joint is the most famous of a slew of trendy restaurants and shops spouting up around the 'hood. Celebrity residents include jazz singer Betty Carter and trumpeter Terrence Blanchard. But the highlight here is the architecture. Check out the wooden houses on Adelphia and Lafayette. The last surviving stand of trained spruce trees is at South Portland near Lafayette. Kalb Avenue off Lafayette has some incredible mansions, including the official residence of the bishop of Brooklyn. Pratt Institute is nearby. There's also great mansions on Clinton between Lafayette and Myrtle.

> **The Frathead District.** Between 79th and 96th sts. and First and Third aves. (Upper East Side, Manhattan).

This is our own invented neighborhood designation, but the city might as well make it official, given that most of the very straight heterosexual types living here exhibit a herd-like, clean-cut, collegial frat boy/sorority girl mindset. You'll find everything and everyone you abhorred back in Evanston or Lexington or Madison right here on the sidewalk—drunk chicks, boring stockbrokers, posses of aggressive, inconsiderate half-wits whooping it up. In one sense it's gratifying that New York actually has a neighborhood for these people, with their own comedy clubs and Irish pickup bars, the better to name and clearly identify them, so one can clearly see what's in store if one moves back to the Marina District of San Francisco. "PAR—TEEEEEEE!!!!!!!!!" Two excellent places to watch fratheads in action are Babka (2372 Broadway near 86th on the Upper East Side) and Greenbergs (2187 Broadway at 78th, outside the District on the Upper West Side).

> **Garment District (a.k.a. The Kathy Lee Gifford Memorial Garment District).** In the vicinity of Seventh Ave. and 34th St. (Midtown Manhattan).

Sweat shop capital of America. Here's where many of the major fashion designs originate and are fabricated in less than glamorous surroundings. Nowhere is the separation between the workers and the ends of production more clearly delineated.

Name: Miss Understood   **Occupation:** Drag Queen

"Being in drag this many days a week is kind of exhausting. It's a job. It's a job, but do you know what? Somebody has to do it. . . .

"There are very different crowds of drag queens. There are the people who work in nightclubs and in the East Village. Then there are the Imperial Court queens, who wear the beaded gowns and have their Night of a Thousand Gowns. I don't really know many of them. We travel in separate circles. In the Forties there's a club called Esquelita, and all the Latino queens hang out there. They have their own crowd, and I know a few of them. They have their own style. We mix at certain occasions, we see each other here and there.

"It's interesting being a drag queen. You learn so much about people. You meet these guys, you know, cab drivers—everyone comes on to you. To me it says something. All this stuff that they call feminine—it's all artificial. Women weren't born with makeup or big hair or long nails or any of that stuff. So when you strip it all away, what do you have?

"I find it amusing when men think it's sexual. I don't see it that way. But I play with it. It's fun. I wouldn't really date them because, you know, I take this off when I go home. And when you come down to it, you have somebody with a penis, no matter how you decorate it."

Name: Anonymous   **Occupation:** Hustler

"I'm a drag sniffer. You hear that. Official drag sniffer. I'm a guy who sniffs around drag queens. Like sort of a straight guy, I guess, picks himself a drag queen and sniffs around her and stuff.

"When a drag queen is into me, I know it's the greatest fuckin' compliment, because drag queens only go for the hottest guys. I've seen drag queens look better than fuckin' models. I appreciate them because they work so hard at what they fuckin' do. More hard work than women have to put into being a woman. Transvestites work a lot harder, and I can appreciate someone who works hard, hard to look good for men.

"So I got attracted to drag queen penis, feminine penis. I got attracted to it, you know what I mean? Everybody called it bisexual. I don't know. I'm into women too, man. I got a girlfriend right now, matter of fact. The whole situation is this: These old fucking men cruise around 14th Street, down at the belly of the beast, by the meat district. These straight-O guys who are fucking married. Old fucking guys. Pick up drag queen prostitutes.

"I'm gonna go to Stella's later, Trixie's—make some money. Place they used to call Rounds. Make a lot of money there. Gay for pay. Anywhere I can make money. Five hundred dollars a night I make. Put it toward my music, record deals, mass-produced CDs. I'm a hustler. I'll do anything for money. I don't steal. I don't steal and I don't kill. I run con games and shit like that. Regular hustler, man. Watch out for me in Midtown Manhattan, Lower East Side, Village. I'm all over the place. Watch out for me. Coast to coast, man."

Name: Beckett   **Occupation:** Drug Addict

"William Burroughs used to live right around the corner. My dad used to publish his books. My name is Beckett, named after Samuel Beckett, the playwright. My dad used to own a press. Kerouac, D. H. Lawrence, Henry Miller— all those people. I guess I took a little too much to heart what his authors wrote. You know, when you start doing drugs you kind of romanticize it. You know, from reading Burroughs and all that stuff. I thought it was cool. I don't really think it's cool anymore. I'm a strung-out drug addict who steals to support my habit."

Name: Gene Pool   **Occupation:** Can Man (also makes grass suits)

Jim Monk: When was the Can Man born?

Gene Pool: In Chicago, in 1989. I was in this big building where there were like nine bands, and they drank a lot of beer, and I would take all the recycling over to this center because there was no recycling, and then I thought, well, I'll make a can suit. I wanted to make it huge. You know, big, but it seemed like a lot of work, so I put maybe 50 cans on the front, and then I said, "Forget it." When I moved here I just was inspired to finish it and really work it into an act. I would go to the recycling center and lie down.

Jim Monk: How do you go to the bathroom?

Gene Pool: I have a colostomy bag.

> **Gramercy Park.** In the vicinity of Irving Place, between Park and Third aves. (Manhattan).

This is getting picky, but the area that is considered Gramercy Park centers a few blocks in either direction from the park itself. And, boy, is it getting yuppie. You can tell because there's a slew of new gourmet restaurants and small boutiques spread all over this area, which only those locals that live near Gramercy could possibly afford on a regular basis. From Moreno to the ubiquitous Sal Anthony, the Gramercy area offers the adventurous well-to-do a chance to dine out "downtown" without all those unsightly downtown people. For the rest of us, it is still a calm, hassle-free oasis (especially the traffic-free Irving Place), even if we can't afford to eat out. Nineteenth street near the Park is known as "block beautiful." See for yourself why.

> **Gravesend, Sephardic Jew Community.** In the vicinity of Stillwell Ave. and 86th St. (Brooklyn).

When Israel was founded, there were 25,000 Jews left in Syria. A steady stream has been coming out ever since, and many have been heading for the Gravesend neighborhood of Brooklyn—and not just visiting either. They've been buying expensive houses, tearing them down, and replacing them with even bigger houses. Currently, these houses occupy 3 or 4 blocks of prime ocean parkway.

> **Greenpoint (a.k.a. Little Warsaw).** In the vicinity of Greenpoint Ave. (Brooklyn).

Don't pity the Polish. They always look so worn down by it all, but that is their scene. This area is Pirogi Central, where thousands of Eastern Europeans share family, friends, and misery; a deindustrialized white enclave, with dozens of businesses—from travel agents to lawyers to a local Polish paper—catering solely to the community. Everything is in Polish. Everything. Also nicknamed "Little Krakow," the neighborhood pointedly refuses to have anything to do with American culture, forcing itself into a time warp, becoming more Polish than Poland is today. A symbol of the Balkanization of America and evidence of a country so big, a city so big, one can carve out an insular ethnocentric niche like this.

> **Hamilton Heights.** Convent Ave. between 140th and 145th sts. (Manhattan).

Area north of Harlem, featuring the blossom-lined Convent Avenue and the warm and inviting City College, considered at one time—long before Professor Jeffries— "the Harvard of New York City."

> **Harlem.** In the vicinity of 125th St. (Manhattan).

Main Street USA for New York's large black population. Compared to Bed-Stuy and the Bronx, Harlem seems white-bread. Places to check out: Lenox Avenue between

120th and 121st streets (great architecture) and Striver's Row (138th between Powell and Eighth Avenue), which got its name because this is where black professional "strivers" of the early part of this century lived.

> **Hell's Kitchen.** Area approximately between 34th and 52nd sts. and Eighth Ave. and the waterfront.

The thing about Hell's Kitchen, New York City's original working class ghetto, is that it is quickly becoming Swell's Kitchen, what with the Disneyfication of the 'hood. Locals are trying to fight the good fight, but, it's like that boardroom scene from *Network,* when Ned Beatty intones, "Beale, you're MESSING WITH THE FORCES OF NATURE!" Forget about preserving the character of good ole Clinton. It's over, folks. Move to Red Hook.

> **Hoboken, New Jersey.** Just across the Hudson via the PATH train.

Remember *Yuppies Invade My House at Dinnertime?* That was the book and the phenomenon that described New York's "6th Borough" in the '80s. The early '90s turned Hoboken into "Slackers Invade My Neighborhood at Sleeping Time." Only to evolve into the horrific "Fratheads Invade My World at All Times." Hoboken ain't what it used to be, that's fer darn sure. But Yo La Tengo is based out of there, so it can't be all bad.

> **Inwood.** Area around the far, far northern end of Broadway (Manhattan).

Once a big secret, now widely known as the neighborhood with the cheapest rents on the island. There is a good reason for this: It's close to an hour commute to downtown and there ain't much in the way of modern amenities. Though near the crime-ridden Washington Heights and the always challenging borough of the Bronx, Inwood is surprisingly tame and, for those needing an escape, tolerably mundane. Though with the exception of the trashed but still natural Inwood Hill Park (with its riot of old couples and lawn chairs), some nice brick houses on Park Terrace West and West 217th Street, and the Lawrence A. Wien Stadium at Baker Field (the field of futility for the Columbia Lions football team), it's not a place I'd want to call home. However, the nearby Dyckman House (the last remaining colonial farmhouse in Manhattan) does offer the one oasis of history in the area.

> **Little India.** Lexington Ave. between 27th and 29th sts. (Manhattan).

It seems everyone knows of the stretch of Indian and Pakistani restaurants on 6th Street in the East Village (what we refer to as the Mulberry Street of the Punjab), but less know of an even better collection of restaurants on Lexington between 27th and 29th streets, which are funkier, cheaper, tastier, and far less touristy. And they're open 24 hours to boot to accommodate all the Paki and Indian cabbies. The Annie

"We're the Monks. We live in this thing. That's Harrod Blank. He lives in that thing. That's the camera van."

Jim Monk: You've been decorating art cars for the past decade, or longer, right?

Harrod Blank: Since 1981. Fourteen years.

Jim Monk: Where'd you get your start?

Harrod Blank: Just the old Bug. It was all white, and I didn't feel it represented who I was. I didn't feel like an all-white-VW-Bug kind of guy. So I just started painting it first and then gradually started adding objects until it had a globe and a TV set and all kinds of weird shit all over it.

Jim Monk: How many cameras do you have on here?

Harrod Blank: Somewhere between 1700 and 2000. I have never counted them because I'm just not interested in counting, but someone counted 1700.

Jim Monk: Where did you get all these cameras?

Harrod Blank: At a thrift store in Santa Cruz, the Bargain Barn. I started with thousands of cameras on a sidewalk, in a big pile, and I had to figure, "Well, I'm going to put these on this van and make it mean more than just throwing cameras on a van." So I had to organize them, and the different types of cameras became my palette. These Polaroids became one color, and the lenses became a color.

Jim Monk: You mentioned earlier that you had a little accident.

Harrod Blank: I hit a deer. It knocked off all these cameras. Like 30 cameras in all. They were just totally crushed to smithereens. I pulled over and looked behind me, and the road was covered with camera parts, little springs and lenses and wires. [He points to a camera.] There! There is proof. That is a deer hair from Fredericksburg, Texas.

Jim Monk: Do you have any decorating tips for the Monkmobile?

Harrod Blank: Silicone caulk.

Michael Monk: A silicone cock?

Harrod Blank: Just get a tube of silicone and start gluing road kill, road stuff you find.

Michael Monk: Oh, silicone caulk! I thought you said "cock."

A passerby spots the Monkmobile. Stops to talk.

Passerby: You get asked questions everywhere you go, all the time, I bet.

Jim Monk: No, actually, I don't.

Passerby: You pull into town in a giant pink van and people don't come up and say, "Who are you, and what's this about?"

Jim Monk: Okay, they do. You're right.

Passerby: You should probably have a printout.

Jim Monk: [Pointing to Harrod Blank] He does. The camera van's got it together. He has the answers to the 20 most frequently asked questions.

Passerby: Do you know people all over the country?

Jim Monk: Every damn town. Not every town, but a lot of places, yeah.

Passerby: Where have you had the most fun?

Jim Monk: Right here, right now.

Passerby: And where have you stayed the longest?

Jim Monk: We were in New York once for a year.

Passerby: If you sleep in a place like Manhattan or New York where do you park?

Jim Monk: We used to stay at the New Yorker Trailer City [now called the New Yorker RV Park and Campground] over in North Bergen, New Jersey, and we also parked here. Actually, we were here during the Tompkins Square riots.

Passerby: So you're not living any particular philosophy. You're just having fun?

Jim Monk: Just trying to make a buck. Actually, I have been living out a philosophy for many years, and now I'm trying to sell that philosophy to the world.

Passerby: How do you put it into words, the philosophy?

Jim Monk: Live simply and carry a big schtick.

Passerby: All of a sudden, you make me question myself: What's my schtick?

Jim Monk: You've got to have a schtick. Actually, we have a motto: simple, mobile, and true.

Passerby: I bet everybody's like that, they just don't admit it.

Jim Monk: You think we're all nomadic by nature?

Passerby: Well, we walk. Mobile to one person might be—to the little old lady with osteoporosis, getting from here to the corner deli is incredibly mobile. You're strong, you're healthy, you have all these skills and capabilities, so your mobility is much broader. But you haven't been to the moon.

Jim Monk: We're thinking about it. Are there any RV parks on the moon?

(E-mail Harrod Blank and the camera van at eccentrix@aol.com.)

Monkmobile meets Camera Van in the East Village

Sprinkle Salon was located on the 11th floor of 90 E. Lexington. Many a memorable evening was spent there, meeting the outrageous members of New York sex and performance art community. In addition, several S&M dungeons are located in this area, some right above Pakistani restaurants.

> **Little Italy.**

See "Mulberry Street."

> **Little Japan.** E. 10th St. (East Village, Manhattan).

This is where the hip kids from Tokyo and Osaka hunker into what for them are reasonably sized apartments with equally reasonable rents and soak in the East Village scene. Part and parcel of our belief that foreigners are what will sustain the Village long after the Yanks have tired of it. There's even a Web site for and about the hipster Japanese living in exile in the East Village (officially known as the "otaku"): www.iijnet.or.jp/tko.rockin.

> **Loisaida.** Avenue A going east, between Houston and 14th sts. (Manhattan).

This is a particular subset of the East Village, traditionally populated by Hispanics, squatters, and young urban junkies, with a few ancient Jewish elderly hanging on because of rent control. It starts at Avenue A and goes clear to the East River. Any trip through this area late at night used to be rightly looked at as The Loisaidan Adventure. Today, it's as safe as midtown Park Avenue.

> **Lower East Side.** Houston toward Canal, east of Allen St. (Manhattan).

While everything east of Fifth Avenue and south of 23rd Street is often called the Lower East Side, it has in recent years been narrowed to everything south of Houston to Chinatown. This was New York's original immigrant neighborhood, where the poorest of the poor scraped by in cold water tenements, with shared bathrooms and little heat. In fact, it was the first non–English speaking neighborhood in the New World. A few of the original Jewish establishments remain—including Katz's Delicatessen, Sammy's Romanian Restaurant, Sol Moscot Glasses, and Schapiro's House of Kosher Wines—but most of the original Jewish settlers have moved out, and many of their synagogues are going condo as the Lower East Side evolves into a place where New Jersey comes to be entertained. Yet, despite these developments, the Lower East Side retains its gray, dark, and funky ethnic ambiance, except filled now with Hispanics and Asians, a sizable contingent of crackies, smackies, and slumming artistes (often all three combined), and a growing number of gentrifying trust funders. Of all the scourges that have befallen this neighborhood, the last of those might very well be the worst.

> **Ludlow Street.** Between Houston and Rivington sts. (Manhattan).

A kind of new nightlife stronghold that is really just an extension of Avenue A in cheaper environs—and not all that friendly, either.

> **Madison Park.** 23rd to 28th sts. between Broadway and Lexington Ave. (Manhattan).

One of those picky distinctions realtors love to make, but which means nothing to the average New Yorker. Not that it won't soon enough. It's essentially the area that goes from 23rd up to 28th, between Broadway and Lex, a no-man's land by night, except for a smattering of largely mediocre hotels in architecturally rich buildings, and a growing number of pricey restaurants. By day it's heavy boring business, huge insurance companies and the like. One could argue that the view from the northeast side of Madison Square Park is spectacular given its vantage point on the Flatiron Building. Or at least it's beautiful enough to keep area condo sales strong for awhile.

Historically, back in the early part of this century, this area provided the architectural training wheels for the huge skyscrapers still to come.

> **Meatpacking District.** Area around Washington St. and W. 12th St. (West Village, Manhattan).

Come at 3am and catch the unloading of huge red meat carcasses into the area's meat lockers. The mixture of bloodied meatpackers, Stetson-wearing ranchers, black transvestites on the prowl, and hipster photographers documenting the scene is our favorite New York tableau. Not to be missed.

> **Midtown.** South of Central Park to approximately 42nd St. (Manhattan).

I guess one could call this a neighborhood, but there's nothing neighborly about it. Unfortunately, it's all most visitors to New York see, outside of a brief run to Wall Street and the Statue of Liberty. If this is all I saw of Manhattan, I wouldn't live here either.

> **Mulberry Street.** Area around Mulberry and Grand sts. (Little Italy, Manhattan).

File Mulberry Street (a.k.a. Via San Gennaro) under Idiotic Waste of Time. The only reason this stretch of the old "Little Italy" still exists at all is because of a pact between the Little Italy Business Association and the Chinatown Merchants Association. Otherwise, the area would be totally Asian by now. What's left is an overpriced mecca for gullible tourists, who don't know tacky Italian when they see it. At least the ever popular and relatively reasonably priced Luna doesn't try to hide the fact. Nor the over-the-top El Mella, which makes no bones about its status as a overexuberant family-style tourist trap. All the others seem to cater to John Gotti wannabes. They've perfected a basic Mulberry Street formula: A Venus Di Milo fountain, fake flowers, overattentive waiters, and a menu 30 years out of date. (See "Food.")

> **Murray Hill.** Area around Park Ave. and 34th St. (Manhattan).

If bland is beautiful, file this neighborhood under Masterpiece. Sort of a muddle of mixed nationalities and income groups that comprises the area between Park and First and 34th and 42nd. The lone highlights are the old historic buildings and town houses that run up the hill near lower Park Avenue.

> **96th St.** (Upper East Side, Manhattan).

This is not a neighborhood but a complete and total paradigm shift. They say that in New York, rich and poor live side by side, and nowhere is this more dramatically

---

That Area Between 14th and 42nd

Let me tell you about these "downtown" neighborhoods, especially those between 14th and 42nd: They ain't made for peoples. They made for bizness. Of course, if your idea of a comforting, ethnic, thriving, vibrant community is a huge insurance building or an all-night photo-developing lab, then these areas are for you. Otherwise, stay below 14th and above Canal, and if you need to live between 14th and 42nd, go far east or far west, where at least there's a warm diner open till 4am or a corner grocer that knows your name, or at least your face.

demonstrated than in this transition zone, on one side of which is the old money and/or yuppified Upper East Side and on the other, Spanish Harlem.

> **NoHo.** North of Houston to Astor Place, between Broadway and Bowery (Manhattan).

While some might consider it the playground of NYU, for most it's the transition zone between East and West Village. Broadway and Lafayette snag their fair share of megachains, bad restaurants, attitudinal clubs, and annoyingly hip boutiques. The preponderance of single-office entrepreneurs that crowd the 10-story buildings are what give this area its lifeblood during the day, with the attendant pedestrian traffic jams. At night, it's a cultural vortex for the cocktail-swigging bridge-and-tunnel crowd while its hipper denizens exit toward neighboring 'hoods.

> **Nolita** (Northern Little Italy). The area around Spring St., between Lafayette and Bowery (Manhattan).

A new improved retirement village for thirtysomething yuppie art scum and attendant fashionistas. They come in search of that ethnic neighborhood thing, and, of course, like all tourists, destroy the very thing they seek.

> **NYU Area of the Village.** Area around Broadway and W. 4th St. (Manhattan).

A highly overrated and aesthetically dull university is the backdrop to the coarsest and tackiest stretch of bad restaurants, bad clubs, and annoying bridge-and-tunnel people anywhere. Some charm along lower Fifth Avenue, 10th Street, and a momentary stretch of University Place, but otherwise give it a miss.

> **Orchard Street.** Above Canal St. (Manhattan).

This is the old business street within the greater Lower East Side. Remarkably, it still retains the grungy ethnic character that has characterized it for years, selling old ties, shirts, suits, bras, you name it, in styles that are at least 10 years out of date. Sundays are the best.

> **Park Avenue above 42nd St.** (Midtown/Upper East Side, Manhattan).

I pity the ridiculously rich denizens of Park Avenue. They've made all this cash, either by inheritance or actual work. They hold these swank dinner parties where women arrive in furs. And yet, they still have to put up with obsequious doormen who work hard at figuring out a million and one different ways to kiss ass—from putting on a woman's fur (which the "gentleman" or "madam" is perfectly capable of doing his or herself) to holding open easily opened doors—for which they expect to be tipped. Thanks to Giuliani, the rest of us have been spared the intrusive nuisance of panhandlers, but they're alive and well in the lobbies of Park Avenue.

> **Park Slope.** Area around Prospect Park West (Brooklyn).

While never much to write home about, its hype always bigger than its hep, Park Slope has become an *Utne Reader* wet dream come to life—featuring PC moms with baby strollers, über eco-consciousness, an overabundance of educated white people, and, of course, GARDENS!!

> **Red Hook.** Area southwest of the Gowanus Expressway along the South Brooklyn waterfront (Brooklyn).

They say the road to big, cheap artists' space leads now to Red Hook—the same way it used to lead to the East Village, Tribeca, and Williamsburg. The difference here is that Red Hook is so cut off from all things Gotham that it doesn't even seem to be in New York. The place is more like Oz—some weird, postindustrial, rust belt Oz—so ill-serviced by public transit it might as well be in Michigan rather than within easy sight of Wall Street and the Statue of Liberty, which it is.

It's almost a quest of faith. You get off the subway in pretty, Old World Carroll Gardens and begin walking southwest, crossing the Gowanus Expressway as if it were the Berlin Wall into a sprawl of disused factories, crumbling warehouses, four-story tarpaper shacks, and the occasional incongruously well-kept 19th-century brick house, sitting as if it had been nabbed by aliens in 1860 and redeposited just as you turned the corner. Keep going to where the streets revert to cobblestones and there's not another soul in sight and eventually you get to the grail: a string of renovated warehouses and artist spaces around the intersection of Van Brunt and Beard streets. New York harbor stretches out right at your feet, and behind you the warehouses are so thick with the past that you half expect crowds of Italian immigrants in overalls to push through the door at the five o'clock whistle. This is the frontier, baby—the intersection of time and tide, decay and modernity—and unless somebody builds a new subway line, the yuppies ain't gonna be moving in soon.

> **Roosevelt Island.** In the East River, below the Queensboro Bridge.

Not so much a neighborhood as a separate country, Roosevelt Island sits in the East River off Manhattan's eastern shore, paralleling the 50s up to the 80s, and might be the only place in America that looks and feels like Communist Germany circa 1972. The buildings are sterile and austere. Pavement runs everywhere there should be grass, or at least bricks. The security cops are omnipresent. The shops are from some creepy mall of no imagination—functional places like dry cleaners, The Grog Shop, and Roosevelt Nails in flashing neon (perhaps the only time the illustrious Roosevelt name was used for something so pedestrian). There is no nightlife. Maybe a loner hanging in the shadows, looking desperately for some action that will never come. Teenagers don't use the basketball courts. It feels most days like a ghost town instead of a vibrant community. Think Alphaville. Think East Berlin, before the Wall came down. Think a cold, soulless police state, where in the background, at the far end of the island, some top secret and sinister operation goes on, as an empty cruel wind blows through the concrete canyons. That most people take a romantic tram to and from the island only adds to the dark surreality. Fact: The island's Octagon Tower, built in 1839 by Alexander Jackson Davis, is what's left of the New York City Lunatic Asylum. We find it apropos.

> **SoHo.** Area around W. Broadway, between Houston and Canal sts. (Manhattan).

The name should be changed to SoWhat? Or rather, SoWhat Happened?! This famous artsy boho mecca has rapidly transformed into a conventional art and "yuppie porn" shopping district (Eddie Bauer, The Nature Company, Smith & Hawken, Evolution, and the like), catering to one commercial fetish or another. The cobblestone streets remain (kept clean by hired teams of homeless), as well as some of the cool warehouse ambiance, amazing cast iron architecture, not to mention Pearl Paint at the south end, but the stores are way overpriced, and on weekends the neighborhood is filled with people you just don't want to know. Stay away from West Broadway at all costs—it's schmoozing grounds for a sizable quotient of Eurotrash.

What is ironic about SoHo's current upscale incarnation is that back in the 1850s, the neighborhood was the city's main red light district, with over 30 brothels on Mercer alone, and another 14 each on Greene and Wooster. Go to 105 Mercer, an ex-brothel that's one of the oldest buildings in the city.

> **South Street Seaport.** Area around South St. near Fulton (Financial District/Downtown Manhattan).

Not a neighborhood per se, though it was at one time. A tourist mecca that is a harbinger of things to come. Run by the Rouse Corporation ("good mall developers, bad seaport developers"), featuring expensive fast food, a ridiculous number of mall stores, and a thriving seaport that is a shell of its former self. There are great views of the East River and the Watchtower sign across the way, but if you're a tourist and you come here without a shred of irony, you're either braindead or brainwashed.

> **Stuyvesant Town.** Area from E. 14th to E. 23rd, between First and Avenue C (Manhattan).

Sort of a defiantly indefinable mixed-use area of hospitals, churches, synagogues, and various ethnic and economic groups—and some of the cheapest rents in Manhattan. Waiting list to get into one of the 110 buildings of Stuy Town and Peter Cooper Village is between 8 and 10 years. Fact: Stuy Town was the original home of the notorious Gas House Gang when the area was the location of the city's major gas works.

"What we would like to do today is to tell you what you will not see in the art world when you come to New York."

They wear gorilla masks and go by pseudonyms: Georgia O'Keefe, Ana Mendieta, Käthe Kolwitz. They call themselves the conscience of the art world, masked avengers who are fighting sexism and racism. Not everyone agrees. The art dealer Mary Boone says they are an "excuse for failure"; artist Mark Kostabi says they are women who "don't have any talent" and are "taking it out on men." But one thing is certain: The Guerrilla Girls have almost single-handedly kept activism in the art world alive. They started in the mid-'80s in response to a show, An International Survey of Painting and Sculpture, at the Museum of Modern Art, and they have been going strong ever since. For more than a decade the Guerrilla Girls have been papering the walls of SoHo with posters bearing such snappy sayings as "Do Women Have to Be Naked to Get Into the Met Museum?" "These Galleries Show No More than 10% Women Artists or None at All," "Women in America Earn Only 2/3 of What Men Do. Women Artists Earn Only 1/3 of What Men Artists Do," and "Relax Senator Helms, the Art World Is Your Kind of Place!" They also publish a newsletter, *Hot Flashes*, and in 1995 their first book, *Confessions of the Guerrilla Girls*, appeared.

Over the years, the Guerrilla Girls have broadened their scope somewhat to include targets outside the art world: They've taken on former President George Bush, the military, the Republican Party, the Catholic church, and, most recently, the Internet.

Two of the Guerrilla Girls, Frida Kahlo and Violet Le Duc, agreed to meet us back in their original stomping ground, SoHo.

Guerrilla Girls: I'm Frida Kahlo. And I'm Violet LeDuc. And we're an anonymous group of women artists, and for 10 years we've been doing posters and graphic projects exposing all forms of racism and sexism in the New York art world.

Michael Monk: Why gorillas? [they are wearing gorilla masks]

Guerrilla Girls: Well, why else would you be talking to us?

Michael Monk: I mean, you could have chosen bunnies or leopards or bears.

Guerrilla Girls: The Bunny Girls. I think they've done that. I think—wasn't that Hugh Hefner?

Michael Monk: Oh, right. Yeah.

Jim Monk: We're coming into SoHo. Come on, tell us about SoHo. What will we not find in SoHo, the trendoid art capital?

Guerrilla Girls: Well, you have to understand how museums work. For artists to be shown in museums usually they have to be shown in commercial art galleries, and commercial art galleries are under no pressure to be fair or inclusive or anything. They can show whatever they want. They're private businesses. What doesn't get shown in the galleries doesn't get shown in the museums. And galleries are very reluctant to promote and show the art of women and artists of color, especially during the 1980s when there was so much speculation and money in the art world.

You have to realize that most art collectors are white males, so they would tend to buy art that reflects their own values. Every few years we do a report card and rank the top galleries, or the most influential galleries, and we've found that they're not getting any better at all. The museums are getting a little bit better, but galleries are not. So what you can't see in SoHo is what's really going on in the art world.

The closer you are to New York, the worse it is for women and artists of color. We're not exactly sure why, but we think it has something to do with the center of the art market being in New York, and when money is involved, money is very conservative, and when big money is involved, it's extremely conservative.

Jim Monk: Isn't there some sort of like, some sort of affirmative action, in a way, that you're supporting?

Guerrilla Girls: No, we've never mentioned quotas, we've never mentioned affirmative action, we've just always pressed the responsibility of cultural institutions to truly represent the culture that they're charged to represent. We should really talk about the situation of artists of color, because, you know, people of color, African-Americans, have played a very important part in our history, and their voices need to be told. Certainly in our popular culture and music their voices have been extremely important, but when you get to the visual arts, they tend to be ghettoized into a separate history. And we're going to be working on a history project next, and talking about some of the weaknesses in art history and how we should not believe art history as we're told it.

Jim Monk: This whole area where we're in, SoHo, is really the breeding ground for the New York art scene still, or not? Is it just where it's shown?

Guerrilla Girls: No one can afford to live here anymore. This is where people who sell and collect art live and come.

Guerrilla Girls: We figure that now that Disneyland—Disney has bought up all of—

Jim Monk: Times Square.

Guerrilla Girls: Well, everything. This is going to become like Culture Land. Like there's going to be Frontier Land. This'll like sort of seem like—

Jim Monk: This will be Art Land.

Guerrilla Girls: This will be Culture Land. High Culture Land.

Newly sanitized for your protection: Times Square

> **Sunset Park.** Area around Fourth Ave. south of 39th St. (Brooklyn).

This is Chinatown Junior, with many of the same shops, markets, and restaurants as in the original Chinatown. Much like the Richmond is to San Francisco's original Chinatown, Sunset Park is friendlier and easier to navigate than New York's Chinatown. And, most importantly, it's relatively undiscovered. True to its name, Sunset Park is also an excellent place to catch a spectacular sunset (go to Eighth Avenue between 50th and 60th streets).

> **Times Square.** Area around 42nd St. and Broadway (Midtown Manhattan).

The overall theme of this theme-driven area is "Reclaiming 42nd Street for the Tourists." The New Victory Theatre sort of sums it up. While old standbys like **Hotalings News** (142 W. 42nd, ☎ 212/840-1868), **Howard Johnson's** (1551 Broadway, ☎ 212/354-1445), and **Jimmy's Corner Bar** (140 W. 44th; ☎ 212/221-9510) still hang on, don't let anybody tell you differently: Disney et al are determined to turn what was the last bit of New York–style sleeze into the Great Middle Class Way. The preservationists hoodwinked into helping the big corporations restore the old theatrical palaces are duping themselves into thinking something of true cultural value will come of all this, and most of New York is completely asleep to the insidious transformation. *Beauty and the Beast* and The Official All-Star Cafe are the harbingers of what's to come. Think of it as South Street Seaport North. Caveat: In researching the Ziegfeld Theatre, preservations found the office of Mr. Ziegfeld, which was entered through a large, 1-foot-thick door. It was behind this door that Mr. Ziegfeld "interviewed" potential dancers. (For an anthropological view of Times Square, see the interview with Terry Williams later in this section.)

> **Tribeca.** Area around W. Broadway south of Canal toward the World Trade Center (Manhattan).

Quickly following in SoHo's footsteps, one of New York's few remaining outposts for the grungy artist set has seen its cost of living skyrocket and its cozy funky feel co-opted by pricey trendoid hot spots. No longer a friendly place to live, though still an occasionally fun place to dine.

> **Union Square.** Area around 14th St. and Broadway (Manhattan).

Primarily a gourmet restaurant ghetto—from Union Square Bar and Grill to Steak Frites to Coffeeshop and farther beyond to the plethora of good eateries lining Irving Place—Union Square is the new swingin' yuppie playground. With an organic Greenmarket a few times a week and less and less of those unsightly pot-smoking ne'er-do-wells that used to hover around the park, the well-heeled and conventional can safely walk their Dobermans at all hours now, enjoying the nearby Toy 'R' Us and a nice Starbucks latte.

> **Upper East Side.** East of Central Park, between 59th and 96th sts. (Manhattan).

This section of Manhattan gets stereotyped and ridiculed as the land of the social x-ray and the omnipresent doorman. And that it is. But there is more. First, a sense of calm and refinement one finds missing from all other parts of the city, save certain parts of the West Village. Secondly, some of the finest museums in the world. Third, the best part of Central Park. Fourth, the most architecturally interesting part of the city, from the historic town houses around Sutton Place and Carl Schurz Park to the outrageously expensive condominiums on Park Avenue. Plus the Carlisle, the Roosevelt Island tram, and Cordelia Roosevelt's childhood home. It gets a bad rap from the liberal PC police, but after awhile its easygoing comfort starts to attract. However, there is an ugly selfish mean streak beneath a lot of this wealth. And the tacky overpriced Shopping District in and around Madison Avenue is enough to make us perform Bushashita.

> **Upper West Side, part 1.** West of Central Park from 59th St. almost up to 125th St. (Manhattan).

Once a heavily artistic community (with artist havens like the Hotel Ansonia predating Lincoln Center by ages) and then a nesting-ground for cardigan-wearing, mussed-hair, cigarette-smoking, McGovern-voting, lit crit PhD, rent-controlled old-school liberals, the Upper West Side has become balkanized these days into several zones: Down in the area from 59th to the low 70s you've got Lincoln Center, some good movie theaters, and some really, really rich people clustered around the Cafe des Artistes; in the 90s and low 100s east of Broadway you've got a decent-sized Hispanic community; up above 110th you've got Columbia University; and in the low- to mid-70s into the 90s you've got a lot of well-paid, well-scrubbed young folks. Which leads us to . . .

> **Upper West Side, part 2.** Indeterminate area stretching from the low- or mid-70s to the low 90s, primarily between Broadway and Columbus Ave. (Manhattan).

Think of this area as a petri dish in which to study yuppie evolution. In the single-celled stage you've got a string of bars in the 80s along Columbus and Amsterdam that are a cruising ground for post–Ivy League second-year investment banking analysts. Here, these organisms meet other single-cell organisms and begin the breeding process, which in turn leads to the cocoon stage, referred to in scientific parlance as the Pupal Pottery Barn Phase. During this period the organisms typically discover golf and begin making weekend trips to their spiritual home in the Hamptons.

Our resident social anthropologist conjectures that there's actually a giant Budweiser blimp hovering over this whole area, trailing a long "Straight White People Wanted" sign that's visible only to those with sufficiently thick portfolios. No wonder JFK Jr. used to live nearby (in a relatively humble pad at 56 W. 91st).

> **West Broadway.** Between Houston and Canal St. (SoHo, Manhattan).

Eurotrash Central. Need we say more?

> **West Village (a.k.a. Greenwich Village).** West of Sixth Ave. between 14th St. and Houston. The area around NYU is technically also known as Greenwich Village, but we're choosing to ignore that fact for now. (Manhattan).

In our renegade East Village days we looked at the West Village as some other world, and snidely dismissed it as the tres precious bedroom for the soft and prissy bourgeoisie liberal of means. As we get older, we start to understand what makes it so special. Yes, the quaint little streets that wind in and out, the sense of history, the surprising little pockets of beautiful architecture, but, most of all, the almost total absence of that pan-hassling street element. Plus, you can feel calm and at peace here without giant

Michael Monk: Last night I went to West Broadway looking for Eurotrash. I turned the corner, and I said, "I want to find a Eurotrash male wearing slacks with no back pockets and no wallet." The first restaurant I looked in there was a guy in a red shirt wearing slacks with no back pockets and no wallet.

Jim Monk: Did he have a good ass?

Michael Monk: He had one of those low, saggy asses that are held together by tight slacks. He had a big watch. He was about to smoke a Gitane.

Jim Monk: Let's elucidate the elements of Eurotrash style.

Michael Monk: Eurotrash men love to wear no underwear.

Jim Monk: Is that true? That's not true. How would you know that?

Michael Monk: You can see the outline. And they always have these stupid little—what are those shoes that you slip your feet in?

Jim Monk: The little loafers, Italian loafers, with the tassels.

Michael Monk: They always have a chain. Here it is, 20 years after the '70s, and they're still wearing chains.

Jim Monk: They have nice, expensive watches. They usually are smoking a cigarette. Often they open up their shirts to reveal a little hair there. They're big on attitude. They hang out on West Broadway. What else?

Michael Monk: Their hair. We can't forget their hair.

Jim Monk: We've got to have the hair.

Michael Monk: Their hair is always greased back. They might as well wear grease nets.

Jim Monk: They don't like grungy Americans like us. They just don't.

Michael Monk: The very last thing about them is that they don't have a sense of humor.

Jim Monk: Zero irony. Irony quotient zero. The babes love them.

Michael Monk: They're very sexy.

Jim Monk: The chicks just go mad for them.

Michael Monk: They're really, really sexy.

Jim Monk: Especially when they wear those purses. You know, the men wear those purses. They have little gold chains on their purses. The women love that.

Michael Monk: They love men with purses.

Trumpified apartment complexes towering overhead, making you feel about as important as a mole rat. The place is civil, livable, and neighborly. A perfect spot for those of us who want to remain human while remaining in the vortex of city life.

> **Williamsburg, North Side.** Area around Bedford Ave. between Metropolitan Ave. and McCarren Park (Brooklyn).

In recent years Williamsburg has become known as the New Bohemia, the Ellis Island of Art, now that SoHo/Tribeca has become prohibitively expensive and the East Village overrun. But what sets Williamsburg apart are not the swarms of cafe culture kids and regimentally dressed artistes, but the native Polish population, which was here long before nose piercings, Bukowski, and chic Thai restaurants. They are what give this quiet, pleasant Brooklyn oasis such genuine appeal—from the amazing prices at Tops Supermarket (more akin to what you get in the Midwest, as opposed to the fleece jobs at A&P and Food Emporium) to the fresh pirogis at Kasha. It reminds me of Chicago's Wicker Park pre-1982, another sweet Polish neighborhood eventually overtaken by the art/yup factor. Go while there are still real people left.

Williamsburg Highlights

To us, Williamsburg is the perfect New York neighborhood: not only close to Manhattan, but close to the ethnic roots of the city. And cheap too (for now, anyway). Here's some highlights.

1. Decrepit warehouses on Kent—empty, rusty, and totally noir. On a misty rainy night the sight of them along the river is one of the coolest things in all of New York.

2. The squatter down on the water with a cell phone and computer.

3. The Chinese takeout, which also has menu selections written in Polish.

4. Just one subway stop to "the city."

5. Views of the East River.

6. Views of the Manhattan skyline.

7. Nearby Greenpoint, with a Polish radio station, Polish newspapers, and real live Polish angst walking around McCarren Park.

8. "Voodoo Volleyball Ballet" in McCarren Park in spring and summer.

9. Oznot's Dish restaurant at North 9th and Berry. (See "Food.")

10. A great crowd of eccentrics—from Gary Panter to Gene Pool.

> **Williamsburg, South Side.** Area around Bedford and Broadway (Brooklyn).

Home to the "Pious Ones," the Satmar branch of the Hasidim (a.k.a. "The Urban Amish"). They live in Brooklyn by night and in the Diamond District of Manhattan (West 47th between Fifth and Sixth avenues) by day. Wanna feel old-fashioned New York rejection? Try engaging one of these characters in affable conservation. Boychiks in the Hood this is not.

> **Yorkville.** Area around E. 86th St. and York Ave. (Upper East Side, Manhattan).

This expensive Upper East Side enclave with the British-sounding moniker was originally a major German settlement, and a hotbed of Nazi activity during WWII. Today, a few of the German proprietors remain (**Schaller and Weber** at 1654 Second Ave., **Bremen House** at 218 E. 86th St., **Cafe Geiger** at 206 E. 86th St., and **Ideal** at 238 E. 82nd St.), though the area is now more Jewish than German goy.

Times Square, Drugs, and Tunnels:
An Interview with Sociologist
Terry Williams

Professor Terry Williams is a tall, handsome, erudite man who comes from a strong southern family. But as a late teenager he tired of the confining milieu of his Mississippi hometown and migrated north to New York City, where he became enthralled with the dark, seedy side of Times Square and the various subcultures that fed into it. Through a thesis project on the intranasal cocaine culture in after-hours clubs, Terry was led to various other subcultures, most notably those centered around the purchase and consumption of crack cocaine. The result was the book *Cocaine Kids* (Addison Wesley, 1992) and the critically acclaimed *Crack House* (Addison Wesley, 1994).

But Terry was not through. Building on the pioneering work of journalists Samme Chittum and others, and from his own experience working with drug users at Grand Central Station, Terry became entwined with a group of homeless living underground in the subways and abandoned railroad tracks of the city. The fruit of his research will be the forthcoming *A Life Under the Streets* (due out in 1999).

Early on, what set Williams apart from other urban ethnographers was his non-judgmental view of his subjects and his willingness to go beyond scholastic voyeurism into honest and authentic engagement with those he met. As a result, he was shown a world few outsiders have ever seen before—a whole community of people living underground, some of whom haven't seen the light of day in years, and others living in crack houses, spending every waking hour in service to the almighty "rock." He found that these people had developed their own lexicon, rituals, and customs. And they were people who, but for the grace of God, could be you or me.

Terry Williams is one of those rare intellectuals, a bridge between academia and street life. Listening to him talk is like wandering in some kind of labyrinth. Although we're not moving at all (we're just sitting in his bland, standard-issue office at the graduate center of the New School for Social Research, where he teaches), the conversation gives a strange, almost disorienting sense of movement. Williams meanders from Times Square—its sad, insistent transformation, which began many more years ago than a lot of us think—to the dark tunnels beneath Grand Central Terminal and Riverside Park, which some 5,000 New Yorkers once

called home, to the city's complex, sprawling drug trade. One has the sense that this is just the beginning: There are 1,000 or 100,000 cities within the city, each culturally distinct from but intersecting with the others.

TIMES SQUARE

Terry Williams: Times Square became the front, became the campus for my graduate education. On 42nd Street between Fifth and Sixth. This is called the Graduate Center of the City University of New York. The Deuce, as we called it. The Deuce was the campus. So any given time you were hanging out in Bryant Park at that time was like drug city. And all the buyers were coming out of the buildings, they were coming out and buying drugs and really supplying the basis for the drug market, and the executives were going into the porn places and they were supplying the money, the income for the pornography establishment. So all of this behavior was just an intriguing thing. So I started to look at this as a graduate student. Just one world after another that I was trying to explore. I went from the top to the bottom. I mean, I interviewed corporation heads, the head of the Ford Foundation, you know, the Brant family, who ran the theaters along the street. I wanted to understand the economics of Times Square, the economics of a major city's entertainment district.

Monk: Has the Deuce changed a lot? Has it become more middle class, in fact?

Terry Williams: Well, yeah, it has, and it will become even more middle class. It will become the Disneyland East. I think Disney has the wherewithal to do exactly that. You've seen these sort of improvement zones happen, and certainly that will be one soon, which means it will have its own police force, it means it will have its own cleaning force. So certainly it will keep out anybody it doesn't want in, and you can see that happening rather quickly.

Monk: How do you feel about it?

Terry Williams: Well, I mean, I'm somewhat saddened because I kind of like the way Times Square was. I certainly don't like to see a Disney come in and kind of homogenize it. I kind of like the mix that Times Square had. I like the cheap theaters that they had. So I don't particularly care for the change. See, Times Square to me was never really only a place. It was always a state of mind. And so the idea that one could totally transform that state of mind by shifting markets from 42nd Street between Seventh and Eighth, for example, was never fully something that I believed in, because we now have a Times Square in the Village. So it was always more a state of mind than a place.

TUNNEL PEOPLE

Terry Williams: So around three o'clock in the morning I saw some of the men move down the tracks, and I discovered that there were five levels under the floor of Grand Central Terminal, and those levels were where people were sleeping and staying.

Monk: Like, what kind of levels?

Terry Williams: Just levels, just levels, I mean, they're just levels.

Monk: Floors?

Terry Williams: Yeah, like, you go down and it's this circular kind of phenomenon. And so you keep going in a circle. You end up—the tracks are all there, but you end up with these small what I call colonies of people. So I'm going down, and I see one cluster of about 25, 30 people, who—first of all, there was no movement, so I didn't know whether—because it was all garbage lined and next to a track and under a platform. But as I walked, something moved. I thought it was rats. And then as I looked closer and closer, like a camouflage, there you could see people's faces, and they began to peer out from behind this garbage, which was as tall as, almost as tall as you are.

Monk: Jesus, it's like hiding from Nazis.

Terry Williams: It was something that was so bizarre to me. I mean, nobody said anything. They just looked at me.

Monk: Because they didn't—the idea was to stay quiet, because they didn't want to be discovered, right?

> *"There's a whole hierarchy about how people perceive others in the tunnels."*

Terry Williams: Yeah, but one time they moved, and I kept looking because I heard that, and slowly but surely these faces started to emerge. I had noticed in all these tunnel spaces that there were several levels of people. There's a kind of hierarchical arrangement. Clearly, there were new arrivals at the top of these tunnels. And I'm talking about now a more vertical descent as opposed to a horizontal one, because the West Side is more horizontal. Where you had the new arrivals almost always accessed at the top. And they're the ones who—you know, you use the notion of margin versus mainstream. There is always this connection between what goes on in the margin and the mainstream, because they would come up, they would have cans, they would beg, and that sort of thing. Then you had another level of people who were just simply recluses, and you rarely, rarely saw them, and they had very little connection to—

Monk: And how did they survive?

Terry Williams: They either had some connection to the new arrivals or made some connection to the new arrivals, because there clearly was a community there, as I could see it, where arrangements were made for them to help in some way. Maybe they helped them with the cans, maybe they did other things, so that they would provide them with food. And there is another group of people who are simply, how do you, what do I call them? These were folk who just simply never showed their faces above ground. And they might have been wanted from the police. They might have just not had the wherewithal physically to continue to make the trek back and forth. And so these various levels seemed to be operating. Then there's another kind of hierarchy, which is a social hierarchy. I mean, clearly the bibliophiles—those who sell books—for example, consider themselves superior to all others. The bottle men were considered to be more, they looked down upon the can men, and the plastic sellers are looked down upon by—so there's a whole hierarchy about how people perceive others in the tunnels. There are communities that are almost set up, set up somewhat ethnically, because in the first part of the tunnel you have what I call Cuban Arms, and that's mostly Cubans. Cubanos, they set up these very interesting lean-tos, and that's the beginning, that's the mouth of the tunnel. And then you go in and you start to see more, you might see some adobe-style structures up above the tracks about 30 feet with almost no movement.

There's an immediate sensory deprivation. Light deprivation creates hallucinations, both visual and auditory. So I'm walking down from light to darkness, and the first thing that happens to me is I think I see somebody crossing the tracks. And I'm walking, and the rocks are under my feet, and I think I hear somebody behind me, and I'm stopping, and I'm looking, and I'm looking around. I mean, it is so bizarre. I mean, because you think that you are just a rational, thinking sober person, and suddenly you see this image, and when you get to where you think the image is, it's impossible for it to have been there. There's nowhere for it to have gone. It couldn't go up because there's nowhere to go. It couldn't have gone to the side because there's nowhere for it to have gone. It is unbelievable.

DRUGS

Terry Williams: People would go to a base house, and they had to take their own paraphernalia. At the first place, the base galleries, before you took your paraphernalia, you had to rent it. You went there, you rented it. Remember, there were no head shops selling these pipes and pipettes and stuff at that time. So you had to go in there, you had to rent it, and then the people had cooks in there that would cook the cocaine for you. You had to buy the cocaine there. You had to smoke it there, and then when you used up all your money you had to leave. Then a few years later, base houses emerged. By this time now you can go to a head shop, you can buy your own pipe, people usually had their own stems with them, they had their own pipettes with them. They usually had their own drugs. But now you had other activities associated with the use of it. Sex, for example. So the base houses had rooms, and women there who could get serviced when you used the drug, or after you finished using the drug. So you took your own pipe. You usually paid a fee to get in. Often times, when you ran out, they had stuff for you to use or buy there. You had different levels of base houses. You had base houses that were pretty raunchy, and you had some that were very elegant. Fifty dollars a night and $100 for the girl. I mean, you know, you had big-time hustlers who went to very elegant ones on Central Park West. And then after the drug price dropped around 1984, '85, you had a huge diminution in the price of crack cocaine.

Monk: Which was caused by what?

Terry Williams: Oh, wow, a lot of things. One, overproduction in the producer countries for the most part. You had about 500,000 acres of coca being produced around 1985. The price dropped from $100 a gram to about $60 a gram. So all of this created a situation where people could literally burn the drug up, and that's what they started to do, because it was so cheap, and the crack houses emerged right around that time, because then you could take your own drug, because it was cheap now, everybody had it. You could buy it very cheaply, took your own paraphernalia there, but there was still a need for a community. There was still a need for a kind of social interaction.

Monk: Because crack made you very social, no?

Terry Williams: Yeah, it made you social. Because at the beginning of crack use everybody was extraordinarily niggardly about it. I mean, they would take it and they would hide in a little corner. It was theirs and they didn't want to share it with anybody. Slowly but surely, you start to have the same elements that you had in the intranasal culture. People wanted to interact with other people. This is somewhat because the sex-driven element of crack use began to really play a powerful role by '85, '86. People wanted to express themselves, particularly men wanted to express themselves. Women, too, but because men controlled the venue, women had to go through the men in order to get the chemical, and so you saw more and more young women giving themselves over to whatever the men wanted to get to the drug. And so crack houses emerged as a result of all of this stuff, and so you started to see more and more people interact in these places called crack houses. And they would meet, they would interact, get high, share whatever they had, engage in various kinds of sexual activity.

Monk: What's your take on the state of the drug underworld today? Because I have the sense that a lot—like, you know, it's like heroin—people are going out to nightclubs and using heroin.

Terry Williams: It is a chic drug. It is. America seems to go through these 20-odd-year cycles of depressants or stimulants. And hallucinogens have never taken off in the same kind of way, like LSD, that sort of thing, peyote, or PCP. But cocaine and the heroin seem to always pop in in these 20-year cycles, and we've moved out of the stimulants cycle. We're now into the more depressants cycle again. And sure enough, it's here. We need 20 years of amnesia to understand what the devastation of these drugs seems to be. People don't know because in the 1960s there was no teenage cohort that picked up the heroin. You just didn't see it. So we have a whole generation that has no clue about what heroin actually does. It is 10 times worse than crack. There is a 20-minute to an hour window of a crack high for a person. That is to say, during that 20 minutes to an hour, they usually come really down. They want to maintain it within that limit. In other words, what they want to do is try and find something else to get high with within that 20 minutes to an hour, so it keeps them up there. Okay. If they don't get anything after 20 minutes to an hour, basically they don't care. It's all right. I'm not thirsty anymore. I might be thirsty but I can live without it. But the heroin craving is so intense that the person must find a way to get money to pay for that to get high again, because the craving is intense and it doesn't let up. It just goes on and on and on.

"We have a whole generation that has no clue about what heroin actually does."

Parks

When there's so much gray—gray buildings, gray sidewalks, even gray air sometimes—green becomes a deeply important color. At one time the city recognized this—that's why we have Central Park, Prospect Park, and most of the others. Today, it's the people on the ground that realize it, which is why we have the community gardens in the East Village and elsewhere. In recent years, though, the city administration has been mounting an effort to close the gardens to make way for more buildings. One guess as to who has the moral high ground on this one.

> **Astoria Park.** Between Hoyt Ave. and Ditmars Blvd., along the East River (Astoria, Queens).

Two main reasons to go to Astoria Park, one visual, one sociological. Visually, the park is totally dominated by the Hell Gate and Triborough Bridges, both of which have huge towers jutting right up out of it, throwing your perspective off and making you feel Lilliputian. It's also got one of the better views of Manhattan, especially from the north end. Sociologically, on any given summer weekend, the place is like a Whitman's sampler of millennial Queens. You've got South and Central Americans playing soccer, multiracial homeboys hanging by their rides, yuppies jogging on the track, Indian and Middle Eastern families picnicking, old Greeks playing bouzoukis, and kids splashing in Astoria Pool.

> **Bryant Park.** Sixth Ave., between W. 40th and W. 42nd sts. (Midtown).

The renovation a few years back has improved the environment dramatically. Unfortunately, now it's espresso hell, with the expensive Bryant Park Grill perched on its southeastern edge, against the back wall of the New York Public Library. Is there no middle ground? Why can't there be a public space that belongs neither to criminals nor to latte-sucking bores?

> **Carl Schurz Park.** East End Ave., between E. 84th and E. 90th sts. (Upper East Side).

Our second favorite park in the city. It's small and green, and the promenade, which overlooks the East River, is splendid. There are views of the Triborough and Queensboro Bridges, plus beautiful walkways. Adjoining this simple oasis is the unassuming expanse of Gracie Mansion, official residence of "da mayah."

> **Central Park.** Between 59th and 110th sts., Fifth Ave. and Central Park West.

Given how money-grubbing this island can be, it's something of a miracle that Central Park remains relatively intact more than a century after it was constructed.

Consider this: Way back in 1904 one Ernest Flagg proposed a Champs Elysées–style boulevard right through the center of it. The city almost bought the idea. Among other suggested "improvements": trenches in one of the park's meadows, to give a sense of what our soldiers were experiencing in World War I; an airport near what is today Tavern on the Green; housing projects; underground parking garages; and a plan to fill in the Reservoir to make way for another field. Thankfully, the Parks Department and the Central Park Conservancy have resisted them all. The park's highlights include the Great Lawn and the jogging track around the reservoir, but the most intriguing is the area (on the park's western edge between 74th and 79th streets) known as the Rambles. Originally conceived as a wild garden preserve for native plants, it's evolved into a cruising ground for men who either enjoy having sex in bushes or, for one reason or other, can't have it in the privacy of their home. Fact: Beneath the park lie 122 miles of pipeline. Fact: Although Central Park has been the site of numerous rapes and muggings, its police precinct is statistically the safest in the city.

> **Gramercy Park.** Lexington Ave. and E. 21st St. (Gramercy Park).

This is certainly one of the natural jewels of the city, and a beautiful and quaint symbol of a time when "people of quality" and civilization inhabited the area. Some of the civilized still live nearby, but the park has not been properly maintained—the fences and birdhouses are in disrepair, and many of the park's trees are endangered. Gramercy is the last private park in New York. You must have a key to enter. A statue at the center of the park depicts Edwin Booth, an accomplished 19th century actor and brother of John Wilkes Booth, Lincoln's assassin.

> **Hudson River Park.** River Terrace between Chambers and Vesey sts. (Financial District/Downtown).

This park can quite rightfully make a claim to being Monk's favorite Manhattan park. It is as though the nouveau-riche of Battery Park City tried to have the city's most picturesque park, but have been cleverly pranked. Or, maybe, someone has a wicked sense of humor down there. There is a perfectly groomed triangle of emerald green with long park benches, a jogging path right on the esplanade, a sculpture garden, a basketball and handball court, and a view over the Hudson River. Or so the plans must have looked, but the view is also of industrial, ugly Jersey City, the courts are taken over by street kids (Jim Monk looked on the game with longing, still fancying himself the next Larry Bird), and the sculpture garden is a subtle critique of the financial district—it's worth the trip alone: Miniature bronze workers mine, push, and collect pennies while squirrels, turtles, and other cartoon animals play around them.

> **Inwood Hill Park.** Area around Dyckman St. at Payson Ave. (Inwood).

While all the yuppies jog at nearby Ft. Tryon Park (home of the Cloisters), the real nature freaks (and there are very few up here) head for Inwood Hill, the last true nature refuge in Manhattan. If you go on a weekday, you will be guaranteed a level of peace and solitude unheard of elsewhere in the city. You can hear the roar of traffic on the Henry Hudson just west, but you can't see a trace of civilization anywhere you look. And forget about interruptions—at most, someone walking their dog once every 20 minutes, maybe some neighborhood Hispanic kids catching a buzz. You can actually gain some perspective on life in the city—quite literally, too, especially if you walk to the park's far western edge where, if you wind your way along, you will come to a fence with a hole in it, leading you out onto a ledge of boulders perched over the roaring traffic below. From this promontory you can not only see the George Washington Bridge to the south and the Palisades to the west, but even a good stretch of the Hudson as it heads north. You will notice too that others have preceded you to this stop, their markings engraved on the rocks—"Pedro," "Kenny, The Only One," "Spellman Prom '93"—giving the place a special *A Separate Peace* quality. It was here, back in 1626, in what is now Inwood Hill Park, that a savvy Dutchman named Peter Minuit bought Manhattan Island from the local Indians for a handful of beads.

> **Liberty Island.** In New York Harbor.

Most New Yorkers shy away from this overwhelmingly popular tourist destination. Which is too bad, because as crowded and touristy as the Statue of Liberty is, it is the very symbol of what this country is all about. The poem inscribed at the base written by Emma Lazarus to help raise funds for construction of the pedestal in 1903 is matchless in its compassionate beauty: "Give me your tired, your poor, your huddled masses yearning to breathe free, The wretched refuse of your teeming shore, Send these, the tempest-tossed, to me: I lift my lamp beside the golden door." You go, girl! Lost in the frenetic rat maze of Manhattan, one can easily forget the noble promise of this city, and what an arrival here meant to millions who came before us.

Some facts: The seven points of Lady Liberty's crown ostensibly represent the seven seas and seven continents. The original name of Liberty Island was Bedloe's Island. The official name of sculptor Frederic-Auguste Bartholdi's statue is Liberty Enlightening the World.

> **Lower East Side Gardens.** Various locations throughout the East Village and Lower East Side.

This is the last place you may expect to find nature. Nevertheless, the East Village has close to 30 small gardens, most of them carved by local artisans and residents from vacant lots and backyards. There are too many to name, but one of the best is on the corner of East 6th Street and Avenue B; in this once abandoned lot a nearly 3-story structure has been decorated with hundreds of old toys. If you'd care for a more comprehensive tour, attend the annual Rites of Spring (Procession to Save Our Gardens) in May. (See Spring under "Calendar.")

> **Madison Square Park.** E. 23rd St. and Madison Ave. (Flatiron District).

Most New Yorkers overlook this beautiful square-block park adjacent to the New York Appellate Building and diagonal to the legendary Flatiron ("home" of Monk Magazine). For me, it conjures up images of old New York, particularly Alfred Steiglitz's photographic images of the park from the early part of the century. Today, it's as dignified as ever. And relatively free of riff-raff. Unless the bevy of expensive dogs scurrying around the small dog run count as "riff-raff."

> **Prospect Park.** At Flatbush Ave. and Eastern Parkway (Brooklyn).

Still wild in spots, and with a very '90s-Brooklyn combination of young profession-als and Santeria practitioners, this is also one of the few parks in the city where you can legally barbecue—there are designated areas, but no one ever bothers staying in them, and as early as 10am you'll see family-reunion-sized groups staking out spaces and firing up the coals. Take your blanket to one of the remote spots (try Lookout Hill), find a secluded bit of lawn, and savor the combination of steel drums and "Pop Goes the Weasel" jangling from a far-away ice-cream truck.

> **Riverside Park.** West Side, from 72nd St. up along the Hudson (Upper West Side to the Bronx).

This is Central Park's long, skinny cousin, slinking up the Hudson all the way to the Bronx. Because of the natural slope from Manhattan's hillier areas down to the water, parts of the park have a kind of outsized rice paddy feel, with basketball courts and lawns stepped into it and trails snaking down to the promenade along the river's edge. At 79th Street, the park serves as a backyard for the Boat Basin, where dozens of boats—some of them looking like set pieces from *Waterworld*—house hundreds of salty New Yorkers year round.

> **Socrates Sculpture Garden.** 31–34 Vernon Blvd., at Broadway (Long Island City, Queens). ☎ 718/956-1819.

A strange, surprising oasis on the waterfront in Queens, the place was a vacant lot until artist Mark DiSuvero got hold of it. Now it's home to numerous large outdoor sculptures, some made from steel, others dug into the earth. Socrates is an artist's playground, and the works are like gigantic jungle gyms. The perfect getaway from—as well as complement to—the city's urban jungle.

> **Tompkins Square Park.** Between E. 7th and E. 10th sts., Avenues A and B (East Village).

For years Tompkins Square Park was the closest New York came to Copenhagen's Christiana district: a lawless area where drug users, dealers, and squatters went about their business unchecked. Several years after the riots (brought on by the forced removal of hundreds of homeless who had created shelters in the park) and by the police crackdown that brought an end to the whole scene, Tompkins Square is a gentrified, pleasant shell of its former grungy self. You'll still find all the vices; they're just not so in your face. The park's redesign may have something to do with this: It used to have an open center, which permitted everything from demonstrations to Wigstock; now it's been broken up by low fences.

> **Washington Square Park.** Fifth Ave., between W. 4th St. and Waverly Place (West Village).

Alright greenhorns, this is the spot. Pot for cheap. Folk musicians. Tourists who think the combination of jugglers, fire-eaters, dope dealers, and extras out of *Kids* is oh-so-bohemian. We consider it oh-so-passé. And so, evidently, do neighborhood community boards, which have spurred the NYPD to totally clean the place up. Look for a grand old tree in the northwestern corner of the park called "The Hangman's Elm."

Observation

"The weird mix of self-loathing and arrogance that has been so often marked in the New York identity—'I live in a tough, rotten city, so I must be better than you'—simply does not hold up at a time when many visitors say that New York has grown almost, well, NICE."

—Kirk Johnson and Marjorie Connelly in *The New York Times*, March 13, 1998

> **Wave Hill.** 252nd St. and Independence Ave. (Riverdale, Bronx). ☎ 718/549-3200.

At this sprawling estate overlooking the Hudson River, an ongoing calendar offers top-flight performances by some of the world's most promising artists. When we were there, Remy Charlip and Friends gave a dance recital ranging from ballet to gymnastics to angst-ridden story-telling. The pastoral setting seems more like New England than New York. An oasis within the city.

An Interview with

Gene Pool,

the Can Man and Grass Suit Guy

We are deep in the rusting core of North Williamsburg, Brooklyn. Flies are buzzing outside a car repair shop, mechanics bent low under hoods. There is the sound of metal on metal. We enter through a door adjacent the shop, climb a steep flight of stairs, and are shown into a loft by a gentle, smiling man. Inside, the floors are covered with cans, bottles, grass, and other urban detritus. There are piles of junk everywhere. At least, that's what the piles appear to be. But then the man, Gene Pool, lifts one, a pile of cans, and it miraculously becomes a suit, and then he lifts another, this one of grass, and it becomes a jacket. He likes to wear these outfits around town, while riding a unicycle. The Can Man, as he calls himself when he is wearing his can suit, appears all over New York: on top of buildings, in Tompkins Square Park, in the subway.

Other peculiar things Gene Pool does: He organizes an annual art show in a Brooklyn hardware store (see Crest Hardware Show under "Calendar"); he grows grass on cars and shoes, and even on Drew Barrymore's bikini.

We have come to Gene Pool for a simple reason: It seems an odd thing for a person to do—grow grass on suits, mount art shows in hardware stores, wander around town dressed in aluminum cans—and we want to know what makes him do it. The answer, at least as far as the grass is concerned, is simple: "I love growing grass clothes and wearing them and walking around and letting people try them on."

Gene Pool: June of '81 I grew my first grass suit and had someone chase me around with a lawn mower in Kansas City at the farmers' market.

Jim Monk: That is so damn funny. Now, were you living there at the time?

Gene Pool: Yeah, I—

Jim Monk: Are you from the Midwest?

Gene Pool: I'm from Ohio. I grew up in Ohio, and then I went to art school in Kansas City.

Jim Monk: Oh, my God, there's art in Kansas City.

Gene Pool: And I graduated in '81 and just started doing all kinds of spectacles and things on the street, and that was one of them.

Jim Monk: What's your real name?

Gene Pool: My real name was Bill Harding. It's not a name, you know, that you can remember or want to remember, and I thought, "Well, I need a better name," so I put out a reward for a new name and some people in Seattle—I was doing a thing there, and I did the worst performance of my life. One review said. "So bad we're not even going to talk about [it]." And I thought that'd be a good time to change my name. So I came back to Chicago—I was living in Chicago—and I changed my name to Gene Pool, and then when I lived here in '89 I changed it legally. So legally my name is Gene Pool Harding.

There was a guy named Michael Paha who was doing a lot of outdoor sculptures with grass, and he was growing grass on screens and in jars without any soil, and so he helped me grow grass in a briefcase for my very first grass performance. And I had this guy come out on the stage with a briefcase and he opens—you know, loosens his tie and takes off his shoes and socks, and he steps into this briefcase, and there's grass growing in there, and that's like his little portable park. So that was like the first thing I did. And then I grew the grass suit, had someone chase me with a lawn mower, and then I decided to grow grass on a car.

The grass, all it needs really is water, and in about twelve days you have a grass car or a grass suit, and so like that whole next year I went on all these shows, and each one was like worse and worse, you know, until I went on this show called *The Claim to Fame Show*, in Toronto, with the female pig mud wrestling champion of the world.

So when I moved here, I didn't quite know what to do. Me and my wife moved here to be rock and roll stars, and then it was just so unbelievably competitive and hard that I just gave up, and I stopped trying to have a band, and I started volunteering for Greenpeace, doing recycling. And there wasn't curbside recycling in Brooklyn at the time, so I was driving all my recycling into Manhattan, to Village Green. And then they got curbside here.

So I made a point of putting on this can suit and going to all the community recycling efforts and just kind of being the mascot and just giving them support, you know. Because this is like, there's the highest concentration of artists here, there's also the highest concentration of, like, environmental faux pas. You know, there's a huge oil spill under Williamsburg and Greenpoint, there [are] all these garbage transfer stations. You know, it's just one thing after another.

Michael Monk: What's next?

Gene Pool: Well, I'm working on that cork suit right there, which I can—I'm going to try and float in. And I have this fork suit, too.

Jim Monk: There's a magazine suit there.

Gene Pool: Yeah, I made the magazine suit.

Jim Monk: It looks like there's a plastic fork suit.

Gene Pool: Yeah, so I'm trying to like—anything that is disposable, I'm trying to kind of collect it. I have a collection of disposable lighters. I'm collecting crack vials.

"And then I grew the grass suit, had someone chase me with a lawn mower . . ."

The Press

New York is meta-media capital of the planet. Nowhere is there more media analysis of the media itself. And nowhere else is the press, the written press in particular, held in such high regard. So we add to the general spew, with our unabashed review.

Dailies

› *The Daily News.* 450 W. 33rd St. ☎ **212/210-2100.**

Recent Promise: Pete Hammill signed on as editor. Recent Disappointment: Pete Hammill quits after 9 months on the job. Add in the ownership of Mort Zuckerman and the editorial directorship of Harold Evans (husband of former *New Yorker* boss Tina Brown) and you have a paper that we don't have much to say about—so we won't.

› *New York Post.* 1211 Sixth Ave. ☎ **212/930-8000.** www.nypostonline.com

Hilariously paranoiac view of the city, with some of the most famous headlines in history (for example, "Headless Body in Topless Bar"). You'd think it would be the last publication to congratulate Mayor Giuliani on any decrease in crime, since the *Post* depends on urban degradation for most of its anxiety-inducing stories (seeing one of its headlines in passing can totally wreck one's day), yet the *Post* is firmly, if incestuously, in Rudy's court. The "Page Six" gossip column is a must for local PR mavens.

› *New York Times.* 229 W. 43rd St. ☎ **212/556-1234.** www.nytimes.com.

The world's premier daily has only gotten better with age, with radically improved coverage of pop culture and the net. But, above all else, the *Times* serves one indisputable function. Obsessed as New York is with career over community, the final arbiter of whether one has lived a good life is the size of the obit one receives in the *Times*, or, better yet, whether one receives an obit at all. For telling us whether we have lived an "important" or "newsworthy" life, the *Times* truly is "the paper of record."

Weeklies

› *New York Observer.* 54 E. 64th St. ☎ **212/755-2400.**

The salmon-colored paper all the satirists love to read is in some ways what *Spy* aspired to be without the groovy graphics (in fact, it's long been a pit stop for former *Spy* employees on the way to bigger gigs). For those deep inside the New York media hive and all those fascinated with highly detailed celebrity esoterica, this entertaining and intelligent weekly is a must.

> **New York Press.** 333 Seventh Ave., 14th floor. ☎ **212/244-2282.** www.adone.com/nypress. Available free on streetcorners.

At first their wily more-right-wing-than-thou tone was a welcome antidote to the über-left leanings of the *Voice,* but now the rantings of these Baltimore refugees seem rude, crude, and just as knee-jerk in their reaction as the *Voice* is in its political correctness. After awhile the ad hominem attacks seem gratuitously immature, as if the *New York Press* recognizes they never will become the city's dominant weekly and are taking their frustration out on all of us as a result. In addition, their yearly attempt to provide genuine service journalism (the Best of New York issue) suffers from the endless stream of weird invented categories, like Best Veal or Best Tuna Tartare, which seem to be created to woo local advertisers ("Let's see, if you buy a quarter page, we can probably fit you into The Best Sports Bars With One Television category") rather than to be useful to a reader (like, am I really going to search for a restaurant simply because they have the best goddamned veal?). Though the 10th anniversary was very entertaining, and the writings of Sifton and Strassbaugh are often quite trenchant, on the whole the *New York Press* is proud of itself in that cheap, blunt, AM talk radio way. This is mainly due to the tone set by its editor and cofounder, one Russ Smith, a.k.a. "Mugger." After awhile, all the boozy angst just comes off as insecure Balto blather—writers screaming so loud they start to get very annoying. While Smith is an eminently readable crank (we've always enjoyed his long-winded thuggery), H. L. Mencken he is not.

> **Time Out.** 627 Broadway, 7th Floor. ☎ **212/539-4444.** ww.timeoutny.com.

While the ridiculously PC *Voice* and the absurdly vitriolic *New York Press* have staked out the political left and right, *Time Out* cruises right up the middle, perfectly in tune with the apolitical "Lettuce Entertain You!" zeitgeist of Disney-Giuliani New York. It's the ultimate commentary on the new improved Gotham that all other weeklies have become quaint anachronisms, while *Time Out* is the harbinger of what's to come. Seek it out if you want to know what's happening free of ideological cant, but don't go expecting razor sharp social commentary. While the design of the guides and the brevity of the articles make this far more user-friendly than any other New York weekly (think *USA Today*), the content needs a lot more than a British imprimatur.

> **Village Voice.** 36 Cooper Sq. ☎ **212/475-3300.** www.villagevoice.com. Available free on streetcorners.

Look at Manhattan right now, at the geeks drinking Ketel at the Monkey Bar, at the Prada-clad caption writers at Ace Gallery for a Friday night magazine party, at account executives driving Explorers and flying west to go snowboarding and even at people just getting by on putatively low-level salaries and long-money dinner tabs 4 nights a week, and you'll see where the yuppie is now. Among us all, anonymous and relatively doing-all-right, buying shit at Tower, heading home to an overpriced apartment on the train. Among us all, living on Ludlow Street, in Battery Park City, on the Upper West Side, shacked up with four artists in a Williamsburg loft: living a middle-class American fantasy, circa 1955. A chicken on every menu, a cab on every street corner.

Have a job in Manhattan, an apartment, don't live in a squat? You're doing okay, and a decade ago you would have been called a yuppie, even if your work's welding widgets to poles and calling it art. A number to consider while you think about it: 45% of people aged 18–30 invest in the stock market now, averaging 19% returns. Approach crucifixion age in Manhattan with a rug in your living room and a 401(k) in your drawer, and you're a yuppie, an internalized one: part of the game.

There's a sense of inevitability to low-level financial success in New York just now, a belief in the right to a 20% return. That's bond in New York right now. It's bond for whole squads of hipster New Yorkers and nerd New Yorkers and New Yorkers of all shades of white who have IRAs and stock portfolios and the generally exuberant feeling that everything's okay. It's okay for those without annuities, too, for those making money and blowing and making more and paying off credit cards and doing it all over again. Think about it. Where'd you have dinner last night? The night before that? It was okay, it wasn't okay, you'll find an okay place pretty soon, you'll try things out. Everything's cool.

Look at the papers, the polls, the TV. The president gets blowjobs in the Oval Office? Who gives a shit? We're doing all right. Giuliani's an asshole? Does not matter. We're doing all right. Microsoft rules the world? No way! Who wants some oysters?

This is not romantic stuff, not by a longshot. What we're looking at in New York in 1998 is actually quite the opposite of that: an unromantic middle-class realism of a sort that 40 years ago would lead to hippies, now with a side of beer-batter onion rings and homemade ketchup. Everyone's okay. Party's not over. Party's just droning on.

—Sam Sifton, *New York Press*, April 22–28, 1998 (reprinted by permission)

I've got to hand it to the *Voice*—they have refused to even acknowledge the loud and boorish noises emanating from the Baltimore refugees at *New York Press,* who think they are about to dethrone the king of alternative weeklies. The folks at *New York Press* are a lot like Pat Buchanan—full of bluster, very entertaining, turning an inevitably losing battle into a heroic struggle of right and wrong, but in the end shooting themselves in the foot because there is no real muscle behind the threat. The *Voice* will survive and even prosper not only because of its superior investigative reporting, but because people forget that New Yorkers can be quite loyal and provincial—and no true New Yorker is going to allow a glossy import or a prickly Balto "newspaper" to completely dethrone a local liberal institution.

Monthlies and Bimonthlies

› *City Limits: New York's Urban Affairs News Magazine.* 40 Prince St. ☎ 212/925-9820.

Way before you were born, cities had newspapers that were different from one another. But, with the discovery of the futon-buyin', bar-hoppin', latte-drinkin' demographic, even the ubiquitous Free Urban Weeklies of America began to look alike. This makes sense since many of them have the same owner (search Yahoo under "New Times"). Serious local news coverage has suffered. While there is no real substitute for weekly events listings, "Anything Goes" personals, or Ask Isadora, at times the inquiring New Yorker may crave a bit more, shall we say, reportage. At times like these, *City Limits* fills the gap on the local front. It is a source of in-depth information about tenants' rights, social services, and neighborhood issues. *City Limits* moves past the easy hype of crime statistics to make sense of New York's dizzyingly complex local politics and Byzantine bureaucracy. If only it were a weekly.

› *George.* 1633 Broadway. ☎ 212/767-6100. Online at AOL, keyword George.

This exercise in Kennedy largesse should probably go the way of all other overblown and essentially pointless New York rags started by the rich and famous (think *Egg*), and yet somehow soldiers on. For this reason alone, it's a marvel, even though it seems mired more in the Bissette model of vacuous celebrity worship than in the traditional Kennedy model of intelligent liberal discourse.

› *Interview.* 575 Broadway. ☎ 212/941-2900.

The ballooning Ingrid Sischy says her magazine covers "people who are doing things for the right reasons." Give me a break. Anybody who says Warhol's New York was a "lifesaver" needs to have her sense of history examined. *Interview* really has no purpose anymore, and slags on in the hopes that the Warhol era might be recycled once again.

> ### New York Independent Film Monitor. 244 Fifth Ave., Suite 2310.
> ☎ 212/865-0164. www.nyfilmmonitor.com.

It is now widely regarded that New York is the center of independent film, usurping formerly creative hotbeds like San Francisco. And the newly launched *New York Independent Film Monitor* documents the scene. From reviews of festivals to using the Web as a film medium, to a comprehensive production guide to crew calls, pre-production, and shoot listings, this little paper is a must for the independent film person. Of course, the whole notion of "independent film" is so bogus and old hat by now it's questionable whether the term has any meaning left at all.

> ### Paper. 529 Broadway. ☎ 212-226-4405. www.papermag.com.

Packed with far more puffery than the other downtown periodicals (it reads like one big advertorial), *Paper* still keeps on vogueing thanks to the indomitable will of its two founders and principal editors, the friendly Kim Hastreiter and the more reserved David Herskovits. *Paper* was never a media darling like *Spy* or the original *Details*, but it always positioned itself as if it was. The problem with *Paper* is that, instead of rein-venting a downtown-style magazine to meet the complex cultural ethos of the late '90s, it often reads as if it wants to be the original *Details*, circa 1989. But who the hell cares where Eurotrash, supermodels, and other assorted "power hitters" shine their shoes, eat their steak frites, and wipe their smug and stupid butts. *Details* was bought out by Condé Nast, the real *Spy* was sold to the stupidest bidder, and so should have ended attitudinal publishing in '80s New York. At that point all talk of celebs, posing, and words like "dish" should have ended too. Most people of any spiritual depth weren't part of the culture of repugnant drug-addled snobbiness that characterized New York from the early days of Studio 54 to 1988, but those that were still part of it come 1989 recognized the shallowness of their ways and either went on a long Vipassana retreat, flew out to SF to fashion something digital, or made babies. *Paper* goes on assuming that the nightclubbing trendoid "model-fueled fabulosity" of the '80s still rules. Nineties early adapters want publications that are smart and real. And *Paper* is neither. ("Work it girl"—NOT!)

> ### Screw. Milky Way Productions, P.O. Box 432, Old Chelsea Station, New York, NY
> 10113. ☎ 212/989-8001.

Loathsome free-speech crusader Al "Be Your Own Cock" Goldstein would be the first to admit exactly what he is: an enormously fat, cigar-chomping, pastrami-juice-and-mustard-stained pornographer. Similarly, his brainchild, *Screw*, is a repulsive but irresistible icon of the American dream gone awry. "The world's greatest newspaper" has been on New York newsstands weekly since 1968, covering the rise and fall of New York's swing clubs ("All-night orgy plus all-you-can-eat buffet!"), dungeons, and the commercial sex industry in general, outlasting most other "alternative" papers of its generation. The argument of Goldstein is that *Screw* makes no pretense of respectability. By contrast, *Hustler* is very L.A.: colorful, glossy, redneck, racist, and cinematic. Models are sprayed with glycerin and photographed by the pool. *Screw* is New York: newsprint monochrome photos taken from stock archives, Borsht Belt racist, but unexpectedly literate and compassionate. Gay and straight ads are listed side by side as equal partners in degradation. The list of regular contributors contains such underground heroes as R. Crumb, painter Joe Coleman, and writer Danielle Willis. Feeling kinda lonely? Check out Al's "TV Guide."

> *Silicon Alley Reporter.* Free all over town.

Forget for a second that there really isn't any place that can rightfully be called Silicon Alley, despite desperate attempts to claim that it's 28th and Broadway on down (it's all over town, folks, c'mon!), and forget all those prejudices you might have against technoblathering publications written by and for the undersexed overpixelated Ronin jitterati, and take a look at this freebie. It's not great—a lot of bogus hype about New York's still fragile Internet industry. (You want quid pro quo blurring of church and state? You got it here, Shogun.) But occasionally, OCCASIONALLY, perhaps because it's a New York mag, and not a bratty Silicon Valley rag, it just cuts loose and tells it like it is. Such as in this selection from the Editor's Desk: "Ten years from now people will laugh when they read about all the attention given to the browser wars. Give me a break, is *Seinfeld* funnier on a Sony TV rather than JVC? New York and Los Angeles are becoming the driving force in the Internet Industry for a very simple reason: they are the talent and media capitals of the world. Would you rather make the camera that shot *Citizen Kane,* or make *Citizen Kane*? Which has done more for the film industry? For history?" Amen, Brother Calacanis. Is the crackie gonna kill for the pipe or the rock?

Sex

Amsterdam it ain't.

First, the **Times Square revitalization plan**—which had been kicked around so long that no one took it seriously—*actually went through,* whipping the area into a makeover so complete that a New Yorker returning after 10 years away would have a hard time recognizing the place. The core of the area's sleazy X-rated theaters—Adonis, Avon, Capri, Circus, Eros, the Hollywood Twin, Kings, Victory, and the Show Palace (where Annie Sprinkle got her start)—have all been either boarded up, demolished, or magically transformed into something more G-rated. Used to be you couldn't go three steps down 42nd without someone hissing "smoke, coke, switchblades" at you; now, instead, you've got the Disney store hawking a fine selection of Mickeywear.

Then, in mid-1998, Mayor Rudy G. turned his Quality of Life campaign loose on the area, imposing new rules that ostensibly apply to all residential neighborhoods in the city but seem targeted mainly at the remaining shops along newly valuable Eighth Avenue. Interestingly, though, the rules have set in motion a nicely surreal capitalist situation in which sex emporiums have to limit their supply of dirty videos, inflatable sex dolls, dildos, and butt plugs to 40% of their total stock, devoting the rest to whatever family-friendly merchandise they choose.

While at first most shops responded by stocking either remaindered novels, cheap tourist gimcracks, or mainstream videos (posters of Brad Pitt in *Seven Years in Tibet* appeared in the windows of half the adult video shops in town), some have been a little more creative. **Show World Center,** 303 W. 42nd St., at Eighth Avenue (☎ 212/247-6643), the king of the remaining sex emporiums, has apparently gone into the luggage business, judging by their window display, while **Amsterdam Video,** 287 Amsterdam Ave., between West 73rd and West 74th streets (☎ 212/580-4900), now stocks a selection of original art ("SPECIAL—$1,000!"), with the "other" merchandise relegated to the back of the store, behind a beaded curtain.

You gotta love that Rudy.

An Interview with
Annie Sprinkle

If there is one person from the New York avant-garde who has the potential to charm the Christian Right into submission, it would be Ms. Annie Sprinkle. Annie has this uncanny ability to make the most edgy subject seem perfectly normal and palatable.

The last time we saw Annie she was performing her Post-Porn Modernist show, during which she invited audience members to view her cervix through a speculum. But in the mid-'90s, feeling weary of New York, the legendary porn-star-turned-performance-artist closed up her cervix (at least to the public), packed up, and moved lock, stock, and dildo out of the city.

We caught our old friend in a new mode, shorn of all her post-porn trappings—Annie as Nature Girl, or, rather, Nature Goddess, finally doing her *Green Acres* thing. She hasn't given up sex or orgasms, however. In fact, she had one for us, albeit a somewhat earthier orgasm than we had expected. It was a tantric energy orgasm, performed picnic style on a blanket on the lawn. "I've had better," she said, upon finishing. "I've had worse."

Monk: Do you still do the [Post-Porn Modernist] shows?

Annie Sprinkle: No, I don't. I haven't done that performance in a few years.

Monk: By the end of its run, what was it about? Did it still have the public cervix announcement and all that?

Annie Sprinkle: It had evolved. Yeah, it still had the public cervix announcement, but I grew and matured. I was just going so much more towards women, and a lot of that show is about my experience with men. So that was a big change. Because when I started doing that performance I was pretty much heterosexual. When I ended doing that performance I was a staunch lesbian. Now, I have a much different focus and different interests and things have changed. Things I liked years ago, now I couldn't stand.

Monk: For example?

Annie Sprinkle: Humiliating someone. I used to be a professional dominatrix. A guy would come and pay me, and I'd say, "Kiss my feet, you asshole," and slap his face and call him a piece of shit. I would get turned on, he would get turned on, and [we thought], "Isn't this fun, aren't we learning, aren't we healing ourselves here?" So I did all this kinky stuff. And in a way, maybe it worked, or maybe I made a mistake. This is what I'm questioning.

Maybe that isn't such a healing thing, and maybe that's perpetuating deep neuroses of being in a society that's sex negative and sexually abusive and patriarchal. I used to do all these things that I thought were intimate. I thought I was really being intimate because I was piercing someone or because I was licking their anus. That's all very nice and wonderful, but that's not really as deep and intimate as eye-gazing, for example.

Monk: Earlier today you said that we all carry wounds, and I wondered what your wounds are.

Annie Sprinkle: As a prostitute, there were good days, and there were bad days. It took me quite a while to get the nasty, painful sexual experiences out of my system. The people that were too rough and the people who were clumsy or the people who wanted to rip you off or the people that didn't respect you. It took me a long time to get that out of my system, and I did, for the most part.

Monk: How are you bringing politics into what you do? How are you going about trying to change those situations—for example, how women are treated? Are you being very political in what you do now?

Annie Sprinkle: I feel like the erotic massage rituals are [a] very political act because they're so empowering of women, and personally, I think my politics has to do with teaching women about their sexuality and creating environments where women have space to heal their sexuality and to use the power of their sexuality to heal themselves, to grow, to become more enlightened. So it's more like the personal is political. It's like creating environments and spaces [for] women [that are] like training soldiers, so to speak, helping to train the troops and creating boot camps for women-warriors that are strong and glowing and full of energy. A sexually satisfied woman is a happy woman. That's political.

Monk: Have you done everything that can be done in terms of fetishes or in the realm of sexual experience? Like in the Hellfire days, did you do practically anything that could be done?

Annie Sprinkle: Well, I think I participated in a lot of things. I know I've done some things that at the time seemed perfectly fine and wholesome and great. Like, my lover Les, he used to like [it] when I punched him in the stomach. And I'm looking back thinking, that's what he wanted, that's what he liked, that's what turned him on. And I'm thinking, now wait a minute, this is someone I really loved. Just because he was an abused child and his father and mother used to beat on him doesn't mean that I should give him what he wants. Because it's not really what he wants. What he really wants is what we all want, [which] is to be loved. I thought to give him what he wanted was to love him. I was wrong. To love him would be to try to show him a new way.

Monk: So your new criteria would be if there's not love, it's not okay.

Annie Sprinkle: Well, everything I did was with love, but I don't think I looked deep enough into what, or thought seriously enough about what I was doing.

Monk: Do you think you'll be performing again, and what shape do you think your performance would take?

Annie Sprinkle: I have a nice new little show. It's called Annie Sprinkle's Herstory of Porn, Reel to Real. It's part film diary, performance, and a play about my 25-year evolution through the sexual revolution. In it I explore three different archetypes: the girl next door, the slut, and the goddess. Using my film diary, I take you through seven different phases of my sexual performance, represented by seven different movie theaters, and I interact with the film clips. So, I'm touring with that show. [Plus, I did my] tarot card deck, a sexual healing tarot card deck, of photographs of women. But not pin-uppy. My pin-up days are over.

"*I think my politics has to do with teaching women about their sexuality . . . to heal themselves, to grow, to become more enlightened.*"

Spirituality

Christ is present in New York. Buddha, too. And Mohammed. Even a Jewish messiah. As rich in character as its greatest attractions, here are the city's finest places of meditation and worship.

Buddhist

> **Eastern States Buddhist Temple of America, Inc.** 64B Mott St., at Canal (Chinatown). ☎ **212/966-6229.**

For the average Chinese person, Buddhism is little more than a devotional religion: You give money and light candles for good luck. The heart of the teaching—hardcore sitting meditation—is gone. Still, this temple, with its authentic monk standing guard out front, has a certain charm and quiet power.

> **New York Shambhala Center.** 118 W. 22nd St., 6th floor, between Sixth and Seventh aves. (Chelsea). ☎ **212/675-1231.**

Michael Monk at the Saint Frances Cabrini Shrine

A more secular approach to Tibetan Buddhism, animated by the teachings of the late, great, overweight, and alcoholic Chogyam Trungpa (author of the modern Buddhist classic *Myth of Freedom*).

Christian

> **Abyssinian Baptist Church.** 132 W. 138th St. (a.k.a. Odell Clark Place), between Lenox Ave. and Adam Clayton Powell Jr. Blvd. (Harlem). ☎ **212/862-7474.**

Not the first place we'd go for a rousing black Baptist service, but the church does have an important history, and the young, debonair Pastor Calvin Butts ably carries on its agitprop tradition. Though it has become a favorite stop for European tourists in sandals, shorts, and T-shirts, the Abyssinian still offers an established, mainstream version of the black Baptist tradition. While the choir doesn't sway quite as far, the clapping is not quite as boisterous, and parishioners don't shout quite as loudly for salvation as in other Harlem churches, it is, nevertheless, the real article and, by all accounts, a positive force in rebuilding the long-neglected Harlem community. (See also Calvin Butts interview later in this section.)

Services at the Abyssinian Baptist Church, Harlem

> **Friends Meeting House.** 137–16 Northern Blvd., near College Point Blvd. (Flushing, Queens). ☎ **718/358-9636.**

The oldest place of worship in the city, built in 1694.

> **Saint Frances Cabrini Shrine.** 701 Fort Washington Ave., at W. 192nd St., just south of Fort Tryon Park (Washington Heights). ☎ **212/923-3536.**

Mother Cabrini, the patron saint of immigrants—and, some say, of parking—is the only saint whose remains are in New York. She's there, in a glass case (although most of her is wax) in the center of the St. Frances Cabrini Shrine. Parishioners come from far and wide to pray for miracles. She's known for one in particular: allegedly, after her death, a lock of her hair restored sight to an infant.

> **Trinity Church.** Broadway and Wall St. (Financial District). ☎ **212/602-0700.**

This, dear friends, is the spiritual center of Wall Street, if you can imagine such a thing. It is where traders go, not to pray for a bullish stock market, but to expurgate the darkness in their souls. The conventional wisdom seems to be that a good trader can't get emotionally attached to a stock. Success requires one to compartmentalize emotions like compassion. Trinity Church is the compartment where a trader can let those feelings flow. Try the 12:15pm daily service, a model of Wall Street deadline concision.

Jewish

> **Lubavitcher Hasidim World Headquarters.** 770 Eastern Parkway, at Brooklyn Ave. (Crown Heights, Brooklyn). No phone.

To our surprise, the Lubavitchers were welcoming, if not overly friendly. A wispy-bearded boy greeted us at the door and invited us to hang out during postservice activities. I was wearing a stocking cap to cover my head, but the young boy offered his yarmulke, deftly slipping it off his head without removing his hat. "Love the stranger," we later learned, is part of Jewish teaching. And boy were we strangers. Bearded men in dark suits and black hats were reading from the Torah and Talmud and praying, while older members sat at the table drinking vodka and telling stories.

> **Chabad of the West Side.** 101 W. 92nd St. and Columbus Ave. (Upper West Side). ☎ **212/864-5010.**

These Manhattan Lubavitchers offer the free weekly Torah Fax, "a 3-minute infusion of Jewish content in your day." Just call with your fax number. Now, no matter how busy you are, you "can always have a dvar Torah to say at your shabbos table."

CHABAD-LUBAVITCH

Hat: Wide black fedora, sometimes knit kippah in summer

Beard: Not always

Dress: Often modern business clothes, sometimes black caftan

Peyes (sidecurls): No

Dynasty descended from: Lithuania

Neighborhood: Crown Heights, Brooklyn

Commentary: The best known of the Hasids, thanks to their Mitzvah Tank RVs, subway ads, and huge Hanukah menorahs. Their late Rebbe, so they say, is the Messiah, and they are evangelists (they're quickly becoming Jewish Moonies). And—surprise, surprise—they're on the Web, "Chabad-Lubavitch in Cyberspace," at www.chabad.org.

SATMAR HASIDIM

Hat: Black and round, sometimes tall fur hats

Beard: Always

Dress: Long black coats, white shirts, work coveralls, black knee socks and knickers

Peyes (sidecurls): Yes

Dynasty descended from: Hungary

Neighborhood: Williamsburg, Brooklyn, Midtown diamond district

Commentary: Back in the shtetl again. Living on the other side of the bridge from the Williamsburg hipsters, they have huge families, speak Yiddish at home, and don't watch TV. They drive to work in school buses with a curtain down the aisle, dividing men from women. They don't want to know you and you probably don't want to know them. No Web site.

Muslim

> **Islamic Center of New York.** 1711 Third Ave., at 97th St. (Upper East Side/Spanish Harlem). ☎ **212/722-5234.**

It's hard to miss this cross between the Citicorp building and the Taj Mahal. Taking up a full city block, it sits right on the line that divides the Upper East Side from Spanish Harlem. Construction of the center was halted for a while in the early '90s when financier Kuwait was invaded by Iraq, but after the war, New York finally got its first mosque big enough and grand enough to rival the city's churches and synagogues. Except for the actual prayer rooms, the center is open to non-Muslims.

> **Masjid Malcolm Shabazz.** 102 W. 116th St., at Malcolm X Blvd. (a.k.a. Lenox Ave.) (Harlem). ☎ **212/662-2200.**

That a place of worship and the street it's on are both named after the same person shows how important the man who was born Malcolm Little, became Malcolm X, and died al-Hajj Malik Shabazz was to Harlem. For years, the original building on this site, a former casino, was Elijah Mohammed's Temple Number 7 and Malcolm X's base. However, having broken with the Nation of Islam, the new mosque on this site is now part of mainstream Sunni Islam, and is under the leadership of Imam W. D. Mohammed. Still an important cultural and spiritual center, it welcomes appropriately dressed visitors.

Treatment

> **Smithers Alcohol and Drug Treatment Center.** 56 E. 93rd St., between Madison and Park (Upper East Side). ☎ **212/369-9566** rehab, 212/523-6491 for immediate detox.

If you're going to detox in the city (a bit of a contradiction), you might as well do it in style. This renowned clinic, where Dwight Gooden, John Cheever, Truman Capote, and Darryl Strawberry all took the cure, is located in a 40-room mansion, with a beautifully landscaped garden in back.

Zen

> **Chogye International Zen Center.** 400 E. 14th St., Apt. 2D, at First Ave. (East Village). ☎ **212/353-0461.**

While this place may not fit your picture of Zen (pristine and oh-so-Japanese), the funky, friendly Kwan Um school offers some of the finest, most down-to-earth Zen teaching in the Northeast. The newly expanded New York center has seen some ups and downs, but it's coming into its own again.

> Dai Bosatsu New York City Center. 223 E. 67th St., at Second Ave. (Upper East Side). ☎ **212/861-3333.**

This handsome, tightly maintained, and very Japanese center offers the Northeast's premier Rinzai experience. The place doesn't give an inch on any of its many rules of conduct and doesn't tolerate slackers who won't cough up the high meditation fees ($10 a visit). During retreats, you are advised literally to run to the interview with Eido Roshi (to show you are eager for the teaching).

> Village Zendo. 15 Washington Place, no. 4-E, near Washington Square Park (West Village). ☎ **212/674-0832.** www.villagezendo.org. E-mail: ohara@is.nyu.edu.

Shifting their allegiance from the angular, severe-looking John Daido Loori to the loopy and roly-poly Bernie Glassman hasn't changed the direction of this zendo in the heart of NYU. Strong common sense teaching from Pat O'Hara, and very gay-friendly.

> Zen Center of New York City (a.k.a. Fire Lotus Zendo). 119 W. 23rd St., Room 1009, between Sixth and Seventh aves. (Chelsea). ☎ **212/642-1591.** www.zen-mtn.org/zcnyc/firelotus.shtml.

Run by Bonnie Mytotai Treace, wife of photographer/Zen Master John Daido Loori of the Zen Mountain Monastery in Mount Tremper, this Chelsea zendo emphasizes art as an expression of Zen realization. Sometimes the art dharma gets a bit too precious and earnest (my major beef with the likes of Natalie Goldberg, author of *Writing Down the Bones*), but at least you can count on the calligraphy being top notch. Since we're talking aesthetics, you might find this low-key zendo less appealing than the stiff, pristine, money-grubbing Dai Bosatsu Zen Center on the Upper East Side, but the natives are far more friendly.

Calvin Butts:

The Monk Interview, Summer 1995

Sunday morning. We're at the Abyssinian Baptist Church, in Harlem, the oldest black church in New York City. Its pews, the color of wine, are packed—with Harlem matriarchs dressed in white (white gloves, white hats, white purses and shoes) and with white tourists (lots of white tourists).

The choir bursts into song. The Harlem matriarchs praise the Lord, they shout amen. The tourists look pleased. This is Harlem to them, something to write home about. Then the pastor, the Reverend Calvin O. Butts III, appears. He is a powerful man, with a powerful voice. At the church for more than 20 years and at its helm since 1989, Butts has kept up Abyssinian's longstanding activist tradition. Butts calls himself "an advocate for black people," and he has taken up numerous causes in the name of the African-American community. He has mounted campaigns against cigarette and alcohol advertisements in black neighborhoods and, more recently, against rap lyrics ("I . . . believe," he wrote in a letter to *Billboard* magazine, "that African-American women . . . did not struggle and jeopardize their lives to give young black music artists the temerity to refer to [them] as bitches and whores"). Through the Abyssinian Development Corporation he has been involved in the redevelopment of Harlem. The organization has bought Harlem landmarks, has created about 600 units of housing, and has opened a school, the Thurgood Marshall Academy for Learning and Social Change.

Butts is charismatic and proud. He could be a politician, but he says he's not. "I never felt called" is the way he puts it. "I don't make any bones about this. Everything that I have, everything that I am, I owe to God."

As the sermon comes to a close, the late morning arrivals cause even more congestion in the back of the pews. By sermon's end there is scarcely breathing room. Rounds of cameras click away at the emotional outpouring near the altar, as Reverend Butts brings his sermon to a close.

Later, upstairs in his private office, following an endless parade of the worshipful, we finally sit down with Calvin Butts. He at once chastises us for our casual dress and then somberly, if not skeptically, lends us his ear.

*"If you want to reduce crime,
you've got to put people to work."*

Interview

Jim Monk: When did you become minister?

Reverend Butts: I have been a minister at Abyssinian Church for 23 years. I became the pastor, the senior minister, in 1989.

Jim Monk: What is the focus now, politically, of the church?

Reverend Butts: Well, we are focusing on several things. Of course, we had—well, one of our major points is, we believe that the criminal justice system is anything but just, especially where people of color are concerned. When you look at the numbers of people in prison today, they are overwhelmingly people of African descent. But people of African descent are not the major perpetrators of the crimes. Now, people say, "Well, no, that's not true, Reverend . . . You know that black people are in jail because they are selling drugs and using drugs and committing crimes to get drugs." In the state of New York, 70% of all the people who sell drugs are white, and 80% of all the people who use drugs are black, but only 9% of those in jail are white, and 90% of those in jail are black. Now, that's true. I mean, I'm not trying to make it up. I mean, it's absolutely true. We also know that prisons are not serving to help rehabilitate people. When you go into prison, you literally come out worse. We also know that these prisons are costing the taxpayers huge amounts of money. It really does cost less to educate a person or rehabilitate a person than it does to incarcerate somebody. So if you really want to talk about bridging the budget gap in the state of New York, for example, let's start talking about closing some of these prisons and stopping the construction of some of these prisons.

> *"I believe deeply in America, with all of its faults and problems, because it's my country."*

But we think that if children can be taught how to resolve their conflicts without violence, this will help to reduce crime. We're trying to give children more to do. If you walk around Harlem during the week and especially on weekends, there are not enough centers, not enough people in the parks. Our children don't have anything to do. The schools have taken away the musical instruments. They've taken away the art classes. In fact, one of the things people say that came out of not having any instruments, they started scratching the records, you know, in the kind of hip-hop tradition. So we're trying to bring those things back as a way of reducing crime. Creating jobs. We have an economic development arm. That economic development arm is helping. We've already created about 16 new businesses. These new small businesses, they employ four or five people in jobs. We have several major construction projects coming up, one being a Pathmark supermarket. That's 200 construction jobs and 200 regular full-time union jobs. If you want to reduce crime, you've got to put people to work. So we're trying to do that.

Jim Monk: Now, there's a recent study that came out that showed that crime in New York had gone down 27% to 35% in the last year, and it's still been going down since Giuliani has been mayor. First of all, do you believe that's true; have you noticed crime reductions in this community? And, if it is true, what do you attribute it to?

Reverend Butts: Well, one of the things that you can attribute to the Giuliani administration that I think has helped to curb crime somewhat is a police force that is helping to reduce crime by striking a sense of fear into people. The police force under Giuliani has been extremely insensitive. But also what I think is that this reduction in crime is a smoke screen. Yes, crime has gone down, but when you cut education as it's been cut, when you cut social welfare programs as they've been cut, and when you cut other types of programs that are designed for helping people, you're not going to maintain that reduction. And I think that Giuliani hopes to maintain it by having the police beat up on people and curse people. But that won't last, unless you begin to put into place the real, substantive things that take care of people who are hurting, that house people who are homeless, that provide jobs for people who need work. And those kinds of things are not being done now.

Jim Monk: In the last 5 years, 6 years, since you've been around, Pastor, has the quality of life improved in Harlem? Have you seen things get better?

Reverend Butts: Well, yes. You know, you can see them get better in spots. Overall, I think that there have been some tremendous changes. I can look right across the street and much of that housing was abandoned. It's now all full.

Jim Monk: Exactly.

Reverend Butts: So, yes. But there's so many other things that need to be done. For instance, I watched the drug problem improve, then I watched it get dramatically worse. What happened was there was a heroin problem that was terrible. Then for a while, that heroin problem seemed to subside, and then, just as soon as that happened, the crack problem popped up. And I think that it's going to be hard to get a grip on that. I don't know what the answer is.

Jim Monk: I see, though, just walking around Harlem I sense, I don't know what it is— maybe I'm way off base here, but I sense something's improved. I really do.

Reverend Butts: Well, a lot of things. I mean, there's hope.

Jim Monk: Yeah, I sense that.

Reverend Butts: You know, I mean, like I say, we're building new supermarkets, we're restoring the Renaissance Ballroom, we're restoring Small's Paradise. We're building and creating new businesses, the congregations are vibrant and alive, and I live in Harlem, other people are starting to live in Harlem. Yes, Harlem itself—hope springs eternal. There's always that resiliency, that fight back. We've got to overcome a drug problem here as the rest of the country has. We've got to.

If I could just find a way to create more jobs. America couldn't be America without our labor, our sweat, our contribution [but] I am not for any rhetoric that puts down other people. I don't agree with that. You know, I don't believe in calling the—you know, the whole white race is not a devil race, as far as I'm concerned. I don't believe that. I am an advocate for black people. Now, because I'm an advocate for black people doesn't mean that I hate anybody else. But as an advocate for black people, I work, I see my calling as to work to redeem and empower people of African descent. In that work, I work along with whites, I work along with Asians, I work along with Latinos, I work along with Jews, you know. I believe deeply in America, with all of its faults and problems, because it's my country. And there's no place else that I want to go. I like to visit other places. I love Africa. But this is my country. I didn't choose to come here, I was brought here against my will, but I'm here now. And so, as the expression goes, we've come over on different boats, but we're all in the same boat now.

Michael Monk: In the congregation today there's a lot of tourists. How do you feel about that, that your congregation is subjected to a lot of people just coming here sightseeing?

Reverend Butts: I've got two feelings. One, they're always welcome. We like to be thought of as a place that people want to see. I hope that many of the people who come go away having felt welcome and inspired. I hope they understand our worship. A lot of people who come, come simply because they think they're going to hear gospel music. I'm a little miffed at that. Because we sing a wide variety of music here. We sing European classical music, we sing Negro spirituals, we sing inspiration music, we sing traditional gospel music. We have very, very good musicians. And we have a good time. So if they just want to come—for instance, one [German] woman called yesterday and said, "Will there be Negroes there?"

Jim Monk: She did not!

Reverend Butts: "Will there be Negroes there?" So, I said, "Well, are you coming to see Negroes or are you coming to worship God?"

After the interview, we stroll outside, where a coterie of Calvin's friends and family are waiting to join him. Calvin Butts strikes a charismatic pose—solid, confident, methodical, and a tad bit skeptical. He is a proud man. And, from what we garnered, a happy man. He is also a man who knows how to work it.

"Monk," he says gently, after a long pensive pause.

"Yeah, we live on the road and write about life on the road. Simplicity, simplicity, simplicity," says Jim enthusiastically.

"That's what I should do," concurs the preacher par excellence, placating the Monks with a Thoreauian rap about "getting a smaller car," knowing full well he'll never dump his beautiful Cadillac.

Above all else, Calvin Butts is the consummate politician.

"I am not for any rhetoric that puts down other people. I don't agree with that."

Sports and Recreation

Amusement Parks

› **Astroland.** 1000 Surf Ave. (Coney Island, Brooklyn). ☎ 718/372-0275.

Forget Great America; this is the place true Monks go to have fun. It's not an amusement park by today's standards. Whether by choice or not, Astroland is amusement park as historical document. It limps along, steadily decaying, never improving its facilities. A word of advice from Dick Zigun, founder of Coney Island's Sideshows by the Seashore: "Everybody goes on the Cyclone, everybody goes on the Wonder Wheel. Let's go a little more offbeat. Go underneath the Wonder Wheel; go on Spook-a-Rama, the world's strangest leftover, 1960s, day-glo-in-the-dark spook house ride. It smells like cat piss."

Pickup Basketball

› **Carmine Rec Center.** 1 Clarkson St., at Seventh Ave. (West Village).
☎ 212/242-5228.

We like the camaraderie here. Some great half-court games, although you have to watch your head. A high leap in the corner can land you at the chiropractor's. Did we mention it's cheap? $25 a year buys you everything: pool, basketball, workout room. The best deal in the city, bar none.

› **4th Street Courts.** W. 4th St. and Sixth Ave. (West Village). No phone.

It gets all the hype, but we usually give it a miss. Either it's filled with overzealous and overserious NBA drop-outs, or it's occupied by school tournaments. Rarely available for a simple pick-up game. Besides, the cage is too confining for all but the most graceful players, although if you're any good or at all vain, it's fun to have a crowd watch your every move. Anthony Mason is rumored to have made his mark here.

› **Holcombe Rucker Memorial Playground.** 155th St. and Eighth Ave. (Harlem).
☎ 212/408-0204.

A court for serious hoops, used mostly by area homeboys, although the occasional Billy Hoyle will make an appearance. Famous for its annual Entertainer's Basketball Classic.

> **Tompkins Square Park.** Between E. 7th and E. 10th sts., Avenues A and B (East Village). No phone.

We recommend the west side of the park, where half-court games rule. The full-court games, next to the roller basketball, are lame. Young studs hog, show off, and play squat for defense.

Billiards

> **Amsterdam Billiard Club.** 344 Amsterdam Ave., at 77th St. (Upper West Side).
☎ 212/496-8180.

For the hard-core aficionado. The players are devoted. They bring not only their own cues but also specially made gloves and glasses.

> **Chelsea Billiards.** 54 W. 21st St., between Fifth and Sixth aves. (Chelsea).
☎ 212/989-0096.

The Rolls Royce of billiard halls. This is the largest, cleanest, most professional hall in the city. The place stinks of success, with gorgeous full-size tables. Unfortunately, the same white fratheads and yuppies who now think it's cool to smoke fat cigars are likely to be shooting, loudly, next to you.

> **Mammoth Billiard 26.** 114 W. 26th St., between Sixth and Seventh aves. (Chelsea). ☎ 212/675-2626.

A funky, fun spot, with billiards, an indoor driving range, and four Ping-Pong tables. Most important, it's relatively cheap (pool is $3 an hour, Ping-Pong is $5 per table for 30 minutes) and open 24 hours, 7 days a week.

Bowling

> **Bowlmor Lanes.** 110 University Place, at W. 12th St. (West Village).
☎ 212/255-8188.

We came for the Monday night disco bowling. The music was loud and tribal. Our neighbors wore their hair slicked back. They bowled, danced (sort of), kissed, and chain-smoked. A Guess jeans ad come to life.

> **Gun Post Lanes.** 1213 E. Gun Hill Rd., near Boston Rd. (Bronx). ☎ 718/881-0331.

These lanes would be standard stuff in a mall, but here, in the heart of the Bronx, they're a gratifying find. Forty-eight lanes on two floors, with pool tables, pinball, and a bar/restaurant. They say they're open 24 hours, "if necessary" (whatever that means).

> **Leisure Time Bowling & Recreation Center.** 625 Eighth Ave., at 41st St. (in the Port Authority bus terminal). ☎ **212/268-6909.**

A clean, modern, upbeat bowling alley, like any you'd find in the 'burbs, but with one crucial difference: It's on an upstairs floor of New York's miserable, decaying Port Authority bus terminal. A bit of perverse middle-class irony, given all the other stuff that goes down inside this hellish gateway to Jersey.

Boxing

> **Gleason's Gym.** 75 Front St., just north of the Brooklyn Bridge (Brooklyn Heights, Brooklyn). ☎ **718/797-2872.**

Gleason's has the Raging Bull ambiance you'd expect from a New York gym (in fact, Jake LaMotta trained here). It's one of the oldest gyms in the country, and it shows: The staircase is grimy; the walls and floor are gray cement; yellowed newspaper clippings of past champions are tacked to the walls. About $10 will buy you an hour's worth of help from one of the house trainers, who will set you up with head gear, a cup, and a partner for sparring. (For $2, you can just watch.)

Chess

> **Washington Square Park and Bryant Park.** Washington Square: Between W. 4th St. and Waverly Place, University Place and MacDougal St. (West Village); Bryant Park: Sixth Ave., between W. 40th and W. 42nd sts. (Midtown).

Chess is popular these days. The last time world champ Gary Kasparov was in town to defend his title, he was mobbed by high school kids, just like a rock star. There is some disagreement over where the best players play out-of-doors, but we've seen some amazing games in both Washington Square and Bryant Park. Speed chess (on the clock, with only 5 minutes maximum thinking time allowed per player, per game) is not for the timid.

Sports Trivia

*The **Brooklyn Dodgers** were originally called the Brooklyn Trolley Dodgers because one couldn't cross a street in Brooklyn without dodging a trolley. Ironically, the Brooklyn Dodgers left Brooklyn and moved to Los Angeles, which had killed its trolley system years before.*

Fishing

Nine a.m. We're at the Bethesda Fountain, in Central Park, dressed in chest-high waders and John Deere caps. Even here, in the heart of New York City, we can't resist the urge to cast a line. Michael especially. He was the 1993 champion of the Kingston, Arkansas, Fly-Fishing Cast-Off. Our guide, Edwin Valentin, gives Jim a lesson in fly casting, while Michael, using the same arched back, pointed toe, and trailing hand that gave him the Olympian edge in Kingston, fishes a lake nearby. Edwin talks about tying flies. Michael spots a man half-exposed in a bush; he seems to be getting a blow job.

"You've got to watch out for that," says Edwin. "Sometimes they go right up to the rocks, plain as day."

"What day is that?" Michael asks.

The fresh air, the sunshine: fishing in Central Park

> **Urban Angler.** 118 E. 25th St., between Lexington and Park Ave. South (Flatiron District). ☎ **212/979-7600.**
You can book Edwin Valentin, New York's (actually, make that the world's) only fly-fishing guide to Central Park, through this place. They can provide other things, too: fishing licenses, gear, the works. Edwin's expensive, though; the last time we checked, he cost $100 for a half-day fishing some of Central Park's numerous ponds.

Health Clubs

> **Johnny Lats Gym.** 7 E. 17th St., between Broadway and Fifth Ave. (Union Square). ☎ **212/366-4426.**
Cabbies, towel-heads, and buffed-up, mean-ass mothafuckas populate this ugly, second-floor pump shop. No fancy Nautilus here. Just free weights, a few bikes, and one little George Jetson–style treadmill. But it's open 24 hours.

Russian and Turkish Baths

> **10th Street Baths.** 268 E. 10th St., between Avenue A and First Ave. (East Village). ☎ **212/473-8806.**
It's easy to imagine Al Capone visiting this legendary Turkish bathhouse. For 20 bucks you can lie in a very hot steam room while a fat old man beats you with scented birch leaves (they're called plotzas) and enjoy ice-cold pools, saunas, Jacuzzis, Swedish showers, and all the rest. It's all very 1930s. Lots of men with toothpick legs and huge bellies that shake like Jell-O.

Surfing

> **Fort Tilden.** All the way at the south end of Flatbush Ave., right on the Atlantic Ocean (Breezy Point, Queens).

An Interview with

Edwin Valentin,

Central Park Fly-Fishing Guide

Edwin Valentin is the real thing: He actually takes people fly-fishing in Central Park. He takes them other places, too, but he is best known for his excursions to Central Park. He is, in fact, Central Park's only fly-fishing guide. He's not cheap, though. A hundred dollars, not including license and equipment, will get you a half day wandering the park, pond to pond. But for the price you will get more than just fishing. Edwin will talk, too. (Book Edwin through Urban Angler, 118 E. 25th St., 3rd floor, ☎ 212/979-7600.)

Jim Monk: When was the first time you ever went fishing?

Edwin Valentin: On Coney Island, when I was 14.

Jim Monk: So what'd you take?

Edwin Valentin: String with a can. That's the first thing I fished with, a can and string.

Jim Monk: And you caught a fish?

Edwin Valentin: Yeah, with a can.

Jim Monk: You love to fish.

Edwin Valentin: Oh yeah, man.

Jim Monk: What's the strangest thing you've ever caught in here?

Edwin Valentin: The strangest thing? You want me to say? A condom.

Jim Monk: You caught a condom. Was the person still attached?

Edwin Valentin: And then a turtle. I caught a big turtle.

Jim Monk: Did you ever catch a rat?

Edwin Valentin: No. No rats.

Jim Monk: How'd you get started fly-fishing?

Edwin Valentin: One day I was fishing here for like a year, I see some guy fishing a fly rod, and I was talking to him. He was catching bluegills. And I told him he could catch bass. Then I made a little fly. I went home, took a duster, with a feather, peeled it, made my own fly.

Jim Monk: What's the biggest fish you ever caught here?

Edwin Valentin: Nineteen-inch bass.

Michael, who has been watching a mysterious object float by, suddenly turns.

Michael Monk: The biggest fish I caught in my life was when I was down in Louisiana, south of New Orleans, going toward Grand Isle. They've got bayous there. I was out there fishing one day with—nothing like this—just a little bamboo rod with a worm on the end. And then I put some bread with peanut butter on it. And I put this pole in the water. I was just settin' there. And I caught a catfish that was as long as my arm. It was like a big old ugly catfish. Have you ever seen a catfish? Catfish are monsters. Big old whiskers. Really, really ugly fish. That was the biggest fish, and it almost pulled me in. It caught me, I didn't catch it. 'Cause I lost it. It took my pole with it. It went off swimming with the pole.

Both Jim and Edwin stare at Michael for a moment.

Jim Monk: Is there a spirituality to fishing for you?

Edwin Valentin: I like the sport. And then the flies—when you make your own flies. You catch a fish with your fly. That makes me feel better. Much better, man.

Jim Monk: What do you like more, sex or fishing?

Edwin Valentin: That's a hard call. I don't mind having the two at the same time.

Jim Monk: If you were to describe the number one girl, like best girl, would you have her as a bass, a perch, or what kind of fish would she be?

Edwin Valentin: Muskie. Mean, rough, and vicious. That's what I love. I don't need no soft girls. I want hard, vicious girls. And they can fight, they can fight.

Awesome site of abandoned nuclear missile silos that once "protected" New York harbor from Soviet attack. The base was closed in the 1970s as part of the Salt II treaty, though there are tours available, and, just as important, a great clean beach, which, according to local surfers, has "the best waves on the east coast."

Swimming in Ice Cold Oceans

› **Polar Bear Club.** Contact Ken Krisses, ☎ 718/748-1674.

They get their name from swimming in icy cold waters during the coldest months of the year. We met the Brooklyn contingent of the Polar Bear Club at an early Mermaid Parade back in the summer of 1990, and we never forgot this motley crew of middle-aged ambassadors of good cheer. They have the same go-for-it gusto and Old World joi de vivre as some eccentric nudists we've met. They made us honorary members of their venerable club, though swimming in the ocean in June was hardly a test of our monkhood. No doubt they'd heard rumors of our protean feats at other times of year—swimming in Lake Superior, skinny-dipping in Sommes Sound, Michael Monk's yearly ritual of taking a dip on January 1 (no matter where he is on the planet). We recommend you connect with these fine folk too, assuming you are a true Monk, and not one of those shallow, image-conscious, comfort-seeking pansies unwilling to grapple with the demons of bone-chilling cold.

Swimming in Pools

› **Asser Levy.** E. 23rd St. and Asser Levy Place (Midtown South). ☎ 212/447-2020.

What makes this far–East Side rec center famous is its Old World indoor pool. It's a beaut: high-vaulted ceiling, sunlight streaming through a skylight, and, at the foot of the pool, a marble lion's-head spigot. The indoor pool is open only after Labor Day, although the outdoor pool isn't bad either. Fact: Asser Levy was America's first Jewish citizen.

› **John Jay Pool.** John Jay Park, Cherokee Place, E. 77th St. and FDR Dr. (Upper East Side).

Perhaps the nicest outdoor public pool in Manhattan. It's surrounded by playgrounds, park benches, and, unexpectedly, a lush canopy of trees. Open after July 1, and it's free.

Tic-Tac-Toe

> **Chinatown Fair.** 8 Mott St., just north of Worth St. (Chinatown).

Trivia Trivia

Just down the street from the Mei Dick barbershop, in the heart of old Chinatown, Chinatown Fair would be nothing more than a run-down video arcade were it not for one peculiar distinction: a live, caged chicken that plays tic-tac-toe for 50¢. You'll never win; at best, you'll tie. PETA would almost certainly have a fit—that is, if it could stomach confronting the surly low-lifes who run the joint, not to mention the ferocious chicken itself.

Scrabble was invented in Queens.

Stores

Art Stores

> **Industrial Plastics.** 309 Canal St., at Mercer (SoHo). ☎ **212/226-2010.**

Where else can you buy 10 feet of iridescent mylar and gaze at a replica of *David* in space-age polymer?

> **Pearl Paint.** 308 Canal St., just west of Broadway (SoHo). ☎ **212/431-7932.**

It's so well known we almost don't want to include it out of some knee-jerk desire to be difficult, but the red-and-white-painted Pearl Paint really is the very bedrock of the old SoHo, with six floors of art supplies catering to all those "SoHo artists" who actually now live in the Village or Long Island City or Dumbo or Williamsburg. When the sun is out, head to the back of the fourth floor. If the door is open, you will catch one of the best views of the World Trade Center in the city.

Books

Even with the demise of New York City's major independent bookstores (Shakespeare & Co. uptown, Endicott Booksellers at Columbus and 81st), there still remains a plethora of unique bookshops in this city. Here are some of the best.

> **Alba House Book Center.** 2187 Victory Blvd., just north of the College of Staten Island (Staten Island). ☎ **718/761-0085.**

Publisher of "fine Catholic books," housed in a bizarre poured concrete structure with Flying Nun–like buttresses. Equal portions trippy and atrocious.

> **Gryphon Bookshop.** 2246 Broadway, between 80th and 81st sts. (Upper West Side). ☎ **212/362-0706.**

This is the kind of bookshop New York used to be famous for: tiny, packed with used volumes stacked two layers deep on the shelves and wherever else there's space, usually an animal or two wandering around or asleep under a desk, clutter everywhere, employees (and customers) who look like they never see the light of day but have read almost any book you ask about. Pray that they have a long lease.

> **Labyrinth Bookstore.** 536 W. 112th St., between Broadway and Amsterdam. ☎ **212/865-1588.**

A lot of heart, a lot of books: scholarly books. It has the feel of a down-to-business real-intellectual's honest-to-god bookstore. Metal bookshelves in rows, library-style. A good selection of just-in academic books, older academic books, literature, poetry, art books, etc. The hard cement floor adds to the bohemian atmosphere, but isn't very comfortable if you're the sort who likes to stand around browsing for hours—and there's no chairs, so you'll definitely be standing. When it opened, the PR said it was the largest scholarly bookstore east of Chicago. That was in news stories over and over—"Largest Scholarly Bookstore East of Chicago."

> **Printed Matter.** 77 Wooster St., at Spring St. (SoHo). ☎ **212/925-0325.**

As befits SoHo, this store is the focal point of the artist publication universe. Everything from Phil Zimmerman's *High Anxiety* to Jenny Holzer's *Laments* to *The Adventures of Go-Go Girl*. It's pretty much guaranteed you won't find their stock anywhere else in town.

> **Revolution Books.** 9 W. 19th St., between Fifth and Sixth aves. ☎ **212/691-3345.**

This is definitely NOT the place for politically incorrect humor or a venue to spout your dittohead devotion to Mr. Limbaugh. These folks take Marxism, Socialism, Anarchism, and every other left-wing ism very seriously, and very

New York in Literature

The propaganda is right on the money: New York *is* book country. New Yorkers are religious about books. Of the many thousand titles which feature the city as a subject, these few capture the spirit of the city best.

The Age of Innocence, Edith Wharton

The Alienist, Caleb Carr

American Psycho, Brett Easton Ellis

Bartleby the Scrivener: A Story of Wall Street, Herman Melville

The Basketball Diaries, Jim Carroll

Bonfire of the Vanities, Thomas Wolfe

The Book of Daniel, E. L. Doctorrow

Bright Lights, Big City, Jay McInerney

Call It Sleep, Henry Roth

Catcher in the Rye, J. D. Salinger

The Chosen, Chaim Potok

Christopher Morley's New York, Christopher Morley

Damon Runyon: A Life, Jimmy Breslin

Flood!, Eric Drooker

From the Mixed-Up Files of Mrs. Basil E. Frankweiler, E. L. Konigsburg

Fudge, Judy Bloom

The Godfather, Mario Puzo

The Great Gatsby, F. Scott Fitzgerald

Great Jones Street, Don DeLlilo

Guys and Dolls: The Stories of Damon Runyon, Damon Runyon

Harriet the Spy, Louise Fitzhugh

The Invisible Man, Ralph Ellison

Journey to the End of the Night, Celine

Ladies Man, Richard Price

Low Life, Luc Sante

MacDoodle Street, Mark Alan Stamaty

Manhattan Transfer, John Dos Passos

McSorley's Wonderful Saloon, Joseph Mitchell

Mercy of a Rude Stream (four volumes), Henry Roth

Moon Palace, Paul Auster

Nexus, Sexus, and Plexus (The Rosy Crucifixion Trilogy), Henry Miller

Old New York, Edith Wharton

Ragtime, E. L. Doctorow

Six Degrees of Separation, John Guare

Slaves of New York, Tama Janowitz

Smoke, Paul Auster

The Subterraneans, Jack Kerouac

The Tenament, Bernard Malamud

Time and Again, Jack Finney

A Tree Grows in Brooklyn, Betty Smith

Tropic of Capricorn, Henry Miller

Up in the Old Hotel, Joseph Mitchell

V, Thomas Pynchon

The Wanderers, Richard Price

Who Needs Donuts?, Mark Alan Stamaty

Winter's Tale, Mark Helprin

For overview of New York in literature, see Shaun O'Connell's *Remarkable, Unspeakable New York: A Literary History*.

literally. In today's ahistorical, post-ideological milieu, Revolution Books is a quaint anachronism, conjuring up images of the day when the local radical bookstore was a major networking center for "the people," before Cocktail Nation, Slackerdom, and TV O.D. destroyed our collective yearning to destroy "the system." According to The Berg Man of Alcatraz, "It's the perfect store for the revolutionary who refuses to admit the dream is over."

> **See Hear Music, Magazines & Books.** 59 E. 7th St., between First and Second aves. (East Village). ☎ **212/505-9781.**

Hard to find, thanks to its basement location, See Hear carries just about every British pop magazine, tattoo journal, music zine, and Asian comic-porn rag you could imagine, all of them stacked tightly along the store's overcrowded walls like some messed-up, over-read teenager's bedroom.

> **St. Marks Bookshop.** 31 Third Ave., at Stuyvesant St. (East Village). ☎ **212/260-7853.**

The job application asks you to match famous and not-so-famous authors with their works. And although the window and floor displays advertise the now cliché East Village canon (Henry Rollins, Nick Cave, Re:Search, and the like), if you head to the back of the store, you'll find a big selection of literary journals and lots of good fiction that you're not likely to find elsewhere.

> **Strand Bookstore.** 828 Broadway, at 12th St. (Union Square). ☎ **212/473-1452.**

Over 8 miles of books, or so they say, loosely organized at best, and even more loosely alphabetized. Not for the weak-hearted. If you stick around, you're guaranteed to find something; it's just not likely to be what you're looking for. What you will find are patrons who rarely, if ever, leave their apartments; they tend to be nervous, have soft, white hands, and smell of baby powder. They take books off shelves and place them on the floor. Old women who smell of booze come in at 10am and ask about acting books; bald men in women's clothing browse the cookbook section.

Call of the Weird

> **Anime Crash.** 13 E. 4th St., at Lafayette (West Village). ☎ **212/254-4670.**

Remember *Johnny Quest?* Well, that wasn't Japanese animation. Remember *Gigantor, Astro Boy, Speed Racer?* THAT was Japanese animation. "Anime," it's called, and this store is devoted to it and such related items as models, books, comics ("manga"), CDs, and the occasional Sega tie-in. The beasty, Queens-born-and-bred Scott Mauriello is hell-bent on expanding Anime Crash into a Japanese animation empire. We liked him— because he was larger than life and could crush us with his bare hands.

> **Dr. Zizmor.** 800 Fifth Ave., between 61st and 62nd sts. (Upper East Side). ☎ **212/688-8326.** E-mail: adamzee@aol.com.

More a dermatological zoo than a store, Dr. Zizmor's, near the Plaza Hotel, is filled with the kind of people you're likely to find sitting next to you on the subway. One woman says to another, "I have a tattoo. I want it removed. I thought I'd have to have plastic surgery, but with this laser surgery, I don't." According to the ads, Dr. Z's "new laser treatment" will take care of that unsightly tattoo for under $200. Imagine the boom when all the postmodern primitives decide to have theirs removed.

> **Flosso Hornmann Magic Co.** 45 W. 34th St., 6th floor, between Fifth and Sixth aves. (Chelsea/Garment Center). ☎ **212/279-6079.**

The oldest magic shop in the world (founded in 1865), its former owners include Harry Houdini. Today it's run by Jackie Flosso, who inherited it from his father, Al, a magician and Punch and Judy puppeteer during the '30s and '40s (he was known as the Coney Island Fakir). The shop is a disheveled mix of antique magic props and cheesy contemporary tricks: One of Houdini's original trunks is in a corner, beneath a pile of rubber chickens; Al's Punch and Judy puppets are on display; and the walls are adorned with banners and photos from the '30s. These days Jackie sells mostly to young adults, but if you catch him at the right time and are willing to spend a little money, you may talk him into putting on a demonstration. Tell him Fredini sent you.

> **Kiehl's Since 1851.** 109 Third Ave., between E. 13th and E. 14th sts. (East Village). ☎ **212/677-3171.**

The original owner, a World War II fighter pilot, liked to display airplanes in the store; today's management, for some reason, shows new and vintage motorcycles. One thing, however, has remained the same: Kiehl's continues to sell handmade cosmetics, in no-frills packaging. A strange combination, cosmetics and motorcycles, but it's not the strangest thing about Kiehl's Pharmaceuticals. This is: The company has sponsored expeditions to Everest and has formed its own stunt-flying squadron. For what it's worth, Kate Moss shops here.

On the Road: Bull Penis in Chinatown

It's hot, the Monkmobile is in the garage, and we have begun to wilt. But just then, as we stagger down Broadway, along comes our friend Reid, whose apartment we've been staying in. Reid tells us to try dried bull penis. "Good for male virility," Reid says. "Great in the heat. You can get it in Chinatown. They sell it over the counter."

Michael is skeptical but eager; Jim does not care. So, on a muggy day, with sweat dripping down our thighs, we make our way to Chinatown to find dried bull penis.

The city is slow and mellow, as if on Demerol, and Chinatown reeks. Orange ducks—plucked, not skinned—hang by their feet in the windows. In the markets, flies swarm around durian, which is, according to Michael, "the stinky fruit."

Our first stop: the Nam Wah Tea Parlor, on Doyers, the crookedest street in the city. The tea parlor, not surprisingly, sells tea. We ask if they have anything to cure baldness, if they have anything to fix our crooked necks. Finally, Jim Monk, our broken English expert, says, "Do you sell anything that helps the men with the ladies?"

Heads shake.

"Do you sell anything that makes men strong?"

Heads shake some more.

We continue our search. We pass the Mei Dick Barbershop and Big Wong restaurant (one wonders if Chinatown merchants give their shops these names on purpose). The Wam Nam Pharmacy has health and beauty aids, ginseng in all shapes and sizes, plus dried worms and horseradish (selling for $250 a package). The worms, which look like shriveled intestines, are supposed to be good for the brain.

But no bull penis.

Chinatown Fair has a live chicken that, for 50¢, plays tic-tac-toe (the chicken beats Michael three times in a row), but again no bull penis.

Hong Kong Market has an assortment of strange foods—but no bull penis.

We become bolder—"Do you sell something for man to make strong babies that comes from a bull?"—and are offered pills for headaches and others to improve concentration. The closest we come is virility pills, at $65 a bottle. At our final stop Jim tries the direct approach: "Do you sell bull penis?" he says emphatically. By now it matters little whether we find what we are looking for. It's the thrill of the hunt that counts. Yet this time the male clerk nods knowingly. "Two doors down," he says.

"You're serious?"

"Two doors down," says the man as he nearly shoves us out the door.

Two doors down is a porn shop. And there, in the window, on a dust-covered calendar, is a picture of an ox.

› Miss Vera's Finishing School for Boys Who Want to Be Girls. P.O. Box 1331, Old Chelsea Station, New York, NY 10011. ☎ **212/242-6449.**

Perhaps the world's only cross-dressing academy, Miss Vera's Finishing School has been around since 1992. Today, it boasts a student body of more than 300 students, with another several hundred participating via telephone extension classes. Course offerings include Maid to Order and the 2-day Femme Intensive (a.k.a. the Cinderfella Experience). Miss Vera also has a 900 line: 1-900/884-VERA; $2.99 a minute, adults only. (See the interview with Miss Veronica Vera, later in this section.)

At Miss Vera's Finishing School for Boys Who Want to Be Girls

> **New York Doll Hospital.** 787 Lexington Ave., between E. 61st and E. 62nd sts. (Upper East Side). ☎ **212/838-7527.**

Pretty much what its name suggests: a hospital for dolls. The place is a mess, with box after box of doll limbs, heads, and eyeballs stacked along the walls. The business was founded by proprietor Irving Chase's grandparents in 1900; today, it is (if you take Chase's word for it) the only operation of its kind in the country. Fact: The New York Dolls named themselves after the place. (See interview with Irving Chase later in this section.)

> **Schapiro's House of Kosher and Sacramental Wines.** 126 Rivington St., between Norfolk and Essex sts. (Lower East Side). ☎ **212/674-4404.**

Once, in a bar in Kansas City, we went to the bathroom. On the wall behind the urinal someone had scrawled this: "If you're one in a million, there are 11 of you in New York." As a general rule, the maxim holds true: In New York there are lots of most things, even rare, one-in-a-million ones. There are, for example, places where a person can buy Miracle Driving Glasses or petrified bull penis. Yet even here some things really are one of a kind, and one of them, perhaps surprisingly, is Schapiro's House of Kosher and Sacramental Wines. It's the city's only surviving winery—

"Everyone loves Schapiro": Norman Schapiro outside the city's only winery

around since 1899 and dispensing wine that, as a sign toward the back of the store proudly boasts, is "so thick you can cut it with a knife"—but the place is a shell, no longer really in operation, so past its prime that it almost brings tears to your eyes. Dust everywhere, no customers whatsoever (at least none when we visited). The place has (we hope) seen better days. One hopes that Norman Schapiro, who runs the place, has also seen better days. When we arrive he is in his office with the door open. He doesn't even nod to us, but sits there discussing an imminent bankruptcy hearing with his lawyer.

"It's like we just walked into history," Michael says. "We took one giant step back. The dust in here has been here for at least my lifetime."

Most of the crushing happens upstate these days, so the tours, on Sundays, consist mostly of wine tasting. "Everyone loves Schapiro," says Norman. "If you look at all the touring guides—Europe or wherever it is—it always has Schapiro's in it." It's worth a visit: How many chances do you get to go wine tasting on the Lower East Side? Call ahead, though—just to make sure the place is still in business.

Camp Lite

> **As Seen on TV.** 401 Fifth Ave., between E. 37th and E. 38th sts. (Murray Hill). ☎ 212/679-0728.

Come here for all your cheesy late-night infomercial needs. The Grass Guy, for instance, or the Bagel Cutter, or Quick 'N' Brite, or Jerome Russell's hair thickener, not to mention the Emerson Speed Peeler (to take the labor out of the arduous, finger-cramping job of peeling oranges), or Map Mate, or Quick Thaw, or (lest we forget) those trusty Miracle Driving Glasses. Technology, as this store attests, will not only save us from needless labor but also heal and entertain us. The store's management seems both to get the joke and to take the products, most of which never made it, seriously.

> **Little Rickie.** 49½ First Ave., at E. 3rd St. (East Village). ☎ 212/505-6467.

The granddaddy of them all, Little Rickie is the store that launched the camp-lite craze across America. Everyone from Archie McPhee and Ruby Montana's Pinto Pony in Seattle to Y-Que and Chicken Boy in L.A. should tip their fez to this pioneer, although they seldom do. Owner Philip Retsky seems a little bitter about it all; he says Ruby visited his store and ripped off the entire concept. Nevertheless, Retsky's shop still offers the best kitsch in town. Highlights include a line of twisted back-to-school supplies and more Elvis and Jesus paraphernalia than even the most devoted of devotees could desire.

An Interview with

Irving Chase

of the New York Doll Hospital

It may go without saying that Irving Chase's New York Doll Hospital is one of a kind. Actually, it's something of a miracle that one even exists. The place is pretty much what its name suggests: a hospital for dolls. Sick, broken, headless, limbless—dolls of all shapes and sizes, with all conceivable maladies. It doesn't look like a hospital, though; what it looks like is a mess. A mess of doll limbs and heads and eyeballs, box after box of them, stacked along two rooms' worth of walls, nearly to the ceiling. The hospital is a family operation, founded by Irving Chase's grandparents in 1900, taken over by his parents, and then, in 1946, by Irving himself. It has had three homes over the years, but the mission has remained unchanged: The New York Doll Hospital repairs and restores, buys and sells dolls. "We've never lost a patient," Chase says, "and we don't bury our mistakes. One hundred percent success. How do you like that?"

Monk: Who are some of your bigger-named, well-known clients?

Irving Chase: We've had at least several hundred well-known, very important VIPs. For me to start going through them would be impossible. Anybody that's anybody comes to the New York Doll Hospital, because we are it. You go from Florida to Maine, I don't think you'll find two.

Monk: People must be very happy when they get their dolls back.

Irving Chase: Nobody grows up. We've had 70-year-old men coming in here with their little monkeys and little teddy bears. "I love him. He's been my buddy. I sleep with him." As a matter of fact, a young lady came in a couple of weeks ago. She was stunning, beautiful. And she brought her little monkey, and the head had come off. She wanted the head put back on again. I said, "All right, I'll have it for you in a couple days." She says, "No, I have to have it now, because I sleep with him." So I said, "What a lucky monkey this is."

Monk: Do you have dolls of your own that you play with?

Irving Chase: I'm not crazy about dolls. I like to work with them, I enjoy them, I appreciate them, I can understand them, we talk to each other and have very lengthy conversations, but I don't love dolls.

Monk: Do any of your dolls talk back to you?

Irving Chase: Of course, all the time.

Monk: What do they say?

Irving Chase: They speak mostly in German.

Monk: What do they say in German?

Irving Chase: They say, "Ich liebe dich. Ich will spazieren gehen." They want to take a walk with me.

Monk: Is Barbie banned from this shop?

Irving Chase: No, I've got Barbies. If a serious doll collector comes in looking for Barbies, I've got them.

Monk: Who are your favorite dolls?

Irving Chase: My wife and my two daughters . . .

Monk: I love it . . .

Irving Chase: And my three girlfriends . . .

Monk: Yeah, you've gotta have three.

"Anybody that's anybody
comes to the New York Doll Hospital,
because we are it."

". . . I document the real condition of the city," Clayton Patterson tells us.

We're inside his shop, Clayton's Hats, on Essex Street. It doesn't really look like a shop. It looks like some kind of front. In a sense, it is one. Although hats are sold here, Patterson's real passion is for things beyond his shop's doors. In his view, New York's Lower East Side is the center of just about everything—from entertainment and culture (the neighborhood is a "creative crucible") to the crack cocaine and heroin trade ("America comes here for its drugs").

Patterson, who can often be seen wandering the neighborhood with his hi-8 video camera, has appointed himself the area's documentarian—an in-your-face obstreperous documentarian, as a passing film crew found out when Patterson insisted on his right to "document" them. However, Patterson's bullish approach has its upside: He's best known for having been on the scene with his video camera—a la George Halliday (who shot the Rodney King beating from his apartment)—during the 1988 riots in Tompkins Square Park.

"Things start down here. What happens is the bubbles come up to the top. And that's what I document. A lot of people come down here, and they sort of get this burst of creativity and inspiration and think, 'Wow, this is great stuff.' But then they're allowed to take that idea, and with money and with managers and with the proper ingredients, they're able to turn that into something that becomes internationally known and recognized. The most creative doesn't make it out because the most creative is the most complicated and the hardest for people to deal with.

"People take the little bits of the creativity. Somebody like RuPaul would come down here and get into the drag scene. And what happens is the generic part gets out. RuPaul learns how to dress like a woman and look like a woman. You know what I mean? But that's not the drag that he comes out of. That's the little piece that gets stolen, that becomes generic and acceptable to the larger public. And what America gets is a little tiny spin-up: Madonna with a bra that sticks out, that's pointed. But the whole world that that came out of is much bigger."

Fashion and Accessories

> **Amy Downs Hats.** 103 Stanton St., at Ludlow St. (Lower East Side).
☎ **212/598-4189.**

The hats are outrageous and exceptional, and Amy makes them all herself. Try the I'm-getting-married-in-the-morning hat.

> **Center For The Dull.** 216 Lafayette St., at Spring St. (SoHo). ☎ **212/925-9699.**

This excellent store—a consolidation of the former Arkle & Sparkle and Smilonylon—specializes in swingy, groovy stuff from the '60s and '70s: bell bottoms, go-go boots, nylon shirts, hip huggers, for the Austin Powers in all of us.

> **Century 21.** 22 Cortlandt St., between Broadway and Church (Financial District).
☎ **212/227-9092.**

Every guide to the city will tell you to go here for alleged discounts on designer threads, but we say, "Why bother?" The atmosphere is standard issue Ross meets Monkey Wards, and the prices, while cheaper than Midtown department stores, are not so cheap as to justify schlepping all the way down to Wall Street. If your idea of fun is spending 5 hours sorting through racks to save 30% on some mediocre Calvin Klein, then you shouldn't be reading this book.

> **Clayton Hats.** 161 Essex St., at Stanton St. (Lower East Side). ☎ **212/477-1363.**

The fact that Clayton Patterson makes and sells hats seems almost secondary; he's best known for (and most interested in) being a kind of roving documentarian of life on the Lower East Side. He's shot hours and hours of video, capturing on his hi-8 camera the 1988 riots in Tompkins Square Park, among other events, and has an amazing collection of heroin wrappers. Nevertheless, he does make custom-embroidered baseball caps, which he's sold to the likes of Keith Haring and Mick Jagger.

> **Domsey's Warehouse.** 431 Kent Ave., along the Williamsburg waterfront (Williamsburg, Brooklyn). ☎ **718/384-6000.**

The best thrift shop in the city. Well, not the store itself but the warehouse next door, where you can buy clothes by the pound, at ridiculously low prices. We do all our shopping here, though recent reports of mistreatment of store workers may dampen our enthusiasm. (To get there, take the J train to the Marcy Street stop. Walk west on Broadway, then left on Kent. It's 2 blocks down on the left.)

> **Kaufman's Army & Navy.** 319 W. 42nd St., between Eighth and Ninth aves. (Theater District). ☎ **212/757-5670.**

It was 6:05pm, the eve before Christmas Eve. The store was supposed to be closed, but it was not. We entered, looking for a cotton, hand-stitched, made-in-the-USA American flag, 3 by 5 feet, with embroidered stars. Two salespeople went to great lengths to find one in the "bunker." No dice. Disappointed, we settled on a nylon job with no embroidery. At the checkout stand, the harried owner, also named Jim, caught my disappointment. "Wait a minute," he said, "let me call a few of my competitors"; he then proceeded to find exactly the flag I was looking for. The "competitor's store" would be open Christmas Eve. We bought our flag there, on Grand Street, but if we're ever in New York again, we'll return to Kaufman's on 42nd.

> **Liquid Sky Design.** 241 Lafayette St., at Prince St. (SoHo). ☎ **212/343-0532.**

When we arrived at this clothier to the club kids, DJ Slinger, the colorful Brazilian owner who believes in aliens and sponsors a weekly rave at the Cooler, was absolutely determined not to let us in. The clothes were put away, he said (although they were not), and we wouldn't get the whole effect. You know, the smell and the lighting and the jungle beat. He was definitely right about the smell: It was ganja all the way. Rave on. Fact: The store was named for the cult movie of same name.

Observation

"When you walked the streets of New York in the '40s, you could tell at a glance who was a prostitute and who was not. Now all the girls dress like whores. Even many older women dress that way. It's sometimes very confusing."

—Painter Richard Lindner, as reported in Hilton Kramer's column in the *New York Observer*, 1/12/98

> **Pops.** 7 Franklin St., northwest of McCarren Park (Greenpoint, Brooklyn). ☎ **718/349-POPS.**

Located in the heart of the Brooklyn industrial wasteland, Pops offers nothing special in the decor department, but it's got—at unbelievably cheap prices—everything the rave and skater kids are paying top dollar for in the East Village and SoHo. Clean, cool Levi's for only $3; workwear of all kinds for under $20 (and often under $10).

> **Salvation Army.** 536 W. 46th St., between Tenth and Eleventh aves. (Hell's Kitchen). ☎ **212/664-8563.**

A tower of salvation, perched in its own warehouse building on the far west edge of Midtown, where the glitz of international commerce gives way to Latino record shops and corner bodegas. This place has an entire huge floor of second-hand clothes, everything arranged by type, and another entire floor of furniture. They're a little skimpy in the knickknacks department, though, unless you want commemorative coffee mugs from a 1987 Christian retreat or 1992 insurance convention, or cheap glassware. Lots of cheap glassware.

Odds and Ends

> **Dart Shoppe Ltd.** 30 E. 20th St., between Broadway and Park Ave. South (Gramercy). ☎ **212/533-8684.**

We hate darts. Can't stand them. Can't think of a more boring way to spend our time, even 5 minutes of it. Nevertheless, there are something on the order of 17 million dart players in the United States alone, and 17 million people (we guess) can't be wrong. Jim Birmingham, the owner of the Dart Shoppe, is one of them. Not just any one, but the 23rd ranked dart player in the world. His store sells everything you might need, from sisal dart boards to shafts, barrels, flies, and tips. He's also got a list of every bar in the city that has a dart board. Allegedly, Wednesday nights at **Kettle of Fish** (130 W. 3rd St.) draws the city's best players, but you won't catch us there any time soon.

Veronica Vera

of Miss Vera's Finishing School
for Boys Who Want to Be Girls

"This is our student Pat," says Veronica Vera, Dean of Students at Miss Vera's Finishing School for Boys Who Want to Be Girls. "Soon to be Patricia. Patricia is actually one of the supermodels of the academy."

"Really?" Michael says, somewhat skeptically. "Supermodel?" The man before him is tall, thick-chested. Bigger than Michael in nearly every respect, he looks— despite his gentle, sad face—like he could hurt someone if he wanted to.

"She's one of the models in our ad campaign."

Miss Vera opens her press kit and removes facsimiles of her advertisements, designed by the firm Griffith/Lovering. Indeed Pat, or Patricia, is there, in an ad whose copy reads "What Every Girl Should Know About Her Five O'clock Shadow." (Another ad reads: "Be the Sister You Never Had.")

Miss Vera's Finishing School has been around since 1992 and now, according to its founder, boasts a student body of more than 300 students, with another several hundred participating via telephone extension classes. Course offerings include "Maid to Order," an 8-hour campus visit that teaches, among other skills, walking, curtsying, carrying trays, answering doors, washing lingerie, and giving pedicures. For out-of-town students who want a lot in a short time, Miss Vera recommends the 2-day Femme Intensive, also known as the Cinderfella Experience. For $2,500, "students stay at a lovely guest house 1 block from the Academy. We decorate your room for you. Except for a brief stroll to the Academy each morning, you remain en femme the whole time."

We visited Miss Vera on the last day of class before summer break. "It's starting to get hot," she explained. "Our girls melt, you know." During the visit, Jim, with the able instruction of Miss Vera, tried on a gaff. "It's quite simple," says Miss Vera, her voice an exercise in campy cordiality and charm. "You step into this, you tuck your penis between your testicles, and it holds you down there for hours."

"I am the worst advertisement you ever had," says Jim.

Miss Vera: The Academy began first as a way to help finance a book I was writing about my personal sexual evolution. I had written hundreds of articles for different sex magazines and researched sex, human sexuality, interviewed people in peep shows and swingers and SM aficionados, written about my own sex life and about my different experiences with different artists like Annie Sprinkle and Robert Mapplethorpe. So I wanted to write a book about it. And around the same time I met a woman who was helping cross-dressers with their hair and makeup, and she introduced me to my first cross-dressing client. She had someone who wanted to come to New York and stay dressed for a full weekend. And she was leaving town, and she felt she couldn't take that responsibility. So I talked to him on the phone. He called himself Jamie Sissyribbons. He was a professional, a lawyer from out of state. And I said, "Well, if you come to town for this particular weekend," which was—there was a fetish ball coming up that weekend called Dressing for Pleasure—"If you come to town for that weekend, I'll organize a great weekend for you with the ball as the focal point."

Part of what they learn when they come here is that the line between who is straight, who's gay, who's bisexual, these lines are all very blurry, especially when it comes to the world of fantasy. I think about 60% of the students are married; about 5%, I would say, identify as gay . . .

Monk: Five percent. You're serious.

Miss Vera: Yeah. Oh, yeah.

Monk: In many ways, do you look at your finishing school as therapy for some? Like, is there a percent who come here as a way of working out some—

Miss Vera: I call it therapy with props. Because you can learn a lot from exploring this territory. I mean, the femme self is really there for a reason. She's connected with feelings, and the main feelings are sensuality, sexuality, and also security and safety. Most of the people who come here have been dressing in some form since early childhood, and that's when their feelings got hooked up with the affinity for clothing. The clothing isn't, you know, it's not just about looking like a female; it's about being connected to a lot of feelings. So what they learn when they come here is to let their femme self be a guide to their feelings. Help open them up to the world.

Preferably, a student meets me for a half-hour consultation. That takes place outside the Academy in just a coffeehouse, a lovely coffeehouse nearby. I bring the enrollment application and brochure. And we chat. And this way I can make sure the student does not have a

beard or a mustache, you know. But most of the people who make it to that step are already, you know, ready to come to the Academy. Over the phone I rule out people who want to be forced to dress or humiliated, and I tell them that's not the experience that's offered here. So first they meet me for the initial consultation, then we set up an appointment for either our Sudden Beauty Seminar or the Femme Intensive.

Monk: The Femme Intensive?

Miss Vera: That's the Cinderfella experience. They come here for a couple of days and have a whole curriculum of classes. We also have Miracle Miss. That's a popular course, that's 4 hours. And at Miracle Miss, they have makeup application and transformation, bodybuilding, walking in high heels, and then they have an option of choosing a voice class. We also have a voice teacher. And a female sexual energy class or Ballet One and Tutu. They have an option there.

About the only thing that I would say, in the beginning, you know, that people had in common, was that they were about the age of 40, 35 to 40. And I felt like that was because 40 I see as the age of self-acceptance. It's like, you know, you get to be 40 and you think, "Okay, now I kind of know who I am." And so they reach around this age and it's like, "Okay, I've been doing this since childhood, it's not going away, so let me find out more about it, let me share it with somebody." A lot of people have never shared this with anybody. A lot of the people who come here have never seen themselves totally transformed. So when they look in the mirror for that very first time, they're confronting their greatest desire and their greatest fear at the same moment. I think that men for the most part experience what I call Venus envy. And our students are very in touch with it. I see it as the flip side of the women's movement.

Most of the women I know, who are very strong feminists, all want to come here. They want to learn how to do their makeup, they want to learn how to walk in high heels. But my point is that it's not women that I'm teaching; it's men that I'm teaching to have this experience. You could say I'm reinforcing stereotypes or an aspect of femininity that the women's movement put down or treated as less important over the years, but that's where women were at. We had gone through that. It's different for men. And yes, I am affirming those parts of femininity that have kind of been put down as stereotypes. And I'm saying yes, the homemaker is great. Yes, the glamour girl, it's a powerful place to be, especially if you understand it.

"It's not just about looking like a female; it's about being connected to a lot of feelings."

Telephones

The Best Phones

Access to a telephone is never guaranteed in our lifestyle, so we're always on the prowl for the nearest call box. When we find a good one, we set up shop, bring in paper, food, a change of clothes, even leave Post-Its for each other. On average, 1.2 million calls are placed from New York's public phones each day, so it's no surprise the city has some great places to reach out and bug someone.

> **Empire State Building.** 350 Fifth Ave., at 34th St., 86th floor (Murray Hill).

Beats all. Easily the best pay-phone vista in Manhattan.

> **Hotel Chelsea.** 222 W. 23rd St., between Seventh and Eighth aves. (Chelsea).

The lobby has two stand-ups and two booths. It may be too much to handle during business hours, but it's great fun when you're relaxing at the receiver.

> **International Phone Center.** 544 Tenth Ave., near the Port Authority Bus Terminal (Midtown).

One of our favorite places in Manhattan. Here a Senegalese cabby can call home to the wife and kids cheaply, and in nice, clean, private rooms (also good for peep shows).

> **New York Life Insurance Building.** 45–55 Madison Ave., at 26th St. (Gramercy/Murray Hill).

We'll always remember this Gothic moderne monolith because we used their pay phones when we visited the nearby Sprinkle Salon. Tucked discreetly into the basement of this 1928 Gothic masterpiece, these are the best vintage pay phones in the city—17 of them in an old room, with lime green walls that remind us of the telephone room at the Subway Inn. Plus, they work. Delightfully 1930s.

> **Pagoda Pay Phones.** Confucius Plaza and environs, below Canal St. (Chinatown).

Elegant and charming—a more fitting symbol of transcontinental communication is hard to find.

> **Telephone Bar & Grill.** 149 Second Ave., between E. 9th and E. 10th sts. (East Village). ☎ **212/529-5000.**

Owner Rudy Mosney went to Plymouth, England, found some old, red pay phones, and decided to build a restaurant around them. The place has three of them, fronting onto the street. Appearances to the contrary, you'll need to go inside and face the yuppies before you can use these beauties. On Mother's Day the Telephone Bar & Grill hands out quarters, so patrons can call home to mum.

The Best Phone Numbers

> **AAAAAAA Alternative Furniture Rentals.** ☎ **212/924-4800.**

Apparently, the real name is I.S. Furniture Rental Co. They've been in business 30 years and insist no one has called and asked for AAAAAAA Alternative Furniture Rentals—despite the fact that they're listed as that in the phone book.

> **AAAAAA Dating Service.** ☎ **212/382-2560.**

I woke the proprietor while she was sleeping. I asked her how business was doing. She said, "Business is slow, honey." I said, "Is it because of Giuliani?" She said, "WHO?!" "Mayor Giuliani, he's cracking down on escort services." "I don't care who the fuck it is. Business is slow. I gotta sleep now, honey," and she hung up. Apparently, the six As haven't done much to attract customers.

I'm in a phone booth, Baby . . .

Hell, much as we'd like to think we know what our readers want, there's always the possibility of holes in our multi-million-dollar market research. So, to be sure we've covered all the angles, here's some choice entries from the New York phone book.

- Cephalos Cephalonian Society of America Inc. (☎ 718/204-8491)
- Dear Foam Slippers (☎ 212/244-3145)
- Mr. Softee of the Bronx (☎ 718/328-9500)
- Ms. Buffy's French Cleaners (☎ 212/586-3945)
- National Association of Independent Interventionists (☎ 212/696-9161)
- Negro Plastic Covers (☎ 212/923-5248)
- Old Bohemian Meat (☎ 212/989-2870)
- Older Women's League (☎ 212/496-1409)
- Professional Women in Construction, Inc. (☎ 212/687-0610)
- S&M Dental Laboratory (☎ 718/495-2664)
- Velvet Voice Association (☎ 212/289-4748)

> **Ben Brafman, Defense Lawyer.** ☎ 212/750-7800.

Keep this number handy in case the victim-culture of our times puts you in deep doo-doo. In New York, four out of five criminal cases that go to trial end in convictions. With Brafman as your defender, those odds are almost exactly the opposite.

> **Celebrity Service.** ☎ 212/757-7979.

For $250 a week, you'll get a list of five celebrities' phone and fax numbers a day. The service was started by an out-of-work actor who opened his black book to the public.

> **Check-a-Mate.** ☎ 800/734-2660.

With some of our bad luck, we could have used this service. They do extensive background checks on potential mates and spouses, and they cut to the chase, with initial questions like "What are your suspicions, exactly? Murder? Previous marriages? Love child of Elvis? Xanex freak?"

> **Dial-a-Prayer.** ☎ 212/246-4200.

Need a quick hit of Jesus? This taped message offers inspirational words of wisdom from the pulpit of the Fifth Avenue Presbyterian Church.

> **Flat Earth Organization.** ☎ 212/750-7829.

Devoted to proving, once and for all, that the earth really is flat. Still going strong after all these years, and they have photos to prove it taken from the Space shuttle. Turns out it's shaped like a CD.

> **Fat Man and Little Boy.** ☎ 212/481-3056.

A real-estate agency, run by an "ex-military guy."

> **Knights of Baron de Kalb Inc.** ☎ 718/743-6626.

Who is Baron de Kalb? A German soldier who aided the United States in the Revolutionary War. Why is he associated with a chapter of the Knights of Columbus? Anybody's guess.

> **Miss Vera's Finishing School For Boys Who Want to Be Girls.** ☎ 900/884-VERA.

Telephone extension courses from the world's only cross-dressing academy. Learn to curtsy, carry trays, wash lingerie, or give pedicures. (See also Call of the Weird under "Stores.")

> **Peak Season Hotel Hotline.** ☎ 800/846-ROOM.

These are the folks to call when you're desperate for a good clean place to spend the night when almost all the city's 59,000 hotel rooms are sold out. At other less busy times of the year they can find a place that's also relatively cheap.

> **Poemfone.** ☎ 212/631-4234.

A new poem each day.

> **Screaming Queens.** ☎ 212/714-8097.

Book a drag queen for your next event.

The Best Useful Phone Numbers

New York City **directory assistance** (☎ **411** in the city, 212/555-1212 out of state) is by far the best in the country. Why? (1) It's always free from any Bell Atlantic pay phone; (2) they will give you not only the phone number, but the address, zip, and even the cross streets should you want them. A bona fide public service.

Here's a few others that might come in handy:

- New York City Department of Transportation Pot Hole Problems Hot Line (☎ 212/768-4653)
- New York City Department of Sanitation Street Cleaning Complaints Line (☎ 212/219-8090)
- Original Roommate Finders (☎ 212/489-6918)
- Time of Day (☎ 212/976-0001; 212/976-6000 without propaganda; 212/976-1616 with propaganda)
- Weather (☎ 212/976-1212)

Theater and _Performance_

Every New York visitor knows about Broadway and Off-Broadway. Buck the trend: explore the true cutting edge of the city's performance scene.

> **Collective Unconscious.** 145 Ludlow St., at Rivington St. (Lower East Side). ☎ **212/254-5277.** www.weird.org.

A funky space for theater so far off Broadway it could be in China. Avant-garde maybe, but the vibe of some of the actors was bewilderingly bad.

> **Dixon Place.** 258 Bowery, between E. Houston and Prince sts. (Lower East Side).
☎ **212/219-3088.**

It's run by Ellie Covan—out of her living room. She just pushes the sofas back, unfolds some chairs, and allows fringe performers—gay, straight, bi, whatever—to work out their material. A friendly, comfortable space, and a surprise to find in a city like New York.

> **Franklin Furnace.** ☎ **212/766-2606.** www.FranklinFurnace.org. E-mail: ffurnace@interport.net.

Martha Wilson, the founding director of this pioneering arts organization, has been a tireless champion of performance art, kick-starting the careers of such performers as Annie Sprinkle and Karen Finley. In keeping with the budget-conscious and digital spirit of the times, she's shifted her focus from literal site-based performance to virtual web site performance. The Furnace has sponsored online performances of artists ranging from Nancy Spiro to Patricia Hoffbauer to Bingo Gazingo. Those seeking grant or programming information can visit the Web site or write to Franklin Furnace, 45 John St., no. 611, New York, NY 10038.

> **La Mama Experimental Theatre Club.** 74A E. 4th St., at Second Ave. (East Village). ☎ **212/475-7710.**

Despite budget cuts, despite Mayor Giuliani, Ellen Stewart's experimental theater has managed to survive (since 1962). Today, La Mama is among the last of a dying breed.

> **Nuyorican Poets Cafe.** 236 E. 3rd St., between Avenues B and C (East Village).
☎ **212/505-8183.** www.nuyorican.com.

This pioneer of the so-called poetry slam used to be the city's most important venue for the newly hip art form of spoken word or performance poetry. In the old days—this is 3^1/$_2$ years ago, mind you—writing students from Columbia University would be mocked at the Nuyorican; these days, it's the other way around. Today, a slam at the Nuyorican feels like a cross between stand-up comedy and group therapy. To be sure, founder Miguel Algarin has his heart in the right place.

> **Surf Reality.** 172 Allen St., 2nd Floor, at Stanton St. (Lower East Side).
☎ **212/673-4182.**

This 50-seat space showcases pansy punk anarchists, Jewish cross-dressers, knife-wielding dykes, and an occasional earnest poet. The Sunday we visited included an agitated monologue from a man who was painting his penis purple and the dismemberment of a black Barbie doll.

> **Theatre for the New City.** 155 First Ave., at 10th St. (East Village). ☎ **212/254-1109.**

Housed in a former pushcart wagon storage facility (in a space it used to share with the Department of Sanitation), Theatre for the New City has two theaters, a cabaret, and a community space. It mounts an eclectic, reasonable selection of plays and throws a kick-ass, not-to-be-missed Halloween party.

> **WPA Theater.** 519 W. 23rd St., between Tenth and Eleventh aves. (Chelsea). ☎ **212/691-2274.**

The exterior hasn't changed since the days of the Great Depression. Productions are neither as dated nor as dreary as you might expect of a self-proclaimed "workers' theater."

Toilets

Allegedly, the psychic Oric Bovar could go a full year without taking a dump. He'd do all right wandering the streets of New York. The rest of us, however, aren't so lucky. At least once a day, we've got to find a place to dispense with our basic bodily functions, and in New York that can be a real problem. Of all the world's great cities, the Big Apple is about the lousiest when it comes to toilets. Public facilities are hard to find, and if you happen to find one, it's likely to be either closed or foul; and private toilets, such as those found in restaurants, are often policed. A few years back, the city almost got its act together and installed efficient, self-cleaning toilets, but the project, which was mired in controversy from day one, never got beyond the prototype stage.

So what's a person to do?

City Toilet and the Municipal Building, City Hall Park

One enterprising New Yorker, Vicki Rovere, took matters into her own hands, as it were. She self-published a book, *Where to Go: A Guide to Manhattan's Toilets,* and we highly recommend it (order a copy from her at 339 Lafayette St., New York, NY 10012, or pick one up at a local bookstore). On the Web, ALLNY has assembled an equally, if not more, comprehensive list, at **www.allny.com/bathroom.html**; it names hundreds of bathrooms in the city, with addresses, and—for the scatologically minded—lists links to a handful of bathroom-related Web sites (you've got to wonder about the person who assembled this material).

Below are some of Vicki Rovere's favorites, mixed in with some of our own.

> **Bar 89.** 89 Mercer St., at Spring St. (SoHo). ☎ 212/274-0989.

A great toilet, and perhaps the only real attraction of this chic downtown eatery. The stall doors are glass, transparent, but when you enter and lock the door behind you, the glass suddenly clouds over, becoming opaque. We never did figure out how it works (some kind of electronic sensor, we imagine).

> **Barnes & Noble** and **Starbucks.** Actually, almost any chain or superstore. Located all over.

Vicki Rovere: What's made a big difference are the Barnes & Nobles and Starbucks.

Jim Monk: They let you use the toilets without buying anything?

Vicki Rovere: Yes. And now they're strewn all over the city. More commercial enterprises like that that will welcome the public are going to make a big difference. So that's been a boon to toilet users, yes.

> **Bowlmor Lanes.** 110 University Place, between W. 12th and W. 13th sts. (West Village). ☎ 212/255-8188.

Ideally situated between the East and West Villages, Downtown and the Flatiron District. Nothing special in the decor department, but when you've got to go you won't care. Take the elevator to the fourth floor. No questions asked.

> **Bryant Park.** Sixth Ave., between W. 40th and W. 42nd sts. (Midtown).

A working public toilet—and it's clean.

> **City Toilet.** On the northeast corner of City Hall Park, corner of Chambers and Centre sts. (Financial District).

This green-granite, glass, and steel structure is one of the few operational self-cleaning prototypes in the city.

Vicki Rovere: This is a test model of the new coin-operated, self-cleaning toilet that they want to install in New York City.

Jim Monk: Do you think there will be lots of sexual rendezvous in these toilets?

Vicki Rovere: That was one of the issues—would it be used by prostitutes? Would it be used by people smoking crack? It opens automatically after 20 minutes, so there's a limit on what you could hope to accomplish.

> **Islamic Center of New York.** 1711 Third Ave., at E. 97th St. (Upper East Side/ Spanish Harlem). ☎ 212/722-5234.

Vicki Rovere: I went in there, sort of as a tourist, just to take a look at the place. They let me use the bathrooms, and those bathrooms are really unusual, because there are washing things that have to do with the religious ritual. You have to be clean in order to pray, so it's a much more elaborate bathroom than most.

> **New York Public Library, Mid-Manhattan Library.** 455 Fifth Ave., at E. 42nd St. (Midtown). ☎ 212/340-0833.

Our personal favorite. Great for both atmosphere and tea-party potential.

> **Old Town Bar and Grill.** 45 E. 18th St., between Broadway and Park Ave. South (Union Square). ☎ 212/529-6732.

Massive urinals, from the days when men were men and H. L. Mencken was a menace.

> **Royalton Hotel.** 44 W. 44th St., between Fifth and Sixth aves. (Midtown). ☎ 212/869-4400.

Vicki Rovere, on the women's room: "Very modern, with lots of mirrors and etched flower vases." We, of course, weren't dressed for the women's room, but the men's, in our estimation, is worth a leak. Watch your step, though: The sink looks like the urinal, the stalls like a wall.

> **Trinity Church.** Broadway and Wall St. (Financial District). ☎ 212/602-0800.

Vicki Rovere: This is one of the limited number of churches that are really tourist attractions. They expect tourists to be coming in to use the toilets, so you don't have to be embarrassed about doing it.

Jim Monk: Is there a stained glass in the Trinity Church bathroom?

Vicki Rovere: Yes, there is. It's to bring you closer to the Lord while purging yourself.

> **Tunnel.** 220 Twelfth Ave., at 28th St. (Chelsea). ☎ **212/695-4682.**

How we landed here is hard to say. We're old men, yet there we were, late one night, before a velvet rope, with a bouncer standing guard on the other side. We were about to turn away. We don't like bouncers; we like velvet ropes even less. But then, like magic, the bouncer whistled to us. There was a crowd of people waiting, but he whistled to us, as if we were somebody. But then we looked around, thought to ourselves, *If we're someone, what the fuck are we doing here?* We went in, anyway. After all, he let us in and not them, and we were already there. The point of this is the bathroom and bar; bathroom and bar, together; that is, in one. Whose idea was that? On the other hand, bars generally have bathrooms in them. Why not a bathroom with a bar in it? We met some friends. We talked while having a drink, drank while having a pee. It makes sense, actually.

Tours

Tours aren't always predictable, touristy, or cheezy, as the following one-of-a-kind New York tours demonstrate.

> **Discovery Tours.** 1775 Broadway. ☎ **212/474-8800.**

This outfit offers tours of New York "gang territories" and East Harlem "graffiti messages." You know Giuliani's Quality of Life program is working when the criminal element becomes a relatively safe tourist attraction. "Look, Ma, a crackie!"

> **The Fulton Fish Market Tour, South Street Seaport Museum.** South Street Seaport (Financial District/Downtown). ☎ **212/748-8590.**

Though one of the best New York tours, it is not worth getting up at 4:45am to get there at 5:45 to go on the 6am tour. A pleasant but sleepy Roger Lasoff wound us around and through the very active fish market, prodding and pointing out red snappers, shark, swordfish, blue fish, salmon, barracuda, buckets of live crayfish, crabs, and the ugly monk fish, while the fish market workers followed us, steering us out the way of loaded dollies and Mafia strong arms, teasing Mr. Lasoff with difficult questions, while expertly cutting filets, showing off their catches of the day (the biggest, the most obscure, etc.) and still haggling their part of half-a-million pounds of wholesale fish that every day finds its way to top New York restaurants, gourmet delis, supermarkets, Chinatown, Paris, and Hawaii.

The Fish Market has been a "family" business for generations (Mayor Giuliani has recently attempted to rid the market of one particular family's influence) and due in part to this the atmosphere is friendly, and the entirely male work force shows immense pride in their work. However, South Street Seaport is no longer a working port and the catches are now flown or trucked in from Maine, Canada, the Caribbean, and freshwater farms around the country. Yet the sales still continue as if it were 2 centuries ago: The fish aren't priced; instead, the asking rate is constantly changing depending on size, amount, season, time of day, demand, and who they are selling to. The tour is on the first and third Thursdays of the month. Call in advance.

Three fish facts: first, the definition of fresh is only that it was never frozen. Second, fresh salmon should smell like cucumbers. Third, the monk fish is sooo ugly that it is never shown whole, because then it would never be bought.

> **Kramer's Reality Tours.** ☎ **800/572-6377** (KRAMERS) or 212/268-5525. www.kramer.com.

Offered by Kenny Kramer, inspiration for the *Seinfeld* character of same last name. We don't care much for Jerry Seinfeld's middle of the road humor, yadda, yadda, yadda, but we know that many of you do. Not that there's anything wrong with that. For us, the highlights of the show were always Kramer and Costanza. Kenny said, "Getting Larry David [the real George Costanza, and co-creator of the popular sitcom] an apartment across from me was the best thing I ever did." You got that right. The delightful real-life Kramer admits to "shamelessly" milking the show for all the money it's worth, meaning he charges $37.50 for his tours—which, since the show's demise, are booked solid for months. For *Seinfeld* groupies, it's well worth it. The 3-hour tour includes "Original Kramers Famous Pizza," beverage, dessert, and a visit to all the *Seinfeld* sites, where you will discover from the real Kramer "what's factual and what's fantasy in the *Seinfeld* universe." Stops include Joe's Fruits, Monk's Restaurant (in real life known as Tom's; see The Seinfeld Restaurant under "Addresses"), and, of course, the infamous Al Yeganeh, whom Kramer calls a "schizophrenic soup savant" (see Soup Kitchen International under "Food").

> **Radical Walking Tours.** ☎ **718/492-0069.**

Led by Bruce Kayton, these tours offer the most alternative political information on New York of any tour we took. We took Bruce's Central Park tour, which was remarkably free of cant, though the leftist leanings of Mr. Kayton are never fully obscured. The value of this tour cannot be overestimated, since the hidden political history of Central Park is never ever told in any of the guidebooks to Manhattan— namely, that there were several different communities of people on or near what became Central Park (including Seneca Village, an old black settlement between

79th and 86th and Sixth and Seventh avenues). And, at first, the rich folk who lived on the park went to great pains to keep the hoi poloi out. In addition, you will learn of the pioneering work of Joseph Papp, creator of Shakespeare in the Park, who was once fired by CBS for his alleged Communist leanings; the perfidious Warner LeRoy, who brings in $30 million a year from Tavern on the Green restaurant; the controversial Robert Moses, the former Parks Commissioner and force behind an incredible number of New York public works, including the Verrazano-Narrows Bridge, the Cross Bronx Expressway, Coney Island Beach, and the New York world's Fairs of 1939 and 1964, plus hundreds of playgrounds and dozens of swimming pools, golf courses, and state parks; and the fascinating and daring 1950s Arbor Day protest by area women, who blocked bulldozers and dealt the powerful Moses his

The Late Great Lou Singer of Lou Singer Tours

Lou Singer was the kind of New Yorker you just loved. Not afraid to tell an off-color joke or nosh on a variety of ethnic cuisine. Most importantly, like any true New Yorker, he loved all of New York, not just Manhattan. Singer's forte was Brooklyn. The man knew it inside and out. He also did colorful tours of the Lower East Side, the Upper West Side, and Old New York, as well as specialty tours of Jewish New York and Erotic Art in the New York City streets. But it was his Brooklyn tours that I loved—everything from Brooklyn Heights to the industrial waterfront to New York's version of Hollywood.

Lou had a resonant voice that got more and more resonant the more he talked, especially when the subject was food. (The guy went subtly orgasmic when talking of Theresa's blueberry blintzes or the farmer's cheese at Ben's Cheese Shop or the crispy egg rolls at Ho Chi Shieh.) For this reason, fans also loved his East Village Noshing Tour, with the requisite stops at Black Forest, Russo's, Di Roberti's, Russ and Daughters, Hunan Garden, and McSorley's Ale House, the oldest saloon in the U.S. Lou's signature Brooklyn Noshing Tour included Moishe's Bakery, K&K in Greenpoint, MacDonald's Dining Room in Bed-Sty, Lebanese food on Atlantic Avenue, and Jean Venee's Pastry Shoppe in Bay Ridge.

Lou tried to come off as a low-key, regular ole mensch (he was a former news-paper route driver), but the guy really knew his history. There was absolutely no way you could walk away from one of his tours without learning something new about the city. Unfortunately, as this book was in the final stages of editing, Lou Singer passed away. He was a living treasure of the city while alive, and will remain so in the hearts of all those who knew him now that he has passed over to the great noshing tour in the sky.

first major defeat; plus the hidden stories behind several of the 51 sculptures in the park, including the memorial at Columbus Circle dedicated to the sinking of the battleship Maine, which launched the Spanish-American War. (When told by a reporter there was no war in Cuba, William Randolph Hearst allegedly shouted "Make a war!") Mr. Kayton does several other radical tours, including Greenwich Village (John Reed, Provincetown Playhouse, Emma Goldman's House, The Shirtwaist Factory Fire of 1911, Stonewall), Wall Street (the first organized slave revolt, the J. P. Morgan & Co. bombing), and the Lower East Side (the Rosenbergs, the Anti-Inflation Riots, Rose Pastor Stokes). From what we've heard, they are all as informative as the one we took—and they only cost $6.

Toxic Tourism

> **Fresh Kills Dump.** 310 W. Service Rd., Staten Island. ☎ **212/788-3919.** Take the Victory Blvd. exit off the 440 (West Shore Expressway) to W. Service Rd. (take it straight to the end where you will see a guard booth—do not follow signs to Fresh Kills Household Disposal).

Fresh Kills, the largest landfill in the friggin' world

It's a friggin' landfill, but by the time our likable guide, Happy Dave Hendrickson, was done you'd have thought it was Aspen. The guy wouldn't admit to even one scintilla of doubt about the hazards there. He pooh-poohed the smell. He pooh-poohed the size. (He was proud of it, in fact: "Fresh Kills is the largest landfill in the world, incorporating over 3,000 tons of trash.") He pooh-poohed it all, from the threat of spontaneous combustion to worker safety to pollution in the Kills to the ominous prospect of a planned 500-foot mountain of garbage. Dave pooh-poohed everything but the poop. Horse poop that is, which the landfill recycles, along with grass and Christmas trees. Yes, Christmas trees. Dave was very proud of the Christmas tree recycling program. He had us stick our Monks' hands in the compost made from them, which winds up on gardens all over the city. All of it donated by the landfill. A nice gesture, we thought.

Except for one thing: It's a drop in the bucket compared to the endless barges of refuse that find their way here—plastic bottles, pipes, newspapers, baby diapers, and a few items that people actually come and pull out of the mess. Dave says he's fished out $20,000 worth of jewels, $400 in rent money from a box of Lipton soup, and a pair of false teeth. He even helped a 70-year-old woman recover a bag of raffle tickets.

Fresh Kills does a few other good things, too: They crush and recycle rock, they trap and resell methane released from the landfills, which heats over 12,000 homes. And they are shockingly open about the entire operation (on the tour you can get pretty darn close to the mighty bulldozers and the giant smelly barges, not to mention the seagull-infested landfills). It's a sanitized tour, but a revealing one nonetheless.

Security is tight, and city bureaucracy appears unavoidable. The only way in is to call the city's **Department of Cultural Affairs** at ☎ 212/788-3916. Their educational tours are free but only available to special interest groups or schools. If you qualify as one of those, be sure to request Dave Hendrickson as your guide.

Transportation

There are many ways to get around New York City. Each has its use, and its lore. We suggest you try them all.

City Buses

There's a substantial percentage of New Yorkers that won't ever go near a city bus. Too slow. Gotta get there. Hurry, Hurry, Hurry. Gotta meet Robert at Nobu. Where's my damn cigarettes? Taxi!

Maybe for that very reason there's something reassuringly therapeutic even about the boxy new East German–looking city buses. In Manhattan (below 96th Street, at least) it's like hopping the trolley in 1898. Nobody seems to mind that the thing stops every couple blocks. Nobody's in a rush. You got your *Times,* you got a 110-year-old Austrian woman sitting next to you, you got an actual view out the window.

Get into the outer boroughs, though, and the vibe changes. There, where subway stops are sometimes nowhere near convenient, the buses are actually vital. Get up into the Bronx and the Bx12 bus from 207th Street, Manhattan, along Fordham Road and Pelham Parkway to Baychester is as busy as a Manhattan subway line. Lifeblood, baby. (And it'll take you right to Arthur Avenue, the Bronx's own Little Italy—see "Neighborhoods.")

Long-Distance Buses

You got three basic types here: (1) the New Jersey Transit–type buses you muscle your way onto at the Port Authority to go watch the ponies race at the Meadowlands or visit your friend Sammy out in the burbs; (2) the great Greyhound/Trailways/Peter Pan net that connects the flightless multitudes from sea to shining sea; and (3) the whitebread cruisers that yuppies take on summer Fridays from Midtown to their time shares in the Hamptons.

There's also a fleet of spotless Neoplan buses that ferry German tourists around the city. We don't know where those come from.

Cars

New York is a city where 75% of the people don't own cars. In fact, they're considered more burden than status symbol. To us, though, this means 75% of the people have their freedom of movement and choice severely curtailed, which is why we say that if you really want to experience New York in its vast multi-borough entirety, you gotta get a car.

"A CAR?!" you shriek. "New York has the best public transportation in America. The subways run all night. To wherever you want to go. The price of parking is prohibitive, plus there are very real dangers of having your car damaged or broken into. Why a car?"

Because without a car you will not experience the pockets of diversity and high weirdness that make the city so amazing. Without a car you simply won't escape your usual haunts. New Yorkers find it daunting to head far uptown to hear a concert—and forget about the outer boroughs. If you hear of some great event in Queens, chances are that even the most adventurous local won't go because the subway ride will take at least an hour. In addition, most New Yorkers are very confused about what trains or buses to take to get there anyway. Third, once you finally get there, that's it. Forget trying to do anything else for the evening.

With a car, however, you can bop around very quickly to several outer-borough places in a night, as you can do in many other American cities. Without a car, you just won't be able to bop around, unless you are a trust funder with oodles of dollars for cab fare. Get a car, get a car, get a car! It's pure heresy in this town. Trying to park in Manhattan can drive you to tears and I don't recommend it for your daily commute, but if you plan to do a lot of running around to the far reaches of this city, nothing beats it.

Car Services

I am waiting for the definitive guide to New York car services because these companies are among the most pathetic in town. The concept goes like this: Car services operate mostly in the outer boroughs, where cabs are less common. The driver must have his own car. Since most car service drivers have a low income to begin with, their cars tend to be in pretty bad shape. If you don't think cabbies make a lot of money, check out the car services. The worst and yet most hilarious service I ever encountered was the North Side Car Service in Williamsburg. Invariably, their cars will break down just as you're trying to catch a flight at La Guardia.

RVs

Not recommended. (See "On the Road.")

Subways

New, improved, and a helluva lot more sane now that panhandlers have been whisked away—though that whiny, deliberately pathetic bearded guy hawking the homeless newspaper and the grating fat female still seem to be doing brisk business on the L line, and the "Vietnam vets offering free food to anyone homeless riding the subway and asking for our money to keep this food drive alive" scam is still going strong.

When you really study the question, New York subways are often the fastest

Transit Trivia

Seventy-eight percent of Manhattan households do not own a car. Shuttling passengers between home, office, entertainment, and other destinations, taxis have become the urban equivalent of the suburban family car.

and most economical way to any one point in the city. However, if you want to cover several points in one outing, we recommend a car (see above). Subways do offer a few salient advantages over other forms of transport: You can read on them, you receive outstanding free entertainment courtesy of the many subway musicians, but, most importantly, you rub shoulders and thighs with the great washed and unwashed masses. And, for obvious social, political, and cultural reasons, this simple sociological fact is what sets New York apart from L.A. and almost any other city on the planet: No matter how educated or rich, if you choose to ride the subway you will have to confront your fellow man. Which, in my opinion, is the reason L.A.-style riots could never happen here: We know each other too well. You can't live inside your stereotypical brain in New York. Everything you thought was ironclad and true is eventually proven false or limited. Especially on the subway. Loud as those screeching trains can be, as horrible as the public address system is, as annoying as those remaining panhandlers can be, the New York subway system is still the most colorful, enjoyable, and fastest in the world. Try the N & R line, which takes you from Wall Street to Midtown to Coney Island and Queens.

Taxis

I love cabs. If I had the money, I'd probably take them all the time. New York cab drivers are historically a fascinating bunch, though these days the cranky storytelling Irish cabbie of lore is almost completely gone, replaced more and more by a steady stream of Pakistanis, Indians, Bangladeshis, and Haitians. Still, the wit and wisdom that comes out of taxi drivers is as high as ever, as duly noted in Risa Mickenberg's *Taxi Driver Wisdom:* "A cabby is a kind of confessional-mobile. Musky with incense or poppy air freshener, somber with soft music (Lite FM), sealed off from the rest of the world, you slide open that glass divider and it's just you and your guru, sharing a few minutes of reflection and advice."

Here are our picks for the most fascinating cabbies and/or cabs in the city:

- **Cesar D, Yellow Cab Driver:** Badass Brazilian with a cab decorated with badges and pins, inside and out. He's a big Palmeiras fan from way back, though he's been in the States over 13 years.
- **Checker Cabs:** These used to be everywhere, and are still the cab of choice for every movie set in New York, but today there are only about 12 left. It's become a source of pride among New Yorkers to be lucky enough to ride in one.
- **Pedicabs:** Or, to put it in more politically correct terms, "human-powered tricycles." There's no way these modern rickshaws will compete with the

furious pace of a Pakistani cabbie eager to make a big tip, but that's not the point. Pedicabs point the way to a more sensible, non-polluting transportation alternative, especially in areas like Wall Street, where the only other reliable option is walking. In addition, like the carriages through Central Park, they are just plain fun, although in appearance, they can seem distressingly colonial. (Call ☎ 212/PONY-CAB.)

- **The "Please Don't Talk To Me" Lady Cabbie:** A woman cabbie with a wildly decorated cab, who asks that you don't talk to her.

Trains

When New Yorkers get on a train, either at Grand Central for the Connecticut- or Westchester-bound lines or Penn Station for everywhere else, it's like stepping out of reality. Their minds are conditioned to think all trains are like the subways—harsh, noisy, windows scraped with some kid's tag and Doctor Zizmor ads along the walls. Then they hop on a Metro North car. The seats are *cushioned*. When the doors close there's this little hermetic "whoosh" and most of the outside noise goes away. Homeless crackheads don't go from car to car, asking you for money. And you can go so *far* between stops. We suspect it was too much riding the trains that made New Yorkers go soft and allowed T J Maxx and Kmart to establish beachheads in town.

Walking

Though we're big on cars, alas, as a car culture, New York is definitely minor league. Compared to the vast swaths of mega-freeway that engulf L.A., New York's streets and highways seem quaint by comparison: narrow, suitable at times for horse and buggies but not streams of traffic. For this reason, New York is first and foremost a walking town. The other transportation alternatives are simply means to ease the walking burden. We have a pet theory that this is why New Yorkers, as a rule, are less fat.

Transit Trivia

Forty-three percent of all applicants for a taxicab drivers license in 1991 were born on the Indian subcontinent (up from 10% in 1984). Between July 1993 and March 1994, 30% of all taxicab driver applicants failed the English test.

Best of NYC Transit

Here are several key aspects of New York transportation culture.

- **Best Subway Line:** No doubt about it. It's the **N & R.** Along this route you catch every major part of New York—Coney Island, Brooklyn Bridge, Tribeca, SoHo, NYU, Union Square, Flatiron District, Times Square, and the south end of Central Park—and all this before it scoots over to Queens and becomes a righteously evocative elevated line. Also, for whatever reason, it seems to arrive far more frequently than either the 6 or the 1 and 9.

- **Best Match of Subway Line with Destination:** The **B to Coney Island.** Catch it southbound from West 4th Street and Sixth Avenue. After quick stops at Broadway-Lafayette and Grand Street, it climbs into the open air and begins rattling up onto the Manhattan Bridge like a roller coaster car heading for The Big Plunge. Sit on the left side of the train for a mobile view of the Brooklyn Bridge or the right side for the Williamsburg before heading back underground. After 36th Street, the train pounces back into the sun like that moment in the funhouse when your car heads straight for the wall, the wooden doors shotgun back, and you're twirled past your parents' faces before carooming back into the dark. Add in the way the train rocks from side to side going into the Bay 50th Street station and you've got a fine précis of mechanized carnival theory for only a buck and a half.

- **Best Bus Line:** Catch the M4 bus at its southern terminus at West 32nd and Seventh Avenue. It heads up Madison past the Morgan Library and Grand Central Terminal, all the way up past the Whitney Museum at East 74th, heads into East Harlem, banks a left and runs across Central Park north, passes Malcolm X and Frederick Douglass boulevards and the Cathedral of St. John the Divine, makes a beeline up Broadway past Columbia U and all through Harlem, then cuts over to Fort Washington Avenue for the final run into Fort Tryon Park and a victory lap around the Cloisters Museum. Take it the other direction and it runs south along Fifth Avenue (and Central Park) instead of Madison, and brings you home right past the Empire State Building.

- **Port Authority Bus Terminal** (Eighth Avenue between West 40th and 42nd Street): A Cold War–era experiment. Got to be. Take a block-large enclosed space; fill it up with Jersey commuters, homeless folks (deranged and otherwise), leftover small-change Times Square hoodlums, and low-budget tourists doing *On the Road* by Greyhound; toss in a few trembling, fresh-faced, baggy-pants teens from Pleasantville; then just throw the switch and see what happens. Get there around rush hour, when the scientists rev

the thing up to speed. Or come in the middle of the night, when they rean-
imate their dead.

Oh, yeah: You can get the bus here, too.

- **Penn Station** (Seventh Avenue between West 32nd and West 33rd streets):
  The most depressing place in New York, but you wouldn't know that unless
  you have a mental picture of what it should look like. Now essentially the
  basement of Madison Square Garden, Penn used to be the grandest of the

Monks on the water: Staten Island Ferry

grand, a cavernous stone, metal, and glass sculpture of a building—a rail station that actually elevated the human spirit. Then some brainless schmucks came along in the early '60s, said, "Who needs elevated spirits?" and tore the whole thing down. Today, its stairways lead to flat, dead-end ceilings and cheap food stands instead of to the original vaulted domes. A metaphor for foreshortened expectations? And how.

- **Grand Central Terminal** (Park Avenue between 42nd and 46th streets): Pretty much the last bastion of 19th century railroad spirit left in New York, Grand Central remains what Penn Station was: a building that says to people stepping off trains, "You have now entered New York City. You have our permission to be impressed." It's a beaux arts wonder, with a huge central hall, vaulted tunnels and hallways that bring mosques to mind, and a sky-blue central dome with gold stars shining in its firmament. Stone, marble, light, and air combine to make a space that mirrors the almost spiritual turn-of-the-century regard for transportation and industry.

  A rarity: The place was refurbished over the last several years, and they did it *well*.

- **Staten Island Ferry** (South Street at State Street): Literally the cheapest ride in the city: 50¢, round-trip—actually, if you don't leave the terminal on the Staten Island side, it won't cost you anything, and you'll still get the great view of Manhattan.

- **Roosevelt Island Tram** (Second Avenue at 60th Street): The air is not usually considered a medium through which to commute in New York. Nevertheless, this tramway hovers over the East River, linking Manhattan with somnambulant Roosevelt Island (see "Neighborhoods"). Actually, it's probably the best thing about the island. Romantic, to boot, especially on a cool night, after the Rooseveltians have already come home to roost.

- **New York City Transit Museum.** See "Museums, Galleries & Other Landmarks."

Transit Resources

> *Taxi Driver Wisdom,* by Risa Mickenberg, photography by Joanne Dugan (Chronicle Books, 1996).

Risa Mickenberg is a highly respected New York copy writer who made her mark at New York's Kirshenbaum and Bond. This book, so smartly designed by Brian Lee Hughes (the colors are taxicab yellow and black; the black cover feels like cab upholstery) and expertly photographed by Joanne Dugan (to convey the feel of what New York looks like from inside a taxi) is both delightfully wise and subtle. The wisdom comes from the cabbies whom Risa queried while jaunting about the city working for K&B. For instance, "on 20/20 vision" one cabbie responds: "As soon as you meet someone, you know the reasons why you will leave them." "On starting a relationship" a cabbie reflects, "new shoes always hurt." And the wisdom comes from Risa, who's framing of the questions reveals a thoughtful person looking at her own life and loves with depth, humor, and integrity. While some might claim that the short aphoristic quotes reveal her copy writer's bent, there is so much heart and truth in this small book you will keep coming back to it again and again. Like great advertising that way, don't you think? As the driver says, "We all connect, like a net we cannot see."

> **Taxi Talk.** 175 Fifth Ave., Suite no. 2108. ☎ 212/505-0604 or 212/560-0107.

This is an 8-year-old trade publication targeting the New York City yellow cab driver. In its "Ms. Taxi" column it often features half-naked women who have only a tangential connection to the taxi industry. There's also a related TV show of the same name on Manhattan Cable 17, every Thursday at 11am. The editor, Michael Higgins, has been a cabbie for 15 years. Star writer William Mercy has been around just as long.

> **Taxi and Limosine Commission.** 221 W. 41st St. **212/302-8294.**

Judge, jury, and executioner for cabbies. To illustrate: "For a cab driver, everything is upside down. If a person has $4 and the meter says $4 and they want to go a few more blocks, I will take them, but I have to shut my meter and if I shut my meter, TLC (taxi and limousine commission) will give me a ticket for $100. This is what I mean about a society that values money over love." (From Risa Mickenberg's *Taxi Driver Wisdom,* illustrating the relative values of love and money.)

Five Great Places to Catch Cabbies

1. Car wash at Houston and Broadway
2. Sixth Avenue cab depot, north end of Canal
3. Any of the 24-hour Indian or Pakistani restaurants that line Lexington Avenue from 25th to 28th
4. Mobile Station on Sixth Avenue right below Spring Street (see "Food")
5. McDonald's at the corner of 34th and Tenth Avenue

Views

Some cities—say, San Francisco—are what you might call topographically democratic. Climb a hill, get a view. In New York, the best views (or at least the most famous) cost money; you've got to pay, for example, to go to the top of the Empire State Building or the World Trade Center. We don't have much money and, even if we did, Michael is afraid of heights. If you, too, are poor or acrophobic and still want a view of the city, you might try some of the following.

> **Bradlee's.** 40 E. 14th St., at Broadway (Union Square). ☎ 212/673-5814.

Ride the escalators to the top floor for a great view north that includes Union Square and the Empire State Building.

> **DIA Center for the Arts.** 548 W. 22nd St., at Eleventh Ave. (Chelsea). ☎ 212/989-5566. www.diacenter.org.

From the roof, there's a view of the East River and New Jersey. Also a rooftop cafe and an installation by the artist Dan Graham. "DIA" is a Greek word meaning "conduit."

> **Kmart.** 770 Broadway, at Astor Place (East Village). ☎ 212/673-1540.

A Kmart on Astor Place? Like it or not, it's arrived. At the Kmart Cafe, on the store's second floor, you can mourn the death of the East Village while sipping coffee and peering south along Lafayette Street, fondly remembering the days when skater kids terrorized the Cube.

> **Liberty State Park.** Off exit 14B of the New Jersey Turnpike (Jersey City, New Jersey). ☎ 201/915-3400.

A great, free view of Manhattan from the park's esplanade.

> **Marriott Marquis Hotel.** 1535 Broadway, between 45th and 46th sts. (Times Square). ☎ 212/398-1900.

Ride the glass elevators for a view not of the city but of the hotel's lobby. Michael Monk rode them: "I don't know what to say about glass elevators with circus lights around them. You see this all over the country. This is high class in the Midwest. I feel sick. I am literally hanging hundreds of feet above the ground, and it's making me very nervous. We're at the top now? Good. Can we go back down to the lobby?" Also in the Marriott Marquis is New York's only revolving restaurant; it's called, appropriately enough, the View. If you squint hard down at the lights of

Times Square while rubbing your ass against the seats, you may convince yourself you're in Vegas.

> **Pen Top Lounge.** 700 Fifth Ave., at 54th St. ☎ **212/247-2200.** Closed for renovation until 1999.

The crowd is gold-chained salesmen from God knows where. The decor is '70s Bad Taste Moderne. But the Pen Top's selling point is that it has an amazing view of the Fifth Avenue canyon and the surrounding skyscrapers. Unlike the views from the Empire State Building and the World Trade Center, this view puts you right in the middle of Manhattan's high-rise action. A must-see. And no fee.

> **Ralph DeMarco Park.** Along Shore Blvd. between Ditmars and Twentieth Avenue (Astoria).

About 4 blocks long and maybe 15 feet wide, this is really just a northern spur of Astoria Park. The quality of the view—across the Hell Gate and Triborough Bridges

Astor Place

toward Manhattan—is testified to by the wedding parties that appear out of nowhere most weekends to have their photos taken here.

> **Socrates Sculpture Garden.** 31–34 Vernon Blvd., at Broadway, along the East River (Long Island City, Queens). ☎ 718/956-1819.

Hang from the jungle-gym-like works of art in this vacant lot turned artists' playground on the banks of the East River.

> **Staten Island Ferry.** South St. and State St. (Battery Park). ☎ 718/390-5253.

Literally the cheapest ride in the city. See the "Transportation" section for details.

> **Williamsburg Waterfront (including Grand Street Park).** Williamsburg, Brooklyn.

Michael Monk: Here we are today in my favorite wino park in all of New York City, at the end of Grand Street. This is a major dog dumping park. Behind me and to my right is the Williamsburg Bridge. You should be able to see Manhattan, but you can't. That's because it's a very, very polluted day, and there's mist coming up from the water, and there's smoke belching out of an indeterminate number of incinerators. Actually, this is one of my least-favorite parks in New York, because of all the pesky planes that keep flying overhead. The East River, behind me, is a dirty river. You can smell the dirt in this river.

Sunbathers on the Williamsburg waterfront

'Zines

It'd probably be impossible to calculate the number of words printed and circulated in New York City each day. There are, for example, 6 local Russian-language newspapers and 11 Chinese. In English, *The Village Voice*, *The New York Press*, *New York* magazine, and *Time Out* all exist for more or less the same purpose: to cover the city. Most national magazines are headquartered here and they're as likely as, say, the editors of *Popsmear* to show up at an event on the Lower East Side, so it can get kind of tricky to define either a local scene or a local 'zine. But we've done our best. Some of the publications that follow are for a New York audience; others are nationally distributed and have nothing to do with New York, except that they're published here. They've all got one thing in common, though: They spring from the world's media capital and, in some way, reflect its intense and varied spirit.

> **2600: The Hacker Quarterly.** P.O. Box 752, Middle Island, NY 11953-0752. www.2600.com. E-mail: subs@2600.com.

The best hacker magazine in the world, period. Named for the old 2600 Hz tone that was once standard on all U.S. telephones (a hacker named Captain Crunch discovered he could make free calls with the plastic whistle included in every box of cereal), 2600 is about computers and the phone system. Perhaps a bit technical for the uninitiated, the 'zine is nevertheless coveted; apparently, it's the only place off the Net where information about hacking the phone systems is exchanged. It's got a libertarian bent and is clear-headed about the absurdity, not to mention impossibility, of federal cyberspace policies. ($4 each, $21 a year.)

> **Bad Seed.** 45 Attorney St., no. 6C, New York, NY 10002.

Bo Wakeman's 'zine is a collection of lurid sex tales, page after page of the author's exploits around New York. We only hope he practices safe sex. Features include "Yesterday I Came Out . . . Tomorrow I Go Back In," "The Top Ten Most Asinine Queer Role Models," and "The Men of Bad Seed—John Waters, Mike Diana (author, *Boiled Angel*), Brad Pitt, Jean Genet, and Russ Meyer." The highlight of the Number 3 double issue is David Svehia's tale about working as a Vegas stripper: "Usually I'd fuck the old guy's face, as old guys are hungry, appreciative, experienced, and often have removable plates that make their palates soft and roomy." ($4 each.)

> **Beer Frame: The Journal of Inconspicuous Consumption.** 160 St. John's Place, Brooklyn, NY 11217. E-mail: krazykat@pipeline.com.

A well-written homage to the stuff we buy (or don't buy, as the case may be). Editor/publisher Paul Lukas takes on things that are either so obscure nobody has noticed them or so ubiquitous everybody has stopped noticing them. Issues have covered such diverse topics as the differences between Oreo and Hydrox people, the design of dental floss dispensers, and the brannock device (which measures shoe size). How about a visit to the Frigid Fluid Company in Chicago, the nation's leading manufacturer of embalming supplies? Or an esoteric essay on the kraut juice market (even its manufacturers wouldn't drink the stuff). If you can appreciate the wonder of God's creation in a single grain of sand, why not the terrifying monstrosity of late-20th-century consumer culture in a Twinkie? ("Published now and then by HyperTensive Products"; $2 each—issues 1–3 are $3 per.)

> *Bust.* P.O. Box 319, Ansonia Station, New York, NY 10023.

Tiger Beat for girls who prefer Iggy Pop, Henry Rollins, and Thurston Moore. From issue Number 6: "My Friends Don't Touch My Boobs" and "A Vindication of the Rights of Cunt." Says Mike Kassner: "If I had a teenage daughter I'd get her a subscription." Thank God (for her, for him?) he doesn't. (Quarterly, $2.50 each, $10 a year.)

> *Crank.* P.O. Box 757, New York, NY 10009. www.btf.com/crank. E-mail: crank@inch.com.

The crank in question is Jeff Koyen, who likes to tell stories about drinking and driving and getting his license suspended (one page of issue Number 5 is titled "Dear DMV: Fuck You"). He also likes to fill the pages of his 'zine with games: "Word Find," for instance, in which you are asked to find 62 words and phrases that Nicholson Baker uses to describe sexual organs and activities in his novel *The Fermata;* or "Crankyland," which is like the board game Life except the goal is "to make it to the bar." Jeff says the first 1,000 subscribers will get an iron-on decal, although he offers this rejoinder: "Let's face it, the idea of more than even 100 people subscribing to *Crank* is a fucking pipe dream." ($3 each, $12 for 4 issues, "published 2–3 times a year.")

> *The Curse.* 158 Grand St., Brooklyn, NY 11211.

What makes this monthly Williamsburg 'zine sing is its bippity boppity British editor, Daisy Decapite. By her own reckoning, she's the unofficial "Mayor" of her little nook of Brooklyn, where her quirky and playful hand-drawn 'zine (think *Nancy's*) can be found at all the local haunts—from Teddy's to the Right Bank to Ugly Luggage—whose funky ads (do they actually pay for these?) adorn every issue. Occasionally the writing in *The Curse* strikes a deep, resonant chord, such as Greg Cornell's "A Letter, A Life." *The Curse* is published every full moon and is free. Best line: "May we recommend trying not to space out." (Make checks out to Decapite for a $10 subscription; $1 per back issue.)

> **Fat.** 18 Spring St., no. 2F, New York, NY 10012. www.thing.net/fat.
E-mail: fat@thing.net.

What we like about this one: It's got a cheap tabloid-style layout (a cross between *Weekly World News* and Soviet socialist realism) and feature articles with such titles as "NYPD Kills Their Cash Cow" and "Turning on Fame's Spit." Gritty street tales, articles that blur the already blurry line between fact and fiction. Best of all are the disturbing photos and the mock ads. *Fat* captures the hollow and greedy Zeitgeist of Clinton America. Anecdote: After a visit with the editor of *Fat* at the Pink Pony Cafe and a drive past a store called Accident Prone, a van crashed into the side of Mrs. Kassner's car, sending Jim Monk to the New York downtown emergency room in the care of two paramedics, Rocco Cassetta and Dan Mandel. We blame *Fat* for this. ($4.95 each, $8 a year—meaning 2 issues.)

> **Fishwrap.** 2130 Broadway, no. 915, New York, NY 10023. www.fishwrap.com.

We should admit to a conflict of interest straight off: There's a phone interview with Jim Monk in the issue that has Bob Guccione, Jr., on the cover. *Fishwrap* is a magazine about magazines, but it doesn't read like an insider trade rag. Publisher Marty Wombacher is just too far out of the loop for that. 'Zinesters should find a lot to like. There's Marky Ramone on rock magazines and Jeff Foxworthy on the Unabomber: "Ladies and gentlemen, if you've ever had the urge to pack explosives up in the mail and then send them to innocent people, you just might be a Unabomber." Actually, for many years, Jim's family thought *he* was a Unabomber. (Quarterly, $2.95 each, $15 for 6 issues.)

> **Meshuggah: Humor Treats and Thought Droppings.** Feh! Press, 200 E. 10th St., no. 603, New York, NY 10003-7702.

Meshuggah has a circulation of 300; it deserves better than that. It's well

Brain Trivia

According to the May 10th, 1997, New York Times, **Stuyvesant High School** *in Manhattan lands more students in America's top colleges than any other high school in the country. "From the class of 1996, 36 students were accepted at Columbia, 28 at M.I.T., and 20 at Harvard." However, Brooklyn's Midwood High School beat out Stuy at the 1997 Westinghouse Science Awards.*

written and funny and offers hours of mind-churning weirdness. Some stories from issue number 13: "Why I Want to Live in a World Filled with Pinheads," "Why People Like Suffering," and "Shopper's Delight—A Tasteless Response to the Commodification of Sustenance." Highly recommended. ($2 each, $7 for 4 issues.)

> *Popsmear.* 648 Broadway, no. 909, New York, NY 10012.
E-mail: POPsmear@sonicnet.com.

Popsmear operates on the always provocative, nearly always profitable, credo: WE WILL, WE WILL, SHOCK YOU. The photographic reenactment of the Jersey high schooler aborting her baby in the bathroom on prom night would push anybody's buttons. But there's more here than salacious journalism for the hyper-ironic Jägermeister set. There's actually intelligent writing, some insightful spite courtesy of founder and editor James Popsmear, and a pretty darn captivating faux tabloid design. And unlike virtually all other scene mags, *Popsmear* does not interview local bands. Articles are wide ranging: There are updates on the cyberworld, reports on shopping at thrift stores around the world, tips on the art of evading transit fares across Europe (Amsterdam is "easy," Budapest and Copenhagen are "iffy for evasion," London is "way vigilant"). If there's a unifying theme, it seems to be hostility towards the music business and Hollywood. *Popsmear* instructs band publicists in the art of exploiting local fanzines and regularly provides the home addresses and telephone numbers of such luminaries as David Geffen, Richard Gere, Michael Eisner, and, last but not least, Sharon Stone's parents.

> *Prometheus.* P.O. Box 2763, New York, NY 10163-2783.

The kids just can't get enough of that crazy, decadent, leather-and-chains thing. *Prometheus* is the *Time, People,* and *Sports Illustrated* of New York's bondage scene. Lots of discipline-craving boys, and the women who beat them. Fans of *Prometheus* might also like *Funeral Party,* a "colorful gothick [sic] extravaganza" published by Rude Shape Productions (511 Sixth Ave., no. 325, New York, NY 10011; www.rudeshape.com).

> *Rumpshaker.* 72–38 65th Place, Glendale, New York 11385.

From Queens, the borough that gave us Donald Trump and the Ramones, comes *Rumpshaker.* Wayne and Garth and Beavis and Butthead don't come close to *Rumpshaker* for real-life, outer-borough delinquency. Very Queens: multicultural and white-bread, urban and suburban. For bored kids who are too young to drive. ($3 each.)

> **See Hear Catalog.** 59 E. 7th St., New York, NY 10003. Fax 212/387-8017.

By the same guys who brought you the See Hear store (see Books under "Stores"), the catalog offers all sorts of 'zines, from the merely obscure (*Teenage Gang Debs*) to the pathologically obsessive (*Mister Density*, the unofficial Crispin Glover fanzine). Their bestseller? *Murder Can Be Fun.*

> **The Shadow.** P.O. Box 20298, New York, NY 10009.
http://MediaFilter.org/MFF/mfhome. E-mail: SHADOW@MediaFilter.org.

If you thought old-style political radicalism was dead, wake up!!! *The Shadow,* in the venerable New York Anarchist tradition, reports on the latest activities of the surveillance state. The cover of the issue we read memorializes the legendary New York defense lawyer and founder of the Center for Constitutional Justice, Bill Kunstler. "Pillage Void" is a scathing and cogent critique of the once important *Village Voice.* The mail-order section offers such titles as Squatter Comics, *The Complete Manual of Pirate Radio,* and "The Battle of Tompkins Square Park," a taped analysis by veteran local journalist Paul DeRienzo. Grimy, ranting, essential. (50¢ in NYC.)

> **Shock Cinema.** P.O. Box 518, New York, NY 10009.

Thoroughly researched, informative, and way out of the mainstream, *Shock Cinema* is "devoted to the most obscure films and videos imaginable." Editor/publisher/writer/designer Steve Puchalski reviews such forgotten gems as *Blazing Stewardesses, The Candy Tangerine Man, Madam Kitty, Guyana: Cult of the Damned,* and Andy Warhol's *Lonesome Cowboys.* Proof that there is still some very weird stuff out there. ($4 each.)

> **World War 3 Illustrated.** C/O Four Walls Eight Windows, 39 W. 14th St., Room 503, New York, NY 10011. www.bookworld.com.

World War 3 Illustrated is to the '80s and '90s what *The East Village Other* was to the '60s: a politico-artistic forum for the diverse communities of the East Village and Lower East Side. There are plenty of low-budget, angry 'zines out there, but few boast such a wealth of talent. *WW3* has launched a number of important comic artists and illustrators: Seth Tobocman (*You Don't Have to Fuck People Over to Survive*), Peter Kuper (*The Building, Bleeding Heart,* plus covers for *Time* and illustrations for *The New York Times* op-ed pages), and Eric Drooker (*Flood*).

Gary Panter:

The Monk Interview

>interview

Painted in the stairwell outside Gary Panter's studio in the Williamsburg section of Brooklyn is a sign that reads: "If we catch you doing drugs, we will paint you blue." This, according to Panter, is supposed to make the junkies want to "leave the building as soon as possible." Whether it works—and how well—isn't clear to us. As if to refute (or support) our skepticism, Panter adds, "There's a Courtney Love cover of *Spin* covering some feces up there." Michael nods, a little perplexed. "Well, welcome," Panter continues, and shows us into his hot, cluttered studio.

In the world of comic art, few have gone as far out as Gary Panter. His strip "Jimbo" has achieved almost mythic status among commix fans. He is also the man behind the hysterical, gaudy sets of *Pee-Wee's Playhouse* and the crazed playroom at the Paramount Hotel.

Panter was raised in East Texas, in the stern, fire-and-brimstone Church of Christ ("You can't dance. You go to church on Sunday mornings and Sunday evenings, and then you go on Wednesday night"). As it turns out, he and Michael have much in common: Both grew up in the same church, on a "no lettuce, grease diet" ("Elvis's diet," as Michael is quick to point out), and both, because of either the religion or the food, developed ulcers in their teens.

Jim Monk: That's where you grew up, in East Texas, right?

Gary Panter: Yup, in Brownsville. We moved around a lot when I was little, and then we settled in Sulfur Springs, Texas—in this dairy country, you know. Real safe and square, and time moves slowly and safely, with a lot of attending church and schools.

Jim Monk: Michael grew up in Arkansas.

Michael Monk: Yeah, not too far from there. I grew up in the Church of Christ.

Gary Panter: Yeah, that's the church I grew up in.

Michael Monk: All right. What do you know.

Jim Monk: Two absolutely strange people came out of that.

Gary Panter: It's like we were wearing the brain trap. The trap still fitted into certain holes in the brain.

Michael Monk: At what point did you finally figure out that there was something basically wrong with the cosmology of no dancing and no musical instruments?

Gary Panter: Well, I started noticing religion when I was really young, and then it progressively just got weirder until I found I had ulcers in junior high school, and then kind of like went along with it through high school and then went to college and stopped going to church after a couple of times, you know.

Jim Monk: Was that scary for you?

Gary Panter: Yeah, it was really scary. Sure, sure.

Jim Monk: Did you like hear your father's voice admonishing you?

Gary Panter: Yeah, I continue to hear it all the time; I still hear it.

Jim Monk: To this day?

Gary Panter: He's still admonishing me, yeah.

Michael Monk: So, when you were a teenager, did you start creating then through art?

Gary Panter: Yeah, I started when I was younger, you know, like drawing strips and then kind of forgot about it and then rediscovered it. Mostly when I got out on my own, I guess. But I had my hippie pad in my garage, and I started this surf, hot-rod, fink, rat-fink pad. I just took over the garage and painted on the walls, and then it gradually

became more like the hippie garage, and my friends and I built this thing we called Able that was this steamer trunk up on chrome exhausts with a big light. Well, like the MTV dancing water jug thing, that's what it was. It was a water jug bottom lit that we—we probably like built a hookah in the top and tried to smoke Lipton tea or something. You know, I could be in bands. Like I had my band in junior high school, the Radiations. We got those little Beach Boys shirts and—

Michael Monk: Are you serious?

Gary Panter: Yeah. And we played Beach Boys tunes, but then we tried to play for the eighth-grade banquet, but my parents came and like jerked me off the stage.

Jim Monk: They took you off while you were playing?

Gary Panter: Yeah, right. Yeah, they did. Because these girls were dancing, you know, so that was the end. They snuck in and took the enemy.

Jim Monk: So not everybody in the town was as fundamentalist as your parents.

Gary Panter: No, not really. But they all had their own brand of truth, you know. Every building had its own shining truth that said, "Kill everyone else." Destroy the infidels, you know, in the next building, the next shack. But they all get along. They just, like, tend to buy their cars from their own church, you know. For a time I wanted to run off and be a hippie because the hippies were going to change the world and build geodesic domes and everything was going to be groovy.

Jim Monk: You know, it's not that they're really being vindicated, but your parents are seeing some of their views being mirrored in the political and cultural climate of the times now. It's very conservative. Do you feel yourself—you've done all this escaping from your parents and their fundamentalist creed, but now you're in this culture which is so—this Newt Gingrich culture which is so fundamentalist in a way. Are you, has your art been affected by that at all, do you think?

Gary Panter: Well, my art's kind of reactionary stuff, you know, I guess, so it's affected by stuff like that. But I think that my parents aren't as conservative as the climate of the times, in a way, you know. They're very religious, but I don't see them like getting ready to march out and do a bunch of stuff, alter the Constitution or something. Although my father did say that the people who burned flags should be shipped out of the country, you know, whereas I would just say if everyone burned a flag every day, we'd have this great industry of, you know—flag production would be way up.

Jim Monk: What brought you to New York? You were afraid to come to New York before, but then you came. What was the reason?

Gary Panter: Yeah, I was just like a small-town guy, and I came to New York, and I went over to—my friends were staying at the Chelsea Hotel, and so I thought, "Well, I don't really have any money, but I'll go look in the *Voice* and see what the cheapest thing was." And it was like this $300 downstairs apartment, and so me and my friend went over to look at it. This was like 1974 or something like that, '73 or something, and these girls, this girl answered the door, and she was bald, and her body was all tattooed blue, her whole body and her hands and everything, and she was pierced—in like '70, whatever it was, '74. And so we went, "Oh, okay." Well, then we went in. Just two hicks, you know. And there was another girl just like her on this chair, and so she said, "Well." I said, "Is this the place? This looks kind of good, you know." And she said, "No, it's the room in the back." And so then they took us into the room in the back, and there was this room totally covered with shit all over the walls, and there was a giant cage in the—

Jim Monk: Literal shit?

Gary Panter: Literal shit.

Jim Monk: It was feces.

Gary Panter: There was this cage in the middle of the room with a great ape sitting there unhappily, sitting there in that back room. And that was the—they were going to get rid of the ape, you know.

Jim Monk: And give you the room.

Gary Panter: Yeah, right, that was the room.

Jim Monk: Did you take the room?

Gary Panter: No, I went—I moved to L.A.

> "If everyone burned a flag every day,
> we'd have this great industry of, you know—flag
> production would be way up."

> interview

> back
on the road

eight a.m. and the phone rings, stirring up flies as jim picks up the receiver. he's sprawled out on the floor surrounded by 3 weeks of the new york times and a bad cough from the dusty air. • "your van's ready," says the voice on the other end. • "my what?" says a sleepy jim. • "your van, you know, like, what is it, the pinkmobile!" • "oh, the monkmobile," mutters jim. "yeah, sure."

Mike rouses from another sweaty sleep, sheets soaked, covered in cat hair, with dark circles the size of teacups under his eyes.

"I'll go get it," Mike says, pulling on the same shorts and T-shirt he's worn for the past few days because he can't bear the heat of the Laundromat to do a load of clothes.

It's Saturday, the day the working class sweep their sidewalks and scrub their walls. Old Polish women in hiked-up skirts and whiskered chins sit cross-legged on steps, fanning their necks under the early morning shade. For a record fifth day, ridiculous heat settles across the city like an oppressive God, choking the air and pounding the pavement with relentless waves. Old men in unbuttoned shirts, rolled cuffs, and ruddy faces sit at windows, yelling across streets, sharing complaints. Today is the feast of Our Lady of Carmel. Despite the humid air, workmen several blocks away are putting finishing touches on a large platform on Havemeyer Street, which 100 strong Italian men will use to hoist and carry a 12-piece brass band, an emcee/crooner, and a giant 5-story sacred monument made of painted wood, with a saint perched on top.

Up tree-lined streets the rest of the melting pot of Williamsburg rolls slowly awake. The resident artists file into the L Cafe, in messy hair and careless attire, picking their scabs and tapping dirty fingernails. Casual hipness, slightly lean and mean, seems the rule of the day. Newspapers unfold as smoke curls from the lips of the morning crowd.

Back on the street, immigrants wear nice cotton skirts, and scarves on their heads. Women with loaves of bread, 10 to a sack, are headed toward the fair on Havemeyer. Their swollen ankles fold over their Old World shoes as they hobble hip-heavy toward the curb.

Turning up Metropolitan, Mike passes shopkeepers unlocking their gated doors, pulling up the bars and turning on their signs. The derelict binges of the night before are swept to the curb and the strong aroma of coffee blankets the neighborhood.

Joe is floating in a pool of grease under a truck when Mike arrives. "You can pay the guy in the office, he'll fix you up," Joe yells from underneath.

The guy in the office sits sweating under a mound of paper, a phone propped to his ear as he shuffles through the yellow receipts looking for the Monk bill.

"Twelve-hundred dollars?!" Mike yells. "You gotta be kidding me. Eight-hundred dollars in labor!?"

"Whaddaya expect. This thing was a bitch to take apart. You want to talk to my man, he'll tell you."

Mike looks at the lineup of gnarly mechanics and leaves it unchallenged. "Does it still sound like a lawnmower? What about starting? Is it still blowing black smoke?"

"It's running good enough!" he says. "Maybe you should trade it in."

Mike doesn't like the sound of that. He climbs in to take it for a test spin around the block. Grease marks cover the floor, and it looks like someone's had a beer or two, maybe even a romp on the back bed. The starter turns and the engine revs up to a nice high idle. Mike feels relief that the Monkmobile is up and running again.

A caravan of rambling trucks bounce along the potholed street as Mike backs out from the garage. As soon as he's out, he waves to an Irish mechanic as he shifts out of reverse back into drive. Suddenly the Monkmobile lunges forward with a radical start. The engine is racing, and before Mike knows it, he's cruising down Metropolitan at increasing speed.

Pedestrians scatter everywhere as the mammoth pink beast plows ahead.

"Jesus Christ, the throttle's stuck!"

The gas pedal is stuck to the floor and is revving at high speed. Traffic crawls ahead, and he blindly swerves to the left to avoid a string of cars, driving down the wrong way of the street. He honks his horn as he cruises at 40 mph through an intersection, running a red light. Pedestrians scatter everywhere as the mammoth pink beast plows ahead. By the time he's back on the other side of the street, he's jammed on the brakes and is tearing the transmission while the engine continues to rev. His long arms reach down, yanking furiously on the pedal, and it comes unlodged in his hand.

Now people are cursing at the Monkmobile and smoke is billowing from the engine as Mike throws it into neutral and takes his foot off the brake. He's in the middle of the street while traffic backs up both ways. Slowly he shifts back into drive and lunges off again, the engine squealing from the stress while he holds the brake to the floor. An acrid smell of burning gears and rubber pollutes the air. He pulls over in half a block and throws it in neutral again and is down at the floor trying to put the pedal back on. But it won't go back on. He stares dumbly at the pedal in his hand as the engine continues to race, making a high-pitched whining sound. Pedestrians walk by casting dirty looks at the whole scene.

He shuts it off with a "kaplunk," the engine creaking and moaning from the high-stress torque.

"Hello, Joe, it's the Monkmobile—you know, the pink piece of shit you just charged me $1200 to fix. It's seriously messed up!"

"Just bring her in," Joe says.

"I can't, the gas pedal came off and it's revving at high speed."

"Well, call a tow."

"Can't you tow it?"

"We don't do towing."

Mike's back on the phone, fuming, as he calls a dozen tow trucks. It'll take 4 hours and $300 if he wants to get it towed this morning. He hops back in the Monkmobile, takes a deep breath, and turns it back on with his foot firmly on the brake. It jumps forward as he throws it into drive. Riding the brake to the floor, he turns the block and drives back in front of the garage. He shuts off the engine with a loud backfire and stomps back in.

Joe sees him coming and says, "Don't worry, we won't charge you. I'll have one of my men take a look."

"I could have killed somebody."

"Did you?"

"No!"

"Then it's your lucky day!"

A mechanic is soon pulling things apart and finds the culprit, a spring that's stuck. He's explaining everything to Mike, who's already cursing the day he and Jim decided to buy a used class-A motor home.

Twenty minutes later, the mercury hovering around 94, the itinerant Monk and Monkmobile are once again back on the streets of New York, running like a charm.

Monks at Wigstock

"How's it working?" Jim asks.

"Sometimes I just wish somebody would steal it so we could collect the insurance," says Mike.

That night, as the empty Monkmobile sits quietly on a street facing the East River, with a cool breeze blowing, a full moon overhead, and the Monks asleep a few blocks away, an early morning prowler breaks a window and lets himself inside, ripping open cupboards, thrashing around, and helping himself to a thing or two. But instead of taking the Monkmobile, or the stereo, he steals the one most cherished possession in the Monk universe, the most indispensable item on board: Jim's coveted Dust Buster.

Wigstock

Finally, the heat wave lifts. Arms and faces open to the breeze as the heated rock of Manhattan finally begins to cool off. Children play in the parks, mothers push strollers, roller bladers jump stairs.

Windows are open everywhere. The drone of air conditioners is silenced for the first time in months. Curtains wave like arms, dancing with the birds that glide in the wind. Bare chests stride seductively down the streets. Without the heat, the whole city has a smile. You can breathe, you can think, you can touch and hug without sweaty regret.

As the sun sweeps across 14th Street, the Monks cruise along arm in arm with wide-open smiles on a window-shopping spree.

Today's a special day. It's the crowning moment of the summer, the peak of the year.

Today is Wigstock.

"This is bigger than the Pope as far as I'm concerned," says Mike.

He's wearing second-hand clothes rummaged from the bins of Domsey's Warehouse. Decked out in a pair of black velvet bell-bottoms, he towers dangerously high on 4-inch platform shoes with extremely square toes. Jim does better in green stretch pants, polyester and tight, an orange ribbed sweater and a pair of low-heeled shoes. The only thing missing is *the wig*.

"Where are we going to find a wig at nine o'clock on a Sunday morning?" says Jim.

"Listen, we'll find a wig or this isn't New York," says Mike.

Nose pressed against glass, Mike scours the passing shops of Manhattan's 14th Street, looking for signs of wigs—banged, curled, teased, or sprayed. After 3 blocks of window shopping, he suddenly stops and shouts. "Holy Giuliani!"

It's a wig shop. Layers of wigs on six tiers of shelves wrap around the room, advertising a hundred different looks for the wig-wearing guy. The Monks enter. Mike spots a deep burgundy wig with a square cut bob and a nice price tag.

"Fourteen dollars. That's a steal. Do you think it looks real?" Mike queries, putting it on.

"It's totally you, Twiggy," answers Jim.

The Monks rummage through a dozen different looks until Jim grabs a shoulder-length wig, looking about as natural as a bleached blonde.

"Orange? You look like a clown."

"And you don't?" says Jim.

Purchases made, the Monks return to the Monkmobile and lumber along 14th toward the Christopher Street Pier. All along the Hudson, barricades and police line the highway, holding back the mid-morning crowds. At the pier, hundreds of people put final touches on the towering stage.

Mike flashes a Wigstock parking pass, and the Monks drive through the barricades and start setting up for the throngs. "Sorry, you can't park in here," says a monitor 10 minutes later. "No vehicles on the pier, you'll have to park a half mile away."

"Listen, we'll find a wig or this isn't New York."

Trucks are parked everywhere, so Michael moves slowly away until the monitor's out of sight, then re-parks again. At noon the gates are thrown open, and thousands of queers and queers-for-a-day begin streaming through the turnstiles and along the river walk toward the faraway stage. Hundreds of drag queens in full day drag, plucked and tweezed, corseted and heeled, follow suit. Seven-foot divas in pinafores and sailor suits, night gowns and wedding dresses, petticoats and bell-bottoms, flaunt a million permutations of the Wigstock look.

At around one o'clock the inimitable Lady Bunny takes the mic and brings the crowd to its feet. The Monks swing out of the Monkmobile as the heat of the day warms the cool river air. Thousands of wigs saunter by. Mike turns red as 1 wig in every 10 is the same cut, style, color, and curl as his. Jim tosses his orange mane around like a mop on a stick as he shakes his bottom to the pounding disco coming from the stage.

Jim and Mike stand pinned against the wall of the Monkmobile, unshielded from the sun, as the wig-adorned run wild. Mike is casually enjoying the passersby, inspecting their get-ups, laughing at their attitude, when he hears a strangely familiar set of voices . . .

". . . and I's goin' downtown One for the cross-town to the Four at Union Square when I see that girl like she be doing that shit down Third and I'd be like, wassup with that?"

"Uh huh, you mean that same one that be down Tenth and Second?" says the other.

Mike cowers beneath his wig, desperately seeking to avoid the attention of the chatting black babes, who've now stopped right in front of the Monkmobile.

"No, what chu talking, I mean that one, you know, the other day down Third and First."

"You crazy, that was Second!"

"No, First."

"Tenth and Second, you crazy?"

"No, no, no you're thinking that shit we saw up First and Tenth, you know what I'm talking."

Suddenly they turn. And look straight at the Monkmobile.

"What kind of motherfuckin' piece of shit is this?"

Michael Monk is now turned completely to the side.

"Hey, girl," they shout at Mike, "get yourself a real wig! Ain't nobody gonna look at your sorry ass looking like that."

And off they go, laughing their loud donkey laughs, prancing down the pier, much to Mike's relief.

"I don't know what you're talking; that shit wasn't never down First."

"Oh, maybe Third?"

"No, girl, 'less you're talking Tenth and First like that day you and I saw her and that shit."

"That wasn't even me; who you thinking?"

"Down Tenth?"

"No, down First, with that piece from Bleecker. Girl, you're rockin' my heels. Where's your head?"

Conclusion

As always with New York, there's a lot we just didn't see over the 6 months we spent here, and there's a heckuva lot that's new since this book went to press, but these omissions are what give us the incentive to come back for more—and also give you an opportunity to help us find and fill in those inevitable gaps. We may not have visited your favorite watering hole, old donut shop, or quirky novelty store, but chances are we covered something equally great.

For the full-tilt Monk experience, we encourage all you Monks and Monkettes who have grand illusions about the great highway to join us online at www.monk.com, or through subscription by sending $10 (for 4 episodes) to **Monk**, 175 Fifth Ave., Suite 2322, New York, NY 10010 (☎ **212/465-3231**; E-mail: monk@monk.com). All checks should be made out to Monk. Foreign subscribers add $10. Visa and Mastercard warmly accepted.

And don't forget to purchase the companion CD-ROM to this guidebook, appropriately entitled *Mad Monks' Guide to New York City CD-ROM*, which has hours of extraordinary audio, video, and photographs of one-of-a-kind people, places, and events in and around New York. A true collector's item, and available for only $19.95 from the above address.

Finally, we want to know what you think is the best of quintessential New York. If you have any additions or corrections, don't hesitate to let us know. We'd love to hear from you!!

From all of us to all of you . . . Happy Tales!!

—The Monks (Jim Crotty and Michael Lane)
Dolly Lama (our cat)

How to Talk New York

Sometimes it's a matter of pronunciation, sometimes it's just a matter of hanging around long enough to get the hang of it. As one native New Yorker advised, "Speak fast, sharp, and rudely, and take it from there."

- **Substitute K for P:** "He bunked into a car."
- **Drop words at will.** Don't "play the piano." Simply "play piano."
- **D is often unnecessary.** "She dint come over for dinner."
- **R is a free agent.** On the one hand, it appears everywhere. "My wife's a lawryuh. Lovely Riter meter maid. Linder Ronstadt. Atlanter Braves. Bar, bar, black sheep, have you any wool? He's drawring pikshuhs of pigeons in the park. Gimme a slica pizzer anna soder." Then it suddenly disappears when you most need it: "Will you get us some cawfee down on toidy-toid street?" Or the unforgettable Brooklyn sportscaster's line, "Oh, no—Hoyt is hoit!" But then, just when you've figured out to pronounce every "er" word like "oi," suddenly you've got a bunch of "oy" and "oi" words that are pronounced "er" (as in "erster" for oyster and "berl" for boil).
- **Liberally season sentences with the all-purpose "fuck."** Only in New York and parts of New Joisey is "fuck" not taboo. It is taboo on stretches of Park Avenue, but that's New England, not New York, so don't sweat it.

Pronunciation guidelines excerpted from Jim's *How to Talk American* (Houghton Mifflin, 1997).

Absofuckinglutely: Absolutely, but more so.

Alphabet City: Avenues A through D in the far east of the East Village. Ten years ago parts of it looked like Beirut; today it's gentrified by yups and bups looking for a colorful address.

Alright, already: "Calm down, I get your point."

Are you talkin' to me?: Line made famous by Robert De Niro in *Taxi Driver*. Must be said while grabbing one's testicles.

Avenue of the Americas: Otherwise known as Sixth Avenue. Only tourists and corporate letterheads ever say "Avenue of the Americas."

Bed-Sty: Bedford-Stuyvesant, a primarily African-American neighborhood in Brooklyn.

Big Apple, The: Old-time slang for New York resurrected by the tourist board about 20 years back and now used only by tourists from Iowa. One theory is that it came from the slang of black jazz musicians: a booking at a New York club was "the big apple," while bookings at clubs in smaller cities were known as "the branches."

Bloomie's: Bloomingdale's, an Upper East Side department store.

Bodega: The Hispanic version of "delicatessen."

Boids: Birds. Usually pigeons, sometimes sea gulls.

BQE: The Brooklyn-Queens Expressway.

Bridge-and-tunnel people: Mutants who work or party in Manhattan but live on the far side of the rivers, usually in Long Island or Jersey.

Brits: Limeys hired by gullible New York executives impressed by their accents.

Bronx Bombers, the: The New York Yankees.

Brothuh or brudda: Brother. "I got an 8-year-old brothuh who's got no accent whatsoevuh."

Brown, Tina: Brit brought in to edit *The New Yorker* earlier this decade. Roundly despised for blowing beloved cobwebs out of corners. Left the job in 1998.

Brownstone: A type of 19th-century house with a facade of brownstone (sandstone). Real estate agents have broadened the definition to mean any row house or town house.

Bullwinkle District: The racially gerrymandered 12th Congressional District, so named because it really is shaped like Bullwinkle's head and antlers.

Canyon of Heroes: Lower Broadway in the Wall Street area, where parades are held in honor of returning war heroes, visiting dignitaries, or champion local sports teams.

The City: New York City, or, more precisely, Manhattan. Even when you take the subway from Brooklyn to Manhattan, you say you're going to "the city"; the designation only includes the outer boroughs when it's used in political speeches. As far as most Manhattanites are concerned, there are no other boroughs.

Coney: A hot dog.

The Cube: Bernard Rosenthal's giant black rotating sculpture (officially called the Alamo), nestled in the center of Astor Place in the East Village.

CUNY: The City University of New York. Originally "the Harvard of the poor," now a stronghold of bigoted professors and less than stellar students.

Da Bronx: The Bronx.

Dapper Don: Big-time Mafia godfather John Gotti, once known for his fine tailored suits, now (and for the rest of his days) modeling the latest in prison couture.

Dinkins, David: Low-key, nattily dressed former mayor.

The Donald: Tacky, cheeseball billionaire real estate tycoon Donald Trump. So named by his former wife, Ivana.

DUMBO: Acronym for Down Under the Manhattan Bridge Overpass (on the Brooklyn side).

Ebbets Field: Home to the Brooklyn Dodgers. Once stood at the corner of Bedford and Sullivan streets in Brooklyn, but was demolished in 1960, after the Dodgers moved to Cali. Today there's a huge housing project on the site, and across the street is the Ebbets Field Donut Shop. The door was locked when we tried to go in, and the man inside waved us off when we made "you open?" faces.

Egg cream: Beloved New York drink made from seltzer, milk, and chocolate.

El Barrio: Section of Manhattan above 96th Street on the Upper East Side, where many Dominicans and Puerto Ricans live.

ESSO: "East of SoHo." Another annoying appelation given to an un-trademarked neighborhood by New York realtors.

Eurotrash: Trash from Europe (see box in "Neighborhoods and Streets" section for tips on spotting them). Nothing pisses off a real Manhattanite like a Gucci-clad Frenchman or a snobby Italian art girl.

Fegedaboudit: Forget about it. An all-purpose expression with positive and negative connotations. See Johnny Depp's explanation in *Donnie Brasco* for the whole scoop.

Fuck: The litmus test of a true New Yorker is how many you can pack into a sentence. "Fuckin' A, didja see the way I fuckin' pounded on that motherfucker? Holy fuckin' shit, he was fuckin' pissin' in his fuckin' pants. You shoulda fuckin' seen his fuckin' face. He was like, 'Oh shit, don't fuck with me,' and I was like, 'Motherfucker I'm gonna fuckin' kill you you fuckin talk to me like that.' Fuck. That was fucked up."

Gedouttahea: Expression of derisive suspicion, as in "You're pulling my leg." Can also be used to express surprise, as in this exchange: "Hey, Hank, I'm gettin' married tomorra." "Gedouttahea!" Usually following in this instance by a fuck line (see above); i.e., "Holy fuckin shit! You're fuckin' kiddin' me. Oh, fuck."

Gotham: Informal name for the city, now in vogue as a kind of retro thing.

Greengrocer: A 24-hour grocery store usually owned by Koreans. Carry a selection of natural foods and unnatural foods and an extensive buffet of food selections that all look different but taste exactly the same.

Gridlock: Traffic snafu in which an intersection becomes completely jammed with vehicles; what happens when drivers don't heed the "Don't Block the Box" street signs.

Gwan: "Go on," or "come on." I.e., "gimme a break."

Hah-rubble: Horrible; not pleasant.

Hero: A submarine sandwich or grinder.

The House That Ruth Built: Yankee Stadium, made famous by Yankees slugger Babe Ruth.

How-ston: Houston Street. "How-ston," not "Hyew-ston."

I got news for you, bud: You are about to be informed by a knowledgeable New Yorker that what you thought was true is, in fact, not.

I'm going down: "I'm going outside," which means down to most apartment dwellers.

Kuhnish: Knish. Dough filled with meat, grains, and/or vegetables. A New York Jewish favorite. You pronounce the "K."

Kvetch: Complain. From the Yiddish.

Ladies' Mile: A fabled stretch of opulent department stores on Sixth Avenue between West 14th and West 23rd streets. It once catered to women, and has now been remade into the home of Bed, Bath and Beyond; T. J. Maxx; Old Navy; Today's Man; and other quaint suburban outlets.

La Guardia, Fiorello: Mayor from 1934 to 1945. Famed for reading the comics over New York public radio station WNYC during newspaper strike. Derided by some for bad public transit policy and for naming the airport after himself while he was still in office.

Lawn-Giland: Long Island.

Lex: Lexington Avenue.

Loisaida: Puerto Rican corruption of "Lower East Side."

Luima, Abner: Haitian alleged to have been sexually assaulted with a broom handle by New York City cops while under arrest in 1997.

Manahatta: The Native American name for Manhattan, meaning "hilly island." Go to Broadway and 160th Street to see what they meant.

Mensch: A good guy. From the Yiddish. "He's a real mensch."

MTA: The Metropolitan Transit Authority, which runs New York's bus and subway lines.

New Amsterdam: Original Dutch name of city. Changed after British took control in 1664.

No problem: "You're welcome."

NoHo: North of Houston.

Nolita: Northern Little Italy.

Noo Yawkah: New Yorker.

Noodge: A pest. "Don't be such a noodge."

Nuyorican: New York Puerto Rican.

Off-off-Broadway: Small theaters far, far away from the whole Theater District, much less Broadway. Many are in the Village.

On line: For the rest of America, on line means being on the Web; in New York it means standing and waiting in a line, often at the post office. "On line," not "in line." In line is a kind of skate.

Or what?: Suffix to an accusing question. "Are you deaf, or what?"

Outer Boroughs: Brooklyn, Queens, the Bronx, and Staten Island. Every one but Manhattan, which is the center of the known universe, and probably even of the unknown. Fegedaboudit.

The Paper of Record: The *New York Times*.

Pataki, George: Tall, hangdog Republican governor. His defeat of former governor Mario Cuomo in 1994 refuted the theory that superior products always come to dominate the marketplace.

PATH: Port Authority Trans Hudson, the commuter train linking Manhattan and New Jersey. The line that makes Hobokenites think they live in the city's sixth borough.

Pisser: Either a real bummer or a truly great person or thing. "My RV's a real pisser."

Please: As in "Oh, please." Delivered in a subdued, understated huff and meaning, "I question your veracity." Not to be confused with "puhleeez."

Puhleeez: Don't waste my time with this bullshit.

Quality of Life Campaign: Mayor Rudy Giuliani's plan to make New York nice for the tourists (and, ostensibly, for New Yorkers). Targets have included drug dealers, threatening panhandlers, squeegy people, sex shops, cabbies, loud music clubs, and jaywalkers.

Queen of Mean, The: Leona Helmsley, tax-evading dominatrix of Helmsley Hotels.

Regular coffee: Coffee with milk and sugar.

Riker's: Riker's Island Penitentiary, located in the East River just northeast of La Guardia Airport.

Rudy: Da Mayuh. Rudolph Giuliani, mayor-cop of New York. Took on the mob as federal prosecutor, now intent on making non–New Yorkers feel comfortable when visiting. See "Quality of Life Campaign."

Schlemiels: Yiddish for those who bring on their own misfortune in life. As opposed to "schlimazels," who are born losers and simply cannot help themselves.

Schlepp: To cart or drag something (or oneself) around.

Schmeer: The cream cheese spread on a roll or bagel, or the sum total of things. "I want the whole schmeer."

Schmooze: To stand around and chat. A Yiddish word used in the broader goy culture to mean to push for something, to network, or to persuade.

Schnoz: Nose. From the Yiddish. "Oy, did ya see the schnoz on him?"

Schrager, Ian: Owner of high-concept, low-content properties like the Royalton and Paramount hotels.

Smatter wid you?: "Hey, don't you know any better?"

SoHo: South of Houston.

Squeegee People: Dying breed of street people who'd smear your windshield with rags and dirty water under the pretense of cleaning it. Ubiquitous at traffic lights until Rudy cracked down. See "Quality of Life Campaign."

Stat'neyelan: Staten Island, the neglected borough of New York.

Stoop: The staircase/porch leading to the entrance of many buildings or houses. "I was sittin' on da stoop watchin' da sunset. It was be-ootiful."

Stuyvesant, Peter: Director general of the Dutch New Netherlands (including New Amsterdam) from 1647 to 1664. Many properties around town still bear his name.

Sty Town: Stuyvesant Town, a complex of 8,755 moderately priced apartments between East 14th and East 20th streets and First Avenue and the FDR Drive.

The Tombs: The New York Criminal Courts Building, downtown.

TriBeCa: Triangle Below Canal Street. Once the next SoHo, now not much better. The parade has passed on.

Welfare Island: Roosevelt Island.

Whaddaya: "What do you want me to do?" An expression of simultaneous fatalism and annoyance. As author Tom Wolfe put it, "It's an age-old New York cry for mercy, unanswerable and undeniable."

>index

Page numbers in *italics* refer to maps.

M

McSorley's Old Ale House, 90–91

Madison Square Garden, 112–14

Madison Square Park, *40*, 211, 233

Madonna, *42*, 74

Magazine distributors, 22

Magazines, 241–43. *See also* 'Zines

Malcolm X, murder site of, *46*, 71

Malibu Studios Hotel, *42*, 59

Malling of Manhattan, 18–24

Mama's Food Shop, *36*, 150

Mammoth Billiard 26, *40*, 260

Manhattan Bridge, *48*, 100

Manhattan Murder Mystery (film), 65

Marble Cemetery, 134

Mare Chiaro, *37*, 93

Mark, The, *42*, 69–70

Market Diner-Restaurant, *40*, 160

Marriott Marquis Hotel, *40*, 63, 306–7

Marshall Chess Club, *35*, 136

Masjid Malcolm Shabazz, 252

Meatpacking District, 211
    bars, 86, 93
    nightclubs, 136
    restaurants, 158

Mercury Lounge, *37*, 189

Mermaid Parade, 123, 176, 178

Meshuggah, 311–12

Met Life clock, 170

Midtown, *40*, *41*, 212

Millenium Hilton, *39*, 63

Millennium Film Workshop, *36*, 144

Miller, Jennifer, 122–23

Miracle driving glasses, 275

Miss Understood, 204

Miss Vera's Finishing School for Boys Who Want to Be Girls, 21, *41*, 273, 282–84, 287

Mobile Gas Station, *38*, 148

Mona's, *36*, 93

Mondo Kim's Video & Music, 187

Monk, corporate headquarters of, *41*, 107

Monk, Jim, first apartment of, 73

Monkey Bar, 91

Montefiore Cemetery, 134

Moon Ska, *36*, 186–87

Morgan Guaranty Trust Company, *39*, 72

Morgans, *40*, 64, 65, 157

Mosaic Man, 21, 78–80

Moshe's Falafel, *40*, 150

Mother, 136

Movies set in New York, 140–42

Movie theaters, 142–45

Mulberry Street, 212
    bars, 92, 93
    restaurants, 148
    sites of interest, 136

Murder sites, 71–72

Murray Hill, 212

Museum of Immigration, *39*, 167–68, 171

Museums, 164–67, 171–77

Music, 182–93
    stores, 186–88
    venues, 188–89

Muslim sites of interest, 252

N

Nam Wah Tea Parlor, 198, 272

Nathan's Famous, 200

National Debt Clock, *41*, 77

Natural foods, 151–53

Navia's Diner, 163

Neighborhoods, 194–223. *See also specific neighborhoods*

Newspapers, 238–39

New York Bed and Breakfast, 59–60

New York City Marble Cemetery, *36*, 134

New York City Transit Museum, *48*, 174, 304

New York Doll Hospital, *42*, 274, 276

New York Earth Room, *38*, 174

New Yorker RV Park and Campground, 60–61

New York Film Academy, 114

New York Independent Film Monitor, 242

New York Kom Tang Soot Bul House, 156

New York Life Insurance Building, 168, 285

New York Observer, 238–39

New York Post, 238

New York Press, 239, 240, 241

New York Public Library, *41*, 106, 292

New York Shambhala Center, *41*, 248–49

New York Times, 238

New York Underground Film Festival, 114

New York Unearthed, *39*, 175

New York University, 213

NoHo, 213
    bars, 88, 92–93

Nolita, 213

Northside Health Food Center, *48*, 153

Nude Cruise in New York Harbor, 126

Nuyorican Poets Cafe, 289

NYPD Blue Police Station, *36*, 74

O

Odeon, The, *39*, 158

Official All-Star Cafe, 156

O'Giglio e Paradiso Feast and Bazaar, 125–26

Old Brewery, 197

Old Town Bar and Grill, *41*, 292

Omonia, *50*, 110

About the Authors

A mutant of Omaha and an adult child of Catholic Republicans, **Jim Crotty** (aka Jim Monk) is one of the most innovative talents Nebraska has ever produced (or at least he thinks so). For 12 years Jim has traveled America in the wildly painted Monkmobile, co-authoring *Monk* (the world's only mobile magazine), pioneering "dashboard publishing," selling thousands of ads from pay phones, revolutionizing the "perzine" or "personal zine" (where the editors are the prime subjects—otherwise known as narcissism), all the while acting as the publicity machine for the mobile monastery. Jim authored the slanguistic classic *How to Talk American* (Houghton Mifflin, 1997) and co-authored the *USA Phrasebook* (Lonely Planet, 1995), *Mad Monks on the Road* (Simon & Schuster, 1993), the *Monks' Guide to New York CD ROM* (Monk Media, 1998), and *The Mad Monks' Guide to California* (Macmillan, 1999). He dreams of holding a steady, high-paying job in corporate America some day, but will invariably be kept from that goal by all those who deeply appreciate his seriously skewed approach to life, death, and real work.

Michael Lane (aka Michael Monk) grew up in trailer parks throughout the South, landed in the Haight-Ashbury scene at 17, rode the wave of the counterculture, and for the last several decades has chased life relentlessly down the road. As co-author of *Monk* magazine, the epic *Mad Monks on the Road* (Simon & Schuster, 1993), and *The Mad Monks' Guide to California* (Macmillan, 1999), Michael's past 12 years—including his inimitable encounters with cultural misfits, rebels, and ordinary folk—have been documented in excruciatingly honest detail. His book *Pink Highways* (Carol Publishing, 1995) chronicled his outlandish pre-Monk adventures, including a near-death experience before a Moroccan firing squad and a marathon evening held at gunpoint under the spell of Jimi Hendrix. Mike currently lives in Los Angeles with his muse and partner, Jim Crotty, though next year he may be living in your backyard.

The Monks have been prominently featured in most national and international media, including *Time, Newsweek,* the *New York Times, Wired News, Rolling Stone, USA Today, Der Stern* (Germany), *Brutus* (Japan), and *Panorama* (Italy), as well as on ABC's *Good Morning America, MTV News, CBS News,* the BBC, CNN, *CBS's Street Stories,* and NPR's *Morning Edition* and *Whadya' Know?*

GET MONKED

Let the journey continue! For the full-tilt Monk experience we encourage all Monks and Monkettes who have grand illusions about the great highway to order our other works.

How to Talk American, by Jim Crotty
(Houghton Mifflin), $12

Pink Highways, by Michael Lane
(Carol Publishing), $20

Monk Magazine, $10 four episodes

Mad Monks' Guide to New York CD Rom,
$19.95 (A multimedia companion to this guidebook.)

You may order by calling 212-465-3231, by mail to 175 Fifth Ave. Suite 2322, NYC, NY 10010 or on our web site (MC/Visa accepted).

Visit us online at www.monk.com